Conceptual Modelling

in Informatic

T0280425

John Krogstie · Andreas Lothe Opdahl
Sjaak Brinkkemper (Eds.)

Conceptual Modelling in Information Systems Engineering

With 75 Figures and 8 Tables

 Springer

Editors

John Krogstie
NTNU and SINTEF
Sem Sælandsvei 7–9
7491 Trondheim
Norway
krogstie@idi.ntnu.no

Andreas Lothe Opdahl
Department of Information Science and Media Studies
University of Bergen
Fosswinckelsgate 6
5007 Bergen
Norway
Andreas.Opdahl@uib.no

Sjaak Brinkkemper
Department of Information and Computing Sciences
Universiteit Utrecht
Centrumgebouw Noord, office B229
Padualaan 14, De Uithof
3584CH Utrecht
The Netherlands
s.brinkkemper@cs.uu.nl

ISBN   978-3-642-09172-8   e-ISBN   978-3-540-72677-7

ACM Computing Classification (1998): D.2, H.1, H.4

Springer is a part of Springer Science+Business Media

springer.com

© Springer-Verlag Berlin Heidelberg 2010

Cover design: KünkelLopka Werbeagentur, Heidelberg

Printed on acid-free paper   45/3180/YL - 5 4 3 2 1 0

Preface

This book is a collection of 20 state-of-the-art contributions in information systems engineering. It was compiled on the occasion of Arne Sølvberg's 67th birthday. 67 is the normal retirement age in Norway, and although Arne has promised to keep working until 70 (at least), we found this to be a good opportunity to honour him, especially since the CAiSE conference will be held in Trondheim this year. The papers will be presented at the Information Systems Engineering Symposium in Trondheim on 11 June 2007 as a pre-conference event to CAiSE'07.

The contributions were invited from the many friends and colleagues that Arne has around the world. During the last 40 years he has made a number of friends in the international research community in his chosen field of study. It has not been an easy task to select whom to invite to contribute. People have been more than eager to contribute. The friends are so numerous that it is not possible to avoid offending many who rightfully may feel that they should also have been invited to contribute.

Arne did not know about this initiative (although he might have suspected something of this kind, being involved himself in a similar book project in connection with the retirement of his colleague Janis Bubenko in 2000). The initiators and editors of this book are John Krogstie of the Norwegian University of Science and Technology (NTNU), Andreas Opdahl of the University of Bergen and Sjaak Brinkkemper of the University of Utrecht. We have selected the contributors ourselves and, given the limited size of a book, we have selected as best we could. We have invited friends from the different realms of Arne's scientific life, from the domestic scene, from VLDB, from IFIP, from ERCIM, and obviously, from the CAiSE community. Some of those invited have jointly written their contributions, some have contributed together with their colleagues, and some have done it alone. We hope that the blend is satisfactory.

When planning the book, we decided on a "free-for-all" attitude regarding the themes, although we asked for a focus on the use of conceptual modelling and an outline of the development from the past to the current and future states in an author's particular field. The papers are fairly coherent in attacking problems in areas related to conceptual modelling and information systems engineering, pointing to further directions for the field.

We are very pleased with the comprehensiveness of this book and are thankful that we have had the good fortune to edit it. We wish to thank Monika Riepl and Ralf Gerstner at Springer for their efficient support in the publication of this book.

It is an honour to be allowed to present this gift to Arne, as a token of our appreciation of his contributions to information systems engineering research and teaching.

John Krogstie   Andreas Opdahl   Sjaak Brinkkemper (editors)
March 2007

Short biography of Arne Sølvberg

Arne Sølvberg was born on 13 February 1940 at Klepp, Jæren in the south-western part of Norway. He was the eldest of five children, with three brothers and one sister. He became Professor of Computer Science at The Norwegian University of Science and Technology in Trondheim, Norway already in 1974, the first professor in the Computer Science Department (IDB), which had been established two years earlier.

Arne Sølvberg began his studies in 1958 and received a Siv.Ing. (M.Sc.) degree in applied physics in 1963 and a Dr.Ing. (Ph.D.) degree in computer science in 1971, both from The Norwegian Institute of Technology (now incorporated in NTNU – The Norwegian University of Science and Technology). Sølvberg's Ph.D., under the guidance of Børje Langefors, was the first doctoral degree in computer science in Trondheim. Between 1963 and 1974 Arne worked at SINTEF Runit, building up and leading their information systems group.

Professor Sølvberg has been Dean of NTNU's Faculty of Information Technology, Mathematics and Electrical Engineering since 2002.

His main fields of research are information systems design methodology, database design, information modelling, information systems engineering environments, and model driven development.

He has been active in several international organizations for research cooperation. He was involved from the start in the establishment of IFIP TC8: Information Systems, and was the Norwegian national representative at the IFIP General Assembly in 1979 to 1982. He was chairman of IFIP WG8.1 for Information Systems Design from 1982 to 1988. He was a trustee of the VLDB Endowment until 1994. He was a co-founder of the CAiSE conference series in 1989 together with Janis Bubenko. Originally a Nordic conference, it quickly was established as an international meeting place for researchers within the area of information systems engineering.

He has been a visiting scientist at IBM San Jose Research Labs, The University of Florida, The Naval Postgraduate School, The University of California at Santa Barbara, and most recently at the University of California at Los Angeles.

During his years as Professor, Arne Sølvberg guided a large number of Ph.D. students to their degrees. He has developed and taught numerous university courses and has inspired generations of students. He played an active role in the development of technical computer studies in Norway. It is specifically worth mentioning the work he did in building up the so-called "customer led projects" already from 1974, giving students real assignments from real customers, introducing to them the wicked problems of information systems engineering first hand.

Arne reached the usual Norwegian retirement age of 67 in February 2007, but is still active as the Dean of the IME-faculty. He is also the current vice-chair of ERCIM and is leading the cross-disciplinary ICT-programme at NTNU.

Arne Sølvberg is married to Ingeborg Sølvberg, also a professor at IDI, NTNU. They have two daughters, Astrid, who has a Ph.D. in pedagogics, and Ingrid, who has a Master's in marine technology (both work in Trondheim). Arne and Ingeborg have three grandchildren and live at Steinan, in the west part of Trondheim.

List of Authors

Nicholas Berente
Information Systems Dept., Case Western Reserve University
10900 Euclid Avenue, Cleveland, Ohio 44106, USA
berente@case.edu

Janis A. Bubenko jr., Professor Emeritus
Dept. of Computer and Systems Science,
Royal Institute of Technology/Stockholm University
Forum 100, SE-16440 Kista, Sweden
janis@dsv.su.se

Jordi Cabot, Dr.
Estudis d'Informàtica, Multimedia i Telecomunicació,
Universitat Oberta de Catalunya
Rbla. del Poblenou, 156, E-08018 Barcelona, Spain
jcabot@uoc.edu

Antje Dietrich
Inst. für Programmstrukturen und Datenorganisation (IPD),
Universität Karlsruhe
Postfach 6980, D-76128 Karlsruhe, Germany
antje@ipd.uka.de

Klaus R. Dittrich, Professor
Dept. of Informatics, University of Zurich
Binzmühlestrasse 14, CH-8050 Zurich, Switzerland
dittrich@ifi.unizh.ch

Johann Eder, Professor
Dept. of Knowledge and Business Engineering, University of Vienna
Dr.-Karl-Lueger-Ring 1, A-1010 Wien, Austria
Johann.Eder@univie.ac.at

Sergio España
Dept. of Information Systems and Computation,
Valencia University of Technology
Camino de Vera s/n, 46022 Valencia, Spain
sergio.espana@dsic.upv.es

Arturo González, Dr.
Dept. of Information Systems and Computation,
Valencia University of Technology
Camino de Vera s/n, 46022 Valencia, Spain
agdelrio@dsic.upv.es

Jon Atle Gulla, Professor
Dept. of Computer and Information Science,
Norwegian University of Science and Technology
N-7034 Trondheim, Norway
jag@idi.ntnu.no

Terry Halpin, Professor
Neumont University
10701 S River Front Pkwy Ste 300, South Jordan, Utah, 84095, USA
terry@neumont.edu

Keith G Jeffery, Professor, Director IT and International Strategy
CCLRC Rutherford Appleton Laboratory
Chilton, Didcot, OXON OX11 0QX, UK
k.g.jeffery@rl.ac.uk

Paul Johannesson, Professor
Dept. of Computer and Systems Sciences,
Stockholm University/Royal Institute of Technology
Forum 100, SE-164 40 Kista, Sweden
pajo@dsv.su.se

Krishna Kavi, Professor
Dept. of Computer Science and Engineering, University of North Texas
3940 N. Elm Street, Suite F201, Denton, Texas 76207-7102, USA
kavi@cs.unt.edu

John Krogstie, Professor
Dept. of Computer and Information Science,
Norwegian University of Science and Technology
N-7034 Trondheim, Norway
John.Krogstie@idi.ntnu.no

David Kung, Professor
Dept. of Computer Science and Engineering,
University of Texas at Arlington
416 Yates Street, NH 300, Arlington, TX 76019, USA
kung@uta.edu

Marek Lehmann, Dr.
Dept. of Knowledge and Business Engineering, University of Vienna
Dr.-Karl-Lueger-Ring 1, A-1010 Wien, Austria
Marek.Lehmann@univie.ac.at

Peter C. Lockemann, Professor
Inst. für Programmstrukturen und Datenorganisation (IPD),
Universität Karlsruhe
Postfach 6980, D-76128 Karlsruhe, Germany
lockeman@ipd.uka.de

Kalle Lyytinen, Professor
Information Systems Dept., Case Western Reserve University
10900 Euclid Avenue, Cleveland, Ohio 44106, USA
kalle@case.edu

Antoni Olivé, Professor
Dept. Llenguatges i Sistemes Informàtics,
Universitat Politècnica de Catalunya
C/ Jordi Girona Salgado 1-3, E-08034 Barcelona, Spain
olive@lsi.upc.edu

Andreas L. Opdahl, Professor
Dept. of Information Science and Media Studies, University of Bergen
N-5020 Bergen, Norway
Andreas.Opdahl@uib.no

Óscar Pastor, Professor
Dept. of Information Systems and Computation,
Valencia University of Technology
Camino de Vera s/n, 46022 Valencia, Spain
opastor@dsic.upv.es

Barbara Pernici, Professor
Dipartimento di Elettronica e Informazione, Politecnico di Milano
piazza Leonardo da Vinci 32, 20133 Milano, Italy
barbara.pernici@polimi.it

Klaus Pohl, Professor, Scientific Director
Software Systems Engineering, University of Duisburg-Essen/
Lero - The Irish Software Engineering Research Centre
Schützenbahn 70 ("Altbau"), 45117 Essen, Germany
klaus.pohl@sse.uni-due.de

Oliver Raabe, Dr.
Inst. für Informationsrecht, Universität Karlsruhe
Postfach 6980, D-76128 Karlsruhe, Germany
raabe@ira.uka.de

Colette Rolland, Professor
Université Paris1 Panthéon Sorbonne
90 Rue de Tolbiac, 75013 Paris, France
rolland@univ-paris1.fr

Ernst Sikora
Software Systems Engineering, University of Duisburg-Essen
Schützenbahn 70 ("Altbau"), 45117 Essen, Germany
ernst.sikora@sse.uni-due.de

Guttorm Sindre, Professor
Dept. of Computer and Information Science,
Norwegian University of Science and Technology
N-7034 Trondheim, Norway
Guttorm.Sindre@idi.ntnu.no

Bernhard Thalheim, Professor
Dept. of Computer Science, Christian Albrechts University Kiel
Olshausenstr. 40, D-24118 Kiel, Germany
thalheim@is.informatik.uni-kiel.de

Anthony I. Wasserman, Professor, Executive Director
Carnegie Mellon West
Moffett Field, CA 94035, USA
tonyw@west.cmu.edu

Patrick Ziegler
Dept. of Informatics, University of Zurich
Binzmühlestrasse 14, CH-8050 Zurich, Switzerland
pziegler@ifi.unizh.ch

Contents

From Information Algebra to Enterprise Modelling and Ontologies – a Historical Perspective on Modelling for Information Systems

Janis A. Bubenko jr

Royal Institute of Technology and Stockholm University, Kista, Sweden

Abstract. Evolution of research and practice in the area of conceptual modelling for information systems during more than four decades is examined. It focuses on activities related to research and practice in the early system development phases. It comments on a large number of modelling methods published in the 1960-ies, 70-ies, and 80-ies as well as on the report "Concepts and Terminology of the Conceptual Schema and the Information Base" reporting the work by the ISO working group ISO/TC97/SC5/WG5 in the early 80-ies. Approaches which are based on a temporal and deductive view of the application domain as well as object-oriented modelling languages are acknowledged. The paper continues with a discussion of principles and research problems related to a topic we call "Enterprise Modelling" and "Ontology Modelling". The *role* of conceptual modelling in information systems development during all these decades is seen as an approach for capturing fuzzy, ill-defined, informal "real-world" descriptions and user requirements, and then transforming them to formal, in some sense complete, and consistent conceptual specifications. During the last two decades an additional role of modelling has evolved - to support user and stakeholder participation in enterprise analysis and requirements formulation and in development of shared conceptualisations of specific domains.

1 Introduction

Modelling has always been an essential part of developing information systems. In the very early attempts of modelling, focus was on describing the domain in strict, formal, and computer independent terms. What were modelled were data and operations on data. Data were modelled in abstract terms using concepts such as information set, entity, attribute, production rule, etc. This kind of modelling started in the late fifties.

The purpose of this paper is to acknowledge the work introducing a large number of basic modelling concepts, some as early as in 1958. Section 2 presents some pioneers: Young and Kent's early approach (1958) towards abstract formulation of data processing problems, CODASYL Development Committee's Language Structure Group's report "An Information Algebra" in 1962, and the *infological approach* and the elementary message concept, presented by Langefors in 1965. Section 3 describes a large number of conceptual modelling styles and approaches introduced during the seventies, as well as a number of activities or special interest groups within IFIP, ACM, and VLDB that were established in order to promote conceptual modelling. Section 4 aims at illustrating the situation during the eighties – method and model comparison and the search for a common framework. This period also gave birth to temporally oriented and object oriented approaches. Section 5 illustrates modelling trends during the nineties: to extend the scope of conceptual modelling, e.g. by modelling organisational intentions and problems, business rules, business processes, etc., and to apply it also in the business and organisational analysis phases of the systems life cycle. The paper is concluded in section 6.

2 Pioneering Work

Already in 1958 two electrical engineers, Young and Kent, [38] argued for the importance of a "precise and abstract way of specifying the informational and time characteristics of a data processing problem". Their notation "should enable the analyst to organize the problem around any piece of hardware". As we can see, their purpose of an abstract specification was to use it as an invariant basis for designing different alternative implementations, perhaps even using different hardware components. Performance and cost of computer equipment were important design factors at that time.

Important concepts introduced by Young and Kent are
- *Information set/item*, e.g. sets of customer numbers (P_2), customer names (P_{10}), order dates, (P_1) etc.
- *Defining relationship*, e.g. $P_2 \leftrightarrow P_{10}$ (where $\leftrightarrow$ denotes isomorphism), $P_1 = P_7 \times P_8 \times P_9$, where the last three information sets denote days, months and years.
- *Document descriptions* using document components explained by the use of definitions of information sets

- *Producing relationship.* e.g. $D_1 \rightarrow D_2$ (where D_1 is the document "shipping notice" and D_2 is the document "invoice"
- *Conditions*, e.g. $t_E (D_2) - t_E (D_1) \leq 2$ days, where t_E denotes the "extrinsic time" of the document, i.e. the time when it was created or produced.

Young and Kent also suggested a graphical notation to represent the different descriptions and relations. These diagrams looked more like electrical wiring diagrams. We believe they were, compared to UML diagrams of today, considerably less user friendly and more difficult (if not impossible) to understand for non-engineers. In any case, it feels important to mention these two pioneers in abstract representation of information systems. They even had the notion of *extrinsic* as well as *intrinsic* time in order to express relations and different kinds of conditions. However, as could be expected, it is impossible to finds any traces of practical use of the above ideas.

The next step in modelling for information systems was taken by the CODASYL Development Committee[1] [10]. The motivation behind the committee's model was essentially the same as for Young and Kent "...to arrive at a proper structure for a machine independent problem definition language, at the system level of data processing". The committee writes: "In general, the underlying concepts of the Algebra have been implicitly understood for years by the business systems analyst. An information system deals with objects and events in the real world that are of interest. These real objects and events, called "entities", are represented in the system by data. The data processing system contains information from which the desired outputs can be extracted through processing. Information about a particular entity is in the form of "values" which describe quantitatively or qualitatively a set of attributes or "properties" that have significance in the system".

Information Algebra is based on three undefined concepts: Entity, Property, and Value. Based on these concepts the Algebra introduces further concepts such as Property Value Set (V) (e.g. employee number sets), Coordinate sets (Q) (e.g. $Q = (q_1, q_2) =$ (employee number, hourly pay-rate) and the Property space (P) of a coordinate set Q (e.g. $P = Q_1 \times Q_2$). A number of additional Algebra concepts such as a "line" (an ordered set of points in P), an "area" (a subset of P), and a "bundle" (a way of relating lines) are defined. All these, and many more concepts, are then used to abstractly define files and operations on data in files. In summary, the Information Algebra is a wonderful example of a strict mathematical formulation of a data processing problem and operations on data. Regretfully, as

---

[1] The mathematical ideas behind the Information Algebra were initially developed by Robert Bosak of the Systems Development Cooperation.

could be expected, it is not possible to find references to realistic, practical use of the Algebra. On the other hand, we can easily imagine how the basic concepts of it inspired a number of followers, such as the relational data model and the semantic data models, developed during the seventies.

The next notable development of the sixties was a number of theoretical notions introduced for information systems by Börje Langefors. They appeared in a number of shorter papers during the early sixties when Langefors was at the Swedish SAAB aircraft company (e.g. [19]). Many of these reports were used for system analyst training at SAAB. In 1967 many of these reports were compiled in the book "Theoretical Analysis of Information Systems"[20], the first university textbook on information systems development in Sweden.

Langefors introduced a number of concepts related to modelling for information systems among others the partitioning of the system development life-cycle in four important *method areas*

- Methods for management and control of organisations
- Methods for analysis and description of information systems at an elementary, "problem oriented" level (the "infological" realm)
- Methods for design and analysis of computerised information processing systems (The "datalogical" realm)
- Methods for implementation of the information system on computer hardware (processors, storage units, communication channels, etc.) and choice of hardware. Methods for installation.

In the infological realm Langefors suggested that the smallest element that could contain any meaningful information was the elementary message. An elementary message is a quadruple <S, T, A, V> where S is the identification of a system point, T is the moment of time, A the name of a state variable, and V is the value of the state variable. The reader recognizes that S is what we nowadays call an entity or an object, A is the name of a property or an attribute, and V is the property value. An interesting notion is the reference to time, the time of the validity of the assertion. A time-less statement in an information base <S, A, V> can, at any time, be true or false. On the other hand a statement with a temporal reference <S, T, A, V> if true when inserted in the information base, is always true. We will return to the use of time in conceptual modelling as well as in data base management in subsequent chapters.

In summary, the important contribution of the sixties was the confirmation of the significance of the infological realm, i.e. the realm where data processing problems were expressed formally in a machine-independent way. This laid the basis for a wealth of new modelling notions during the next decade.

3   Refinement – New Models and Extensions

The decade of 1970 is characterised by introduction of new models as well as refinement and extensions of a number of information modelling languages. Different actors with different ambitions were active here. Perhaps the most enthusiastic data modelling researchers at this time came from the database community. Also the Information Systems community as well as some AI-people joined in. For the database designers, the primary purpose of modelling was the need to define what kind of reality the data in the data base (or in an Information Systems) should describe. This should be described in a machine independent way, i.e. it should not be in terms of records, record descriptions and access links. It should rather be in terms of concepts similar to the ones expressed by the proponents of the Information Algebra, i.e. entities, properties, relationships, and such.

Some important events, which significantly contributed to further developing the field of data modelling, occurred in the seventies:

In the early seventies **IFIP** formed a **Technical Committee 2** (TC2) on **Software**. A few years later TC2 established a Working Group (WG2.6) on Database. WG 2.6 then took the initiative to launch a number of Working Conferences on Data Base Management and Data Modelling. The first four of them had a considerable focus on data modelling issues and problems. The first was held in Cargèse, Corsica [21] in 1974. The second was held in Wepion, Belgium[13], the third in Freudenstadt [25], Germany, and the fourth in Nice, France [26].

The **Standards Planning and Requirements Committee** (SPARC) of the American National Standards Institute Information Processing Systems (ANSI/X3) Committee, proposed in 1975 a three-schema *architecture* for data bases [1]. The architecture defined three separate *schemas,* or *views,* for describing data in a database. They were the External Schema or User View, the Conceptual Schema or the Logical View, and the Internal Schema or Implementation View. A journal publication appeared in 1978 [34]. The architecture had a major impact on thinking about the contents, structure, as well as of the interoperability of data base systems.

The **IFIP Technical Committee 7** (TC 7) on **Information Systems** was formed in 1977. TC8's Working Group 8.1 deals with formal description and analysis of information systems. As databases are natural parts of information systems, many data base researchers joined also WG-8.1. Several of the methods for IS – design and development discussed in WG-8.1 also had substantial suggestions of concepts regarding conceptual data models.

ACM's Special Interest Group on Management of Data (SIGMOD) started its annual conferences in 1975. Besides a large number of technical data base problems, also papers on data base design and conceptual data modelling were solicited. SIGMOD's annual conferences as well as its periodical SIGMOD Newsletter significantly contributed to spreading of data and conceptual modelling ideas on the North American continent as well as in the rest of the world.

The **VLDB series** of conferences started 1975 in Framingham, Massachusetts. The motivation for having a special conference for "very large" data bases was the introduction of powerful disk-based storage devices for direct access. This created a need to develop technology and methods how to structure, store, access, and manipulate large amounts of data. Many of the papers presented at VLDB dealt with data modelling, structuring, and access, as well as with performance issues. VLDB is held annually in the months of August – September. Later VLDB formed an Endowment, consisting of 21 trustees who are responsible for the continuity of the conference series. The proceedings of VLDB were published by Morgan Kaufmann during 17 years. Since 1992 they are published by Springer.

Which were the significant issues, insights and proposals during the seventies regarding conceptual data modelling? In the author's view, the following are candidates:

An "object" and "the name of an object" are different things. This "obvious" insight is still not generally acknowledged even among some "ontology fans" of today. Some of the first data modelling researchers to recognize this distinction were Michael Senko [33] and Sjir Nijssen in his NIAM model [24].

Binary vs. relational models: Many new types of data models presented in the seventies were binary models, i.e. models composed of triplets <A, R, B> where A and B are objects (or entities) and R denotes a relationship (see for instance Abrial's model of 1974 [2]). Some researchers advocated a third node type, a relationship that could be ternary or a higher order relationship (the well known Entity-Relationship model [9] had this property). A substantial part of the data modelling community advocated the relational data model (suggested by [11] at IBM Research), not only for its simplicity, but also for its mathematical strictness. Considerable discussions, pro and contra, took part between followers of both camps. Even at IBM people were in different camps, while the management of IBM Research put considerable resources in developing the relational data base management system R*. Today the battle is settled: conceptual data models are generally used as high-level problem oriented descriptions of organisations and data. Relational models are seen as implementation oriented descriptions.

Specialisation and generalisation, inheritance: Some conceptual models permitted definition of subtypes and supertypes of entities, and definition of how properties of a supertype could be inherited by subtype entities.

Distinction between types, sets, and instances: These notions initially came from the field of Semantic Networks within Artificial Intelligence, primarily used for representation of knowledge and to support automatic systems for reasoning about knowledge.

Constraints and deduction: The purpose of defining constraints is to define which entities, relationships, and property values are permitted in the set of instances of a data model schema. Another type of constraints may define how the set of instances of a data model may change, e.g. by stating pre- and post-conditions for transactions. Deduction in its turn permitted the definition of *derived* entities, relationships and attributes. An example of a data model of the seventies that had a rich language for definitions of this kind is the Semantic Data Model [18]. Also, the use of logic for expressing conceptual models, including rules, was presented [12].

The temporal dimension: The importance of time in conveying information was noted by Young and Kent as well as by Langefors (see above). This notion was further developed by Bubenko [5] who suggested an approach to design a conceptual schema that contained "time-stamped" information including a set of derivation rules. Bubenko also argued [6] that inclusion of the temporal dimension in information modelling improved user understanding and, therefore, also the quality of the conceptual schema.

Data Model Based Data Base Management Systems. Most, if not all, semantic modelling approaches were at this time intended to develop abstract descriptions of the content and the constraints and rules of a data base. Data bases were subsequently implemented using a Data Base Management System (DBMS). The major types of systems were the hierarchical, the network and the relational types of DBMS. There was, however, one exception. The CADIS group in Stockholm developed already in 1970 a DBMS, called CS1 (CADIS System 1) that was based on a binary data model (inspired by the LEAP language [15]). The CS was further developed and supplemented with a procedural data manipulation language [3]. This "fourth generation language" (4GL) later became a Swedish software product, that evidently led to significantly shorter system development times as well as less error-prone software. The CS could not match the marketing effort of relational systems and it did not lead to markets outside

Sweden. Surprisingly enough the CADIS System is still being used for systems development in several sites in Sweden.

Graphical query languages: One very peculiar achievement during the seventies was a graphical query language using a binary data model. Mike Senko introduced around 1976 the light-pen oriented language FORAL LP by which transactions could be defined on a binary data model displayed on a screen by pointing to nodes and arcs of the model as well as to letters and numbers. In this way a transaction was built-up and then translated to the FORAL language. Unfortunately, Senko was years ahead of the rest of the computing community and, therefore not appreciated by some influential colleagues. Also the graphics hardware was extremely primitive at that time. The idea was not further developed until in the late eighties when it was used by SISU[2] [22] to build a graphical query language referring to a conceptual model of a domain. The graphical language was then translated to SQL. This tool was called HYBRIS. The idea was further exploited in a number of EU projects in connection with access to multi-media data.

In summary, we feel that most of the essential basic concepts of modelling were invented and presented during the seventies. Not all approaches presented became practically used, but they formed a solid platform for further developments during the eighties and nineties.

4 The Search for a Common Framework

A large number of more or less similar modelling languages and concepts were published during the seventies. It seems we reached a common desire to compare the different models and try to find a common acceptable framework. At least there was an aspiration to better understand, evaluate, and/or improve parts of existing methods and to harmonize them. Likewise, there was a wish to enhance the requirements capture and validation stage of the systems life-cycle by application of powerful, abstract modelling techniques. In this connection also the question "what are we modelling?" was raised. Is it the data base or the real-world? And whose real world is it?

One notable activity during the end of the seventies is the start-up of a working group WG3 in the subcommittee SC5 of ISO/TC 97. Three years later, in 1981, the working group presented a preliminary report "Concepts and Terminology for the Conceptual Schema" [17]. The overall charter of the group was to prepare for standardisation in the area of data base man-

---

[2] SISU stands for Swedish Institute for Systems Development. Mare about SISU can be found at http://roxy.cnet.se/vnapps/SISUWeb/Frontpage_default.vns

agement. Some important objectives chartered to the group were 1) to define concepts for the conceptual schema language, 2) to define or monitor definition of conceptual schema languages, 3) to develop a methodology for assessing conceptual schema languages, 4) to assess proposals for conceptual schema languages. The group never fully reached these apparently very tough goals. Neither was the preliminary report ever finalized. But the report left, at that time, a heavy impact on the modelling community. The report also became frequently referenced.

Taking the three-schema approach [1] as a starting point, the working group makes a number of important distinctions between the universe of discourse and a universe of discourse description. Two principles, suggested by the group, have been frequently cited.

1. A conceptual schema should be as free as possible of any aspect irrelevant to the universe of discourse, e.g. aspects of internal physical data representation, organization, and access within the data base system, or aspects of particular external user representations, such as external language or message formats, etc.
2. All relevant aspects, rules, etc. of the abstraction system should be described in the conceptual schema. None of them can occur elsewhere, in particular not in application programs formulated apart from the conceptual schema.

The group then examines four classes of modelling approaches 1) the entity attribute relationship, 2) the entity relationship, 2) the binary relationship, and 4) the interpreted predicate logic approaches for their expressive power with respect to a particular domain description. Not surprisingly, the fourth approach was found superior. Considering the principles above, we can also see that the so called "object-oriented" modelling approaches of the nineties, e.g. UML, do not fully match properties required for a conceptual schema language due to some deficiencies regarding its expressive power.

One problem with most modelling approaches seems to be how to express temporal or dynamic rules and constraints, e.g. how to express the rule "the salary of a permanently employed person must not decrease". One way to handle this is to use a deductive, temporal modelling approach [7]. In this approach the conceptual schema consists of time stamped predicate definitions and a set of derivation rules. Predicates define state information, e.g. employed (p, t), as well as events, e.g. employment (p, t). All state information is derived from corresponding events, e.g. a person is employed at time t if s/he has been employed before time t and not fired before time t. The non-decreasing salary rule above could be expressed by stating that the salary of an employee at time t+1 must be greater or equal to that person's salary at time t. Further work on the deductive, temporal approach is reported by Olivé [27,28].

In an alternative approach the entity-relationship model is augmented with time, e.g. a non-permanent, time varying entity, relationship, or attributed is marked as "temporal". Using temporal operators such as "sometime in the past", "sometime in the future", or "in the next state" different kinds of temporal constraints can be defined.

Several other semantically rich and expressive modelling approaches were introduced during the eighties , e.g. RML [16]. RML, in particular, also paved the way for increased attention to requirements engineering as a significant phase in the systems development life cycle. During the eighties an interest was also expressed in the topic of "historical databases". This gave birth to data models that treated several aspects of time, i.e. the *time* of an event, the *observation time* of the event and the *transaction time* of the event. This data base concept was called "multi-temporal databases".

The search for a common modelling and method framework continued during the eighties. One particular manifestation of this is the IFIP WG 8.1 Working Conference series on System Development Methodologies that was initiated in 1982. The series became known as CRIS – Comparative Review of Information Systems Design Methodologies [29-31]. This series exposed a large number of modelling approaches in the realm of information system design. While the comparison between approaches hardly gave significant insights, the discussions among method authors stimulated them to insights that eventually would improve their own approaches. CRIS also stimulated a number of follow-up conferences as well as the forming of a task group FRISCO (Framework of Information System COncepts) that in 1995 presented an extensive report which provides a reference background for modelling in the information system area [14]. In particular, the report[3] "justifies the information system area scientifically by placing it in a more general context, comprising philosophy, ontology, semiotics, system science, organisation science, as well as computer science", thereby anchoring concepts of the information system area to concepts of the other areas.

In this connection we should not forget the "synergy-workshops" started, mainly by North-American researchers, in 1980 in Pingree Park [4] where the aim was to explore advances in: data bases[4], artificial intelli-

---

[3] For the full FRISCO report see: http://www.mathematik.uni-marburg.de/‾ ~hesse/papers/fri-full.pdf

[4] From the data base standpoint it was essentially data modelling that was discussed

gence and programming languages in order to look for synergetic cross-fertilization of concepts and theories. As with the CRIS conference series there were no immediate practical effects of this set of activities. But they brought together scientists with different perspectives and they most likely laid a basis for future innovations. Perhaps the "ontology movement", see below, is such a result.

5   Participation and Understanding

The 90-ties lead to increased development and use of advanced conceptual modelling methods and techniques. One of the main questions during the eighties regarding modelling was "What are we modelling?" The nineties brought new questions in to the inquiry. Why are we modelling and how are we modelling became two of the new issues. Furthermore, we were moving from relatively well defined, limited scope applications into new, less well conceptualised applications and not well bounded problem domains. It was in most cases difficult to achieve full understanding and consensus of the world.

In Europe many collaborative projects in IT were sponsored by the European Union via the European Commission (EC). In its ESPRIT framework, EC argued for increased *focus on organisational aspects, participation and understanding when developing IT-systems for practical applications.* In particular it argued for "increased understanding and support of human activities at all levels in an organisation".

An example of this expressed need is the TEMPORA project where a temporal ER-type of model was developed (see for instance [23], and example in Fig.1). The TEMPORA conceptual model also included submodels of business goals and rules. Goals and rules could be expressed over time using temporal logic as could "derived" entity and relationship types. In this sense we can say that TEMPORA paved the way for extending the scope of modelling. This illustrates the movement from conceptual modelling to "business modelling" or "enterprise modelling".

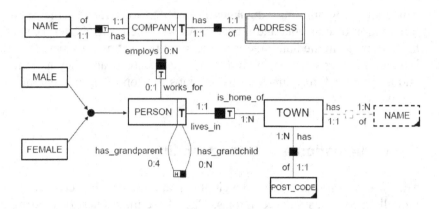

Fig. 1. An ER-type model of TEMPORA with temporal dimension for both entities and relationships (from [23]).

An example of a model with extended scope is the EKD (Enterprise Knowledge Development) approach. EKD is a derivative of the TEMPORA model. The EKD modelling approach was first developed in the EU-project F^3 ("F Cube", EU Nr. 6353) and then further elaborated in the ELEKTRA project (22927) [8] [32]. Later EKD was used in several more projects, national as well as international, for instance in Hyper-knowledge[5] (28401). EKD differs from the approaches discussed earlier in this paper foremost through two distinguishing characteristics.

Firstly, it is an approach strongly based on involvement and participation of "stakeholders" (users, managers, owners …). This means that an EKD model is gradually built by its stakeholders in participatory modelling seminars, led by one or more facilitators. The work mode is using a wall covered with a plastic sheet and posting pieces of paper on it, representing components of the different models. Later the modelling results are documented in a computer by a documentation specialist. Secondly. it is a multi-model approach involving not only a model for conceptual structures but also interlinked submodels for goals, actors, business rules, business processes, and requirements to be stated for the information system, if such is developed. All these models are interlinked, for instance a goal in a goal model may refer to a concept in the concepts model, if the concept is used in the goal description (see Fig. 2).

The EKD approach, or other multi-model, participatory approaches similar to EKD, are now in frequent use in a wide range of practical appli-

---

[5] The latest EKD description can be found at ftp://ftp.dsv.su.se/users/js/ekd_ user_guide_2001.pdf

cations and having a spectrum of purposes. We find uses of this kind of approach not only for information system development, but also for organisational development, business process analysis, knowledge management studies, and many more. We do not have a complete trace of all places where this kind of approach is applied, but we know several instances in Sweden, UK, France, Greece, Austria, and Latvia.

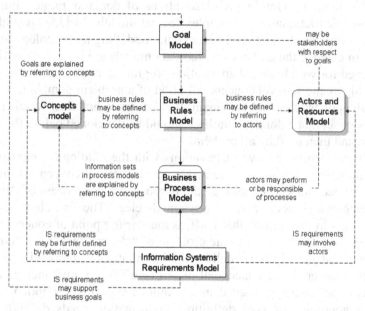

Fig. 2. A top view of the multi-model approach EKD, showing different types of models in interaction. The "Concepts model" can be said to correspond to what was earlier called a data model or a conceptual model.

A quickly developing modelling topic, related to EKD, concerns development and use of "business patterns", i.e. documentation and re-use of successful conceptualisations of subsets of an EKD interlinked model. However, lack of space prevents us from dwelling further into the topic here.

Last in this section, I wish to comment on what might be called "the ontology movement". The concept "ontology" has during the nineties become increasingly popular and used in different kinds of disciplines. What seems to be behind it is the need for better "understanding" and a "shared conceptual view" of different (problem) domains. Another need is to improve understanding, of information on "the Web", i.e. what does a particular page on the web "mean and describe". and perhaps even make the

semantic of it automatically manageable. Naturally, this has lead to increased use of conceptual modelling, not only for development of information systems but for all kinds of organisational or scientific analysis in different application domains, be it medicine, transportation, or defence. The
term "ontology" seems to have as many definitions as there are "ontologists". An oversimplified definition of an ontology[6] is "An ontology of
domain X is a conceptual description, preferably formal, of what "there is"
in the domain". Ontological descriptions of domains range from simple
taxonomic dictionaries to complex logical models. In [35] the authors try
to describe the distinction between data modelling and ontology engineering. In essence the authors say that data models are conceptualisations developed for well bounded application program domains, while an ontology
is a high generic-level conceptualisation of a problem domain to be shared
by all applications of that domain. It is however, not clear whether the authors mean that a domain ontology should be developed before the applications and then used by all of them.

There seem to be two observations with the ontological movement: 1)
not all ontologists seem to be aware of advances in conceptual modelling
several decades earlier, and 2) the purpose and the process of developing
an ontological model is not always made clear. The first observation usually leads to the opinion that UML is the starting point of conceptual modelling. The second leads to the problem of "closure": what is a "complete"
ontological model? In modelling for information systems this question is
easily answered: the conceptual model (see Fig. 2) must include descriptions of all concepts needed in a complete systems description, i.e. concepts appearing in goal definitions, information needs definitions, rule
definitions, process definitions, etc. etc. Since ontologies seem normally to
be developed for domains, without a particular application in mind, this
seems to lead to difficulties regarding the completeness of an ontology.

6   Concluding Remarks and Dedication

This subjective, one man's view of four decades of conceptual data modelling in connection with information systems design is obviously incomplete. It has not been practically possible to tell about all developments and
achievements in the area. It has not been possible to give a fair set of relevant references showing all important work being published and exposed.

---

[6] In dictionaries ontology is often defined as "The branch of metaphysics that
studies the nature of existence or being as such".

Contributions in this widening area during the past forty years are too many. Nevertheless, I hope the reader will find my view of the evolution, influenced by the "Scandinavian school", interesting as a complement to other historical contributions.

A simple conclusion can be drawn from the description above. Starting from simple and well bounded conceptual descriptions of information and data base systems, the area of modelling is exploding and encompasses now many different kinds of "knowledge advancing and building" activities in many possible domains. The importance of stakeholder participation is well recognised (see e.g. [36]) leading to increased use of a participatory work mode. The consultant-type of analysis is being replaced by group-work putting severe demands on availability of skilled facilitators as well as tools for cooperative work. However, due to the immense number of applications being developed, there is a lack of trained and skilled system developers and modellers. The market is open for all kinds of "hackers" that we can observe by the lack of quality and security of many vital public as well as private information and software systems in our society.

This paper is dedicated to my friend Professor Arne Sølvberg. Arne has been in the middle of this evolutionary work, described above, since the late sixties. We have had everlasting discussions in different parts of the world and in different environments such as IFIP, ACM, and VLDB, about numerous issues in the modelling area. Most often we have had similar and compatible views of modelling issues and concepts. Arne has skilfully managed his research teams in national as well as in international projects, in particular in projects supported by the European Commission. He has contributed to projects as well as to promoting scientific communication between people in different countries and continents. He has, in particular, cared to support the new eastern European nations to speed up the process of integration with rest of the EU-countries.

I would like to end this paper with a citation from a paper by Arne [37]: "Computational devices, communication systems and storage devices are becoming commodities. Moore's law is still valid, and price/performance for the equipment decreases by the month. Computers will be so deeply engrained in the fabric of our societies that they will seem to have disappeared as distinct devices. Software, humans and all kinds of intelligent artefacts will be interwoven in information systems of interacting, autonomous subsystems. One of the great challenges ahead is to manage technical complexity. Another is to be able to easily change, in our human societies, what we do and how we do it. Low ability to master technical complexity together with low ability to change our ways, spells disaster. We need to have systems that can evolve as the needs and desires of individuals and organizations evolve. We need to build our societies such that they can change as new technology makes new developments possible".

References

[1] ANSI/X3/SPARC, Study Group on Data Base Management Systems: Interim Report 75-02-08. ACM SIGMOD Newsletter, 1975. 7(2).
[2] Abrial, J.R.: Data Semantics. In: *Data Base Management*, ed. Klimbie J.W., Koffeman, K.L. (North Holland/ Elsevier. 1974). pp 1-69.
[3] Berild, S.,Nachmens, S.: CS4 a Tool for Database Design by Infological Simulation. In: 3rd International Conference on Very Large Data Bases (Tokyo 1977)
[4] Brodie, M.L., Zilles, S. N. (eds): *Proceedings of Workshop on Data Abstraction, Databases, and Conceptual Modelling.* 1981, ACM SIGMOD Record, Vol. 11, No. 2, Feb. (1981)
[5] Bubenko, J.A., Jr.: The Temporal Dimension in Information Modelling. In: *IFIP WG 2.6 Working Conference on Architecture and Models in Data Base Management Systems.* Nice, France: (North Holland, 1977).
[6] Bubenko, J.A., Jr.: Validity and Verification Aspects of Information Modeling. In: *3rd International Conference on Very Large Data Bases.* Tokyo: (IEEE Computer Society, 1977)
[7] Bubenko, J.A., Jr.: Information Modeling in the Context of Systems Development. In: *Information Processing 80.* Tokyo, Japan and Melbourne, Australia: (North Holland 1980).
[8] Bubenko, J.A., Jr, Brash, D.,Stirna, J.: EKD User Guide., Dept. of Computer and Systems Science, KTH and Stockholm University, Sweden.: Kista. (1988)
[9] Chen, P.P., The Entity-Relationship Model - Towards a Unified View of Data. ACM TODS, 1(1) (1976).
[10] CODASYL, D.C.: An Information Algebra Phase 1 Report. Communications of the ACM, 5(2),190-204 (1962)
[11] Codd, E.F.: A Relational Model for Large Shared Data Banks. Communication of the ACM, 13(6), 377-387 (1970)
[12] Deliyanni, A., Kowalski, R.: Logic and Semantic Networks. Communications of the ACM, 22(1), 184-192 (1979)
[13] Douqué, B.C.M., Nijssen,G.M. (eds): Data Base Description. *Proceedings of the IFIP WG2.6 special Working Conference.* (North Holland, 1975)
[14] Falkenberg, E.D., Hesse, W.. Lindgreen, P., Nilsson, B.E., Rolland, C., Stamper, R., Van Assche, F., Verreijn-Stuart, A.A., Voss, K. (eds): A Framework of Information Systems Concepts. The FRISCO Report., The IFIP WG 8.1 Task Group FRISCO (1995)
[15] Feldman, J.A., Rovner, P.D. An Algol-based Associative Language. Communication of the ACM, 12(8): 439-449 (1969)
[16] Greenspan, S.J., Borgida, A., Mylopoulos, J.: A Requirements Modelling Language and its Logic. Information Systems, 11(1), 9-23 (1986)

[17] van Griethuysen, J.J., ed: Conceprs and Terminology for the Conceptual Schema (preliminary report). (ISO TC97/SC5/WG5, 1982)
[18] Hammer, M., McLeod. D.:The Semantic Data Model: a Modelling Mechanism for Data Base Applications. in *SIGMOD 1978*. Austin, Texas: (ACM, 1978)
[19] Langefors, B.:Some Approaches to the Theory of Information Systems.. BIT, **3**(34), 229 - 254. (1963)
[20] Langefors, B.: Theoretical Analysis of Information Systems., Lund, Sweden: (Studentlitteratur, 1967)
[21] Klimbie, J.W., Koffeman, K.L. (eds): *Data Base Management*. (North Holland/American Elsevier, 1974)
[22] Lundh, J., Rosengren, P.: HYBRIS - A First Step Towards Efficient Information Management. SISU, Swedish Institute for Systems Development, Box 1250, S-164 28 Kista, Sweden (1989)
[23] McBrien, P., Seltveit,A-H., Wangler, B.: An Entity-Relationship Model Extended to Describe Historical Information. In: *International Conference on Information Systems and Management of Data - CISMOD '92*. Bangalore, India: (Indian National Scientific Documentation Centre., 1992)
[24] Nijssen, G.M.: A Gross Architecture for the Next Generation Database Management Systems. In: *Modelling in Data Base Management Systems*. Freudenstadt, Germany: (North Holland, 1976)
[25] Nijssen, G.M., ed: *Modelling in Data Base Mangement Systems. Proceedings of the IFIP WG 2.6 Working Conference*, Freudenstadt, 5-8 Jan.(North Holland, Amsterdam, 1976)
[26] Nijssen, G.M., ed: *Architecture and Models in Data Base Management. Proceedings of the IFIP TC2 Working Conference,* Jan. (North Holland/Elsevier Science, New York 1977)
[27] Olivé, A.: A Comparison of the Operational and Deductive Approaches to Information Systems Modeling. In: *IFIP Congress 1986*. (North Holland, 1986)
[28] Olivé, A.: On the Design and Implementation of Information Systems from Deductive Conceptual Models. In *VLDB89*. Amsterdam. (1989)
[29] Olle, T.W., Sol,H.G., Verrijn-Stuart, A.A. (eds): *Information System Design Methodologies: a Comparative Review*. (North Holland, Amsterdam 1982)
[30] Olle, T.W., Sol, H. G. , Tully, C.J. (eds): *Information System Design Methodologies: a Feature Analysis*. (North Holland, Amsterdam 1983)
[31] Olle, T.W., Sol, H.G. , Verrijn-Stuart, A.A. (eds): *Information Systems Design Methodologies: Improving the Practice*. (North Holland, Amsterdam 1986)
[32] Persson, A., Stirna.J.: Why Enterprise Modelling - an Explorative Study Into Current Practice. In: *The 13th International Conference on Advanced Information Systems Engineering, CAiSE '02*. Interlaken, Switzerland (Springer 2002)
[33] Senko, M.E., Altman,E.B., Astrahan, M.M., Fehder, P.L.: Data Structures and Accessing in Database Systems. IBM Systems Journal, **12**(1) (1973)
[34] Tsichritzis, D., Klug, A.: The ANSI/X3/SPARC DBMS Framework. Information Systems, 1978. **3**: 173-191 (1978)

18   Janis A. Bubenko jr

[35] Spyns, P., Meersman, R., Jarrar,M.: Data Modelling versus Ontology Engineering. SIGMOD Record, **31**(4): 12-17 (2002)
[36] Sølvberg, A.: Co-operative Concept Modelling, In: *Information Systems Engineering - State of the Art and Research Themes*, Brinkkemper,S., Lindencrona, E., Sølvberg, A. Editors. (Springer, London 2000) pp 305-317
[37] Sølvberg, A.: Conceptual Modeling: A Key to Quality Information Systems. In: *Proceedings of the Fourth International Conference on Quality Software (QSIC'04)*. Braunschweig, Germany (IEEE Computer Society Press 2004)
[38] Young, J.W., Kent,H.K.: Abstract Formulation of Data Processing Problems. Journal of Industrial Engineering, (Nov. Dec.): 471-479 (1958)

Fact-Oriented Modeling: Past, Present and Future

Terry Halpin

Neumont University, Utah, USA.

Abstract. Fact-oriented modeling is a conceptual approach that enables one to model and query business domains in terms of the underlying facts of interest, where all facts and rules may be verbalized in language readily understandable by non-technical users of those business domains. Unlike Entity-Relationship modeling and object-oriented modeling, fact-oriented modeling treats all facts as relationships (unary, binary, ternary etc.). Grouping of facts into attribute-based structures (e.g. ER entities, UML objects, database relations, XML elements) is considered a lower level, implementation issue that is irrelevant to capturing the essential business semantics. This chapter provides a brief history of the fact-oriented modeling approach, illustrates its main concepts and benefits via a case study, reviews the current state of the art in terms of methodology and tooling perspectives, and identifies several topics for future research.

1 Introduction

Fact-oriented modeling is a conceptual approach to information modeling and information systems engineering [83], designed to promote correctness, clarity, and adaptability. The approach enables one to model, transform, and query information in terms of the underlying *facts* of interest, where facts and rules may be verbalized in language readily understandable by non-technical users of the business domain. In contrast to Entity-Relationship (ER) modeling [17], Unified Modeling Language (UML) class diagrams [71], Relational Database (RDB) schemas and Extended Markup Language (XML) schemas, fact-oriented models are *attribute-free*, treating all facts as relationships (unary, binary, ternary etc.). For example, instead of the attributes Person.isSmoker and Person.birthCountry, the following *fact types* are used: Person smokes; Person was born in Country.

Avoiding attributes in the base model enhances *semantic stability*. For example, if we used a birthCountry attribute and later decided to record the population of countries, then we would need to remodel the information as a relationship and recode any queries based on it. An attribute-free approach also enables all fact structures to be easily *populated* with fact instances to help validate models by discussing concrete examples (more difficult with attributes, especially multi-valued ones), as well as facilitating *natural verbalization* (compare Pat smokes with Pat.isSmoker = true).

For information modeling, fact-oriented *graphical notations* are typically far *more expressive* than those provided by other notations (see later). Fact-oriented textual languages are based on formal subsets of native languages, so are easier for business people to understand than technical languages like the Object Constraint Language (OCL) [88]. However, attribute-based notations provide value in enabling more compact diagrams, and are closer to implementation data structures. For such reasons, fact-oriented modeling is often used in conjunction with attribute-based notations, especially for the original conceptual analysis. Since fact-oriented modeling includes procedures for mapping to attribute-based structures, such as those of ER, UML, RDB, or XML, it may be used productively to front-end such approaches.

Though less well known than ER and object-oriented approaches, fact-oriented modeling has been used successfully in industry and academia for over 30 years. This chapter focuses on *Object-Role Modeling* (ORM), the most popular fact-oriented approach, so-called because it pictures the world in terms of *objects* (entities or values) that play *roles* (parts in relationships). We use the term "ORM" to include a number of closely related dialects, all of which use a similar object-role graphical notation, and stress model validation via verbalization and sample fact populations. Other fact-based (attribute-free) approaches adopting different graphical notations include the Object-oriented Systems Model (OSM) [24], and the fact modeling technique in the Semantics of Business Vocabulary and Business Rules (SBVR) proposal [73]. For a basic introduction to ORM see [44], and for comparisons of ORM with ER and/or UML see [35, 36].

The rest of this chapter is structured as follows. Section 2 sketches a brief history of ORM, section 3 outlines the ORM notation, section 4 illustrates ORM's modeling process via a small case study, section 5 discusses recent and future research initiatives, and section 6 provides a conclusion and list of references.

2   A Brief History of ORM

Research in the 1970s, especially in Europe, developed high level semantics for modeling information systems. Abrial [1], Senko [81] and others
modelled with binary relationships. In 1973, Falkenberg generalized their
work to n-ary relationships and excluded attributes at the conceptual level
because they involved "fuzzy" distinctions and also complicated schema
evolution. Later, Falkenberg proposed the fundamental ORM framework,
which he called the "object-role model" [28]. This framework allowed n-
ary and nested relationships, but depicted roles with arrowed lines.

Nijssen [68] adapted this framework by introducing the circle-box notation for objects and roles, and adding a linguistic orientation and design
procedure to provide a modeling method called ENALIM (Evolving NAtural Language Information Model) [69]. Nijssen's team of researchers at
Control Data in Belgium developed the method further, including van Assche who classified object types into lexical object types (LOTs) and non-
lexical object types (NOLOTs). Today, LOTs are commonly called "Entity
types" and NOLOTs are called "Value types". The late Bill Kent provided
several semantic insights and clarified many conceptual issues [63], the recent republication of his seminal text on Data and Reality testifying to the
continued relevance of his contributions [64].

Meersman added subtyping to the approach, and made major contributions to the RIDL query language [65] with Falkenberg and Nijssen. The
method was renamed "aN Information Analysis Method" (NIAM) and
summarized by Verheijen and van Bekkum [86]. Later, the acronym
"NIAM" was given different expansions, e.g. "Natural language Information Analysis Method". Two matrix methods for subtype determination
were developed, one by Vermeir [87] and one by Falkenberg and others.

In the 1980s, Nijssen and Falkenberg moved to the University of
Queensland, where the method was enhanced by Halpin, who provided the
first full formalization [31], including schema equivalence proofs, and
made several refinements and extensions. In 1989, Halpin and Nijssen co-
authored a book on the approach, followed a year later by Wintraecken's
book [89]. Today several books, including major works by Halpin [24],
and Bakema, Zwart and van der Lek [4] expound on the approach.

Many researchers contributed to the ORM approach, and there is no
space here to list them all. Today various versions of ORM exist, but all
adhere to the fundamental object-role framework. Although most ORM
proponents favour n-ary relationships, some preferred Binary-Relationship
Modeling (BRM), e.g. Shoval [82]. Habrias [30] developed an object-
oriented version called MOON (Normalized Object-Oriented Method).

The Predicator Set Model (PSM) was developed mainly by ter Hofstede, Proper and van der Weide [56], and includes complex object constructors. De Troyer and Meersman [19] developed a version with constructors called Natural Object-Relationship Model (NORM). Halpin developed an extended version called Formal ORM (FORM), and with Bloesch and others at InfoModelers Inc. developed an associated query language called ConQuer [7]. Bakema, Zwart, and Van der Lek [4] recast entity types as nested relationships, to produce Fully Communication Oriented Information Modeling (FCO-IM).

Various *software tools* support different flavours of the fact-oriented approach. The earliest tools developed by Nijssen, Meersman and others at Control Data (e.g. IAST, RIDL*) are no longer available. Bloesch, Halpin, and others developed VisioModeler (discontinued but freely available), ActiveQuery (currently unavailable), and the ORM modeling solution in Microsoft® Visio for Enterprise Architects [48]. The FCO-IM version is supported by the commercial tool CaseTalk (www.casetalk.com) and by the freeware tool Infagon (www.mattic.com). Dogma Modeler (www.starlab.vub.ac.be) and T-Lex [85] are academic ORM-based tools for specifying ontologies. NORMA [15], an open-source plug-in to Microsoft® Visual Studio, is currently under development to provide deep support for the next generation of ORM (http://sourceforge.net/projects/orm).

3   The ORM Graphical Notation

ORM includes graphical and textual notations for specifying models, as well as procedures for creating, transforming, mapping, and querying models. This section outlines the main ORM graphical symbols, and the next section discusses a procedure using this notation to specify models.

For space considerations, we limit our attention to the ORM 2 notation [43], as supported by the NORMA tool. Figure 1 lists the main graphical symbols, numbered for easy reference, which are now briefly explained. The next section illustrates the use of many of these symbols.

An *entity type* (e.g. Person) is depicted as a named, soft rectangle (symbol 1). As a configuration option, the soft rectangle may be replaced by an ellipse (symbol 2), which was commonly used in earlier versions of ORM, or a hard rectangle (symbol 3). A *value type* (e.g. PersonName) is a lexical object type (instances are typically character strings or numbers) and is shown as a named, dotted soft rectangle (symbol 4). Each entity type has a *reference scheme*, indicating how each instance of the entity type may be mapped via predicates to a combination of one or more values.

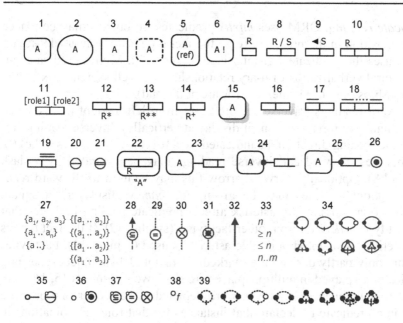

Fig. 1. ORM graphic symbols

A simple injective (1:1 into) reference scheme maps entities to single values. For example, countries may be identified by country codes (e.g. 'US'). In such cases the reference scheme may be abbreviated as in symbol 5 by displaying the *reference mode* in parentheses, e.g. Country (.code). The reference mode indicates how values relate to the entities. Values are constants with a known denotation, so require no reference scheme.

Typically each entity type has a *preferred* reference scheme. Relationships used for preferred reference are called *existential facts* (e.g. there exists a country that has the country code 'US'). The other relationships are *elementary facts* (e.g. The country with country code 'US' has a population of 300 000 000). In symbol 6, an exclamation mark declares that an object type is *independent*. This means that instances of that type may exist without participating in any elementary facts. By default, this is not so.

A fact type results from applying a logical *predicate* a sequence of one or more object types. Each predicate comprises a named sequence of one or more *roles* (parts played in the relationship). A predicate is basically a sentence with object holes in it, one for each role, which each role depicted as a box and played by exactly one object type. Symbol 7 shows a unary predicate (e.g. ... smokes), symbols 8 and 9 depict binary predicates (e.g. ... was born in ...), and symbol 10 shows a ternary predicate. Predicates of higher *arity* (number of roles) are allowed. Each predicate has at least one *predicate reading*. ORM uses *mixfix* predicates, so objects may be placed at any position in the predicate (e.g., the fact type Person introduced Person to Person uses the predicate "... introduced ... to ..."). Mixfix predicates allow natural verbalization of n-ary relationships, as well as non-infix binary relationships (e.g. in Japanese, verbs are at the end).

Forward readings traverse the predicate from left to right (if displayed horizontally) or top to bottom (if displayed vertically). Inverse readings reverse the reading direction, as indicated by a reverse arrow-tip (symbol 9). For binaries, forward and inverse readings may be separated by a slash (symbol 8). Optionally, forward arrow-tips may be used for forward readings. Optionally, roles may be given *role names*, displayed in square brackets (symbol 11). An asterisk after a predicate reading indicates that the fact type is *derived* from other fact types (symbol 12). If the fact type is both derived and stored, a double asterisk is used (symbol 13). Fact types that are only partly derived are marked "+" (symbol 14). Object types and predicates displayed in multiple places are shadowed (symbols 15, 16).

Internal uniqueness constraints are depicted as bars over one or more roles in a predicate to declare that instances for that role (combination) in the fact type population must be unique (e.g. symbols 17, 18). For example, adding a uniqueness constraint over the first role of Person was born in Country declares that each person was born in at most one country. If the constrained roles are not contiguous, a dotted line separates the parts of the uniqueness bar that do constrain roles (symbol 18). A predicate may have one or more uniqueness constraints, at most one of which may be declared preferred by using a double-bar (symbol 19).

An *external uniqueness constraint* shown as a circled uniqueness bar (symbol 20) may be applied to two or more roles from different predicates by connecting to them with dotted lines. This indicates that instances of the combination of those roles in the join of those predicates are unique. For example, if a state is identified by combining its state code and country, we add an external uniqueness constraint to the roles played by Statecode and Country in: State has Statecode; State is in Country. To declare an external uniqueness constraint preferred, a circled double-bar is used (symbol 21).

If we want to talk about a relationship, we may *objectify* it (make an object out of it) so that it can play roles. Graphically, the objectified predicate (a.k.a. *nested* predicate) is enclosed in a soft rectangle, with its name in quotes (symbol 22). Roles are connected to their players by a line segment (symbol 23). A *mandatory role constraint* declares that every instance in the population of the role's object type must play that role. This is shown as a large dot placed either at the object type end (symbol 24) or the role end (symbol 25). An *inclusive-or* (*disjunctive mandatory*) constraint may be applied to two or more roles to indicate that all instances of the object type population must play at least one of those roles. This is shown by connecting the roles by dotted lines to a circled dot (symbol 26).

To restrict the population of an object type or role, the relevant values may be listed in braces connected by a dotted line to the object type or role (symbol 27). For ordered values, a range is declared using ".." between the first and last values. For continuous ranges, a square or round bracket indicates the end value is respectively included or excluded. For example, "(0..10]" denotes a range of positive (hence excluding 0) real numbers up to and including 10. These constraints are called *value constraints*.

Symbols 28-30 denote *set comparison constraints*, which apply only between compatible role sequences (i.e. sequences of one or more roles, where the corresponding roles have the same host object type). A dotted arrow with a circled subset symbol from one role sequence to another depicts a *subset constraint*, restricting the population of the first sequence to be a subset of the second (symbol 28). A dotted line with a circled "=" symbol depicts an *equality constraint*, indicating the populations must be equal (symbol 29). A circled "X" (symbol 30) depicts an *exclusion constraint*, indicating the populations are mutually exclusive. Exclusion and equality constraints may be applied between two or more sequences. Combining an inclusive-or constraint with an exclusion constraint yields an *exclusive-or constraint* (symbol 31).

A solid arrow (symbol 32) from one object type to another indicates that the first object type is a (proper) *subtype* of the other. For example, Woman is a subtype of Person. Mandatory (circled dot) and exclusion (circled "X") constraints may also be displayed between subtypes, but are implied by other constraints if the subtypes are given formal definitions.

Symbol 33 shows four kinds of *frequency constraint*. Applied to a sequence of one or more roles, these indicate that instances that play those roles must do so *exactly n* times, *at least n and at most m* times, *at most n* times, or *at least n* times.

Symbol 34 shows eight kinds of *ring constraint* that may be applied to a pair of roles played by the same host type. Read left to right and top row first, these indicate that the binary relation formed by the role population must respectively be irreflexive, asymmetric, antisymmetric, reflexive, intransitive, acyclic, intransitive and acyclic, or intransitive and asymmetric.

All the constraints so far considered are *alethic* (necessary, so can't be violated) and are coloured violet. ORM 2 also supports *deontic* versions (obligatory, but can be violated) of these constraints. These are coloured blue, and either add an "o" for obligatory, or soften lines to dashed lines. Displayed here are the deontic symbols for uniqueness (symbol 35), mandatory (symbol 36), set-comparison (symbol 37), frequency (symbol 38) and ring (symbol 39) constraints.

4   The ORM Modeling Procedure

The information systems life cycle usually involves several stages: feasibility study; requirements analysis; conceptual design of data and services; logical design; external design; prototyping; internal design and implementation; testing and validation; and maintenance. ORM's *conceptual schema design procedure* (CSDP) focuses on the analysis and design of data. The conceptual schema specifies the information structure of the business domain: the *types of fact* that are of interest; *constraints* on these; and perhaps *derivation rules* for deriving some facts from others. With large domains, the universe of discourse is divided into convenient modules, the CSDP is applied to each, and the resulting subschemas are integrated into the global conceptual schema. Table 1 shows a popular version of the CSDP, which we now illustrate with a small case study.

Step 1 is the most critical. Examples of the required information are verbalized in natural language. Such examples, known as *data use cases*, are often available as output reports or input forms, perhaps from a current manual version of the required system. If not, the modeller may work with the client to produce examples. To avoid misinterpretation, a *domain expert* (a person who understands the business domain) assists with the verbalization. It helps if the speaker imagines he/she has to convey the information contained in the examples to a friend over the telephone.

For our case study, we consider a fragment of an information system maintained by a book publisher. One required service is to provide a report about books, an extract of which is shown in Table 2. In the first phase of Step 1, the domain expert verbalizes the information naturally as they understand it. For example, the subject matter expert might informally verbalize the information on the first row of table 1 thus: "The book with ISBN 1-33456-012-3 is titled 'Mizu no Kokoro' and was published in 2002. This book sold 5000 copies in 2003, 6000 copies in 2004, and 5000 copies in 2005, totalling 16000 copies sold. It is a best seller".

Table 1. The conceptual schema design procedure (CSDP)

Step	Description
1.	Transform familiar information examples into elementary facts, and apply quality checks.
2.	Draw the fact types, and apply a population check.
3.	Check for entity types that should be combined, and note any arithmetic derivations.
4.	Add uniqueness constraints, and check arity of fact types.
5.	Add mandatory role constraints, and check for logical derivations.
6.	Add value, set comparison and subtyping constraints.
7.	Add other constraints and perform final checks.

Table 2. Extract from a report about books

ISBN	Title	Published	Translation of	Sales			Best Seller?
				Year	Nr	Total	
1-33456-012-3	Mizu no Kokoro	2002		2003 2004 2005	5000 6000 5000	16000	Y
2-55860-123-6	Mind Like Water	2004	1-33456-012-3	2004 2005	3000 3000	6000	N
3-540-25432-2	Informatics	2005		2005	2000	2000	N
4-567-12345-3	Informatics	2006					
5-123-45678-5	Semantics						

The second row includes a new kind of fact: "The book with ISBN 2-55860-123-6 is translated from the book with ISBN 1-33456-012-3". We now have examples of all the kinds of facts provided by the table.

In the second phase of Step 1, the modeller rephrases the information as elementary facts, ensuring all objects are *well identified*. Here the term "*fact*" means a proposition taken to be true by the business. An *elementary fact* asserts that an object has a property or that one or more objects participate in a relationship, where that relationship cannot be expressed as a conjunction of simpler (or shorter) facts without introducing new object types. The information expressed informally above may be rephrased into eight elementary facts ("CE" denotes "Common Era"):

> The Book identified by ISBN 1-33456-012-3 has the BookTitle 'Mizu no Kokoro'.
> The Book identified by ISBN 1-33456-012-3 was published in the Year 2002 CE.
> The Book identified by ISBN 1-33456-012-3 in the Year 2003 CE sold NrCopies 5000.
> The Book identified by ISBN 1-33456-012-3 in the Year 2004 CE sold NrCopies 6000.
> The Book identified by ISBN 1-33456-012-3 in the Year 2005 CE sold NrCopies 5000.
> The Book identified by ISBN 1-33456-012-3 sold total NrCopies 16000.
> The Book identified by ISBN 1-33456-012-3 is a best seller.
> The Book identified by ISBN 2-55860-123-6 is translated from the Book identified by ISBN 1-33456-012-3.

The third, fourth, and fifth facts are instances of the same type. There are two entity types, Book and Year, whose reference (identification) schemes may be abbreviated as Book(ISBN) and Year(CE), and two value types BookTitle and NrCopies. Abstracting out the instance data and reference schemes leads to the following six *fact types*. Here the object types are distinguished by starting with a capital letter (other styles may be used instead, e.g. underlining); the rest of the sentence is the predicate reading.

> Book has BookTitle. Book was published in Year. Book in Year sold NrCopies.
> Book sold total NrCopies. Book is a best seller. Book is translated from Book.

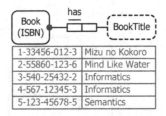

Fig. 2. Populating a fact type with sample data

The third, fourth, and fifth facts are instances of the same type. There are two entity types, Book and Year, whose reference (identification) schemes may be abbreviated as Book(ISBN) and Year(CE), and two value types BookTitle and NrCopies. Abstracting out the instance data and reference schemes leads to the following six *fact types*. Here the object types are distinguished by starting with a capital letter (other styles may be used instead, e.g. underlining); the rest of the sentence is the predicate reading.

Later steps in the CSDP involve diagramming the fact types, adding constraints, noting any fact types that are derived from others, and catering for subtyping. *Constraints are validated with the domain expert by verbalization and population.* As a simple example, Fig. 2 populates the fact type Book has BookTitle with sample data. The uniqueness and mandatory constraints on the left role may be jointly verbalized as "**Each** Book has **exactly one** BookTitle". The lack of a uniqueness constraint on the right-hand role is verbalized as "**It is possible that more than one** Book has **the same** BookTitle".

The sample data illustrates the uniqueness constraint pattern (entries in the left role's column are unique, but duplicate entries occur in the right-hand column). If a constraint is in doubt, negative verbalizations may be used to spell out what it means to violate the constraint, and this can be illustrated by populating with counterexamples [0, 0]. While the example shown here is basic, the fact-based approach enables this validation process to be applied to all its fact types and constraints.

Now suppose the information system is also required to output reports like those shown in Table 3 and Table 4. Here "PNr" denotes a personnel number used to identify people who work in some capacity for the book publisher, as staff and/or authors and/or reviewers. Table 4 lists details about books assigned to people for review. The result column indicates the grade that the reviewer assigned to that book (if known).

An ORM schema for the domain described in the three reports is shown in Fig. 3. Some aspects (e.g. the derivation rule for best sellers) need to be obtained by questioning the domain expert.

Table 3. Extract from a report about persons employed by the publisher

PNr	Name	Title	Gender	Books authored
1	John Smith	Mr	M	
2	Don Bradchap	Sir	M	
3	Sue Yakamoto	Mrs	F	1-33456-012-3
4	Yoko Ohyes	Dr	F	2-55860-123-6
5	Isaac Seldon	Dr	M	3-540-25432-2, 5-123-45678-5
6	Ann Gables	Ms	F	
7	John Smith	Mr	M	4-567-12345-3
8	Ann Jones	Ms	F	5-123-45678-5
9	Selena Moore	Mrs	F	

Table 4. Extract from a report about book reviews

ISBN	Title	Review Assignment		
		PNr	Name	Result
1-33456-012-3	Mizu no Kokoro	1	John Smith	4
		4	Yoko Ohyes	5
2-55860-123-6	Mind Like Water	2	Don Bradchap	5
		5	Isaac Seldon	5
		6	Ann Gables	4
3-540-25432-2	Informatics	1	John Smith	4
		7	John Smith	5
4-567-12345-3	Informatics	1	John Smith	
		5	Isaac Seldon	

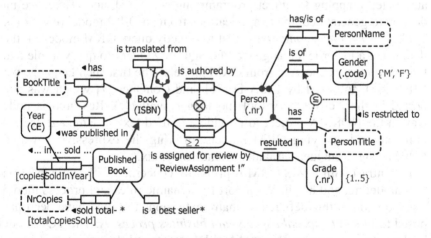

Each PublishedBook **is a** Book that was published in **some** Year.
* **For each** PublishedBook, totalCopiesSold= **sum**(copiesSoldInYear).
* PublishedBook is a best seller **iff** PublishedBook sold total NrCopies >= 10000.

Fig. 3. An ORM schema for the case study

The external uniqueness constraint (circled bar) reflects the publisher's policy of publishing at most one book of any given title in any given year.

The ring constraint indicates that the book translation relationship is acyclic. The exclusion constraint ensures that no person may review a book that he or she authors. The frequency constraint ensures that any book that is assigned for review has at least two reviewers. The subset constraint ensures that if a person has a title that is restricted to a specific gender (e.g. 'Mrs' is restricted to females), then that person must be of that gender—a simple example of a constraint involving a conceptual join path [38]. The textual declarations provide a subtype definition as well as two derivation rules, one in attribute style (using role names) and one in relational style.

5   ORM Research and Practice

Once constructed, an ORM schema can be transformed into logical, internal, and external structures for implementation. Decades of research has gone into *forward engineering* ORM schemas into RDB schemas (e.g. [18], [80]) as well as *reverse engineering* to ORM (e.g. [13, 5, 82]), and automated support for this is provided by various ORM tools. More recently, research has been conducted to transform ORM schemas to other structures, including UML (e.g. [8]), XML schema (e.g. [6]), external forms and web interfaces (e.g. [12, 20, 23]). Some ORM tools also provide automated mapping to object programming code [15], and efforts are underway to generate complete applications from an ORM model (e.g. [74]).

Conceptual query languages exist to directly query ORM models, rather than using a lower level language like SQL or XQuery to query implementation structures generated from ORM models. The first such language was RIDL [65], followed by LISA-D [56], and ConQuer [7] which was supported in the ActiveQuery tool (no longer available). Research is under way in the NORMA project to provide a unified textual language for formulating and querying ORM models, offering the expressive power of FORML and ConQuer but with a friendlier syntax.

In contrast with UML, ORM is primarily concerned with static information modeling, and has little support for dynamic rules and process modeling. To address this deficiency, many extensions to ORM have been proposed to model *temporal aspects and business processes*. The TOP model [29] allows fact types to be qualified by a temporal dimension and granularity. TRIDL [11] includes time operators and action semantics, and LISA-D [56] supports basic updates. Task structures and task transactions model various processes [53], with formal grounding in process algebra. EVORM [78] formalizes first and second order evolution of information systems. Some explorations have addressed reaction rules [52], behavioural extensions [19], and the derivation of activity models from ORM models [79]. Recent research indicates that the fact-oriented approach is even more suitable than UML for adding state machine behavioural semantics [67], and for specifying dynamic rules (e.g. dynamic rules may be declared in the context of a fact type, not just an object type or class) [3].

On-going research is addressing the use of ORM for designing and reusing *ontologies*[e.g. 21, 84, 85], and on transforming ORM models to OWL (Web Ontology Language) and other description logics. Many proposals seek to enrich ORM with additional semantics to address issues such as *context-aware* systems [55], *part-whole* relationships [62], *default* reasoning [51], varieties of *conceptual join s* [38], and *deontic rules* [45]. Various papers have discussed whether to extend ORM with direct support for *collection types*, *higher-order types*, and *algebraic data types* [33, 39, 75].

Because ORM diagrams can rapidly get very large as the size of the domain grows, *abstraction mechanisms* have been proposed for managing very large ORM schemas [14, 60, 61], and some of these techniques are finding their way into ORM tools.

Support for *objectification* (reification of relationships) has been enriched (e.g. by allowing objectification of unaries). FCO-IM treats all entity types as objectified relationships[4], while the version of ORM supported by NORMA supports implicit objectification, based on a new formalization of situational and propositional nominalization [40].

Considerable research has been conducted in the context of ORM on the related topics of *schema patterns, schema equivalence, schema transformation, conceptual optimization*, and *subtyping patterns* [2, 18, 50, 31, 49]. Research efforts have investigated the *use of ORM in conjunction with other methodologies*, such as DEMO [22] and Agent Object Relationship (AOR) modeling [52]. Empirical research has and is being conducted on the use of OR*M in education* [e. g. 27, 9], and on the *modeling process* itself (how to best use the language to construct models) [10, 58, 59].

ORM has been used productively in industry for three decades. Recent case studies on the practical benefits of *ORM in industry* cover topics such as data quality firewalls[77], dynamic multidimensional denormalization[54], requirements engineering [26] and decision support systems[76].

6   Conclusion

This chapter provided a brief historical overview of the fact-oriented ORM approach, explained its graphical notation, illustrated its basic modeling process with a small case study, and identified many of the past, current, and ongoing research efforts to improve the methodology. Industrial use of ORM has repeatedly shown that its main benefit lies in lifting the communication between modeller and domain expert to a level where they can readily understand and validate the model in fine detail.

Although originating over 30 years ago, the fact-oriented approach has only recently begun to enjoy significant adoption. Possible reasons for this increase in popularity include wider penetration of ORM courses in secondary and tertiary education, and the emergence of powerful software tools supporting ORM. Additionally, ORM is now seen as more relevant because of the heightened perception within the information engineering community of the importance of requirements analysis and the productivity benefits of model-driven development. While European pioneers such as Arne Sølvberg, to whom this book is dedicated, have long espoused a conceptual approach to information engineering, due recognition of the value of semantic modeling has only recently arisen in many countries. An ORM Foundation (www.ormfoundation.org) is now being set up to facilitate the continued development of the fact-oriented approach.

References

[1] Abrial, J.R. (1974) Data Semantics. In: Klimbie JW, Koffeman KL (eds) *Data Base Management*. North-Holland, Amsterdam, pp 1–60

[2] Azizah, F.N., Bakema, G. (2006) Data Modeling Patterns using Fully Communication Oriented Information Modeling. In: Meersman R et al. (eds) *On the Move to Meaningful Internet Systems 2006: OTM 2006 Workshops*, LNCS vol 4278. Springer, Berlin Heidelberg New York, pp 1221–1230.

[3] Balsters, H., Carver, A., Halpin, T., Morgan, T. (2006) Modeling Dynamic Rules in ORM. In: Meersman R et al. (eds) *On the Move to Meaningful Internet Systems 2006: OTM 2006 Workshops*, LNCS vol 4278. Springer, Berlin Heidelberg New York

[4] Bakema, G., Zwart, J., van der Lek, H. (2000) *Fully Communication Oriented Information Modelling*. Ten Hagen Stam, The Netherlands.

[5] Bird, L.J. (1997) Data Reverse Engineering: From a relational database system to a 3-dimensional conceptual schema. PhD thesis, University of Queensland.

[6] Bird, L., Goodchild A, Halpin T (2000) Object Role Modeling and XML Schema. In: *Conceptual Modeling – ER2000*, Proc. 19th ER Conference, Salt Lake City, October 2000, LNCS vol 1920. Springer, Berlin Heidelberg New York, pp 309–322

[7] Bloesch, A., Halpin, T. (1997) Conceptual queries using ConQuer-II. In: *Proc ER'97: 16th Int. Conf. on Conceptual Modeling*, LNCS vol 1331. Springer, Berlin Heidelberg New York, pp 113–126

[8] Bollen, P. (2002) A Formal Transformation from Object Role Models to UML class diagrams. In: *Proc. EMMSAD'02 Workshop*, Toronto.

[9] Bollen, P. (2006) Using Fact-orientation for Instructional design. In: Meersman R, Tari Z, Herrero P et al. (eds) *On the Move to Meaningful Internet Systems 2006: OTM 2006 Workshops*, LNCS vol 4278. Springer, Berlin Heidelberg New York, pp 1231–1241

[10] Bommel, P. van, Hoppenbrouwers, S., Proper, H., Weide, Th P. van der (2006) Exploring Modelling Strategies in a Meta-modelling Context. In: Meersman R et al. (eds) *On the Move to Meaningful Internet Systems 2006: OTM 2006 Workshops*, LNCS vol 4278. Springer, Berlin Heidelberg New York, pp 1128–1137

[11] Bruza, P.D., Weide, Th P. van der (1989) The Semantics of TRIDL, Technical Report 89–17, Department of Information Systems, University of Nijmegen.

[12] Campbell, L., Halpin, T. (1993) Automated Support for Conceptual to External Mapping. In: Brinkkemper S, Harmsen F (eds) *Proc 4th Workshop on Next Generation CASE Tools,* Univ. Twente Memoranda Informatica 93–32, Paris (June), pp 35-51

[13] Campbell, L., Halpin, T. (1994) The reverse engineering of relational databases. In: *Proc 5th Workshop on Next Generation CASE Tools*, Utrecht.

[14] Campbell, L., Halpin, T., Proper, H. (1996) Conceptual Schemas with Abstractions: making flat conceptual schemas more comprehensible. *Data Knowl Eng* 20(1): 39–85.

[15] Curland, M., Halpin, T. (2007) Model Driven Development with NORMA. In: *Proc. HICSS-40*, CD-ROM, IEEE Computer Society.

[16] Cuyler, D., Halpin, T. (2005) Two Meta-Models for Object-Role Modeling. In: Krogstie J, Halpin T, Siau K (eds) *Information Modeling Methods and Methodologies,* Idea Publishing Group, Hershey, pp 17–42

[17] Chen, P.P. (1976) The entity-relationship model—towards a unified view of data. *ACM Transactions on Database Systems*, 1(1), pp 9–36

[18] De Troyer, O. (1993) On Data Schema Transformations, PhD thesis, Uni. Tilburg.

[19] De Troyer, O., Meersman, R. (1995) A logic framework for a semantics of object oriented data modeling. In: *OOER'95: Object-Oriented and Entity-Relationship Modeling*, LNCS vol. 1021. Springer, Berlin Heidelberg New York, pp 238–249

[20] De Troyer, O., Castelyn, S., Plessers, P. (2005). Using ORM to Model Web Systems. In: Meersman R et al. (eds) *On the Move to Meaningful Internet Systems 2005: OTM 2005 Workshops*, LNCS vol 3762. Springer, Berlin Heidelberg New York, pp. 700–709

[21] Dietz, J.L.G. (2005) A World Ontology Specification Language. In: Meersman R et al. (eds) *On the Move to Meaningful Internet Systems 2005: OTM 2005 Workshops*, LNCS vol 3762. Springer, Berlin Heidelberg New York, pp 688–699

[22] Dietz, J.L.G., Halpin, T. (2004) Using DEMO and ORM in Concert: A Case Study. In: Siau K (ed) *Advanced Topics in Database Research, vol. 3*, Idea Group, Hershey

[23] Dumas, M., Aldred, L., ter Hofstede, A. (2002) From Conceptual Models to Constrained Web Forms. In: Kashyap V, Shklar L (eds) *Real World Semantic Web Applications*, IOS Press, pp 50–68

[24] Embley, D.W. (1998) *Object Database Development*, Addison-Wesley.

[25] Embley, D.W., Wu, H.A., Pinkston, J.S., Czejdo, B. (1996) OSM-QL: a calculus-based graphical query language, Tech Report, Brigham Young University, Utah

[26] Evans, K. (2005) Requirements Engineering with ORM, In: Meersman R et al. (eds) *On the Move to Meaningful Internet Systems 2005: OTM 2005 Workshops*, LNCS vol 3762. Springer, Berlin Heidelberg New York, pp 646–655

[27] Everest, G. (1994) Experiences teaching NIAM/OR modeling. In: Nijssen GM, Sharp J (eds), *NIAM-ISDM 1994 Conf. Working papers*, Albuquerque, pp N1–26

[28] Falkenberg, E. (1976) Concepts for modeling information. In: Nijssen GM (ed) *Proc. 1976 IFIP Working Conf. on Modelling in Data Base Management Systems*, North-Holland Publishing, pp 95–109

[29] Falkenberg, E., van der Weide, Th. P. (1988) Formal Description of the TOP Model, Technical Report 88-01, Department of Information Systems, University of Nijmegen

[30] Habrias, H. (1993) Normalized Object Oriented Method. In: *Encyclopedia of Microcomputers*, vol. 12, Marcel Dekker, New York, pp 271–285

[31] Halpin, T. (1989) A Logical Analysis of Information Systems: static aspects of the data-oriented perspective, PhD thesis, University of Queensland

[32] Halpin, T. (2000) Integrating fact-oriented modeling with object-oriented modeling. In: Siau K, Rossi M (eds) *Information Modeling for the new Millenium*, Idea Group Publishing, Hershey, pp 150–166

[33] Halpin, T. (2000) Modeling collections in UML and ORM. In: *Proc EMMSAD'00: 5th IFIP WG8.1 Int Workshop on Evaluation of Modeling Methods in Systems Analysis and Design*, Kista, Sweden

[34] Halpin, T. (2001) *Information Modeling and Relational Databases*, Morgan Kaufmann, San Francisco.

[35] Halpin, T. (2002) Information Analysis in UML and ORM: a Comparison. In: Siau K (ed) *Advanced Topics in Database Research, vol. 1*, Idea Group, Hershey,

[36] Halpin, T. (2004) Comparing Metamodels for ER, ORM and UML Data Models. In: Siau K (ed) *Advanced Topics in Database Research, vol. 3*, Idea Group, Hershey

[37] Halpin, T. (2004) Business Rule Verbalization. In: Doroshenko A, Halpin T, Liddle S, Mayr H (eds) *Information Systems Technology and its Applications*, Proc. ISTA-2004, Salt Lake City, Lec. Notes in Informatics, vol. P-48, pp 39–52

[38] Halpin, T. (2005) Constraints on Conceptual Join Paths. In: Krogstie J, Halpin T, Siau K (eds) *Information Modeling Methods and Methodologies,* Idea Group, Hershey

[39] Halpin, T. (2005) Higher-Order Types and Information Modeling. In: Siau K (ed) *Advanced Topics in Database Research, vol. 4,* Idea Pub. Group, Hershey, pp 218–237

[40] Halpin, T. (2005) Objectification. In: Castro J, Teniente E (eds) *Proc. CAiSE'05 Workshops,* FEUP, Porto, pp 519–532

[41] Halpin, T. (2005) Fact-Orientation Meets Agent-Orientation. In: Bresciani P et al. (eds) *Agent-Oriented Information Systems II,* LNAI vol 3508, Springer, Berlin Heidelberg New York, pp 97–109

[42] Halpin, T. (2005) Information Modeling in UML and ORM: A Comparison. In: Khosrow-Pour M (ed) *Encyclopedia of Information Science and Technology,* vol. 3, Idea Publishing Group, Hershey, pp 1471–1475

[43] Halpin, T. (2005) ORM 2. In: Meersman R et al. (eds) *On the Move to Meaningful Internet Systems 2005: OTM 2005 Workshops,* LNCS vol 3762. Springer, Berlin Heidelberg New York, pp 676–687

[44] Halpin, T. (2006) Object-Role Modeling (ORM/NIAM). In: Bernus P, Mertins K, Schmidt G (eds) *Handbook on Architectures of Information Systems,* *2nd edition,* Springer, Berlin Heidelberg New York, Heidelberg, pp 81–103

[45] Halpin, T. (2006) Business Rule Modality. In: Latour T, Petit M (eds) *Proc. CAiSE'06 Workshops,* Namur University Press, pp 383–394

[46] Halpin, T., Bloesch, A. (1999) Data modeling in UML and ORM: a comparison. *Journal of Database Management,* 10(4): 4–13

[47] Halpin, T., Curland, M. (2006) Automated Verbalization for ORM 2. In: Meersman R et al. (eds) *On the Move to Meaningful Internet Systems 2006: OTM 2006 Workshops,* LNCS vol 4278. Springer, Berlin Heidelberg New York, pp 1181–1190

[48] Halpin, T., Evans, K., Hallock, P., MacLean, W. (2003) *Database Modeling with Microsoft® Visio for Enterprise Architects,* Morgan Kaufmann, San Francisco.

[49] Halpin, T.,Proper, H. 1995, 'Subtyping and polymorphism in Object-Role Modeling', *Data and Knowledge Engineering,* 15: 251–281.

[50] Halpin, T, Proper, H. (1995) Database schema transformation and optimization. In: Papazoglou M (ed) *OOER'95: Object-Oriented and Entity-Relationship Modeling,* LNCS vol 1021. Springer, Berlin Heidelberg New York, pp 191–203

[51] Halpin, T., Vermeir, D. (1997) Default reasoning in information systems. In: *Database Applications Semantics,* Chapman & Hall, London, pp 423–441

[52] Halpin, T., Wagner, G. (2003) Modeling Reactive Behavior in ORM'. *Conceptual Modeling – ER2003,* LNCS vol 2813. Springer, Berlin Heidelberg New York, pp 567–569

[53] ter Hofstede, A.H.M. (1993) Information Modelling in Data Intensive Domains, PhD thesis, University of Nijmegen

[54] Hansen, J., dela Cruz, N. (2006) Evolution of a Dynamic Multidimensional Denormalization Meta Model Using Object Role Modeling. In: Meersman R

et al. (eds) *On the Move to Meaningful Internet Systems 2006: OTM 2006 Workshops*, LNCS vol 4278. Springer, Berlin Heidelberg New York, pp 1160–69

[55] Henricksen, K., Indulska, J., McFadden, T. (2005) Modelling Context Information with ORM. In: Meersman R et al. (eds) *On the Move to Meaningful Internet Systems 2005: OTM 2005 Workshops*, LNCS vol 3762. Springer, Berlin Heidelberg New York

[56] ter Hofstede, A.H.M., Proper, H.A., Weide, Th.P. van der (1993) Formal definition of a conceptual language for the description and manipulation of information models, *Information Systems*, vol. 18, no. 7, pp 489–523

[57] ter Hofstede, A.H.M., Weide, Th.P van der (1993) Expressiveness in conceptual data modeling', *Data and Knowl Eng* 10(1): 65–100

[58] Hoppenbrouwers, S., Lindeman, H., Properm H. (2006) Capturing Modeling Processes—Towards the MODial Modeling Laboratory. In: Meersman R et al. (eds) *On the Move to Meaningful Internet Systems 2006: OTM 2006 Workshops*, LNCS vol 4278. Springer, Berlin Heidelberg New York, pp 1242–1252

[59] Hoppenbrouwers, S., Proper, H., Weidem Th.P. van der (2005), Fact Calculus: Using ORM and Lisa-D to Reason about Domains. In: Meersman R et al. (eds) *On the Move to Meaningful Internet Systems 2005: OTM 2005 Workshops*, LNCS vol 3762. Springer, Berlin Heidelberg New York, pp 720–729

[60] Jarrar, M. (2005) Modularization and Automatic Composition of Object-Role Modeling (ORM) Schemes. In: Meersman R et al. (eds) *On the Move to Meaningful Internet Systems 2005: OTM 2005 Workshops*, LNCS vol 3762. Springer.

[61] Keet, M. (2005) Using Abstractions to facilitate Management of Large ORM Models. In: Meersman R et al. (eds) *On the Move to Meaningful Internet Systems 2005: OTM 2005 Workshops*, LNCS vol 3762. Springer, Berlin Heidelberg New York, pp 603–612

[62] Keet, M. (2006) Part-Whole Relations in Object-Role Models. In: Meersman R et al. (eds) *On the Move to Meaningful Internet Systems 2006: OTM 2006 Workshops*, LNCS vol 4278. Springer, Berlin Heidelberg New York, pp 1118–1127

[63] Kent, W. (1977) Entities and relationships in Information. In: Nijssen GM (ed) *Proc 1977 IFIP Working Conf on Modelling in Data Base Management Systems*, Nice, France, North-Holland Publishing, pp 67–91

[64] Kent, W. (2000) *Data and Reality*, 2nd edition, 1stBooks Library, Bloomington.

[65] Meersman, R. (1982) The RIDL conceptual language, Research report, Int. Centre for Information Analysis Services, Control Data Belgium, Brussels.

[66] Mok, W., Embley, D. (1996) Transforming conceptual model to object-oriented database designs: practicalities, properties and peculiarities. In: *Proc ER'96: 15th Int. Conf. on conceptual modeling*, LNCS, vol. 1157. Springer, Berlin Heidelberg New York

[67] Morgan, T. (2006) Some Features of State Machines in ORM. In: Meersman R et al. (eds) *On the Move to Meaningful Internet Systems 2006: OTM 2006*

Workshops, LNCS vol 4278. Springer, Berlin Heidelberg New York, pp 1211–1220

[68] Nijssen, G.M. (1976) A gross architecture for the next generation database management systems. In: Nijssen GM (ed) *Proc. 1976 IFIP Working Conf. on Modelling in Data Base Management Systems*, Freudenstadt, Germany, North-Holland Publishing

[69] Nijssen, G.M. (1977) Current issues in conceptual schema concepts. In: Nijssen GM (ed) *Proc. 1977 IFIP Working Conf. on Modelling in Data Base Management Systems*, Nice, France, North-Holland Publishing, pp 31–66

[70] Oaks, P., ter Hofstede, A., Edmond, D., Spork, M. (2003) Extending conceptual models for web based applications, *Conceptual Modeling – ER2003*, Proc. 22nd ER Conference, Chicago, LNCS vol 2813. Springer, Berlin Heidelberg New York, pp 216–245

[71] Object Management Group 2003, *UML 2.0 Superstructure Specification*. Online at: www.omg.org/uml.

[72] Object Management Group 2005, *UML OCL 2.0 Specification*. Online at: http://www.omg.org/docs/ptc/05-06-06.pdf.

[73] Object Management Group 2006, *Semantics of Business Vocabulary and Business Rules Interim Specification*. Online at: www.omg.org/cgi-bin/doc?dtc/06-03-02.

[74] Pepels, B., Plasmeijer, R. (2005) Generating Applications from Object Role Models. In: Meersman R et al. (eds) *On the Move to Meaningful Internet Systems 2005: OTM 2005 Workshops*, LNCS vol 3762. Springer, Berlin Heidelberg New York, pp 656–665

[75] Pepels, B., Plasmeijer, R., Proper, H. (2006) Fact-Oriented Modeling from a Programming Language Designer's Perspective. In: Meersman R et al. (eds) *On the Move to Meaningful Internet Systems 2006: OTM 2006 Workshops*, LNCS vol 4278. Springer, Berlin Heidelberg New York, pp 1170–1180

[76] Pierson, E., dela Cruz, N. (2005) Using Object Role Modeling for Effective In-house Decision Support Systems. In: Meersman R et al. (eds) *OTM 2005 Workshops*, LNCS vol 3762. Springer, Berlin Heidelberg New York, pp 636–645

[77] Piprani, B. (2006) Using ORM-based Models as a Foundation for a data Quality Firewall in an Advanced Generation Data Warehouse. In: Meersman R et al. (eds) *On the Move to Meaningful Internet Systems 2005: OTM 2005 Workshops*, LNCS vol 3762. Springer, Berlin Heidelberg New York, pp 1148–1159

[78] Proper, H.A. (1994) A Theory for Conceptual Modeling of Evolving Application Domains, PhD thesis, University of Nijmegen

[79] Proper, H.A., Hoppenbrouwers SJB, Weide thP van der (2005) A Fact-Oriented Approach to Activity Modeling. In: Meersman R et al. (eds) *OTM 2005 Workshops*, LNCS vol 3762. Springer, Berlin Heidelberg New York, pp 666–675

[80] Ritson, P., Halpin, T. (1993) Mapping Integrity Constraints to a Relational Schema. In: *Proc. 4th Australian Conf on Inf. Systems*, Brisbane, pp 381–400

[81] Senko, M. (1975) Information systems: records, relations, sets, entities and things. *Information Systems* 1(1): 3–13

[82] Shoval, P., Shreiber, N. (1993) Database reverse engineering: from the relational to the binary relational model. *Data and Knowl Eng* 10: 293–315

[83] Sølvberg, A., Kung, C.H. (1993) *Information Systems Engineering.* Springer..

[84] Spyns, P. (2005) Object Role Modeling for Ontology Engineering in the DOGMA Framework. In: Meersman R et al. (eds) *OTM 2005 Workshops,* LNCS vol 3762. Springer, Berlin Heidelberg New York, pp 710–719

[85] Trog, D., Vereecken, J., Christiaens, S., De Leenheer, P., Meersman, R. (2006) T-Lex: a Role-based Ontology Engineering Tool. In: Meersman R et al. (eds) *On the Move to Meaningful Internet Systems 2006: OTM 2006 Workshops,* LNCS vol 4278. Springer, Berlin Heidelberg New York, pp 1191–1200

[86] Verheijen, G., van Bekkum, J. (1982) NIAM: an information analysis method. In: *Information systems Design Methodologies: a comparative review, Proc. IFIP WG8.1 Working Conf.,* Noordwijkerhout, The Netherlands, North Holland Publishing.

[87] Vermeir, D. (1983) Semantic hierarchies and abstractions in conceptual schemata. *Information Systems* 8(2): 117–124

[88] Warmer, J., Kleppe, A. (2003) *The Object Constraint Language,* 2nd edn, Addison-Wesley

[89] Wintraecken, J. (1990) *The NIAM Information Analysis Method: Theory and Practice,* Kluwer, Deventer, The Netherlands

Data Integration – Problems, Approaches, and Perspectives

Patrick Ziegler, Klaus R. Dittrich

University of Zurich, Switzerland

Abstract. Data integration is one of the older research fields in the database area and has emerged shortly after database systems were first introduced into the business world. In this paper, we briefly introduce the problem of integration and, based on an architectural perspective, give an overview of approaches to address the integration issue. We discuss the evolution from structural to semantic integration and shortly present our own research in the SIRUP (Semantic Integration Reflecting User-specific semantic Perspectives) approach. Finally, an outlook to challenging areas of future research in the realm of data integration is given.

1 Introduction

In today's business world, it is typical that enterprises run different but co-existing information systems. Employing these systems, enterprises struggle to realize business opportunities in highly competitive markets. In this setting, the integration of existing information systems is becoming more and more indispensable in order to dynamically meet business and customer needs while leveraging long-term investments in existing IT infrastructure.

In general, integration of multiple information systems aims at combining selected systems so that they form a unified new whole and give users the illusion of interacting with one single information system. The reason for integration is twofold: First, given a set of existing information systems, an integrated view can be created to facilitate information access and reuse through a single information access point. Second, given a certain information need, data from different complementing information systems is combined to gain a more comprehensive basis to satisfy the need.

There is a manifold of applications that benefit from integrated information. For instance, in the area of business intelligence (BI), integrated information can be used for querying and reporting on business activities, for statistical analysis, online analytical processing (OLAP), and data mining in order to enable forecasting, decision making, enterprise-wide planning, and, in the end, to gain sustainable competitive advantages. For customer relationship management (CRM), integrated information on individual customers, business environment trends, and current sales can be used to improve customer services. Enterprise information portals (EIP) present integrated company information as personalized web sites and represent single information access points primarily for employees, but also for customers, business partners, and the public. Last, but not least, in the area of e-commerce and e-business, integrated information enables and facilitates business transactions and services over computer networks.

Similar to information, IT services and applications can be integrated, either to provide a single service access point or to provide more comprehensive services to meet business requirements. For instance, integrated workflow and document management systems can be used within enterprises to leverage intraorganizational collaboration. Based on the ideas of business process reengineering (BPR), integrated IT services and applications that support business processes can help to reduce time-to-market and to provide added-value products and services. Thereby, interconnecting building blocks from selected IT services and applications enables supply chain management within individual enterprises as well as cooperation beyond the boundaries of traditional enterprises, as in interorganisational cooperation, business process networks (BPN), and virtual organizations. For instance, in e-procurement, supply and demand for producer goods are provided with integrated information and services to streamline the purchasing process for institutional buyers. Thus, it is possible to bypass intermediaries and to enable direct interaction between supply and demand, as in business-to-business (B2B), business-to-consumer (B2C), and business-to-employee (B2E) transactions. These trends are fuelled by XML that is becoming *the* industry standard for data exchange as well as by web services that provide interoperability between various software applications running on different platforms.

In the enterprise context, the integration problem is commonly referred to as enterprise integration (EI). Enterprise integration denotes the capability to integrate information and functionalities from a variety of information systems in an enterprise. This encompasses enterprise information integration (EII) that concerns integration on the data and information level and enterprise application integration (EAI) that considers integration on the level of application logic. In this paper, we focus on the integration of information and, in particular, highlight integration solutions that are provided by the database community. Our goal is to give, based on an architectural perspective, a database-centric overview of principal approaches to the integration problem and to illustrate some frequently used approaches. Additionally, we introduce semantic integration that is needed in all integration examples given above and that forms a key factor for current and future integration solutions.

An outlook to our own approach to personal semantic data integration and future research challenges round off this paper which is an extension of [37].

The structure of this paper is as follows: In the following Section, we sketch the problem of integration. Section 3 presents principal approaches to address the integration issue and in Section 4, the evolution from structural to current semantic integration approaches is discussed. Our work in the SIRUP project is outlined in Section 5 and then, an outlook to challenging areas of future data integration research is given. Finally, Section 7 concludes the paper.

2 The Problem of Integration

Integration of multiple information systems generally aims at combining selected systems so that they form a unified new whole and give users the illusion of interacting with one single information system. Users are provided with a homogeneous logical view of data that is physically distributed over heterogeneous data sources. For this, all data has to be represented using the same abstraction principles (unified global data model and unified semantics). This task includes detection and resolution of schema and data conflicts regarding structure and semantics.

In general, information systems are not designed for integration. Thus, whenever integrated access to different source systems is desired, the sources and their data that do not fit together have to be coalesced by additional adaptation and reconciliation functionality. Note that there is not *the* one single integration problem. While the goal is always to provide a homogeneous, unified view on data from different sources, the particular integration task may depend on:

- the architectural view of an information system (see Fig. 1),
- the content and functionality of the component systems,
- the kind of information that is managed by component systems (alphanumeric data, multimedia data; structured, semi-structured, unstructured data),

- requirements concerning autonomy of component systems,
- intended use of the integrated information system (read-only or write access),
- performance requirements, and
- the available resources (time, money, human resources, etc.) [12].

Additionally, several kinds of heterogeneity typically have to be considered. These include differences in:

- hardware and operating systems,
- data management software,
- data models, schemas, and data semantics,
- middleware,
- user interfaces, and
- business rules and integrity constraints.

3 Approaches to Integration

In this section, we apply an architectural perspective to give an overview of the different ways to address the integration problem. The presented classification is based on [12] and distinguishes integration approaches according to the level of abstraction where integration is performed.

Information systems can be described using a layered architecture, as shown in Fig. 1: On the topmost layer, users access data and services through various interfaces that run on top of different applications. Applications may use middleware — transaction processing (TP) monitors, message oriented middleware (MOM), SQL-middleware, etc. — to access data via a data access layer. The data itself is managed by a data storage system. Usually, database management systems (DBMS) are used to combine the data access and storage layer.

In general, the integration problem can be addressed on each of the presented system layers. For this, the following principal approaches — as illustrated in Fig. 1 — are available:

Manual Integration

Here, users directly interact with all relevant information systems and manually integrate selected data. That is, users have to deal with different user interfaces and query languages. Additionally, users need to have detailed knowledge on location, logical data representation, and data semantics.

Common User Interface

In this case, the user is supplied with a common user interface (e.g., a web browser) that provides a uniform look and feel. Data from relevant information systems is still separately presented so that homogenization and integration of data yet has to be done by the users (for instance, as in search engines).

Integration by Applications

This approach uses integration applications that access various data sources and return integrated results to the user. This solution is practical for a small number of component systems. However, applications become increasingly fat as the number of system interfaces and data formats to homogenize and integrate grows.

Integration by Middleware

Middleware provides reusable functionality that is generally used to solve dedicated aspects of the integration problem, e.g., as done by SQL-middleware.

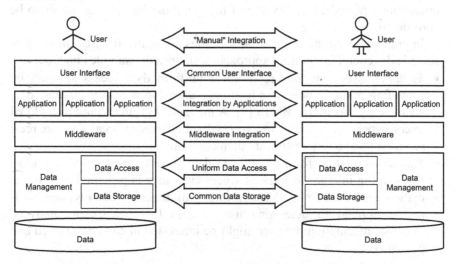

Fig. 1. General Integration Approaches on Different Architectural Levels

While applications are relieved from implementing common integration functionality, integration efforts are still needed in applications[1]. Additionally, different middleware tools usually have to be combined to build integrated systems.

Uniform Data Access

In this case, a logical integration of data is accomplished at the data access level. Global applications are provided with a unified global view of physically distributed data, though only virtual data is available on this level. Local information systems keep their autonomy and can support additional data access layers for other applications. However, global provision of physically integrated data can be time-consuming since data access, homogenization, and integration have to be done at runtime.

Common Data Storage

Here, physical data integration is performed by transferring data to a new data storage; local sources can either be retired or remain operational. In general, physical data integration provides fast data access. However, if local data sources are retired, applications that access them have to be migrated to the new data storage as well. In case local data sources remain operational, periodical refreshing of the common data storage needs to be considered.

In practice, concrete integration solutions are realized based on the presented six general integration approaches. Important examples include:

- *Mediated query systems* represent a uniform data access solution by providing a single point for read-only querying access to various data sources, e.g., as in TSIMMIS [9]. A mediator [34] that contains a global query processor is employed to send subqueries to local data sources; returned local query results are then combined.
- *Portals* as another form of uniform data access are personalized doorways to the internet or intranet where each user is provided with information according to his detected information needs. Usually, web mining is applied to determine user-profiles by click-stream analysis; thereby, information the user might be interested in can be retrieved and presented.

---

[1] For instance, SQL-middleware provides a single access point to send SQL queries to all connevcted component systems. However, query results are not integrated into one single, homogeneous result set.

- *Data warehouses* realize a common data storage approach to integration. Data from several operational sources (on-line transaction processing systems, OLTP) are extracted, transformed, and loaded (ETL) into a data warehouse. Then, analysis, such as online analytical processing (OLAP), can be performed on cubes of integrated and aggregated data.

- *Operational data store* are a second example of a common data storage. Here, a "warehouse with fresh data" is built by immediately [2] propagating updates in local data sources to the data store. Thus, up-to-date integrated data is available for decision support. Unlike in data warehouses, data is neither cleansed nor aggregated nor are data histories supported.

- *Federated database systems (FDBMS)* achieve a uniform data access solution by logically integrating data from underlying local DBMS. Federated database systems are fully-fledged DBMS; that is, they implement their own data model, support global queries, global transactions, and global access control. Usually, the five-level reference architecture by [30] is employed for building FDBMS.

- *Workflow management systems (WFMS)* allow to implement business processes where each single step is executed by a different application or user. Generally, WFMS support modeling, execution, and maintenance of processes that are comprised of interactions between applications and human users. WFMS represent an integration-by-application approach.

- *Integration by web services* performs integration through software components (i.e., web services) that support machine-to-machine interaction over a network by XML-based messages that are conveyed by internet protocols. Depending on their offered integration functionality, web services either represent a uniform data access approach or a common data access interface for later manual or application-based integration.

- *Model management* introduces high-level operations between models (such as database schemas, UML models, and software configurations) and model mappings; such operations include matching, merging, selection, and composition [6]. Using a schema algebra that encompasses all these operations, it is intended to reduce the amount of hand-crafted code required for transformations of models and mappings as needed for schema integration. Model management falls into the category of manual integration.

- *Peer-to-peer (P2P) integration* is a decentralized approach to integration between distributed, autonomous peers where data can be mutually

---

[2] That is, not within the same transaction, but within a period of time that is reasonable according to the particular application requirement

shared and integrated through mappings between local schemas of peers. P2P integration constitutes, depending on the provided integration functionality, either a uniform data access approach or a data access interface for subsequent manual or application-based integration.

- *Grid data integration* provides the basis for hypotheses testing and pattern detection in large amounts of data in grid environments, i.e., interconnected computing resources being used for high-throughput computing. Here, often unpredictable and highly dynamic amounts of data have to be dealt with to provide an integrated view over large (scientific) data sets. Grid data integration represents an integration by middleware approach.
- *Personal data integration systems* (e.g., [38]) are a special form of manual integration. Here, tailored integrated views are defined (e.g., by a declarative integration language), either by users themselves or by dedicated integration engineers. Each integrated view precisely matches the information needs of a user by encompassing all relevant entities with real-world semantics as intended by the particular user; thereby, the integrated view reflects the user's personal way to perceive his application domain of interest.
- *Collaborative integration* (e.g., [25]), another special form of manual integration, is based on the idea to have users to contribute to a data integration system for using it. Here, initial partial schema mappings are presented to users who answer questions concerning the mappings; these answers are then taken to refine the mappings and to expand the system capabilities. Similar to folksonomies, where data is collaboratively labelled for later retrieval, the task of schema mapping is distributed over participating users.
- In *Dataspace systems* [13], co-existence of all data (i.e., both structured and unstructured) is propagated rather than full integration. A dataspace system is used to provide the same basic functionality, e.g., search facilities, over all data sources independently of their degree of integration. Only when more sophisticated services are needed, such as relational-style queries, additional efforts are made to integrate the required data sources more closely. In general, dataspace systems may simultaneously use every one of the presented six general integration approaches.

4 From Structural to Semantic Integration

Database technology was introduced in enterprises since the late 1960s to support (initially rather simple) business applications. As the number of applications and data repositories rapidly grew, the need for integrated data became apparent. As a consequence, first integration approaches in the form of multidatabase systems [21] were developed around 1980 — e.g., MULTIBASE [24]. This was a first cornerstone in a remarkable history of research in the area of data integration. The evolution continued over mediators (e.g., Garlic [8]) and agent systems (e.g., InfoSleuth [4]) to ontology-based (e.g., OBSERVER [26]), peer-to-peer (P2P) (e.g., Piazza [19]), and web service-based integration approaches (e.g., Active XML [1]). Recently, tailored personal data integration (e.g., SIRUP [38]), collaborative integration (e.g., MOBS [25]), and dataspace systems [13] are being addressed by the research community (see Figure 2).

In general, early integration approaches were based on a relational or functional data model and realized rather tightly-coupled solutions by providing one single global schema. To overcome their limitations concerning the aspects of abstraction, classification, and taxonomies, object-oriented integration approaches [7] were adopted to perform structural homogenization and integration of data. With the advent of the internet and web technologies, the focus shifted from integrating purely well-structured data to also incorporating semi- and unstructured data while architecturally, loosely-coupled mediator and agent systems became popular.

However, integration is more than just a structural or technical problem. Technically, it is rather easy to connect different relational DBMS (e.g., via ODBC or JDBC). More demanding is to integrate data described by different data models; even worse are the problems caused by data with heterogeneous semantics. For instance, having only the name "loss" to denote a relation in an enterprise information system does not provide sufficient information to doubtlessly decide whether the represented loss is a book loss, a realized loss, or a future expected loss and whether the values of the tuples reflect only a roughly estimated loss or a precisely quantified loss. Integrating two "loss" relations with (implicit) heterogeneous semantics leads to erroneous results and completely senseless conclusions. Therefore, explicit and precise semantics of integratable data are essential for semantically correct and meaningful integration results. Note that none of the principal integration approaches in Section 3 helps to resolve semantic heterogeneity; neither is XML that only provides structural information a solution.

In the database area, semantics can be regarded as people's interpretation of data and schema items according to their understanding of the world in a certain context. In data integration, the type of semantics considered is generally real-world semantics that are concerned with the "mapping of objects in the model or computational world onto the real world [. . .] [and] the issues that involve human interpretation, or meaning and use of data and information" [27]. In this setting, semantic integration is the task of grouping, combining or completing data from different sources by taking into account explicit and precise data semantics in order to avoid that semantically incompatible data is structurally merged. That is, semantic integration has to ensure that only data related to the same or sufficiently similar[3] real-world entity or concept is merged. A prerequisite for this is to resolve semantic ambiguity concerning integratable data by explicit metadata to elicit all relevant implicit assumptions and underlying context information.

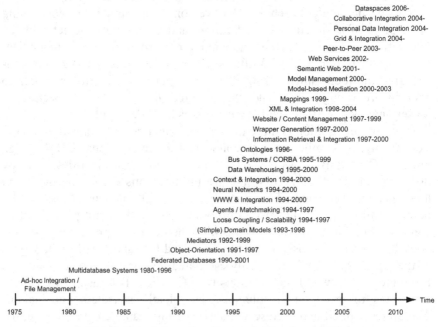

Fig. 2. Data Integration Research Trends over Time

---

[3] How much similarity is considered as sufficient depends on the particular information need and application area.

One idea to overcome semantic heterogeneity in the database area is to exhaustively specify the intended real-world semantics of all data and schema elements. Unfortunately, it is impossible to completely define what a data or schema element denotes or means in the database world [29]. Therefore, database schemas do typically not provide enough explicit semantics to interpret data always consistently and unambiguously [30]. These problems are further worsened by the fact that semantics may be embodied in data models, conceptual schemas, application programs, the data itself, and the minds of users. Moreover, there are no absolute semantics that are valid for all potential users; semantics are relative [15]. These difficulties concerning semantics are the reason for many still open research challenges in the area of data integration.

Ontologies — which can be defined as explicit, formal descriptions of concepts and their relationships that exist in a certain universe of discourse, together with a shared vocabulary to refer to these concepts — can contribute to solve the problem of semantic heterogeneity. Compared with other classification schemes, such as taxonomies, thesauri, or keywords, Ontologies allow more complete and more precise domain models [20]. With respect to an ontology a particular user group commits to, the semantics of data provided by data sources for integration can be made explicit. Based on this shared understanding, the danger of semantic heterogeneity can be reduced. For instance, ontologies can be applied in the area of the Semantic Web to explicitly connect information from web documents to its definition and context in machine-processable form; thereby, semantic services, such as semantic document retrieval, can be provided.

In database research, *single* domain models and ontologies were first applied to overcome semantic heterogeneity. As in SIMS [3], a domain model is used as a single ontology to which the contents of data sources are mapped. Thus, queries expressed in terms of the global ontology can be asked. In general, single-ontology approaches are useful for integration problems where all information sources to be integrated provide nearly the same view on a domain [33]. In case the domain views of the sources differ, finding a common view becomes difficult. To overcome this problem, multi-ontology approaches like OBSERVER [26] describe each data source with its own ontology; then, these local ontologies have to be mapped, either to a global ontology or between each other, to establish a common understanding. Thus, it is now state of the art that information systems "carry with them an explicit model of the world that they operate in, a model of what the data that they carry stand for." [32].

5 Personal Semantic Data Integration in the SIRUP Approach

Mapping all data to one single domain model or ontology forces users to adapt to one single conceptualization of the world. This contrasts to the fact that receivers of integrated data widely differ in their conceptual interpretation of and preference for data — they are generally situated in various real-world contexts and have different conceptual models of the world in mind [17]. These models do not only vary between different people in the same domain, but even for the same individual over time [14]. COIN [17] was one of the first research projects to consider the different contexts data providers and data receivers are situated in.

In our own research, we continue the trend of taking into account user specific aspects in the process of semantic integration. We address the problem how individual mental domain models and personal semantics of concepts can be reflected in data integration to provide tailor-made integration for personal information needs. In the SIRUP (Semantic Integration Reflecting User-specific semantic Perspectives) approach [38], we investigate how data — equipped with explicit, queryable semantics — can be effectively preintegrated on a conceptual level. Thereby, we aim at enabling users to perform declarative data integration by conceptual modeling of their individual ways to perceive a domain of interest.

Origin of our research is the observation that different users often have diverse views of reality — i.e., they perceive and conceptualize the same real world part differently, according to their relative points of view, their information needs, and expectations [23]. Additionally, none of these co-existing views of the real world can be regarded as being more correct than another because each view is intended for a worthy purpose [31]. In general, we refer to this phenomenon as data receiver heterogeneity. Imposing a single global schema for all users can have severe limitations that seriously interfere with the users' individual work because thereby, data receiver sovereignty is violated. Sovereignty of data receivers refers to the fact that using integrated data must be non-intrusive [28]; i.e., users should not be forced to adapt to any standard concerning structure and semantics of data they desire. Therefore, to take a "one integrated schema fits all" approach is definitely not a satisfactory solution. We generally subsume problems that cause a single global schema to be inappropriate for particular users as perspectual integration mistakes [38]. These include:

- *Data selection mistakes* are caused when data that is available through the global schema is, from the users' perspective, inappropriately collected and selected from a given data source — for example, by only including particular local relations in the global schema.

- *Source selection mistakes* occur when the decision of the global schema designer, which data sources to incorporate into the global schema, differs from individual users' preferences for data from various origins (e.g., due to quality or reliability).
- *Entity granularity mistakes* refer to the fact that the degree of granularity in which information is represented in the global schema can be too coarse-grained (general) or too fine-grained (specialized) according to the requirements of individual users — e.g., by integrating a "seminar" and a "colloquium" relation into a general global "course" relation.
- *Attribute granularity mistakes* are problems of inadequate granularity concerning attributes of entities in the global schema.
- *Data semantics mistakes* arise when the global schema provides an integrated view on data that is semantically not related according to the individual perception of specific users. For instance, data concerning lectures and seminars may be globally merged since both represent similar forms of teaching. However, this is not useful for people who are only interested in seminars because seminar information is blurred with lectures.
- Last, but not least, *data taxonomy mistakes* occur when generalization / specialization hierarchies given by the global schema do not fit the perspective of the particular domain according to individual users.

In general, all six integration mistakes presented can be independently combined to form combined perspectual integration mistakes.

To avoid perspectual integration mistakes, we advocate user-specific, personal semantic data integration. However, to be suitable for this, data integration approaches have to meet certain requirements. We summarize these requirements with the ASME criteria [36]:

- *Abstraction* refers to shielding users from low-level heterogeneities of underlying data sources;
- *Selection* means the possibility of user-specific selection of data and data sources for individual integration;
- *Modeling* corresponds to the availability of means to incorporate user specific perception of the domain for which integrated data is desired in the process of data integration;
- *Explicit semantics* refers to means for explicitly representing the intended real-world semantics of data.

As shown in [36], current data integration approaches fail to completely meet these requirements. In response to this, we propose the SIRUP approach to personal semantic data integration to fulfil all the ASME criteria entirely.

In SIRUP, data providers declaratively link groups of attributes representing alphanumeric data for particular real-world concepts (e.g., "database lecture at University of Zurich") to so-called IConcepts (short for "Intermediate Concept"). Each IConcept represents a single, distinct concept of the real world, and for each real-world concept, there is only one single IConcept in a SIRUP integration system. To make its meaning explicit for both, humans and computers, every IConcept is connected to an ontological concept (through the SOQA ontology API [40]) that precisely represents its intended semantics. Thus, by connecting attribute data from diverse data sources to IConcepts, data from these sources is pre-integrated on a conceptual level and its intended semantics made explicit. In order to allow more than one data source to provide data concerning a particular concept of the real world and to distinguish the origin of data, all the attributes from each data source are organized as separate attribute groups in their respective IConcept. In addition, data providers annotate all attributes they provide for IConcepts so that metadata on attribute meaning, data types, key constraints, measurement units, etc. is explicitly available for users.

Based on these foundations, we provide a declarative integration and query language so that users, equipped with suitable IConcept search tools (see [39]), can derive user-specific concepts (UserConcepts) that are tailored to their information needs from the available set of IConcepts. These UserConcepts can be organized in hierarchies so that individually integrated, virtual views (so-called Semantic Perspectives) representing user-specific conceptual domains models to precisely meet personal information needs can be built. In the whole process of UserConcept modeling and combination, all available metadata including ontology links is automatically maintained and propagated; thus, Semantic Perspectives are annotated individual schemas over diverse data sources with explicit semantics. Finally, queries against Semantic Perspectives can be formulated that are processed by the respective SIRUP integration system. If desired, resulting data can be exported in a variety of formats, such as XML documents, relational tuples (through JDBC), and Excel spreadsheets.

6 Outlook

Albeit there is a remarkable history of research in the field of data integration and in spite of significant progress that has been made since the mid-

1990s, ranging from concepts and algorithms to systems and commercial aspects, significant challenges still remain [18]. In this section, we present some areas that exhibit such challenges for future data integration research from our own perspective.

First of all, dynamic markets and increased competition demand for higher degrees of flexibility concerning data access and interoperability in the business domain. Thus, enterprises are faced with the requirement to provide multiple co-existing integrated views on their distributed corporate data sources to flexibly support different information needs. For instance, to enable banks to precisely assess credit risks according to the Basel II standard for risk management[4], a comprehensive and sound basis of inte-grated customer data is necessary. While in most banks, the needed data is available, it is often scattered over distributed sources, can be inconsistent and partially available only in hard paper copies. This alone is a challeng-ing integration task for many banks; however, it is aggravated by the fact that alternative ways to organize the integrated data can simultaneously be necessary to support distinct information needs (e.g., categorization of credit risks according to geographical criteria or based on customer types). Here, personal data integration approaches like SIRUP can contribute.

Fostering agile cross-enterprise cooperation is another area that imposes challenges for data integration. For example, for virtual organizations as sets of organizational units that work towards a common goal, on-the-fly data integration is extremely important due to their dynamic nature [35]. To effectively provide the needed information by all the cooperating part-ners in a timely manner, each of them being situated in a different real-world context having his own conceptual model of the world in mind, flexible and tailored data integration is a prerequisite. Based on adequately integrated data, required applications like supply chain management (SCM), enterprise resource planning (ERP), and customer relationship management (CRM) can be realized.

Another area of inter-organizational cooperation between organizational units is e-science. Here, virtual experiments based on intensive computa-tions and huge amounts of data are performed in grid environments, as, for example, in earth sciences, particle physics, and bioinformatics. Not only is data integration in this field required to meet diverse scientific informa-tion needs, but also scalability and manageability issues rise due to the fact that masses of data need to be handled efficiently. A key factor for inter-disciplinary multi-national e-science projects is the ability to precisely sat-isfy the data integration and sharing needs of the involved research groups from diverse disciplines. Similarly, successful work in life sciences and e-

---

[4] See http://www.bis.org/publ/bcbsca.htm

health relies on integrated access to disparate forms of data that are spread over many biological and medical institutions by taking into account local data semantics. For these areas, user and group-specific integration approaches like SIRUP can be useful.

As one of the goals of data integration is the provision of unified access to multiple data sources, privacy and security are important issues. Thus, flexible yet effective means for access control in integrated systems are necessary [22]. Despite the fact that integration can provide many benefits, data integration and data sharing are often hampered by privacy concerns [10]. For instance, companies abstain from exchanging data because of fear to be exploited by competitors or regulatory institutions. Similarly, integrated access to patient data can advance medical research but may be impossible without proven measures for privacy protection and access control. Therefore, the development of techniques to guarantee data integration and data sharing without loss of privacy is essential.

Data quality, that can be characterized through accuracy, completeness, timeliness, and consistency of data, is of major interest for the usability of integrated data. In the realm of data integration, however, often complex data flows between data producers, data integrators, and consumers of integrated data have to be taken into account to provide appropriate data quality solutions. Fortunately, ontology-enhanced schemas, as used in semantic data integration, represent an important prerequisite for high quality integrated data and can thus ease quality related issues [16]. In particular, the possibility for users to verify where data originates from and how it was combined and converted into its current form are central in enabling users to distinguish between facts and beliefs and, in consequence, to establish trust in integrated data [16]. Therefore, data lineage and traceability issues are likely to play an important role in future integrations systems, especially when complex data transformations over widely distributed data sources are involved. In addition, globally enforcing integrity constraints can help users to trust integrated data from diverse sources [11].

In our own work in the SIRUP project, we focus on personal semantic integration of structured and annotated alphanumeric data. However, unstructured data, such as letters, reports, presentations, emails, and web pages constitute about 80-90% of all the data in enterprises according to current estimates by analyst firms, such as Gartner. Thus, there is a big challenge to transform this into valuable integrated information that precisely serves the needs in a dynamic business world. One approach to manage this may be provided by the emerging concept of dataspaces that postulates co-existing structured and unstructured data sets without initially requiring to integrate all data. Similar loosely-coupled approaches to data integration are represented by social networks and data sharing communities who collaboratively and incrementally contribute to building an integrated set of data. Here, the vision is to provide ease of use in community data sharing so that also non-expert users can manage and share their diverse data with minimal effort [2]. However, the future needs to show to what extent these approaches can contribute to reach the grand challenge as formulated in the Asilomar report on database research [5], i.e., to make it easy for everyone to store, organize, access, and analyze the majority of human information online.

7 Conclusions

In this paper, we gave an overview of issues and principal approaches in the area of integration seen from a database perspective. Even though data integration is one of the older research topics in the database area, there is yet no silver bullet solution and there is none to be expected in the near future. The most difficult integration problems are caused by semantic heterogeneity; they are being addressed in current research focusing on applying explicit, formalized data semantics to provide semantics-aware integration solutions. Despite this, considerable work remains to be done for the vision of truly personal semantic integration in form of easy to use and scalable solutions to become true.

References

[1] Abiteboul, S., Benjelloun,O., Milo.T.: Web Services and Data Integration. In *Third International Conference on Web Information Systems Engineering (WISE 2002)*, pages 3–7, Singapore, December 12-14, 2002. IEEE Computer Society.

[2] Abiteboul, S., Polyzotis, N.: The Data Ring: Community Content Sharing. In *Third Biennial Conference on Innovative Data Systems Research (CIDR 2007)*, Asilomar, CA, USA, January 7-10, 2007. Online Proceedings.

[3] Arens, Y., Chee, C.H., Hsu, C.-N, Knoblock, C.A.: Retrieving and Integrating Data from Multiple Information Sources. *International Journal of Cooperative Information Systems (IJCIS)*, 2(2):127–158, 1993.

[4] Bayardo, R. J.,Bohrer, B., Brice, R. S., Cichocki, A., Fowler, J., Helal, A., Kashyap, V., Ksiezyk, T., Martin, G., Nodine, M.H., Rashid, M., Rusinkiewicz, M., Shea, R., Unnikrishnan, C., Unruh, A., Woelk, D.: InfoSleuth: Agent-Based Semantic Integration of Information in Open and Dynamic Environments. In *1997 ACM SIGMOD International Conference on Management of Data (SIGMOD 1997)*, pages 195–206, Tucson, Arizona, USA, 1997. ACM.

[5] Bernstein, P., Brodie, M., Ceri, S., DeWitt, D., Franklin, M., Garcia-Molina, H., Gray, J., Held, J., Hellerstein, J., Jagadish, H.V., Lesk, M., Maier, D., Naughton, J., Pirahesh, H., Stonebraker, M., Ullman, J.:The Asilomar Report on Database Research. *SIGMOD Record*, 27(4):74–80, 1998.

[6] Bernstein, P.A., Halevy, A.Y., Pottinger, R.A.: A Vision for Management of Complex Models. *ACM SIGMOD Record*, 29(4):55–63, 2000.

[7] Bukhres, O.A., Elmagarmid, A.K. editors. *Object-Oriented Multidatabase Systems: A Solution for Advanced Applications*. Prentice-Hall, 1996.

[8] Carey, M., Haas, L., Schwarz, P., Arya, M., Cody, W., Fagin, R., Flickner, M., Luniewski, A., Niblack, W., Petkovic, D., Thomas, J., Williams, J., Wimmers, E.: Towards Heterogeneous Multimedia Information Systems: The Garlic Approach. In *5th Internationa lWorkshop on Research Issues in Data Engineering- Distributed Object Management (RIDE-DOM 1995)*, pages 124–131, Taipei, Taiwan, March 6-7, 1995.

[9] Chawathe, S., Garcia-Molina, H., Hammer, J., Ireland, K., Papakonstantinou, Y. , Ullman, J., Widom, J.: The TSIMMIS Project: Integration of Heterogeneous Information Sources. In *16th Meeting of the Information Processing Society of Japan (IPSJ)*, pages 7–18, Tokyo, Japan, October, 1994.

[10] Clifton, C., Kantarcioglu, M., Doan, A., Schadow, G., Vaidya, J., Elmagarmid, A.K., Suciu, D.: Privacy-Preserving Data Integration and Sharing. In 9th *ACM SIGMOD Workshop on Research Issues in Data Mining and Knowledge Discovery (DMKD 2004)*, pages 19–26, Paris, France, June 13, 2004. ACM.

[11] Conrad, S., Höding, M., Saake, G., Schmitt, I., Türker,C.: Schema Integration with Integrity Constraints. In *15th British National Conference on Databases (BNCOD 1997)*, pages 200–214, London, UK, July 7-9, 1997. Springer.

[12] Dittrich, K.R., Jonscher,D.: All Together Now — Towards Integrating the World's Information Systems. In *Advances in Multimedia and Databases for the New Century*, pages 109–123, Kyoto, Japan, November 30 - December 2, 1999. World Scientific Press.

[13] Franklin, M.J., Halevy, A.J., Maier,D.: From Databases to Dataspaces: A New Abstraction for Information Management. *SIGMOD Record*, 34(4):27–33, 2005.

[14] Gaines, B.R, Shaw,M.L.G: Comparing the Conceptual Systems of Experts. In *11th International Joint Conference on Artificial Intelligence (IJCAI 1989)*, pages 633–638, Detroit, Michigan, USA, August, 1989. Morgan Kaufmann.

[15] Garc´ıa-Solaco, M., Saltor, F., Castellanos,M.: Semantic Heterogeneity in Multidatabase Systems. In O. A. Bukhres and A. K. Elmagarmid, editors, *Object-Oriented Multidatabase Systems. A Solution for Advanced Applications*, pages 129–202. Prentice-Hall, 1996.

[16] Gertz, M., Özsu, M.T., Saake, G., Sattler,K.U.: Report on the Dagstuhl Seminar "Data Quality on the Web". SIGMOD Record, 33(1):127–132, 2004.

[17] Goh, C.H, Madnick, S.E., Siegel, M.: Context Interchange: Overcoming the Challenges of Large-Scale Interoperable Database Systems in a Dynamic Environment. In *Third International Conference on Information and Knowledge Management (CIKM 1994)*, pages 337–346, Gaithersburg, USA, November 29 - December 2, 1994. ACM.

[18] Halevy, A.Y.: Data Integration: A Status Report. In *Datenbanksysteme in Business, Technologie und Web (BTW 2003)*, volume 26, pages 24–29, Leipzig, Germany, February 26-28, 2003. Gesellschaft f'ur Informatik (GI).

[19] Halevy, A.Y., Ives, Z.G, Suciu, D., Tatarinov, I.: Schema Mediation in Peer Data Management Systems. In *19th International Conference on Data Engineering (ICDE 2003)*, pages 505–518, Bangalore, India, March 5-8, 2003. IEEE Computer Society.

[20] Huhns, M.N., Singh, M.P.: Agents on the Web: Ontologies for Agents. *IEEE Internet Computing*, 1(6):81–83, 1997.

[21] Hurson, A.R., Bright, M.W.: Multidatabase Systems: An Advanced Concept in Handling Distributed Data. *Advances in Computers*, 32:149–200, 1991.

[22] Jonscher, D., Dittrich, K. R.: An Approach for Building Secure Database Federations. In *20th International Conference on Very Large Data Bases (VLDB 1994)*, pages 24–35, Santiago de Chile, Chile, September 12-15, 1994. Morgan Kaufmann.

[23] Kent, W.: *Data and Reality. Basic Assumptions in Data Processing Reconsidered*. North-Holland, Amsterdam, 1978.

[24] Landers, T., Rosenberg, R.L.: An Overview of MULTIBASE. In *Second International Symposium on Distributed Data Bases (DDB 1982)*, pages 153–184, Berlin, Germany, September 1-3, 1982. North-Holland.

[25] McCann, R., Doan, A.,Varadaran, V. Kramnik, A. Zhai, C. Building Data Integration Systems: A Mass Collaboration Approach. In *Sixth International Workshop on Web and Databases (WebDB 2003)*, pages 25–30, San Diego, California, USA, June 12-13, 2003.

[26] Mena, E., Kashyap, V., Sheth, A.P., Illarramendi, A.: OBSERVER: An Approach for Query Processing in Global Information Systems based on Interoperation across Pre-existing Ontologies. In *First IFCIS International Conference on Cooperative Information Systems (CoopIS 1996)*, pages 14–25, Brussels, Belgium, June 19-21, 1996. IEEE Computer Society.

[27] Ouksel, A.M., Sheth, A.P.: Semantic Interoperability in Global Information Systems: A Brief Introduction to the Research Area and the Special Section. *SIGMOD Record*, 28(1):5–12, 1999.

[28] Scheuermann, P., Elmagarmid, A.K., Garcia-Molina, H., Manola, F., McLeod, D., Rosenthal, A., Templeton,M.: Report on the Workshop on Heterogenous Database Systems held at Northwestern University, Evanston, Illinois, December 11-13, 1989. *SIGMOD Record*, 19(4):23–31, 1990.

[29] Sheth, A.P., Gala, S.K., Navathe,S.B.: On Automatic Reasoning for Schema Integration. *International Journal of Intelligent and Cooperative Information Systems*, 2(1):23–50, 1993.

[30] Sheth, A.P., Larson, J.A.: Federated Database Systems for Managing Distributed, Heterogeneous, and Autonomous Databases. *ACM Computing Surveys*, 22(3):183–236, 1990.

[31] Sølvberg. A.:Data and What They Refer to. In *Conceptual Modeling, Current Issues and Future Directions, Selected Papers from the Symposium on Conceptual Modeling, Los Angeles, California, USA, held before ER 1997*, pages 211–226. Springer, 1997.

[32] Sølvberg, A.: Conceptual Modeling in a World of Models. In R. Kaschek, editor, *Entwicklungsmethoden für Informationssysteme und deren Anwendung, EMISA 1999*, pages 63–77, Fischbachau, Germany, 1999. Teubner.

[33] Wache, H., Vögele, T., Visser, U., Stuckenschmidt, H., Schuster, G., Neumann, H., Hübner, S.: Ontology-Based Integration of Information - A Survey of Existing Approaches. In *IJCAI-2001 Workshop on Ontologies and Information Sharing*, pages 108–117, Seattle, USA, April 4-5, 2001.

[34] Wiederhold, G.: Mediators in the Architecture of Future Information Systems. *IEEE Computer*, 25(3):38–49, 1992.

[35] Winslett, M.: Databases in Virtual Organizations: A Collective Interview and Call for Researchers. *SIGMOD Record*, 34(1):86–89, 2005.

[36] Ziegler, P.: User-Specific Semantic Integration of Heterogeneous Data: What Remains to be Done? Technical Report ifi-2004.01, Department of Informatics, University of Zurich. http://www.ifi.unizh.ch/techreports/TR 2004.html, 2004.

[37] Ziegler, P., Dittrich, K.R.: Three Decades of Data Integration - All Problems Solved? In *18th IFIP World Computer Congress (WCC 2004), Volume 12, Building the Information Society*, pages 3–12, Toulouse, France, August 22-27, 2004. Kluwer.

[38] Ziegler, P., Dittrich, K. R.: User-Specific Semantic Integration of Heterogeneous Data: The SIRUP Approach. In *First International IFIP Conference on Semantics of a Networked World (ICSNW 2004)*, pages 44–64, Paris, France, June 17-19, 2004. Springer.

[39] Ziegler, P., Kiefer, C., Sturm, C., Dittrich, K.R., Bernstein, A.: Detecting Similarities in Ontologies with the SOQA-SimPack Toolkit. In *10th International Conference on Extending Database Technology (EDBT 2006)*, pages 59–76, Munich, Germany, March 26-31, 2006. Springer.

[40] Ziegler, P., Sturm, C., Dittrich, K.R.: Unified Querying of Ontology Languages with the SIRUP Ontology Query API. In *Datenbanksysteme in Business, Technologie und Web (BTW 2005)*, pages 325–344, Karlsruhe, Germany, March 2-4, 2005. Gesellschaft für Informatik (GI).

Challenges to Conceptual Modelling

Bernhard Thalheim

Christian Albrects University, Kiel, Germany

Abstract. Database and information systems technology has substantially changed. Nowadays, content management systems, (information-intensive) web services, web information systems, collaborating systems, internet databases, OLAP information systems, distributed and nomadic information systems, etc. have become challenges to current technology. At the same time, object-relational technology has gained the maturity for being widely applied. Conceptual modelling has not (yet) covered all these novel topics. It has been concentrated for more than two decades around specification of structures. Meanwhile, it is accepted that functionality, interactivity and distribution must be included into conceptual modelling of xyz information systems.

In this paper we demonstrate how achievements of conceptual modelling can be exploited for development of user-oriented content management systems and for the development of distributed and collaborating information systems.

Content and content management have become buzzwords. They are still heavily overloaded, not well understood or defined and heavily misused. Moreover, the user dimension is not yet incorporated. We base this approach on proposals made by the Scandinavian school of conceptual modelling and especially on work of A. Sølvberg.

Specification of distribution has neglected over a long period. Instead of explicit specification of distribution, multi-database systems and federated database systems have been extensively discussed in the literature. We develop a specification framework for collaborating information systems by intertwining and integrating specification of communication, coordination and cooperation.

1 Introduction

Database literature and teaching is divided into at least two branches: applications and their formal treatment on the basis of database theory. The first branch uses database theory mainly on the basis of results obtained until the mid-80ies. For computer engineers, logics and algebra becomes more and more a 'Terra incognita'. There are already statements that database theory research is 'dead on its feet' [1]. How-

---

[1] M. Stonebraker, ICDE, Vienna 1993

ever, database theory, database application formalization and database applications have gained from logics and discrete mathematics more than it is acknowledged.

1.1 Information Systems Design and Development

The problem of information system[2] design can be stated as follows:
Design the logical and physical structure of an information system in a given database management system (or for a database paradigm), so that it contains all the information required by the user and required for the efficient behavior of the whole information system for all users. Furthermore, specify the database application processes and the user interaction.

The implicit goals of database design are:

- to meet all the information (contextual) requirements of the entire spectrum of users in a given application area;
- to provide a "natural" and easy-to-understand structuring of the information content;
- to preserve the designers entire semantic information for a later redesign;
- to achieve all the processing requirements and also a high degree of efficiency in processing;
- to achieve logical independence of query and transaction formulation on this level;
- to provide a simple and easily to comprehend user interface family.

Over the last years database structures have extensively been discussed. Some of the open questions have been satisfactorily solved. Modelling includes, however, more aspects:

Structuring of a database application is concerned with representing the database structure and the corresponding static integrity constraints.

Functionality of a database application is specified on the basis of processes and dynamic integrity constraints.

Distribution of information system components is specified through explicit specification of distribution.

Interactivity is provided by the system on the basis of foreseen stories for a number of envisioned actors and is based on media objects which are used to deliver the content of the database to users or to receive new content.

This understanding has led to the **co-design approach** to modelling by specification **structuring, functionality, distribution**, and **interactivity**. These four aspects of modelling have both syntactic and semantic elements.

---

[2] A database system consists of a number of databases and a database management system. An information system extends the database system by the application system and by presentation systems.

1.2 Information System Models in General

Database design is based on one or more database models. Often, design is restricted to structural aspects. Static semantics which is based on static integrity constraints is sparsely used. Processes are then specified after implementing structures. Behavior of processes can be specified by dynamic integrity constraints. In a late stage, interfaces are developed. Due to this orientation the depth of the theoretical basis is different as shown in the following table displaying the state of the art in the 90ies:

	Used in practice	Theoretical background	Earliest layer of specification
Structures	well done	well developed	strategic
Static semantics	partially used	well developed	conceptual
Processes	somehow done	parts and pieces	requirements
Dynamic semantics	some parts	parts and glimpses	*implementation*
Services	implementations	ad-hoc	*implementation*
Exchange frames	intentionally done	nothing	*implementation*
Interfaces	intuitive	nothing	*implementation*
Stories	intuitive	nothing	*implementation*

Database design Database design requires consistent and well-integrated development of structures, processes, distribution, *and* interfaces. We will demonstrate below that extended entity-relationship models allow to handle all four aspects.

Database systems are now extended to web information systems, to data warehouse, to intelligent knowledge bases, and to data analysis systems. This extension can be developed in a conservative fashion or based on novel paradigms. As long as novel paradigms do not overcome the problematic parts of database systems operating, conservative extension must be preferred. In this case we need a good architecture [7, 6] for extensions of systems.

At the same time, we need to model database systems quality . The quality criteria are often stated in a rather fuzzy form. Typical quality criteria are [5] accuracy, changeability, fault tolerance, operability, performance, privacy, recoverability, reliability, resource efficiency, safety, security, stability, and testability.

2 Cultivating Database Research For Content Systems

Content management became vital within the web information systems context. These systems integrate generation, delivery and storage of complex structured objects with rights management, with service management in distributed environment, with customer management, with update and quality management, and with context dependent delivery depending on the user, the HCI, and the actual systems situation. *Content* is complex enriched data and may become ready-to-use data. Information is related to the users dimension. *Information* as processed by humans, is content perceived or noticed, selected and organized by its receiver, because of his subjective human interests, originating from his/her instincts, feelings, experience, intuition, common sense, values, beliefs, personal knowledge, or wisdom simultaneously processed by his/her cognitive and mental processes, and seamlessly integrated in his/her recallable knowledge. Content management systems are thus information systems that support extraction, storage and delivery of complex information.

This section shows that a sophisticated separation of concern allows to develop a flexible, powerful and completely pleasing content management. We separate four dimensions: the media type dimension for data, the concept dimension for theories and semantics, the topic dimensions for annotation and referencing, and the referent dimension for handling the concerns of users. The first three dimensions are the basis for content management. The first and third dimension are classically representing assets in industrial content management systems.

2.1 The Content Trinity: Media Types, Concepts, and Topics

Content is often considered to be a generalization of knowledge, information, and data. This generalization must capture all aspects of concern. We separate three different aspects of concern for content and content management systems: syntactical aspects mainly related to data management, semantical aspects mainly related to the knowledge background, and pragmatical aspects mainly related to the utilization, annotation, and querying of users and user communities. Instead we prefer a separation of aspects of concern:

Pragmatics concentrates on the meaning of terms used by a community of users.
Semantics expresses the interpretation of terms used by a community of users.
Syntax restricts attention to the language, its construction, and the way of using it
    through utterances or expressions.

This separation is expressed in the semiotic triangle in Figure 1. Media objects [9] are associated with concepts that specify the semantical meaning of media object suites and topics that specify the pragmatical understanding of users.

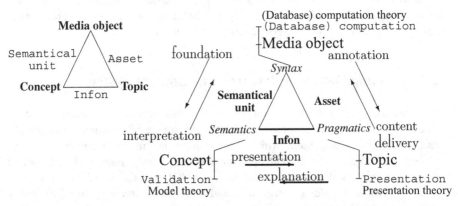

Fig. 1. Separation of concerns based on the semiotic triangle on media objects, concepts and topics

The media object-topic pairs are called assets [10]. The concept-topic terms are called infons [1]. Logics calls concept-media object pairs semantical units. These pairs may be considered as relations or mappings in Figure 1 such as

interpretation that maps concepts to media object suites,
foundation that provides concepts for given media object suites,
explanation that maps topics to concepts,
presentation that relates topic suites to media object suites,
annotation that represents media object suites by topics, and
content delivery that provides media object suites for given topic suites.

Media objects may be structured, semi-structured, or unstructured by the media types. They are data that are generated from underlying databases, ordered, hierarchically representable, tailorable to various needs and enhanced by functionality for its usage. A *suite* consists of a set of elements, an integration or association schema [16] and obligations requiring maintenance of the association[13]. In the case of a media object suite, we specify media objects based on a type system enabling in describing structuring and functionality of media objects, in describing their associations through relationship types and constraints. The functionality of media objects is specified by a retrieval expression, the maintenance policy and a set of functions supporting the utilization of the media object and the media object suite.

Concepts $\mathfrak{C}$ are described by the triple
(meta information, intension specification, extension) .
The intension can be specified by providing the logical theory on the basis of a set of formulas of the predicate logics. The extension of $\mathfrak{C}$ specifies the mappings to the content spaces and is used for associating data or media objects with concepts.
The *concept intension* is given by (1) intext of the concept, i.e., a syntactical description of mandatory, normal and optional parameter, (2) by context of the application area, of the history of things under consideration, (3) by semantics specified through a set of formulas defined over the intext and the context and based on an interpretation theory, and (4) by usage and pragmatics that restricts the application and usage of the concept. Concepts are rather 'small' logical theories representing the meaning of content.

Topics $\mathfrak{T}$ include the annotation of content. They are described by the triple
(user community, topic description, topic population)
for a given user community (or cultural context based on a population that serves as typical examples for the given topic. The topic description is given by
(topicRef, subjectIdentity, scope, baseName, association, roles, member, parameters) .
Topics are given by an ortho-normalized language [8], by a glossary, by a thesaurus, or by an ontology. A glossary is a collection of textual glosses or of specialized terms with their meanings. A thesaurus is a list of subject headings or descriptors about a particular field together with their synonyms usually with a cross-reference system for use in the organization of a collection of documents for reference and retrieval.

2.2 The Referent or User Dimension

Users do not mainly base their utterances on glossaries, thesauri, or ortho-normalized languages. Instead they assume that they will be understood on the basis of context, especially cultural context, their habits, their association to communities or their task background. We may use this association for the development of a user dimensions of advanced content management systems. An advanced content management systems may by based on the content-concept-topic triangle that uses explicit mappings from the user dimension to this triangle. We explore this idea in the next two sections.

The Referent Model Language (RML) is the basis for our model for the user dimension of advanced content management systems. RML was originally developed in order to support work in heterogeneous databases and data warehousing [11]. RML is based on set theory. Our model is based on set and graph theory. The basic constructs of RML are referent sets and individuals, their properties and relations. These corresponds to the need for expressing interpretations in terms of real-world things. From the area of semantic data models, one has identified a set of general abstraction mechanisms: Classification, aggregation, generalization and association, which are all supported by the language.

Humans have their reasoning capabilities, their memory chunks, and their expression capabilities. The memory chunks should be based on the achievement of neural network research. So far, it is assumed that humans based their reasoning and storage on suites of neurons. These suites can be called memes that are specified by

- names or (fuzzy or navigation) identification facilities,
- a number of properties,
- associations with different co-/adhesions and repulsion to other memes,
- activation and deactivation facilities,
- and groupings for different purposes.

In Figure 2 we extend the semantic triangle by the user dimension and relate memes to topics based on user understanding, user enrichment, and user expression capabilities.

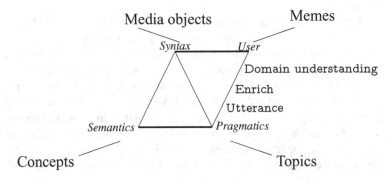

Fig. 2. The tetrahedron for user-oriented content management

This notion generalizes the notion of knowledge objects developed for knowledge maps. Memes are related to their users. We follow the approach of [4] and use a two-step procedure similar to [2] for memes evolution. Memes are extensively discussed and applied in [3, 12]. These resources consider memes to be units of cultural evolution and selection. They can be folded and be used for derivations. The main operations on memes are understanding, enrichment, and expression. These three kinds of operations are similar to the main database operations: read, compute, and write. We extend these operations to general transformations: replication operations depending on replication slots, operations for extracting, transforming and loading memes into other memes, and composition operations.

2.3 Memes of the Referent Dimension and Information

We used a notion of information that is better fitted to the needs of information systems and of content systems. It bases the existence of information for a user on this users abilities for perception (1), abilities for selection (2), the interests (3), the knowledge obtained so far (4), and abilities for integration (5). This notion nicely corresponds to different uses of information as noted in [12]: generation, externalization, recording, protection, communication, distribution, sharing, referencing, editing, search, analysis, management, and annihilation.

Classically memes have been considered as structures that are encoded within a gene or a suite of genes. We may, however, consider also dynamic memes that allow a change over the lifespan of a human organism. The *brain pattern* (b-pattern) consists of a suite of neurons. B-pattern may be stable or instable. Their formation, transformation, and removal requires energy. Therefore, stability and transformation is based on minimal energy consumption. Additionally, b-pattern have their compositionality and replication that is characterized by the general ability for composition or replication the general properties required for composition or replication, the topological and geometrical properties including distance and relative location, and the ad-/cohesion and repulsion within a suite and to other suites.

Using b-pattern we may now characterize the meme as a suite of b-pattern that is enhanced by activation facilities. These facilities support building, removal, and change of memes. Typical activation facilities are based on stimulants such as positive or negative emotions, good or bad practices (for keeping, refining or checking), and requests for change or replacement (delete, store in the background and link, insert, update). Stimulants are usually increasing or decreasing the energy level. Requests for change are often based on imposing some stress to memes. If the energy level becomes too low for a meme then this meme is lost or forgotten. This process can also be explicitly described by deactivation mechanisms.

Memes can be accessed by pattern matching or by navigation. Pattern matching is based on overlay structures that might be applied. The access to a meme may lead to a change of pattern (control memes), to invocation of replication or composition (collector memes), or to orchestration of a new set of b-pattern (information meme). We may now combine composition, replication and query functions to complex functions that represent the users ability for deduction, induction, abduction,

and reasoning such as non-monotonic, approximate, temporal, epistemic, and quali-
tative reasoning. The limited ability of users to apply formal reasoning, their specific
kind of logics, their specific topic landscape can also be represented through suites
of memes.

2.4 An Example

Let us consider two content suites which use the concepts *Person* and *Address*. We
need to characterise each of them by media types, concepts, and topics. Additionally
we might want to give a characterisation through memes. The media type specification of these content suites follows classical schemata which are widely used in
literature, e.g. the one in [14].

Concepts are specified based on the triple

(meta information, intension specification, extension) .

Let us omit the meta information specification and consider the other elements of
concept specification. We may specify the intention by a small theory for the Person concept based on a general database schema that uses parameters (denoted by
_-prefixes), optional attributes (denoted by square bracket) and references to other
structures (denoted by $\rightsquigarrow$), for instance by the schema in Figure 3.

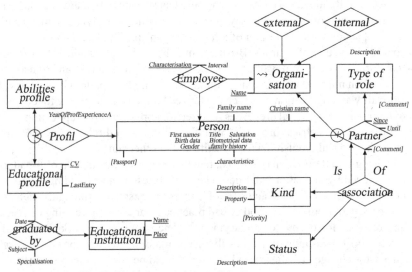

Fig. 3. The concept schema of the Person concept

The intext is usually associated to a context. In this example we relate the person
concept to the parameterised context, e.g.   (_enterpriseIS, _tasksActor) .
This context limits parameters, e.g. the following ones:

τ(_association) = _employee _partner

τ(_characteristics) = _names _birthData _identData _gender
_family _additCharact _profile .

The concept theory is based on explicit specification of axioms $\Sigma_{\text{Person}}^{\text{EpistemLogics}}$ which are formulated in a logical language, for instance in the deontic first-order predicate logic $\Sigma_{\text{Person}}^{\text{DeontTempPL}/1}$, for instance the following formulas:

$F(update(Person._birthData))$

$\alpha_{\text{"divorced"}}(\_person) \rightarrow \exists_{past} \_y$
$(Association(Is.Partner._y, Of.Partner._person, Since, Until) \wedge Until < \_today)$

The first axiom states that a birth date of a person cannot be changed and is preserved in our applications. The second axiom states that divorced people must have ha a partner in the past and belongs to general knowledge and is usually not represented in the database.

Pragmatics and usage of concepts can be given in a similar way. They provide the background for combining concepts like the one at the end of this subsection. The extension of the *Person* concept is give by a set of person models M $_{\text{Person}}$.

Addresses also specify a set of possible addresses under consideration, e.g. M$_{\text{Address}}$.

Concepts and media types are partially associated by instantiation of parameters and by refinement of notions used for concepts. If a concept element is not associated to a media type element then it cannot be instantiated by media object data. If the media type provides more data than requested by the concepts then we may use these data as auxiliary data. For instance, we may associate the parameter _familie with

$\mathcal{T}$ *(BirthName, Father, Mother)* or with $\mathcal{T}$ *(BirthName, { Child })*.

Another more complex association relates _name with

$\mathcal{T}$ *(FirstNames<(FirstName,use)>, FamName, [BirthName,] Title:{AcadTitle} FamTitle)* or more simply with $\mathcal{T}$ *(ChristianName, FamilyName, Nickname)*.

Concepts may be combined. We may, for instance, combine the two concepts *Person* and *Address* by *Practical usage* of the address for a person. This combination is partial and can be given by association schemata like the one in following figure.

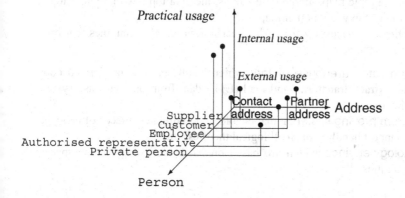

The algebra can also be based on the algebra for extended ER models [13], i.e. has operations such as $\cup, \cap, \setminus, \pi, \bowtie, \mu, \nu, \rho_{\text{NameSpace}}, Aggr$, and src_{h_0, h_1, h_2}.

Topics $\mathfrak{T}$ are described by the triple
(user community, topic description, topic population)
We associate concepts to topics and may thus use the association of concepts and media objects for associating topics with media objects. Some of the topics are not associated and thus not supported by corresponding content. For instance, the *Address* concept considers the address a the main or deputy place where a person or organization may be communicated with or directions for delivery on the outside of an object (or the designation of place of delivery placed between the heading and salutation on a business letter but does not consider the address as a location (as in the memory of a computer) where particular information is stored as the readiness and capability for dealing, as the manner of bearing oneself, as a formal communication or as a dutiful and courteous attention. In the same form we restrict the topic of the *Person* to (a) human, (b) personality of a human being and (c) reference of a segment of discourse to the speaker. We exclude characters or parts in or as if in a play, the topic of abstract person and the the bodily appearance.

2.5 Content Management

A content system [15] consists of a content management system and a set of media object suites, a set of concepts and a set of topics. The content management system uses special subsystems for management of media objects, concepts and topics. The first subsystem is an extended database management system. The concept subsystem has features for export and import of concepts, for recording and archiving concepts, for distributing concepts, for sharing concepts, for quoting and reusing concepts, and for editing fragments of concept suites. Therefore, this subsystem can be understood as a specific knowledge base [12]. The topic subsystem supports functions for merging a topic into a topic map, merge base names, merge a topic with another topic, and merge a topic map with another map.

The functionality necessary for each dimension is based on engines that have been developed in the past:

database and data warehouse system which handle basic data, derived complex data, extract, transform, and load (ETL) data from one database system to the other one,

AI and theorem proving systems that enable in deriving new pieces of concepts and that support handling of small logical theories, and

topic or ontology engines which are based on XML technology, name spaces, linking facilities.

2.6 Data Extraction Frameworks

Surprises, data warehousing, and complex applications often require sophisticated data analysis. The most common approach to data analysis is to use data mining software or reasoning systems based on artificial intelligence. These applications allow to analyse data based on the data on hand. At the same time data are often observational or sequenced data, noisy data, null-valued data, incomplete data, of wrong granularity, of wrong precision, of inappropriate type or coding, etc. Therefore, brute-force application of analysis algorithms leads to wrong results, to losses of semantics, to misunderstandings etc.

We may use approaches known from mathematics for the development of data analysis framework. We thus need general frameworks for data analysis beyond the framework used for data mining.

An approach to semantics- and pragmatics-preserving data analysis we developed in our data mining projects is based on the following steps:

1. Modelling of the tasks and problems and their data requirements.
2. Selection of possible appropriate analysis algorithms, categorisation of their outcome and pitfalls within the task and problem scope, development of an application frame for application of the chosen algorithms.
3. Categorisation, extraction of macro- and meta-data, adaption of the data to the analysis needs and modelling of data semantics and pragmatics.
4. Extraction, transformation and loading of macro-data for the chosen analysis algorithms, including cleansing and adaption of the data.
5. Application, stepwise refinement and correction of the analysis algorithms.
6. Modelling of the obtained analysis results with their semantics and pragmatics.

This approach is based on modelling of data analysis algorithms, on their requirements to data, their functions for analysis and their transformations of the data.

3 Specification of Distribution

Specification of distribution has neglected over a long period. Instead of explicit specification of distribution different collaborating approaches have been tried such as multi-database systems, federated database systems,

3.1 View Suite

Classically, (simple) views are defined as singleton types which data is collected from the database by some query.

```
create view   name (projection variables)
   select      projection expression
     from      Database sub-schema
    where      selection condition
 group by      expression for grouping
   having      selection among groups
 order by      order within the view
```

Since we may have decided to use the class-wise representation simple views are not the most appropriate structure for exchange specification. Instead we use *view suites* for exchange. A *suite* consists of a set of elements, an integration or association schema and obligations requiring maintenance of the association.

Simple examples of a view suites are already discussed in [13] where view suites are ER schemata. The integration is given by the schema. Obligations are based on the master-slave paradigm, i.e., the state of the view suite classes is changed whenever an appropriate part of the database is changed.

Additionally, views should support services. Services provide their own data and functionality. This object-orientation is a useful approach whenever data should be used without direct or remote connection to the database engine.

We generalize the view specification frame used in relational databases by the frame:

    generate MAPPING : VARS → OUTPUT STRUCTURE
     from DATABASE TYPES
     where SELECTION CONDITION
     represent using GENERAL PRESENTATION STYLE
            &   ABSTRACTION (GRANULARITY, MEASURE, PRECISION)
            &   ORDERS WITHIN THE PRESENTATION
            &   HIERARCHICAL REPRESENTATIONS
            &   POINTS OF VIEW
            &   SEPARATION
    browsing definition CONDITION
            &   NAVIGATION
    functions SEARCH FUNCTIONS
            &   EXPORT FUNCTIONS
            &   INPUT FUNCTIONS
            &   SESSION FUNCTIONS
            &   MARKING FUNCTIONS

The extension of views by functions seems to be an overhead during database design. Since we extensively use views in distributed environments we save efforts of parallel and repetitive development due to the development of the entire view suite instead of developing each view by its own.

3.2 Services

Services are usually investigating on one of the (seven) layers of communication systems. They are characterized by two parameters: Functionality and quality of service. Nowadays we prefer a more modern approach [7]. Instead of functions we consider *informational processes*. *Quality of service* is bounded by a number of properties that are stated either at implementation layer or at conceptual layer or at business user layer. Services consist of informational processes, the characteristics provided and properties guaranteeing service quality, i.e. $S = (\mathcal{I}, \mathcal{F}, \Sigma_S)$ where $\mathcal{I} = (\mathcal{V}, \mathcal{M}, \Sigma_T)$.

Informational processes are specified by the ingredients:

Views from the view suite $\mathcal{V}$ are the resources for informational processes. Since views are extended by functions they are computational and may be used as statistical packages, data warehouses or data mining algorithms.

The services manager $\mathcal{M}$ supports functionality and quality of services and manages containers, their play-out and their delivery to the client. It is referred to as a service provider.

The competence of a service manifests itself in the set of tasks $\mathcal{T}$ that may be performed.

Service characteristics $\mathcal{F}$ is characterized depending on the abstraction layers:

Service characteristics at business user layer are based on service level agreements and the informational processes at this layer.

Service characteristics at conceptual layer describe properties the service must provide in order to meet the service level agreements. Further, functions available to the client at specified by their interfaces and semantic effects.

Service characteristics at implementation layer specify the syntactical interfaces of functions, the data sets provided and their behavior and constraints to the information system and to the client.

Quality of service Σ_S is characterized depending on the abstraction layers:

Quality parameters at business user layer may include *ubiquity* (access unrestricted in time and space) and *security* (against failures, attacks, errors; trustworthy).

Quality parameters at conceptual layer subsume *interpretability* (formal framework for interpretation) and *consistency* (of data and functions).

Quality parameters at implementation layer include *durability* (access to the entire information unless it is explicitly overwritten), *robustness* (based on a failure model for resilience, conflicts, and persistency), *performance* (depending on the cost model, response time and throughput), and *scalability* (to changes in services, number of clients and servers).

3.3 Exchange Frames

The exchange frame is defined by

exchange architecture usually provided a system architecture integrating the information systems through communication and exchange systems,

collaboration style specifying the supporting programs, the style of cooperation and the coordination facilities, and

collaboration pattern specifying the roles of the partners, their responsibilities, their rights and the protocols they may rely on.

Distributed database systems are based on local database systems and follow a certain integration strategy. Integration is based on total integration of the local conceptual schemata into a global distribution schema.

Beside the classical distributed system we support also other architecture such as *database farms, incremental information system societies* and *cooperating information systems*. The later are based on the concept of cooperating views [13]. Incremental information system societies are the basis for facility management systems. Simple incremental information systems are data warehouses and content management systems.

Database farms are generalizing and extending the approaches to federated information systems and mediators. Their architecture is displayed in Figure 4. Farms are based on the co-design approach and the information unit and container paradigm:

Information units are generalized views. Views are generated on the basis of the database. Units are views extended by functionality necessary for the utilization of view data. We distinguish between *retrieval information units* and *modification information units*. The first are used for data injection. The later allow to modify the local database.

Containers support the export and the import of data by bundling information units provided by view states. Units are composed to containers which can be loaded and unloaded in a specific way. The unloading procedure supports the dialogue scenes and steps.

The global communication and farming system provides the exchange protocols, has facilities for loading and unloading containers and for modification of modification information units.

We do not want to integrate entirely the local databases but provide only *cooperating views*.

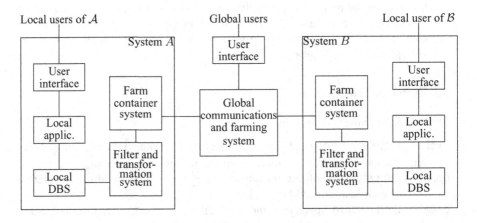

Fig. 4. Database Systems Farm

The exchange architecture may include the **workplace** of the client describing the *actors, groups, roles* and *rights* of actors within a group, the *task portfolio* and the *organization* of the collaboration, communication, and cooperation.

The collaboration style is based on four components describing

supporting programs of the information system including session management, user management, and payment or billing systems;

data access pattern for data *release* through the net, e.g., broadcast or P2P, for *sharing* of resources either based on transaction, consensus, and recovery models or based on replication with fault management, and for *remote access* including scheduling of access;

the style of collaboration on the basis of peer-to-peer models or component models or push-event models which restrict possible communication;

and the coordination workflows describing the interplay among partners, discourse types, name space mappings, and rules for collaboration.

We know a number of collaboration pattern supporting *access and configuration* (wrapper facade, component configuration, interceptor, extension interface), *event processing* (reactor, proactor, asynchronous completion token, accept connector), *synchronization* (scoped locking, strategized locking, thread-safe interface, double-checked locking optimization) and *parallel execution* (active object, monitor object, half-sync/half-async, leader/followers, thread-specific storage):

Proxy collaboration uses partial system copies (remote proxy, protection proxy, cache proxy, synchronization proxy, etc.).

Broker collaboration supports coordination of communication either directly, through message passing, based on trading paradigms, by adapter-broker systems, or callback-broker systems.

Master/slave collaboration uses tight replication in various application scenarios (fault tolerance, parallel execution, precision improvement; as processes, threads; with(out) coordination).

Client/dispatcher collaboration is based on name spaces and mappings.

Publisher/subscriber collaboration is also known as the observer-dependents paradigm. It may use active subscribers or passive ones. Subscribes have their subscription profile.

Model/view/controller collaboration is similar to the three-layer architecture of database systems. Views and controllers define the interfaces.

Collaboration pattern generalize protocols. They include the description of partners, their responsibilities, roles and rights.

References

[1] Al-Fedaghi, S. S., Fiedler, G., and Thalheim, B. Privacy enhanced information systems. In *Proc. EJC'05, Informaton Modelling and Knowledge Bases Vol. XVII, Series Frontiers in Arificial Intelligence,* (Tallinn, 2005), IOS Press.

[2] Bienemann, A., Schewe, K.-D., and Thalheim, B. Towards a theory of genericity based on government and binding. In *Proc. ER'06, LNCS 4215* (2006), Springer, pp. 311–324.

[3] Blackmore, S. *The Meme Machine.* Oxford University Press, Oxford, 1999.

[4] Chomsky, N. *Some concepts and consequences of the theory of government and binding.* MIT Press, 1982.

[5] Jaakkola, H., and Thalheim, B. Software quality and life cycles. In *ADBIS'05* (Tallinn, September 2005), Springer, pp. 208– 220.

[6] Lenz, H.-J., and Thalheim, B. OLTP-OLAP schemes for sound applications. In *TEAA 2005* (Trondheim, 2005), vol. LNCS 3888, Springer, pp. 99–113.

[7] Lockemann,P. Information system architectures: From art to science. In *Proc. BTW'2003, Springer, Berlin* (2003), pp. 1–27.

[8] Ortner, E., and Schienmann, B. Normative language approach - a framework for understanding. B. Thalheim, Ed., LNCS 1157, Springer, Berlin, pp. 261– 276.

[9] Schewe, K.-D., and Thalheim, B. Structural media types in the development of dataintensive web information systems. In *Web Information Systems*, W. R. D. Taniar, Ed. IDEA Group, 2004, pp. 34–70.

[10]Schmidt, J., and Sehring, H.-W. Conceptual content modeling and management - the rationale of an asset language. In *Proc. PSI'03, LNCS , Springer, 2003* (2003). Perspectives of System Informatics.

[11] Sølvberg, A. Data and what they refer to. In *Conceptual modeling: Historical persepectives and future trends*, P. C. et. al, Ed., no. 1565 in LNCS. Springer, Berlin, 1998.

[12] Tanaka, Y. *Meme media and meme market architectures: Knowledge media for editing, distributing, and managing intellectual resources.* J. Wiley, Hoboken, 2003.

[13] Thalheim, B. *Entity-relationship modeling – Foundations of database technology.* Springer, Berlin, 2000.

[14] Thalheim, B. The person, organization, product, production, ordering, delivery, invoice, accounting, budgeting and human resources pattern in database design. Tech. Rep. Preprint I-07-2000, Brandenburg University of Technology at Cottbus, Institute of Computer Science, 2000.

[15] Thalheim, B. The co-design framework to content specification. In *BIS'2004* (2004), W. Abramowicz, Ed., IEEE Press, pp. 326–351.

[16] Thalheim, B. Codesign of structuring, functionality, distribution and interactivity. *Australian Computer Science Comm. 31*, 6 (2004), 3–12. Proc. APCCM'2004.

Interoperable Management of Conceptual Models

Andreas L. Opdahl[1], Guttorm Sindre[2]

[1] University of Bergen, Norway,
[2] Norwegian University of Technology and Science, Trondheim Norway,

Abstract. The paper reviews a line of conceptual-modelling research that originated in Arne Sølvberg's Information Systems Group at the Norwegian University of Science and Technology in the 1980-ies. The line of research has since produced results such as facet modelling, ontological analyses and evaluations of modelling languages and a template-based approach to modelling-construct description. Currently, focus is on developing a revised version of the Unified Enterprise Modelling Language (UEML). Finally, the paper offers paths for further work.

1 Introduction

Several of the most significant breakthroughs in the ICT area in the last decades have originated in *new ways of connecting and integrating* previously disconnected information resources: One breakthrough occurred in the 1970-ies, when advances in data management and data modelling, combined with a better understanding of the practical problems of managing very large databases, lead to the relational model of data and to relational databases, a breakthrough that greatly improved organisations' ability to leverage information resources on structured *tabular* form. Another breakthrough occurred in the 1980-ies and early 1990-ies, when developments in networking technology and middleware, combined with a better understanding of its potential, lead to the emergence of the world-wide web, a breakthrough that greatly improved societies', organisations' and individuals' abilities to leverage information resources on semi-structured *hypermedia* form. Other important breakthrough technologies, which have similarly facilitated integrated use of new types of information resources, include *object technology* and *web services*.

However, no technology or theory yet exists for leveraging another type of information resources that is becoming increasingly important. These information resources are neither tabular nor in hypermedia form, nor objects, nor web services, but represented and visualised as *diagrammatic models*. Already today, diagrammatic languages and models are used widely to develop and manage ISs and for general management of enterprises. Several current trends ensure that diagrams will be even more central in future ISs: model-driven enterprise ISs (including ERP, SCM and CRM systems), model-driven enterprise application integration (EAI) and ontology-driven software interoperability, ontology-driven agents on the semantic web, model-driven engineering and model-driven software development, including the OMG's *model-driven architecture* (MDA) initiative.

When ISs become model-driven, the ability to use and re-use a multitude of models in an integrated manner becomes crucial for developing and maintaining open, adaptable, robust, evolvable and interoperable ISs. Furthermore, and partly as a result, the enterprises themselves and their activities become model-driven too. *Integrated model use* thereby becomes key to both ISs and enterprises, making it necessary to facilitate *integration of the languages* in which the models are expressed.

This paper reviews a line of conceptual-modelling research that aims at developing theory and technology for *interoperable management of conceptual models*. The line originated in the Information Systems Group at the Norwegian University of Science and Technology (then the Norwegian Institute of Technology, NTH) in the 1980-ies, under the leadership of Professor Arne Sølvberg. Along the way, results such as facet modelling, ontological analyses and evaluations of modelling languages, the template-based approach to modelling-construct description and the Unified Enterprise Modelling Language (UEML) will be presented and discussed. The paper will finally outline paths for further work, emphasising opportunities for empirical validation, with the aim of contributing to establishing conceptual modelling as a core for the information systems field.

The paper thus aims to present a line of work as it has emerged over two almost two decades and to trace its roots back to its origin in the Information Systems Group in Trondheim. In consequence, too little space has been left to acknowledge the many other important sources that the authors have been inspired by and built on. The reference list contains a plethora of pointers to earlier efforts and comparisons with related work.

2 Phenomena and Behaviours

During the late 1970-ies and the 1980-ies, research in the Information Systems Group centred heavily around conceptual modelling from structural and behavioural perspectives. Centrally, Sølvberg's [36] *Phenomenon Model* (PM) supported integrated representation of information and material structures. Sølvberg and Kung's [6, 38] *Behaviour Net Model* (BNM) offered an early extension and interpretation of Petri Nets that supported enactable behavioural modelling of informational and material processes formalised using pre- and postconditions. The *Process Port Model* (PPM) (e.g., [4], although the work had started around 1985 and involved many others) offered a DFD-type notation extended with representation of material and informational flows as well as processes with pre- and postconditions. PPM process nodes were also annotated with input and output ports to visualise the allowable combinations of inputs to and outputs of each process step.

When the authors joined Sølvberg's group in the second half of the 1980-ies, they joined a group that would produce results as diverse as the conceptual model quality framework SEQUAL [5, 8], techniques and tools for software performance engineering [14, 30, 31], the misuse-case modelling technique [35], the PPP tool- and languagset [4] and the facet-modelling framework [28, 29]. A large group of master and doctoral students made pointed contributions to these efforts. For example, Sindre [32] developed algorithms for automatically generating pre-and postconditions in multi-level BNM models, which were then implemented and validated [33]. Lindland & Opdahl [7] used a temporal logic language to map semantically between the BNM and PPM models, whereas Opdahl [12] proposed an integrated formalisation of the PM and PPM languages. A few years later, Sindre [34] proposed a new common notation, *Hicons*, with the power to express both structure and behaviour in an integrated manner, whereas Opdahl [13] developed a tool-supported framework for estimating the performance of proposed software during development, based on the PPM language[1]. Continuing the group's emphasis on integrated analysis of informational and materials aspects, Opdahl & Sindre [27] also presented a discussion of basic concepts for representing concrete problem domains.

Although diverse on the surface, we can identify several commonalities among the activities of Sølvberg's group in this period, key to the spread of its results:

---

[1] The international orientation of the group is examplified by both these PhD's being parts of European projects: Tempora (ESPRIT-II Project No. 2469) and IMSE (IST-508011).

- *Problem-domain focus.* At a time when much focus was placed on representing technology artefacts, such as proposed software solutions, almost all the activities in the group were instead orientated towards the problem domain.[2]
- *Operationalism and animation.* Despite they problem orientation, most of the solutions proposed were operational in form, a some of them even amenable to simulation and animation.
- *Formality.* Most of the activities and solutions proposed had at least some degree of formal grounding, contributing to their clarity and applicability.
- *Integrated approaches.* Many projects were tying together already proposed solutions, often across modelling languages and techniques.
- *Continuity and cohesion.* Most of the student projects were building on previous projects. Even when seemingly new activities were initiated or solutions proposed, they would have underlying connexions to past activities.[3]

The line of work presented in this paper originates in and incorporates several of the above themes.

3 Items and Facets

After the explosion of modelling approaches during the 1980-ies, at the start of the 1990-ies it was becoming clear that approaches were needed to integrate diagram languages and models beyond simple bi-language model-to-model translation. A variety of modelling perspectives, or *orientations*, had been introduced, including structural, behavioural, declarative, actor-oriented, business-rule oriented, object oriented ones etc. In [28], the authors argued that "the priorities set by choosing one particular orientation will mean that the aspects not promoted by that orientation will be more difficult to account for during analysis". More specifically, "Orientation means that some aspects of phenomena in the problem domain will be difficult to capture and/or easy to forget because the modelling constructs which represent them are less important in (or even missing from) the modelling approach used" (*representational bias*); "Orientation means that

---

[2] Already in 1979, Sølvberg had argued "that the conceptual schema should contain an ontological subschema (i.e. a 'reality' model)", which could be used to "proving semantical equivalence/difference of databases." [37], thus predating a topical idea in the ontology community by many years.
[3] For example, the software performance work in IMSE followed earlier efforts by [11].

the problem domain will be looked at from one particular perspective the whole time, thus hiding weaknesses that would be more apparent from other perspectives" (*perspective bias*); "Orientation means that it will be difficult to communicate a model to people to whom the particular orientation is unnatural, although easy to others" (*communication bias*); and "Orientation means that the problem-domain models may inherently support the participation and interests of some of the individuals and groups affected by development, but not those of others" (*interest bias*) [28, 29].

They authors instead proposed a *facet modelling* framework from the view "that clearly orientated models are not to be striven for in the early phases of problem analysis, but rather a source of problems on their own" [28]. The goal of facet modelling was to "allow the modeller to (1) choose to represent a wide range of aspects of real-world phenomena depending on the problem at hand, and (2) simultaneously represent several aspects of the same real-world phenomenon whenever needed" [28, 29].

Facet modelling differed from mainstream multi-perspective modelling frameworks because it did not attempt to integrate languages by representing them using metaobjects, -properties and -relationships or similar concepts inspired by ER models or class diagrams. Opdahl & Henderson-Sellers [25] later elaborated this position, criticising mainstream approaches because they easily lead to *referentially redundant* meta models, where several modelling constructs or model elements refer to the same classes, things or properties in the problem domain. Facet modelling instead avoided referential redundancy at the language level by "breaking down" each modelling construct into its "smallest parts" in three steps – where each step eliminated a source of referential redundancy as explained below – and by making sure that each resulting "smallest parts" was never duplicated in a facet model or language.

The details of the framework have been described in detail elsewhere, e.g., [25, 29]. Here, space allows only a brief explanation of the above three steps. *Step 1:* At the instance level, facet modelling assumes that the problem domain consists of classes, things and properties that exist independently of observers, but acknowledges that these classes, things and properties are conceptualised differently by different observers in different situations.[4] The framework therefore distinguishes between *items*, which represent classes, things and their properties *per se*, and *facets*, which represent the various conceptualisations of the classes, things and properties. *Step 2:* Facet modelling also acknowledges that different conceptualisations of the same thing may *overlap* in the sense that they may reflect

---

[4] Facet modelling has evolved since it was first proposed; this paper presents the most current version.

some of the same properties of the thing. The framework therefore lets facets have subfacets, and two or more facets of the same item may share one or more subfacets. *Step 3:* Even conceptualisations of different things may overlap. The framework therefore lets two or more facets of distinct items have one or more subfacets in common. We say that such a subfacet is a link subfacet (or just link) because it is common to subfacets of distinct items. The authors have argued that the concepts of items, facets and subfacets – shared as well as links – thereby provide a minimal set of concepts needed to integrate conceptual models and modelling languages without introducing referential redundancy.

4 The Need for Ontological Foundations

Further work on facet modelling sought to refine it into a practical framework for modelling enterprises and their information systems [15, 16]. This turned out to be difficult in practice. The framework provided a precise view of what the result of language integration should be, but it offered few practical guidelines on how to reach such a result. Given a modelling construct in an established modelling language, which category (or categories) of phenomena did it represent and which aspects? When did aspects overlap and when were they disjunctive? How could the exact overlap between aspects be identified? Questions such as these indicated that the precise conceptual structure of the framework needed to be underpinned by an equally precise semantics. Given the concrete-focus of many of the languages focussed on at the time, the Bunge-Wand-Weber representation model of information systems ("the BWW model", e.g., [39-41]) seemed a suitable platform. This choice emphasised the *referential* aspect of semantics, recognising that concrete concepts draw their meaning in part from the phenomena in and/or aspects of enterprises and information systems that they are intended to represent.[5] The choice also implies a focus on *concrete problem domains*, as opposed to purely conceptual domains.[6]

The match between central facet modelling and BWW-concepts turned out to be straightforward; individual and categorical phenomena corresponded to things and classes of things, whereas complex and primitive

---

[5] We will revisit other aspects of meaning, such as pragmatic issues, in the Discussion.
[6] Other types of domains may need to be treated differently from concrete domains.

facets corresponded, respectively, to compound and non-compound BWW-properties.[7]

As soon as the basic correspondences between facet modelling and the BWW-model had been fleshed out, work could be started on analysing existing modelling languages in terms of the BWW-model, with the aim to prepare those languages for being reformulated as facet languages. The OPEN Modelling Language (OML) was analysed first [21] and the Unified Modeling Language (UML) next [22]. An analysis of part-whole relations in object-oriented languages was also performed [26].[8]

The ontological analyses and evaluations also augmented other ontology work based on the BWW model because the aim was slightly different: Whereas the present work prepared for incorporating the analysed languages as facet languages, other BWW work prepared for empirical evaluations of the same languages. One consequence was that, whereas the present work did sometimes propose improvements to existing languages, other analyses were careful not to add to or otherwise change the languages analysed. (This may explain some of the differences between the UML analyses in [3] and [22].)

5 Describing Modelling Constructs with Templates

The ontological analyses and evaluations of existing modelling languages soon lead to further developments of facet modelling. For example, [17] demonstrated how enterprise knowledge modelling can be animated 3-dimensionally based on facet models, whereas [25] criticised conventional OPRR (object-property-relationship-role) approaches to meta modelling, as already explained, showing how referential redundancy potentially hampers consistency checking, update reflection and reuse of model content across diagrams or models.

Even more effort has been put into a side result of the ontological analyses and evaluations: In addition to clarifying and offering improvements to modelling languages, this work provided useful insights about using the BWW model to describe modelling languages and their constructs. In this respect, a few shortcomings were identified:

---

[7] Indeed, the exercise made it clear that facet modelling had from the start been more strongly inspired by the BWW-model than the authors were aware of.

[8] Although part-whole relations do not play a central role in practical enterprise and IS modelling, they become critical when distinct perspectives represented at different granularities need to be precisely integrated

- A typical BWW analysis describes modelling constructs only at the level of ontological categories (*classes, properties, states, transformations etc.*) but, in many cases, it is also important *which* classes, properties, states, transformations etc. the construct is intended to represent.

- A typical BWW analysis describes modelling constructs only in terms of a single ontological category but, in many cases, the modelling construct may represent a *scene* played by several types of ontological categories together, e.g., one or more classes along with the properties they possess or one or more transformation laws along with the transformations they effect.[9]

- A typical BWW analysis does not take *modalities* into account. But modelling constructs differ as to whether they represent factual assertions about the problem domain, someone's knowledge about the domain, goals that someone wants to achieve in the domain etc.

- Not all BWW concepts are equally important for practical purposes. For example, state and transformation spaces are rarely accounted for by existing modelling languages and this does not appear to be a problem for practical modelling. On the other hand, classes/things, and the various types of properties, states and transformations/events are central.[10]

In response, [23] propose a *template-based* approach to describing modelling constructs. The template is based on the BWW model and, additionally, it offers a structured approach to construct description, where the description of each construct is separated into descriptions of:[11]

- *Instantiation level*: Is the construct intended to represent individual things and their particular properties, states and transformations? Or is it intended to represent classes and their characteristic properties, states and transformations? Or is it intended to represent both levels?

- *Classes*: Which thing or class of things in the problem domain is the construct intended to represent? Even when a construct primarily represents a property, state or transformation, this field remains

---

[9] For example, a whole-part relation describes two specific *classes of things* – a composite and component class – with a particular ontological property – a *part-whole relation* – between them, which also *characterises* the two classes.

[10] In the first volume of his Treatise, when Mario Bunge [2, p. 27] illustrates the hierarchy of objects in his basic ontology, the following four types of extralinguistic factual objects are shown: "Concrete thing", "Property, state, or change of a thing".

[11] The template has evolved since it was first proposed; this paper presents the most current version. For example, *behaviour* was less developed in the first template version, and *transformations* were called "events".

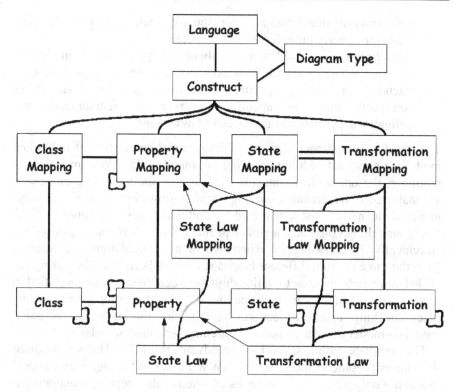

Fig. 1. In the UEML meta-meta model, modelling constructs are mapped onto classes, properties, states and transformations in a common ontology.

relevant, because every property, state or transformation must occur in a specific thing or class. A construct definition can have several class entries, because some constructs are even intended to represent more than one thing or class at the same time.

- *Properties*: Which property or properties in the problem domain is the construct intended to represent? Again, even when a construct primarily represents not a property but, e.g., a state or transformation, this field is relevant, because every state or transformation pertains to one or more properties.
- *Behaviour*: Even when two modelling constructs are intended to represent the same properties of the same things or classes, they may be intended to represent different behaviours. For example, one modelling construct may be intended to represent just their existence, i.e., a static representation. Other modelling constructs may be intended to represent a state of the classes, things or properties, or a transformation, or a process, i.e., alternative dynamic representations.

This entry distinguishes between the four cases and provides sub-entries to specify the relevant case in detail.

- *Modality*: We are used to think about enterprise and IS models as asserting what is the case. However, not all modelling constructs are intended for making assertions. The modality entry distinguishes constructs that are intended to represent recommendations, obligations, permission etc. instead of assertions.

The result is an approach that offers fine-grained description of individual modelling constructs while remaining grounded in the BWW model. Furthermore, the ontological concepts used to describe modelling constructs are maintained in a *common ontology*, which grows incrementally and dynamically as more constructs are added and which ties descriptions of different modelling constructs together in fine detail.[12] It is also organised hierarchically. In consequence, when two or more modelling constructs – from the same or from different languages – have been described using the UEML approach, the exact relationships between them can be identified in terms of the common ontology, paving the way for comparison, consistency checking, update reflection, view synchronisation and, eventually, model-to-model translation across modelling language boundaries.

The template offers several other advantages [23]: The standardised definitions become grounded in the BWW model and Bunge's ontological model not only generally — in terms of whether they represent general ontological categories such as "classes" or "properties" — but also specifically in terms of *which* classes and/or properties they represent. The clarity and precision of the definitions is thereby enhanced. The standardised definitions become more cohesive and, thus, more learnable, understandable and directly comparable with one another. The template can also be seen as a contribution to making the BWW model easier to use because it offers a structured approach to comparing, defining and integrating languages.

The template was validated using example constructs, revised and partially formalised through OCL constraints [24]. Figure 1 shows the *meta-meta model* that ties the approach together. It is called a meta-meta model because it is a model of how to model languages and because models of languages are called meta models. The top part of the meta-meta model is for managing the relationships between languages, their diagram types and their modelling constructs. The bottom part shows the structure of the

---

[12] The common ontology was initially derived from the BWW model and was designed from the start to grow incrementally as additional classes, properties, states and transformations are introduced in order to describe new modelling constructs.

common ontology. The middle part is for breaking down modelling constructs and mapping them onto the common ontology.

6 The Unified Enterprise Modelling Language

The Unified Enterprise Modelling Language (UEML) is an ongoing effort to develop an intermediate language for modelling enterprises and related domains, such as information systems [1]. Hence, its primary aim is not to propose new modelling constructs or new visual notations, but to integrate existing modelling languages in a structured and cohesive way. A first version of UEML was established in the UEML Thematic Network (TN) (2002-2003). A second version is currently being finalised as part of the INTEROP Network of Excellence (NoE) (2003-2007).

The template-based approach was chosen as the starting point for defining UEML 2 according to the following steps [18]: A construct description was first created for each modelling construct to be incorporated. Each construct description had a *presentation part* that dealt with the visual presentation of the modelling construct (covering *lexemes, syntax* and some simple *pragmatics*). It also had a representation part that accounted for which enterprise phenomena the construct was intended to represent (covering *reference*, a central aspect of *semantics*).[13]

The representation part followed the approach presented in Section 5 and used *separation of reference* to break each modelling construct into its *ontologically atomic parts*, i.e., parts that mapped one-to-one with an *ontological concept*, which is either a class, property, state or transformation. Based on the meta-meta model, a prototype tool for managing language and construct descriptions, *UEMLBase*, was developed. UEMLBase manages the representation part of language and construct descriptions using the OWL plug-in for the Protégé tool.

UEMLBase currently contains descriptions of constructs from ARIS, BPML, GRL, IDEF3, ISO19440, KAOS, UEML 1.0, coloured Petri nets and selected UML notations, although not all these languages are yet described in full detail. Less detailed analyses have also been undertaken on other languages. The UEML group currently focuses on finishing the description of these languages and on validating them empirically. Matulevicius, Heymans & Opdahl [9, 10] discusses GRL and KAOS spe-

---

[13] The UEML 2 work in INTEROP has two additional activities: determining requirements for UEML and selecting languages to incorporate. A related task is developing a virtual handboook for enterprise modelling [1].

cifically. Opdahl & Berio [19] discusses the UEML approach in a global setting, based on the SEQUAL framework[5].

7 Discussion

The template-based/UEML approach of sections 5 and 6 differs from facet modelling of section 3 in the following ways:

- UEML was explicitly grounded in the BWW model from the start, whereas facet modelling was coupled to the BWW model later and less strictly.
- UEML treats presentation and representation separately, where facet modelling covers them using the same set of concepts.
- UEML does not attempt to be uniform across instantiation levels, whereas facet modelling uses the same set of concepts at the instance, type, meta type and meta-meta type levels.
- UEML explicitly mentions behaviour, through states and transformations, which are not central concepts in the original facet-modelling framework.

At the same time, the two approaches are essentially compatible:

- They have the same ontological foundation in the BWW model.
- They both focus on breaking modelling constructs down into their smallest parts, in particular on breaking down properties/facets.
- The classes in the common ontology correspond to FM-language phenomena, and common-ontology properties correspond to FM-meta type facets.

In this way, the template-based approach can be seen as a simplified version of facet modelling, better suited for establishing and validating an initial collection of incorporated languages.

Opdahl & Berio [20] propose a roadmap for further evolution of UEML along the following dimensions: (1) Language breadth: include more languages[14]; (2) Ontological depth: refine the common ontology; (3) Ontological clarity: elaborate the common ontology language; (4) Presentation: extend the support for presentation issues; (5) Mathematical formality: define UEML semantics formally; (6) Tool support: provide GUI and validation support; (7) Model management: provide support for model manage-

---

[14] In addition to broadening the UEML to cover additional languages, selected critical language features, such as behavioural execution semantics and part-whole relations could also be analysed in more detail.

ment in addition to language management; (8) Validation: provide structural and behavioural language and model validation; (9) Dissemination: make UEML known in industry and academia and promote it as a standard; (10) Community: establish and maintain a committed and cohesive community for managing and evolving UEML and its approach.

Validation must play a particularly important role in future work. Work has already started on validating UEML by comparing construct-similarity estimates derived from UEMLBase with expert estimates of the same similarities. Further validation attempts should use UEML to facilitate cross-language model-to-model translation and then empirically evaluate the translation results, either by direct evaluation by modelling experts or by systematically comparing UEML and expert translations. Gradually, UEML should then be validated in increasingly realistic industrial settings

As argued by Weber [42], conceptual modelling has the potential to become a core for the information systems field. Many researchers are currently seeking to establish such a core grounded in the BWW model, in corresponding ontological models or in models from the cognitive sciences, often combining analytic and experimental means. Our line of research can be seen as one such attempt. In addition to offering practical solutions for interoperable management of conceptual models, it has the potential to contribute to a core for the information systems field by making the BWW model more amenable to empirical evaluation in two ways: Firstly, the UEML approach analyses modelling constructs in terms of specific classes, properties, states and transformations. UEML analyses thereby potentially become more precise than BWW analyses of the same constructs, and they should thus be easier to falsify empirically. Secondly, the UEML approach has the potential to support practical tasks such as consistency checking and model translation across languages. In consequence, UEML analyses can be evaluated more directly, e.g., as explained above for model translations, by comparing them in practice with the results of experts performing the same tasks. Further work is needed to demonstrate that the UEML/template-based approach – and its cousin, facet modelling – indeed have the power to facilitate such stronger empirical validation.

8 Conclusions

The paper has reviewed a line of conceptual-modelling research that originated in the information systems group at the Norwegian University of Science and Technology in the 1980-ies. The paper has also outlined a few paths for further work. As the above discussion shows that facet modelling and the UEML approach are compatible, the two approaches should eventually be aligned, either using the experience and constructs descriptions from the UEML work to extend facet modelling or by incorporating further ideas from facet modelling into UEML.

Acknowledgments. The authors are indebted to all the participants in the Domain Enterprise Modelling research group within the INTEROP Network of Excellence (IST-805011).

References

[1] Berio, G., A. Opdahl, V. Anaya and M. Dassisti, Deliverable DEM1. 2005, Interop-NoE, IST-508011, Domain Enterprise Modelling.

[2] Bunge, M., Semantics 1: Sense and Reference. Treatise on Basic Philosophy. Vol. 1. 1974, Boston: Reidel.

[3] Evermann, J. and Y. Wand. Towards Ontologically Based Semantics for UML Constructs. in Proc. 20th International Conference on Conceptual Modeling - ER'2001. 2001. Yokohama, Japan: Springer.

[4] Gulla, J.A., O.I. Lindland and G. Willumsen, PPP - an integrated CASE environment, in Advanced Information Systems Engineering (Proc. CAiSE*91), R. Andersen, J.A. Bubenko jr., and A. Sølvberg, Editors. 1991, Springer: Heidelberg. p. 194-221.

[5] Krogstie, J., A Semiotic Approach to Quality in Requirements Specifications, in Organizational Semiotics. 2001, Springer: Heidelberg. p. 231-249.

[6] Kung, C.H. and A. Sølvberg, Activity Modeling and Behaviour Modeling, in Information Systems Design Methodologies: Improving the Practice (Proc. IFIP WG8.1 WC CRIS'86), T.W. Olle, H.G. Sol, and A.A. Verrijn-Stuart, Editors. 1986, North-Holland. p. 145-171.

[7] Lindland, O.I. and A.L. Opdahl, Representation of Diagrammatic Systems Specifications in Temporal Logic. 1987, IS Group, Dept. of Electrical Engineering and Computer Science, Norwegian Institute of Technology: Trondheim.

[8] Lindland, O.I., G. Sindre and A. Sølvberg, Understanding Quality in Conceptual Modelling. IEEE Software, 1994. 11(2): p. 42-49.

[9] Matulevičius, R., P. Heymans and A.L. Opdahl. Comparison of goal-oriented languages using the UEML approach. in Proc. EI2N'06. 2006. Bordeaux.

[10] Matulevičius, R., P. Heymans and A.L. Opdahl. Ontological Analysis of KAOS Using Separation of Reference. in Proc. EMMSAD'06. 2006. Luxembourg.

[11] Oftedahl, H. and A. Sølvberg, Data Base Design Constrained by Traffic Load Estimates. Information Systems, 1981. 6(4): p. 267-282.

[12] Opdahl, A.L., RAPIER - Rapid Application Prototyper for Information Engineering Recourse. 1987, IS Group, Dept. of Electrical Engineering and Computer Science, Norwegian Institute of Technology: Trondheim.

[13] Opdahl, A.L., Performance Engineering During Information System Development, Ph.D. Thesis, IS Group, Department of Electrical Engineering and Computer Science, . 1992, Norwegian Institute of Technology: Trondheim.

[14] Opdahl, A.L., Sensitivity Analysis of Combined Software and Hardware Performance Models: Open Queueing Networks. Performance Evaluation, 1995. 22(1): p. 75-92.

[15] Opdahl, A.L. Towards a Facet Modelling Language. in Proc. 5th European Conference on Information Systems - ECIS'97. 1997. Cork, Ireland.

[16] Opdahl, A.L. Multi-Perspective Modelling of Requirements: A Case Study Using Facet Models. in Proc. Third Australian Conference on Requirements Engineering - ACRE'98. 1998. Geelong, Australia.

[17] Opdahl, A.L., Multi-Perspective Multi-Purpose Enterprise Knowledge Modelling, in Concurrent Engineering: Enhanced Interoperable Systems (Proc. CE'2003), R. Jardim-Goncalves, J. Cha, and A. Steiger-Garcão, Editors. 2003, A.A. Balkema Publishers. p. 609-617.

[18] Opdahl, A.L. The UEML Approach to Modelling Construct Description. in Proc. I-ESA'06. 2006. Bordeaux, France.

[19] Opdahl, A.L. and G. Berio. Interoperable language and model management using the UEML approach. in Proc. First International Workshop on Global Integrated Model Management – G@mma'06. 2006. Shanghai.

[20] Opdahl, A.L. and G. Berio. A Roadmap for UEML. in Proc. I-ESA'06. 2006. Bordeaux.

[21] Opdahl, A.L. and B. Henderson-Sellers, Grounding the OML Metamodel in Ontology. Journal of Systems and Software, 2001. 57(2): p. 119-143.

[22] Opdahl, A.L. and B. Henderson-Sellers, Ontological evaluation of the UML using the Bunge-Wand-Weber model. Software and Systems Modelling (SoSyM), 2002. 1(1): p. 43-67.

[23] Opdahl, A.L. and B. Henderson-Sellers, A Template for Defining Enterprise Modelling Constructs. Journal of Database Management (JDM), 2004. 15(2).

[24] Opdahl, A.L. and B. Henderson-Sellers, Chapter 6: Template-Based Definition of Information Systems and Enterprise Modelling Constructs, in Ontologies and Business System Analysis, P. Green and M. Rosemann, Editors. 2005, Idea Group Publishing.

[25] Opdahl, A.L. and B. Henderson-Sellers, A Unified Modeling Language Without Referential Redundancy. Data and Knowledge Engineering (DKE), 2005. 55(3).

[26] Opdahl, A.L., B. Henderson-Sellers and F. Barbier, Ontological Analysis of Whole-Part Relationships in OO Models. Information and Software Technology, 2001. 43(6): p. 387-399.

[27] Opdahl, A.L. and G. Sindre, A Taxonomy for Real-World Modelling Concepts. Information Systems, 1994. 19(3): p. 229-241.

[28] Opdahl, A.L. and G. Sindre, Facet Models for Problem Analysis, in Advanced Information Systems Engineering (Proc. CAiSE*95), J. Iivari, K. Lyytinen, and M. Rossi, Editors. 1995, Springer: Berlin.

[29] Opdahl, A.L. and G. Sindre, Facet Modelling: An Approach to Flexible and Integrated Conceptual Modelling. Information Systems, 1997. 22(5): p. 291-323.

[30] Opdahl, A.L., G. Sindre and V. Vetland. Performance Considerations in Object-Oriented Reuse. in Proc. Second International Workshop on Software Reuse. 1993. Lucca, Italy: IEEE Computer Society.

[31] Opdahl, A.L. and A. Sølvberg, Conceptual Integration of Information System and Performance Modelling, in Information Systems Concepts: Improving the Understanding (Proc. IFIP WG8.1 WC FRISCO-2), E.D. Falkenberg, C. Rolland, and E.N. El-Sayed, Editors. 1992, North-Holland: Amsterdam.

[32] Sindre, G., Abstraction of Behaviour Network Models. 1987, IS Group, Dept. of Electrical Engineering and Computer Science, Norwegian Institute of Technology: Trondheim.

[33] Sindre, G., RAPACITY - An Approach to Constructivity in Conceptual Modelling. 1988, IS Group, Dept. of Electrical Engineering and Computer Science, Norwegian Institute of Technology: Trondheim.

[34] Sindre, G., HICONS: A General Diagrammatic Framework for Hierarchical Modelling, Ph.D. Thesis, Dept. of Electrical Engineering and Computer Science. 1990, Norwegian Institute of Technology: Trondheim.

[35] Sindre, G. and A.L. Opdahl, Eliciting Security Requirements with Misuse Cases. Requirements Engineering Journal, 2005. 10(1): p. 34-44.

[36] Sølvberg, A., A Contribution to the Definition of Concepts for Expressing Users' Information Systems Requirements, in Entity-Relationship Approach to Systems Analysis and Design (Proc. ER'79), P.P. Chen, Editor. 1979, North-Holland: Amsterdam. p. 381-402.

[37] Sølvberg, A. Software Requirement Definition and Data Models. in Proc. 5th International Conference on Very Large Databases (VLDB'79). 1979. Rio de Janeiro: IEEE Computer Society.

[38] Sølvberg, A. and C.H. Kung, On Structural and Behavioural Modelling of Reality, in Data Base Semantics (Proc. IFIP WG2.6 WC DS-1), T.B. Steel Jr. and R. Meersman, Editors. 1986, North-Holland: Amsterdam. p. 205-221.

[39] Wand, Y. and R. Weber. An Ontological Analysis of some Fundamental Information Systems Concepts. in Proc. Ninth International Conference on Information Systems - ICIS'88. 1988. Minneapolis.

[40] Wand, Y. and R. Weber, On the Deep Structure of Information Systems. Information Systems Journal, 1995. 5: p. 203-223.

[41] Wand, Y. and R. Weber, On the ontological expressiveness of information systems analysis and design grammars. Journal of Information Systems, 1993. 3: p. 217-237.

[42] Weber, R.A., Ontological Foundations Of Information Systems. 1997, Melbourne, Australia: Coopers And Lybrand Accounting Research Methodology Monograph No. 4, Coopers And Lybrand.

Uniform and Flexible Data Management in Workflow Management Systems

Johann Eder, Marek Lehmann

University of Vienna, Austria

Abstract. Various kinds of data are processed in workflow management systems: from case data to control data, from internal data to access to external databases or documents exchanged in inter-organizational workflows. We propose a uniform treatment of all kinds of business data in workflows. This is achieved by an abstraction mechanism which enables the transparent access to data in any source in a uniform way. Moreover, we ensure simplicity by binding the human user interface layer of the workflow system with XML-based forms. The concept contributes to transparency of data location, and logical and physical independence of data, business logic and presentation in workflow systems. It facilitates the reuse of predefined activities and forms on different data sets and eases the interaction of a workflow with its environment by abstracting from the actual representation of data.

1 Introduction

There is already a quite long history of endeavours to model business processes and support their execution. A particular role always played the two intertwined, but separate aspects: the data or structural aspect and the dynamic, behavioural or process aspect [23,24]. Workflow management systems are a successful product of these research and development efforts. As we will argue below, workflow management typically focuses on the process aspect of business processes. In this paper we argue that workflow management systems should improve the management and handling of data and present an approach for uniform and flexible data management in Workflow Management Systems.

Workflow processes may involve different kinds of business data. Each workflow management system(WfMS)[1] must be able to handle these data, which may come from many different sources. These data are used in two different ways. First, they are required by individual activities. Second, the WfMS uses data to make automatically the control flow decisions based on data values. Clearly, workflow management would be not possible without data. It is perhaps surprising, that the data perspective in workflow management was usually left in the background[7].Only quite recently interest in data management aspects of workflow systems increased somewhat with the analysis of workflow data patterns[18] which in particular showed how complex the handling of data in workflow management system actually is.

Workflow Management systems (WfMSs) are not intended to provide general data management systems capabilities, although they have to be able to work with large amounts of data coming from different sources. Business data, describing persistent business information necessary to run an enterprise, maybe controlled either by a WfMS or be managed in external systems (e.g. corporate database).The WfMS needs a direct data access to make control flow decisions based upon data values. An important drawback is that WfMS-external data can only be used indirectly for this purpose, e.g. be queried for control decisions. Therefore, most of the activity programming is related to accessing external databases[3], a great impediment for flexibility, understandability and changeability of workflows[8]. On the other hand, data used within a workflow system may be in different types and formats. Basically each product uses different, proprietary solutions varying from the minimal set of built-in primitive types(number, string, date) to user defined types. This sometimes causes inconsistency with the XML data format used in inter organizational workflows and by web services.

In a typical workflow, performing of a manual task is often associated with filling in some form (e.g. purchase order form).A form has a certain format and is composed of a number of fields with some kind of structure. These fields are mapped to the data used within the workflow. Existing WfMSs support form based manual tasks in two ways: they offer their own proprietary form format or allow web based solutions to be used. The drawback of the former case is, that the client software must understand the form format. The client software must be installed on a machine of each human workflow participant which increases installation and maintenance costs. In the latter case, the workflow management system may offer web based form processing like HTML forms (e.g.PantaRhei[11]).Well accepted and understood web standards enable the use of many design tools and do not require specific client software, except a standard web browser. On the other hand, HTML-based solutions are very limited.

Forms described in HTML are flat, more sophisticated user interface and client behaviour requires lot of programming in scripting languages(e.g. JavaScript) or form processing on the server side. Another important drawback is the necessity to provide the mapping between HTML form fields, represented as a set of attribute-value pairs, and data used internally in a workflow.

We propose to solve all three presented problems. The problematic issue of data location is sorted out by the introduction of data access plug-ins which manage the distributed data sources, so that access to business data is transparent. Limitations of the internal data formats are avoided by basing our system upon XML which provides a flexible data representation. The third problem solved concerns the complexity of the interface layer in most workflow management systems. In order to provide fast and easy communication with the human actors, we use XForms technology to present XML data in a web browser. We validated the functionality of the proposed approach in a prototype WfMS.

Section 2 presents our mechanism for accessing transparently business data stored in many different data sources. An XML based user interface is described in Sec. 3. Both these mechanisms are incorporated into our workflow metamodel in Sec. 4 and the prototype architecture in Sec. 5. We discuss related work in Sec.6 and draw some conclusions in Sec.7.

2 Uniform XML Based Data Access

We propose to provide the workflow management system with a uniform and transparent access method to all business data stored in any data source. The workflow management system should be able to use data coming from external and independent systems to determine a state transition or to pass it between activities as parameters. This is achieved by an abstraction layer called data access plug-ins [13]. Data access plug-ins are reusable and interchangeable wrappers around external data sources which present to the workflow management system the content of underlying data sources and manage the access to it. The functionality of external data sources is abstracted in these plug-ins.

On the other hand, we propose to use XML as the main business data format at every stage of workflow processing. The workflow management system should be able to test conditions on XML data to determine the state transitions, regardless of where these data are stored and maintained. Data passing between activities should also rely on XML-standards, independent of whether these activities are internal to a workflow or external.

Both goals aim at a seamless integration of intra-and inter-organizational workflows and on location transparency of data.

2.1 Data Access Plug-ins

A data access plug-in is a wrapper presenting to the workflow management system the content of external data sources as XML documents. Each data access plug-in provides documents in one or several predefined XML Schema types. Both a data access plug-in and XML Schema types served by this plug-in are registered to the workflow management system. Once registered, a data access plug-in can be reused in many workflow definitions to access external data as XML documents of a given type. A workflow designer specifies in a workflow definition which document should be accessed by which data access plug-in.

Consider the following frequent scenario: an enterprise has a large database with the customer data stored in several relations and used in many processes.

In our approach the company defines a complex XML Schema type describing customer data and implements a data access plug-in which wraps this database and retrieves and stores customer data in XML format. This has several advantages:

- Business data from external systems are accessible by the WfMS. Thus, these data can be passed to activities and used to make control flow decisions.
- Activities can be parameterized with XML documents of predefined types. The logic for accessing external data sources is hidden in a data access plug-in fetching documents passed to activities at runtime. This allows activities to be truly reusable and independent of physical data location.
- Making external data access explicit with the data access plug-ins rather than hiding it in the activities improves the understandability, maintainability and auditability of process definitions.
- Both data access plug-ins and XML Schema type are reusable.
- This solution is easily evolvable. If the customer data have to be moved to a different database, it is sufficient to use another data access plug-in. The process definition and activities remain basically unchanged.

The task of a data access plug-in is to translate the operations on XML documents to the underlying data sources. A data access plug-in exposes to the workflow management system using a simple interface which allows XML documents to be read, written or created in a collection of many documents of the same XML Schema type. Each document in the collection is identified by a unique identifier. The plug-in must be able to identify the document in the collection given only this identifier.

Each data access plug-in allows an XPath expression to be evaluated on a selected XML document. The XML documents used within a workflow can be used by the workflow engine to control the processing flow. This is done in conditional split nodes by evaluating the XPath conditions on documents. If a given document is stored in an external data source and accessed by a data access plug-in, then the XPath condition has to be evaluated by this plug-in. XPath is also used to access data values in XML documents.

Data access plug-ins can be used in workflow definitions described in our workflow definition language WDL-X. A sample WDL-X fragment of an order processing workflow is presented in Fig. 1. There is a declaration of two documents typed with XML Schema. An order document is of type orderType (line 3) and is accessed by a data access plug-in orderDbPlugin, i.e. it is stored outside of the workflow repository. A document describing an invoice is stored in the repository (line 4).

```
1: <process name="processOrder" owner="marek" version="1.0">
2:   <documents>
3:      <document name="order" type="orderType" accessPlugin="orderDbPlugin"/>
4:   <document name="invoice" type="invoiceType"/>
5: </documents>
```

Fig. 1. SampleWDL-Xscriptfragment with a declaration of a document accessed by a plug-in

A data access plug-in can be wrapped around any data source, if it provides the described basic functionality. In particular a data access plug-in can be also wrapped around a web service. In this case the functionality of a data access plug-in is limited only to read mechanisms (i.e. open and retrieve document, test XPath expression) and update operations are not allowed. This limitation is imposed by two facts: the data access plug-ins are intended only to serve data, but the web services offer interfaces to provide services and have active properties. A call to a web service can start an external workflow. Such a behaviour initiated by a data access plug-in would make the workflow definition obscure and very difficult to analyze and maintain. Therefore, we argue that an implementation of a data access plug-in based on a web service should be done very carefully to avoid unwelcome side effects during the workflow execution. On the other hand, the web services are very good sources of data. A recent empirical study shows that majority (up to 84%) of existing public web services are simply data sources, and most of them offer just one operation[14]. Such web services can provide data which are completely managed outside the context of an active workflow instance, e.g. credit card validity, tax rates, metal and oil prices, currency exchange rates.

2.2 Generic Data Access Plug-in

A proposal we described in [13] required data access plug-ins to be defined each time from scratch. On the other hand, most business data remain stored in relational databases. Therefore, a generic and expandable solution for relational data sources was needed. A generic data access plug-in (GDAP) offers basic operations and can be extended by users to their specific data sources. GDAP is responsible for mapping of the hierarchical XML documents used by workflows and activities into flat relational data model used by external databases. Thus, documents produced by GDAP can be seen as XML views of relational data.

The workflows and activities managed by the WfMS can run for a long time. In a loosely coupled WfMS scenario it is neither reasonable nor possible to lock data in the original database for processing time in a workflow. At the same time these data can be modified by other systems or workflows[7]. In order to provide optimistic concurrency control, some form of view invalidation is required[20]. Therefore, GDAP provides a view freshness control and view invalidation method. In case of view update operations GDAP automatically checks whether the view is not stale before propagating update to the original database.

3 XML Based User Interface

We propose an XForms based user interface to the manual tasks. XForms is a new standard[10] for describing forms. It is both XML based and web enabled. These features are very important. First, we use XML as the data format internally in the workflow management system and to communicate with the external systems. Because XForms are designed to work with XML, there are no inconsistencies and no need for special data mappings or transformations. On the other hand, by giving access to manual tasks from a simple web browser, we provide access to workflow applications for a large number of users at very low installation and maintenance cost. Moreover, this enables external users(e.g. customers) to initiate and take part in a workflow, e.g. by submitting an order request from their own web browser. Thus, enterprise-wide and inter-organizational workflows can be easily created with standardized tools [3].

Traditionally such functionality was provided by HTML forms, but for large and complex systems it is obvious, that HTML forms have many disadvantages. Traditional forms remember the data entered by the user in a flat form, as a set of attribute-value pairs. Such data, when received by the server, have to be additionally processed and validated. Another problem was caused by the necessity to provide a mapping between flat HTML forms and data format used internally in the workflow, e.g. hierarchical XML is usually mapped into HTML with XSLT[2]. On the contrary, the XForms standard allows data to be validated on the client side. Moreover, XForms provide a more advanced graphical interface together with data derivation and calculation mechanisms. XForms make clear distinction between the data content and the graphical presentation. What is most important, XForms are designed to work with XML. All these features make XForms an ideal technology for workflow management systems.

An XForm has a set of input and output parameters which are defined in its code. Each XForm parameter has its unique string identifier and is an XML document which may by typed by an XML Schema type. A form can accept a set of XML Schema typed XML documents as the input presented to a user and used for internal calculations. It can also produce XML documents as output.

A manual task has also a set of input and output parameters which are XML documents described by XML Schema types. The user interface to such manual tasks is provided by XForms. When a user chooses a manual task from a worklist, all the required documents are retrieved(possibly with data access plug-ins) and passed to a XForm as input parameters. The parameterized XForm is presented to the user. After the user finishes the interaction with the XForm, the results are sent as one or more XML documents to the workflow management system which saves them in appropriate locations (possibly using data access plug-ins).

A manual task can have associated a default form in its definition as presented in Fig. 2. The important issue is to provide a mapping between the parameters of a manual task and an XForm. Each formal parameter of the task is mapped to a formal parameter of the form. The number of the parameters must be the same, mapped parameters must have the same XML Schema type and same input mode (*IN, INOUT, OUT*). The actual parameters of a task instance are used to parameterize a form template at runtime, and a complete and parameterized XForm is send to the client.

```
1: <manualTaskDefinition name="produceInvoice" owner="marek"
                            defaultForm="invoiceForm">
2:    <formalParameters>
3:      <formalParameter name="order" inputMode="IN"
                            dataType="orderType"
                            mapToFormParam="order"/>
4:      <formalParameter name="invoice"
                            inputMode="OUT"
                            dataType="invoiceType"
                            mapToFormParam="invoice"/>
5:    </formalParameters>
6: </manualTaskDefinition>
```

Fig. 2. WDL-X definition of a manual task with an associated default form

Forms are reusable. The same XForm can be used by different manual tasks and can take different documents as input. A workflow designer specifies a default form for each manual task registered in the workflow management system. When the task is used as a single step in a workflow definition, the system uses its default form to provide the user interface. The workflow designer may override this default form in a particular workflow definition and specify that, a manual task used in a particular step should use a different form. This makes the task independent from the user interface representation. For example the same manual task may have different interface to different users, e.g. different to a secretary and different to a manager.

4 Workflow Metamodel

We propose a new workflow metamodel which captures both data access plug-ins and forms together with reusable workflows and activities and associated data (Fig. 3).The metamodel reflects the nested structure of complex activities and supports the graph representation of workflows. The metamodel is tailored to the purpose of this paper and, therefore, does not contain all components required in a workflow metamodel, e.g. we do not consider the organizational structure.

A *workflow* uses *activities* and can have a set of declared *documents*. Documents can be passed to activities as parameters. An activity is either a task, a complex activity or a (sub-) workflow. An activity can be used to compose complex activities and workflows. An activity occurrence in such a composition is represented by a *step*. One activity can be represented by several steps in one or several other complex activities or workflows. In other words, steps are placeholders for reusable activities. Between the subsequent steps there is additionally a *transition* from a predecessor to a successor. The control structure of a complex activity is described by its *type* (*seq* for sequence, *par* for parallel and *cond* for conditional). We limit our metamodel only to the description of full blocked workflows [26].

In the presented metamodel, workflow graphs can be viewed on different levels of detail. A workflow or a complex activity can be viewed as a composed whole, with all its relations to the subactivities. It can also be viewed decomposed into a full flattened graph. This is achieved by *activity steps* and *control steps*. An attribute *type* of a step can have either a value *activity* (for activity steps) or one of the following for the control steps: *par-split, par-join, cond-split* or *cond-join*. An activity step offers a compact view of a complex activity. In a graph representation it would be a complex activity represented as a single box. An activity step has a method *flatten* which eliminates a level of composition. A control step represents a control element such as a split or a join. As we permit only full blocked workflows, each join has a corresponding split and vice versa. This is represented by a recursive relation *is_counterpart*. Corresponding control steps are the boundaries of a complex activity. The control steps offer a more detailed view on a workflow graph. They have a method *unflatten* which is inverse to the method *flatten*. Both methods are described in [12].

Each *document* used in a workflow definition is typed with an XML Schema type (*DocType*) which has a unique name. The XML documents may be used as variables declared in a workflow definition, or used as formal parameters to activities. An XML document declared in a workflow definition can be accessed by a *data access plug-in*. Each data access plug-in can serve documents of predefined XML Schema types. The XML Schematype of a document accessed by the data access plug-in must by among types supported by this plug-in.

Each workflow can have many workflow instances. Within a *workflow instance* are instantiated documents and steps of a corresponding workflow definition. Step instances represent actual activity instances. Which activity is instantiated by a given step instance is described by the relation between a step instance and a corresponding step and the relation between a step and an activity. A *type* of a step instance is the same as a type of a corresponding step. The step instances form a workflow instance graph. Each step can have predecessors and successors and the transitions between them. The hierarchical structure of activity instances is reflected by the recursive relation *parent*.

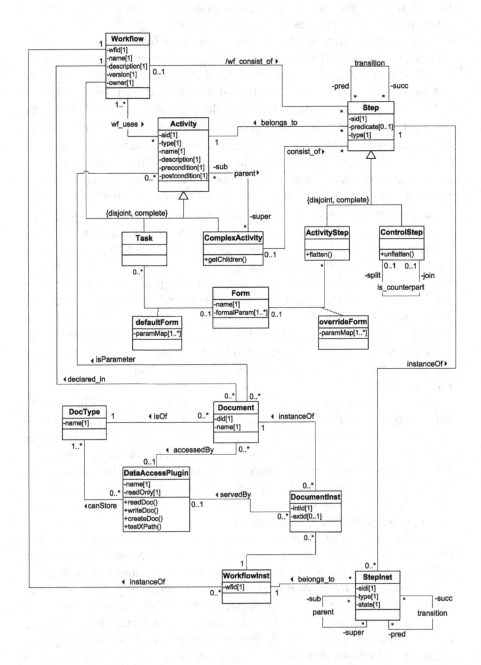

Fig. 3. Workflow metamodel

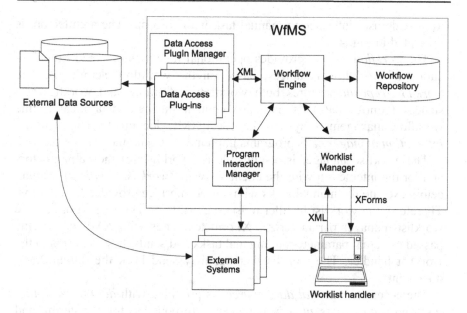

Fig. 4. Proposed WfMS architecture with data access plug-ins

Instances of documents, declared in the workflow definition as accessed with a data access plug-in, are served at runtime by this plug-in. Each document instance has a unique internal identifier, used by the workflow management system. The instances of documents accessed by a data access plug-in have additionally an external identifier, used by the plug-in to identify the document instance. This is a reference to the actual document content in an external data source.

A manual task registered in the workflow management system, may have a default XForm. Each form has a unique name and a set of formal parameters. The parameters of the manual task are mapped into parameters of the form. A workflow designer may override this default form in a workflow definition, and decide to use a different form for a particular step corresponding to this manual task. In this case the parameter mapping must be also provided.

5 Proposed Architecture and Prototype

We propose a new architecture of a workflow management system which supports the usage of XML documents at every stage of workflow processing. This architecture allows the workflow management system to transparently access many sources of business data via data access plug-ins and to provide user interface to manual task with XForms. The architecture is presented in Fig. 4.

The *workflow engine* provides operational functions to support the execution of workflow instances, based on the workflow definitions. The *workflow repository* stores both workflow definitions and workflow instances (control data). It can also contain business data local to the workflow management system, i.e. local XML documents. The *program interaction manager* calls programs implementing automated activities.

The worklist manager is responsible for worklists of the human actors and for the interaction with the client software (*worklist handlers*). Human actors execute the manual tasks with a user interface provided by XForms. Therefore, the worklist handler must be capable of handling XForms. The worklist manager parameterizes XForm templates with XML documents passed as actual parameters to manual tasks and sends these XForms to the worklist handler. The worklist handler may send back the output XML documents.

The access to *external data sources* is provided with *data access plug-ins*. The *data access plug-in* manager is responsible for registering and managing data access plug-ins. The WfMS is extensible, because new data access plug-ins can be registered to the manager and used in the workflow definitions. This architecture is very flexible, because existing data access plug-ins may be replaced by new ones without any integration into existing workflow definitions.

The presented architecture was prototypically implemented [22]. A lightweight workflow engine was implemented as a Java servlet, which produced parameterized XForms instead of standard HTML to communicate with clients. We used Apache Tomcat as a servlet container and the DENG browser[1] to present XForms. The prototype represented internally all business data as XML documents accessed by data access plug-ins. Our implementation included GDAP for relational databases and another one for XML files stored in a file system.

The current implementation of the GDAP for relational databases [9] takes advantage of the XML-DBMS middleware for transferring data between XML documents and relational databases [6]. XML-DBMS maps the XML document to the database according to an object-relational mapping in which element types are generally viewed as classes and attributes and XML text data as properties of those classes. An XML-based mapping language allows the user to define an XML view of relational data by specifying these mappings. The XML-DBMS supports also insert, update and delete operations.

---

[1] See http://sourgeforge.net/projects/dengmx

6 Related Work

In most existing workflow management systems, data used to control the flow of the workflow instances (i.e. workflow relevant data) are controlled by the workflow management system itself and stored in the workflow repository. If these data originate in external data sources, then external data are usually copied into the workflow repository. There is no universal standard for accessing external data in workflow management systems. Basically each product uses different solutions [19]. A chain of so called materialization and dematerialization programs was proposed in [16].Such chains can be attached to activities. On the contrary, we proposed to associate data access plug-ins to documents used in a workflow and not to activities. This has two main advantages. First, it allows a business logic of activities to be separated from a data access logic of data access plug-ins. Second, both the activity and the data access plug-in are independent and can be reused in many workflow definitions and easily maintained and replaced.

The importance of XML technology is increasing tremendously in the workflow management. Workflow management systems [26], B2B standards [21], and Web services [4] use XML as a data format. Methods for integrating workflow management systems with standards for web services are becoming more important [17, 21].Web services are sometimes treated as data sources and composed using data integration techniques [25]. Another approach for processing XML documents in workflow management systems is presented in [5]. The authors proposed to partition a single XML document into several meaningful segments, i.e. units of work that can be performed by an activity in a workflow process.

Forms used for manual tasks can have proprietary format or use HTML like in PantaRhei [11]. PantaRhei used even a form-flow metaphor to provide access to workflow specific data. The authors of [2] proposed to use process aware XSLT style sheets to provide an active user interface to XML data used in workflows. There are also proposals to use XSLT to produce GUI for web services [15]. But mixing XSLT with the business logic can make a workflow definition very obscure. The XForms which provide only presentation and are reusable and data and business logic independent are a great step forward.

7 Conclusions

It was our ambition to show that integrated consideration of the data aspects and the dynamic aspects of workflow systems is possible and that this integrated view can lead to rather lean and flexible systems which are comparatively easy to comprehend and use due to uniform general architectural principles. We did so by designing and implementing a small workflow management system which shows how data management can be both flexible and uniform.

The main contributions of the presented approach for uniform access to data in workflows are:

- Separation of the business logic (activities), data access mechanism (data access plug-ins) and user interface (XForms).
- All data in workflows (application data, workflow relevant data, data in external sources, etc.) are described, represented and processed uniformly.
- We offer a simple and transparent mechanism for accessing data stored in many different data sources (workflow repository, external systems).
- Seamless integration with external systems can be achieved by exchange of process and application data in XML format.
- XML datatypes and data access plug-ins can be reused in many workflow definitions.
- Reusability of activities is made easier and is no longer prohibited by differences in data representation.

Thanks to XForms and the way they are parameterized in our system, the user interface to manual tasks is more flexible and modular. Moreover, the interface is not fixed, as in many typical applications, but the XForms templates can be easily redesigned and improved, without the need to change the implementation. And last but not least, the use of browser ensures portability which is nowadays a very important feature.

The concept and the architecture we propose strives for achieving true physical and logical independence of process and data. The abstraction represented in exchangeable plug-ins for data access frees workflow definitions from the accidentiality of representation formats. Besides the obvious advantages for intra-and interorganisational exchange of data and documents, maintenance and evolution of workflow systems will benefit considerably.

Acknowledgments We would like to thank our students: Christian Dreier, Maciej Siekierski and Aleksandra Wojnowska, who implemented the prototype WfMS and GDAP.

References

[1] van der Aalst, W., van Hee, K.: Workflow Management: Models, Methods, and Systems. MIT press, Cambridge, MA, 2002.

[2] Aberer, K., Datta, A., Despotovic, Z :Separating business process from user interaction utilizing process-aware xslt style-sheets. In WECWIS'02: Proceedings of the Fourth IEEE International Workshop on Advanced Issues of E-Commerce and Web-Based Information Systems (WECWIS'02), page 69. IEEE Computer Society, 2002.

[3] Ader, M.: Workflow and business process management comparative study. Volume 2. Technical report, Workflow & Groupware Strat'egies, June 2003.

[4] Andrews, S., Curbera, F., Dholakia, H.,Goland, Y., Klein, J., Leymann, F., Liu, K., Roller, D., Smith, D., Thatte, S., Trickovic, I., Weerawarana, S.: Business process execution language for web services (bpel4ws). Technical Report 1.1, BEA, IBM, Microsoft, SAP, Siebel Systems, 5 May 2003.

[5] Bae, H., Kim, H.: A document-process association model for workflow management. Comput. Ind., 47(2):139–154, 2002.

[6] Bourret, R.: Xml-dbms middleware. Viewed: May 2005, http://www. rpbourret.com/xmldbms/index.htm.

[7] Bussler. C.: Has workflow lost sight of dataflow?, 1999. High Performance Transaction System Workshop 1999.

[8] Carlsen, S., Krogstie, J., Sølvberg, A., Lindland, O.I.: Evaluating flexible workflow systems. In Hawaii International Conference on System Sciences (HICSS-30), 1997.

[9] Dreier, C.: Generischer datenzugriff in xml-gest"utzten lighweight workflow management system. Master's thesis, University of Klagenfurt, 2005.

[10] Dubinko, M., Klotz Jr. L.L., Merrick, R., Raman, T.V.: Xforms 1.0. W3c recommendation, World Wide Web Consortium (W3C), 14 October 2003.

[11] Eder, J., Groiss, H., Liebhart, W.: The workflow managament system panta rhei. In A. Dogac, L. Kalinichenko, T. "Oszu, and A.Sheth, editors, Workflow Management Systems and Interoperability. Springer-Verlag, 1998.

[12] Eder, J., Gruber, W.: A meta model for structured workflowssupporting workflow transformations. In Proceedings of the 6th East European Conference on Advances in Databases and Information Systems (ADBIS 2002), volume 2435 of Lecture Notes in Computer Science, pages 326–339. Springer-Verlag, 2002.

[13] Eder, J., Lehmann, M.: Uniform access to data in workflows. In Kurt Bauknecht, Martin Bichler, and Birgit Pröll, editors, Proceedings of the 5th International Conference on E-Commerce and Web Technologies, EC-Web 2004,

volume 3182 of LNCS, pages 66–75, Zaragoza, Spain, August/September 2004. Springer-Verlag.

[14] Fan, J., Kambhampati, S.: A snapshot of public web services. SIGMOD Record, 34(1):24–32, March 2005.

[15] Kassoff, M., Kato, D., Mohsin, W.: Creating guis for web services IEEE Internet Computing, 7(5):66–73, 2003.

[16] Leymann, F., Roller, D.: Production Workflow. Concepts and Techniques. Prentice-Hall PTR, Upper Saddle River, New Jersey, USA, 1999.

[17] Lienhard, H.: Web services and workflow - a unified approach. In Workflow-cHandbook 2003, pages 49–60. Workflow Management Coalition, 2003.

[18] Russell, N., ter Hofstede, A.H.M., Edmond, D., van der Aalst, W.M.P.: Workflow data patterns. Proc. of 24th Int. Conf. on Conceptual Modeling (ER05), 3716:353–368.

[19] Russell, N., ter Hofstede, A.H.M., Edmond, D., van der Aalst, W.M.P.: Workflow data patterns. Technical Report FIT-TR-2004-01, Queensland University of Technology, Brisbane, Australia, April 2004.

[20] Rys, M.: Bringing the internet to your database: Using sqlserver 2000 and xml to build loosely-coupled systems. In Proceedings of the 17th International Conference on Data Engineering ICDE, April 2-6, 2001, Heidelberg, Germany, pages 465–472. IEEE Computer Society, 2001.

[21] Sayal, M., Casati, F., Dayal, U., Shan, M-S.: Integrating workflow management systems with business-to-business interaction standards. In Proceedings of the 18th International Conference on Data Engineering (ICDE'02), page 287. IEEE Computer Society, 2002.

[22] Siekierski, M., Wojnowska, A.: Xforms workflow engine. Technical report, University of Klagenfurt, 2004.

[23] Sølvberg, A., Kung, C.H.: Activity modelling and behaviour modelling. In Information Systems Design Methodologies: Improving the Practice, 1986.

[24] Sølvberg, A., Kung, C.H.: On structural and behaviour modelling of reality. In Database Semantics, 1986.

[25] Thakkar, S., Knoblock, C.A., Ambite, J-L.: A view integration approach to dynamic composition of web services. In Proceedings of 2003 ICAPS Workshop on Planning Web Services, 2003.

[26] WfMC. Workflow process definition interface - xml process definition language (xpdl). Technical Report WFMC-TC-1025, Workflow Management Coalition, 2002.

Using Models in Enterprise Systems Projects

Jon Atle Gulla

IDI, NTNU, Trondheim, Norway

Abstract. In enterprise systems projects, modeling is used both to configure the application and work out more efficient work processes. Due to the complexity and volatility of the domain, these projects tend to be very expensive and can easily fail and threaten the whole existence of the enterprise. This paper emphasizes the use of models in these projects and exposes some of the challenges they need to deal with. We present some recent work that may help us apply conceptual modeling more successfully when developing new business processes and configuring new systems. In particular we discuss how models may be expanded with performance-related information that is needed to assess the quality of the business processes supported by the computerized enterprise system.

1 Introduction

Organizations today depend on information systems that help them carry out their operations efficiently and reliably and keep information updated and available. Some of these systems have been developed internally and cover just a small fraction of the organization's processes or data. They are often not well integrated with other systems and require a substantial amount of manual work to complete the business processes. Increasingly, however, large-scale standard packages are replacing the smaller and specialized solutions. From 1985 to 1997 the share of large organizations using packaged enterprise systems rose from about 30% to 95% [15]. When Hydro Agri Europe introduced its SAP enterprise system in 1999, it replaced around 120 applications that were used all over Hydro's 17 sites in

Europe. Whereas the packages in the past were only used by large organizations, we now have software intended for small and mid-size companies as well. A survey of European mid-size companies shows that the adoption of packaged enterprise systems increased from about 27% in 1998 to more than 50% in 2000 [20]. With the introduction of light versions and accelerated implementation tools in recent years this trend has continued and few organizations are now running their businesses without packaged solutions.

An *enterprise system[1]* is a packaged application that supports and automates business processes and manages business data. They come with pre-implemented and customizable modules that reflect best practice for common business operations. Business data from different functional areas are integrated and kept consistent across the organization. A characteristic of enterprise systems is their complexities both in terms of business data and in the way they affect the organization's business practices and individual work tasks.

The functionality of enterprise systems is broken down into high-level *work areas* like logistics, financial accounting, and human resources. Within each area, there are *modules* that tend to correspond to organizations' functional units. There are modules for plant maintenance, sales & distribution, materials management, service management, asset management, finance, etc. Some of these modules are again split into sub-modules that also correspond to organizational units. The Materials Management module contains sub-modules for purchasing, inventory management, and invoice verification, for example.

Enterprise systems are among the largest and most complex IT systems on the market. They process thousands of transactions every day and store information about all aspects of the business. Unified data about materials, vendors and customers need to be defined and maintained as the business evolves. Parts of the organization also have to be modelled in great detail, like the structure and materials used in production plants. SAP R/3, the market leader among ERP systems, offers several thousand transactions that potentially penetrate about every business process of the company. This complexity combined with the generality of customizable modules makes ERP projects large and difficult to control. A survey among Australian companies showed that it took between 6 and 7 years to complete an ERP project from early design to a successful company transformation [2]. In the Hydro Agri project, 120 applications were replaced by an SAP

---

[1] The term *enterprise system* is often used synonymously with *enterprise business application* or with the more restricted term *enterprise resource planning* (ERP) system.

R/3 solution that integrated 47 legal companies [7]. When STATOIL, a Norwegian petroleum company, introduced their integrated enterprise system in 2001, they had around 245,000 sales orders and 11,000 work orders created every month, almost 400,000 materials and 900,000 customers defined, and an underlying database that increased by 30-40 GB every month. The complexity is further increased by cultural and legal differences among the sites to be supported by the enterprise system [11, 16].

The most difficult complexity comes from the intricate relationship between enterprise system and organization.   Organizations with complex structures and processes will necessarily need enterprise systems that are customized to deal with this type of complexity. As the organizational complexities grow, it will be increasingly more difficult to analyze the organization's needs and agree on the requirements to the enterprise system. There are rarely any clear lists of requirements in enterprise systems projects. The organization has vague ideas of how their operations can be made more efficient, but these ideas cannot be directly translated into system requirements. They also depend on the way the organization works, their internal structures and their business processes. An alternative to customizing a strict approval system for purchase orders, for example, is to involve managers directly when purchase orders are created. While defining the system requirements, thus, the project needs to define organizational structures and business processes as well. The fundamental challenge is to find the combination of system customization and business reengineering that optimizes business processes with respect to speed, quality and costs. This involves knowledge of functional areas of the organization, enterprise system technology, technical issues, management structures, and external factors like legal requirements and partnerships. Terminological misunderstandings and cultural conflicts are not uncommon when people from so different backgrounds meet to discuss project objectives.

The issue of wicked problems is also getting more apparent in the enterprise system sector. A system engineering problem is wicked if the system requirements and the implemented system mutually affect each other. As soon as the enterprise system is in operation, thus, new requirements tend to develop, leading to ever new cycles of requirements engineering and system implementation.

Enterprise systems come with pre-implemented customizable modules that do not require any programming to run. The behaviour of each module is controlled by a number of system-defined parameters. To set up the system, the project needs intimate knowledge of the nature of these parameters and how they combine to produce a running enterprise solution. Understanding how business needs map onto these parameters is vital to the project and necessitates experts on both business issues and enterprise system features.

Reference models, or best practice models, document the functionality of the systems in more abstract and comprehensible terms. SAP uses a simple process modeling language, Event Process Chains (EPC), to provide a conceptual overview of their system's capabilities and recommended business processes. As illustrated in Figure 1, these models serve as a bridge from the users' perceived real-world problems to the customization tables implementing the desired application behaviour.

We will in the following see how conceptual modeling supports the customization of enterprise systems and help us reengineer the organizations' IT-supported business flows. Even though enterprise systems projects are more model-driven than traditional software engineering projects, there are still fundamental challenges with using traditional process models in these projects. We discuss some aspects of enterprise models that tend to be problematic in large-scale projects, but also present some recent work that sheds more light on how modeling can be successfully applied to reengineer organizations' processes with information technology.

2 Business Reengineering with Enterprise Systems

Enterprise systems provide a shift of focus from programming special-purpose applications to assessing real-world phenomena with humans interacting with computers or other machineries. Since the systems come with pre-defined packages, the emphasis is on how these packages can be used to fulfil a larger task or process. It may be that they can be combined with other packages in more comprehensive applications, but it might also be that they should be accessed directly by people that do parts of the work manually themselves. This represents a shift from replacing people with software to designing more efficient work processes with the help of computerized systems.

Whereas old applications helped organizations to optimize the use of their resources, modern enterprise systems help organizations optimize their business processes across various resource boundaries. *Resource optimization* leads to improved performance at the departmental level, but may not have a positive effect on the whole organization. Due to interface problems between departments, the result is often additional costs or less efficiency at the company level.

Training is an activity that often suffers from resource optimization. In many organizations the Human Resource department is responsible for all training and career planning. The training costs are part of their budget and affect the overall measured performance of the department. Since the HR department does not generate revenues, its performance tends to be measured in terms of costs and vaguely defined value creation. Since key performance indicators for HR departments often include total training costs, the department's performance may increase by keeping training at the lowest possible level.

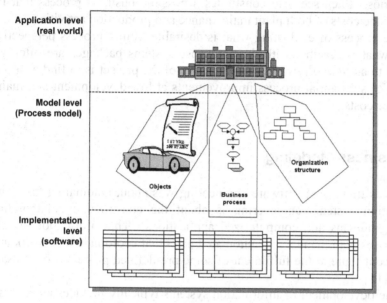

Fig. 1. Three views of enterprise systems

Another example of resource optimization is found in many old production plants with no preventive plant maintenance. Critical production parts are not replaced before they break down and the production halts. It is then important that they can either order the parts very fast or keep sufficient stocks of critical materials at the plant. For the plant maintenance department itself, this may look like a good strategy, as they make full use of all parts, do not need any sophisticated IT support to monitor the use of materials, and can simplify many procedures for maintenance and repair. The costs of a larger inventory of spare parts are often attributed to the warehouse department anyway. What is quite serious, however, is that the strategy may lead to complete process stops if several parts break down simultaneously or unnecessary warehouse costs.

The objective of *business process optimization* is to optimize the performance of processes rather than departments. The efficiency of departmental work is important also in the process optimization philosophy, but we now also have to take into account the interfaces between departments and the way activities are grouped together to create value. In the case of HR and training we now need to analyze how training fits into the process of preparing employees for particular projects and estimate the additional value of having better trained people in these projects. In the plant maintenance case we must compare two production scenarios, with and without preventive maintenance, and analyze the strengths and weaknesses of both scenarios. Each scenario constitutes a possible business process that includes the costs of both plant maintenance and production activities.

The process of evaluating what is desirable from a process perspective with what is feasible with the enterprise systems packages are often referred to as *fit analysis* [7]. The objective of the project is to find a fit that provides substantial process improvements at low development and maintenance costs.

3 Business Modeling

Whereas traditional software engineering was about automating tasks, information systems engineering is about the constructive collaboration among humans and computerized applications. The information system comprises both manual and automated parts that coordinate their work and each contribute to the fulfilment of some pre-defined processes or transactions [18].

The development of information systems typically includes an analysis of some real-world phenomena, a determination of system requirements, and coordinated work among a number of parties. Several kinds of stakeholders may be negotiating in the process, and the result is a product that guides the successive realization of the computerized part of the system. The whole development process has been referred to as a change process due to its overall goal of replacing existing structures or systems with new ones, or – focusing on the intra-dependencies between system requirements and various system representations – as a series of transformations.

The information system is built from a series of increasingly detailed and focused models. By starting from an analysis of a business area, i.e. an unsatisfactory real-world system, a conceptual model is constructed and gradually refined to assess the problems and needs of the system. In the beginning, both the information system and the environment may be included, but as the final conceptual model is finished, automation boundaries are introduced into the model. These decide which parts of the system are to constitute the computerized information system, and they guide the subsequent configuration and implementation stages. From a modeling perspective, we can view these stages as a continuation of the design stage, in which construction details are added to realize the behaviour of the design model. Having implemented the computerized information system, we put it into operation in the larger real-world information system. The whole process is illustrated in Figure 2.

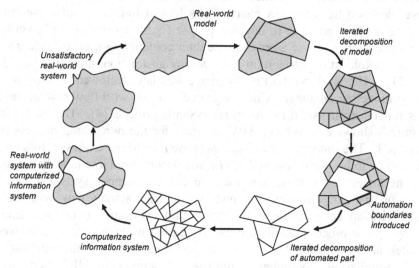

Fig. 2. Information systems development cycle

The modeling approach advocated in information systems engineering has been adopted in enterprise systems projects. The initial real-world model constitutes the AS-IS model of the enterprise, and the final decomposed model – the TO_BE model – determines how the new enterprise system should be configured. However, the TO_BE model is constrained by the functional limits of the enterprise system or the project's willingness to develop additional software to integrate with standard system functionality.

As a bridge between system configuration and real-world problems, the conceptual model needs to satisfy the often conflicting needs for comprehensibility and representativeness:

- *Comprehensibility* refers to the stakeholders' ability to understand the modeling language and correctly read the models constructed
- *Representativeness* refers to the modeling language's ability to represent information systems aspects important to the development of computerized parts and the evaluation of the system as a whole.

A number of formal graphical conceptual modeling languages have been introduced over the years. Many of them build on traditional Petri nets of data flow diagrams, but are extended with more real-world concepts and formalized according to some mathematical or logical theory. Sølvberg's early work on Behaviour Net models, defined as an extension of Petri Nets, was followed by formalized process models that added logical expressions and clear interfaces to data models as well as more low-level decision trees or flow charts. The formal foundation of these languages made it possible to develop proper CASE tools that could verify the models and help the users evaluate their content by means of code generation, explanation generation and various abstraction strategies [8, 13, 17, 21]. His work on the PPP language was later followed by Carlsen's APM modeling language, which is geared towards workflow systems and has proven itself useful in enterprise systems projects [4]. The model in Figure 3 shows a high-level APM diagram for the purchasing process in SAP R/3. The rounded boxes like *Purchase requisition* express a function or activity to be carried out and are further decomposed into new diagrams. At the lowest level, these activities are either enterprise system transactions or basic undecomposed manual work. Each activity may be associated with an actor, some tool support and necessary transaction data, though these process details are usually added when the more low-level models are developed. They may specify, for example, that the purchasers in the purchasing department should use transaction code ME21 and master data about materials, vendors and contracts when new purchase orders are created. Logical ports on the flows between activities are introduced at lower levels to indicate more precisely how activities are triggered and coordinated.

A fundamental problem with all these process languages was the validation against real-world phenomena and user needs. Formal models can be checked for consistency and completeness, but these tests do not reveal whether the model is a suitable representation of the process being modelled. Borrowing concepts from linguistics, Lindland et al. developed a model quality framework that describes the conceptual model's quality in terms of syntactic, semantic and pragmatic quality. Whereas syntactic quality refers to whether the model is syntactically correct, semantic and pragmatic quality reflect the model's capturing of relevant domain aspects and the user's ability to understand its content, respectively [12].

Even though the quality framework has been useful in the analysis of models and modeling languages, it does not say much about the effectiveness or efficiency of the processes being modelled and later supported by the deployed enterprise systems. This depends both on the use of resources internally and the external events, to which the system needs to respond. It is, for example, more important to run frequent processes speedy and economically than processes that are only used every now and then. Also, certain sales processes need to be run extremely fast to generate new revenues, even though it would be cheaper to implement a slower process where all customers are dealt with once a month. Effective and efficient process execution depends on the design of the process, but also on the resources available for executing it and the external load. Theoretical performance models may help us with some of this [3], though we still need real usage data and strategic knowledge of the business.

Another complexity with enterprise systems is the mutual dependency between computerized system and perceived user needs. When the new computerized system is deployed, it allows the users to work differently or do things they could not do in the past. New user needs emerge as the users realize that the new system may generate new opportunities or can be further improved.

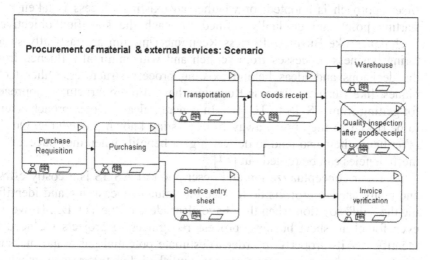

Fig. 3. High-level APM model of the purchasing process (from [22])

Take for example Hydro Agri's SAP system that was developed to integrate production sites all over Europe. The original plan was to source goods from warehouses anywhere in Europe, but keep the familiar separate sales offices. However, as the application was gradually put into operation, the project organization realized that they could simplify both technical, organizational and legal matters by defining one pan-European sales organization rather than keeping all the local national sales organizations. As a result, the development of enterprise systems is never completely finished. Every upgrade generates new user requirements that calls for a later upgrade. The phenomenon is often referred to as the *wicked problem* of information systems development and forces the organization to constantly monitor the use of their enterprise systems [18].

The wicked nature of enterprise systems and the lack of load and resource data in conceptual models has later been addressed by work on process mining and automatic model reengineering.

4 Expanding Models with Performance Indicators

Change projects aim at optimizing business processes and make better use of the enterprise system resources across the enterprise. Hammer [9] and Davenport and Short [6] were the first to describe more or less systematic approaches to improving entire business processes. An important aspect that distinguishes various change project methodologies is whether a *clean sheet* approach is adopted, or whether an existing process is taken as a starting point and gradually refined to reach the specified objectives. Techniques like Business Process Reengineering aim at drastically structuring business processes from scratch and with minimal influence from the decisions and ideas behind existing process structures. Other techniques, like Business Process Redesign, have a more structured approach for getting from AS_IS to TO_BE. In general, clean sheet approaches tend to be riskier as they break away from existing known procedures. On the other hand, they also tend to deliver higher benefits when they succeed, as inefficiencies can be rooted out [14].

A proper conceptualization and description of AS_IS is a costly effort, and many change projects do not see the value of measuring and identifying the "old" solution when they have clear ideas of the TO_BE. However, even for clean sheet business process reengineering projects we need to identify AS_IS properly in order to estimate potential gains and measure these gains when the projects are accomplished. For this reason, most organizations are interested in identifying AS_IS in an objective, representative and, maybe most importantly, cost-efficient manner.

Activities that can be carried out to identify current business process behaviour include on-the-job observations, workshops and employee interviews. The downside of these approaches is that they suffer from subjective, fragmented, and possibly unreliable sources of data. Involving more people may improve the quality of this manual process evaluation work, but the required costs and amount of coordination may soon exceed the gains of this group work. Simulation and cost models have also been used, though they both require very specialized modeling competence and are difficult to use in vague, unclear and wicked system contexts [1, 5].

Automated process mining techniques can to some extent replace the manual approaches and produce AS_IS information that is both objective and structured. Process mining techniques can also be applied to collect and investigate performance indicators related to the business flow. Among the process mining applications available today are EMiT/ProM, Process Miner, EVS, HP Process Intelligence tools suite, and ARIS Process Performance Manager [19].

Empirical business models (EBMs) are business process models where information about historical execution instances is coupled to each activity. Structurally, an EBM shares many commonalities with traditional data flow diagrams. They contain activities that produce specific end results like documents or products and are carried out by certain actors or actor roles in particular departments. Activities depend on each other to the extent that an activity may consume or refer to the end results of others.

Also other model formalisms, like High level Petri Nets, relate context information to the model elements. Specifically for EBMs is that information about the execution instances are stored and kept as an integral part of the model.

From each execution instance we can gather information like execution timestamp, user, user-role, department, and other resources involved in the execution. By keeping this instance information tightly to the graphical model representation, the model can serve as an interactive front-end for more detailed statistical analyses. Including more resource-specific data in the models, we have an extensive basis for uncovering unknown relationships and patterns. Examples of resource specific data include vendors, products, customers, shipping providers, etc. Several studies have been carried out to show the potential of merging data from event logs with other data sources, i.e., a data warehouse.

As described, change projects require information from multiple sources to allow the right decisions to be made and the project to complete successfully. EBMs seek to cover several of the information needs related to change projects and create a dynamic, interactive and model-based basis for AS_IS analysis. We will in the following provide an example model that is extracted using the Enterprise Visualization Suite (EVS) from Businesscape AS [10]. The given case examples are extracted from purchase data in the SAP R/3 implementation at the Norwegian Agricultural and Marketing Cooperative (FKT). A detailed presentation of this case study and a more detailed description of the process mining techniques involved in the extraction process are found in [10].

Figure 4 shows the EBM that was extracted with the EVS tool. The model shows the procurement process from the creation of purchase requisitions to the creation of invoice documents and goods movements. The activities (shown as rounded boxes) represent different transactions in SAP. An arrowed line represents a flow of resources, typically a document. When *ME21N – Create Purchase Order* has an arrowed line to *ME22N – Change Purchase Order,* it means that the first activity produces a document (a purchase order) that the latter activity consumes.

As we can see, the procurement process is fairly complex with numerous alternative process paths and transaction codes. There are several transactions that are related to procurement, and there are several ways of carrying out a purchase. Spare parts to production activities, different types of customer products, and office supplies require different purchasing procedures that are all covered by alternative process paths in the model. Even though the model is dynamically constructed from event logs, it reflects very well the functions in the reference model of SAP R/3.

For each activity box a set of performance indicators are calculated and visualized:

- **Number of monthly executions** – The area of the circular icon at the lower left corner of the activity boxes is an average measure of number of executions per month for the respective activity. The specific area is relative to the largest value that is present in the model, though the exact value is presented as numbers to the right of the circular icon.
- **Average duration** – The size of the dark pie of the circular icons is a average measure of the duration for the respective activity. The size is relative to the largest duration value present in the model, but the exact duration value is also presented to the right of the circular icon.
- **Trends** – The latest trends of throughput and duration are shown as arrows pointing upwards or downwards, depending on the abruptness of the trend.

In figure 4, we can see that the activities *Create Goods Movement* and *Create Purchase Requisition* are executed most frequently, while the activities *ME51N – Create Purchase Requisition* and *MR8M - Cancel Invoice Document* are executed rather infrequently. We notice that created purchase requisitions are changed rather frequently, which may indicate some weaknesses in the way these requisitions are set up. The purchasing process is mostly stock-driven, since most the purchase orders are generated automatically (transaction code ME59) based on stock level. This makes sense, because Felleskjøpet has several warehouses, from which the goods may be sourced without any negotiation.

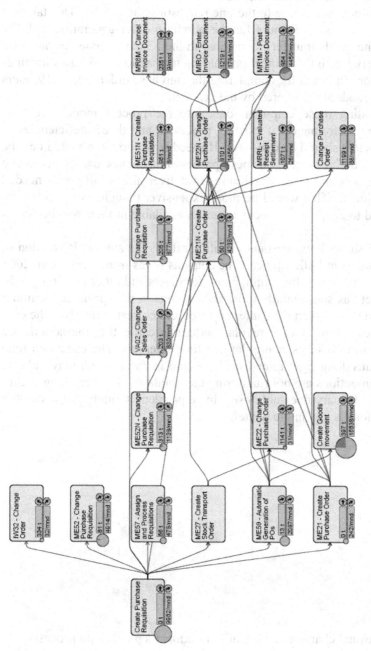

Fig. 4. Empirical process model for purchasing process in Felleskjøpet

The Create Goods movement transaction is simply used to transfer the goods from one warehouse to the one requesting the goods. This takes in total about 17 days (13 hours for the purchase order generation and 397 hours for the goods transfer), compared to the 55 days needed to purchase a new material with the manual purchasing transactions (56 hours for finding a vendor, 50 hours for completing the purchase order, and 1219 hours before the goods are delivered by the vendor).

Incorporating these empirical data into the process model, we may evaluate the performance of existing processes and detect deficiencies or bottlenecks that should be removed. If speed is important, it would here be tempting to define a new business process that makes use of automatic purchase orders and large warehouses to deliver almost all goods needed by Felleskjøpet. This would be more expensive, though, as the company would need to keep larger stocks of goods available in their warehouses at all times.

Figure 5 shows how seasonal variation affects the automatic creation of purchase orders at Felleskjøpet. The analysis spans from week 40 in 2005 to week 36 in 2006. Selling equipment, fertilizers and other farming goods, Felleskjøpet has substantially more transactions in the spring and summer months and should plan their internal resources correspondingly. The execution times follow a very regular pattern, because the transactions are normally run in batches at pre-defined time intervals. The execution time is unnormally long right after Christmas and in July, which may indicate that the transactions are not run during the holidays. The very long execution time in January does not pose a huge problem, though, as the number of transactions is low in the winter.

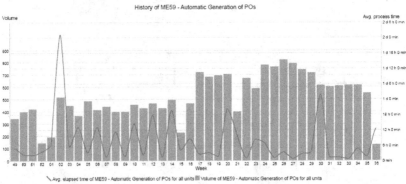

Fig. 5. Seasonal characterization of Felleskjøpet's purchasing process

5 Conclusions

Conceptual modeling is today an integral part of large-scale enterprise systems projects. They allow the project to focus on the reengineering of work processes rather than the technical realization of enterprise transactions. They also provide a uniform formalism for representing the views of all the stakeholders of the system as well as the generic functionality of the enterprise system packages, while still being formal enough to guide the subsequent configuration and tailoring of system functionality. There are today a wide range of tool-supported process modeling languages that lend themselves to sophisticated verification checks, code generation, abstraction and explanation generation. Traditional process modeling languages lack however the means to evaluate the effectiveness and efficiency of business processes. Simulation languages have been introduced in recent years to address this, though it seems hard to describe the organization's resources and the external load in terms of precise mathematical formulas. Research on process mining and empirical business models seems to be more useful in analyzing the performance of processes within a firm conceptual modeling framework. Empirical data about processing times, process frequencies and dependencies supplement traditional process languages' focus on functional issues and are both necessary.

References

[1] Anupindi, R., Chopra, S., Deshmukh, S. D., Van Mieghem, J. A., and Zemel, E.: Managing Business Process Flows. Prentice Hall, 1999.

[2] Booth, P., Matolcsy, Z., Wieder, B.: ERP Systems Survey Benchmark Report 1999. Enterprise Resource Planning Systems Project, University of Technology, Sydney.

[3] Brataas, G., Hughes, P. H. and Sølvberg, A.: Performance Engineering of Workflow Systems With an Integrated View of Human and Computerised Work Processes. In Proceedings of the 9th International Conference on Advanced Information Systems Engineering (CAiSE'97). Barcelona, 1997.

[4] Carlsen, S., Krogstie, J., Sølvberg, A. and Lindland, O. I., Evaluating Flexible Workflow Systems, In: Hawaii International Conference on System Sciences (HICSS-30), Maui, Hawaii, 1997.

[5] Currie, W. L., and Hlupic, V.: Simulation Modelling: The Link Between Change Management Approaches.Knowledge and Business Process Management, Chapter III, pp. 33-50. IDEA Group Publishing, 2003.

[6] Davenport, T. H. and Short, J. E.: The New Industrial Engineering: Information Technology and Business Process Redesign. Sloan Management Review, Vol. 31, No. 4, 1990, pp. 11-27.

[7] Gulla, J. A. and Brasethvik, T.: On the Challenges of Business Modeling in Large-Scale Reengineering Projects. In Cheng (ed.), Proceedings of ICRE'2000, Schaumburg, Illinois, June 2000.

[8] Gulla, J. A., Lindland, O. I., and Willumsen, G.: PPP: An Integrated CASE Environment. In Andersen, R., Bubenko jr., J. A., and Sølvberg, A. (Eds.): Proceedings of CAiSE'91, pp. 194-221, Trondheim, May 1991. Springer.

[9] Hammer, M.: Reengineering work: Don't automate. Obliterate.   Harvard Business Review, July/August 1990, pp. 104-112.

[10] Ingvaldsen, J. E. and Gulla, J. A.: Model Based Business Process Mining. Journal of Information Systems Management, Special Issue on Business Intelligence, Volume 23, No. 1, pp. 19-31, Winter 2006.

[11] Krumbholz, M. and Maiden, N. A. M.: ow Cultuer Might Impact on the Implemenation of Enterprise Resource Planning Packages. In Proceedings of the 12th International Conference on Advanced Information Systems Engineering (CAiSE'2000), June 2000, pp. 279-293.

[12] Lindland, O. I., Sindre, G. and Sølvberg, A.: Understanding Quality in Conceptual Modeling, IEEE Software, 11(2):42-49, March 1994.

[13] Lindland, O. I., Willumsen, G., Gulla, J. A. and Sølvberg, A.: Prototyping in transformation-based case environments. In Proceedings of SEKE'93 pages 696--603, Hotel Sofitel, San Francisco Bay, USA, 1993. Knowledge Systems Institute.

[14] Reijers, H. A.: Process Design and Redesign. Process-Aware Information Systems, John Wiley & Sons, 2005, pp. 207-234.

[15] Robsen, W.: Strategic Management & Information Systems. Second Edition. Financial Times/Prentice Hall. 1997.

[16] Soh, C., Kien, S. S., and Tay-Yap, J.: Cultural Fits and Misfits: Is ERP a Universal Solution? Communications of the ACM, Vol. 43, No. 3, April 2000, pp. 47-51.

[17] Sølvberg A.: Data and what they refer to, in P.P.Chen et al.(eds.): Conceptual Modeling, pp.211-226, Lecture Notes in Computer Science, Springer Verlag, 1999

[18] Sølvberg, A. and Kung, C. H.: *Information Systems Engineering.* Springer-Verlag, 1993

[19] van der Aalst, W. M. P. and Weijters, A. J. M. M.: Process Mining: A Research Agenda. Computers in Industry, Vol. 53, No. 3. Elsevier Science Publishers. 2004, pp. 231-244.

[20] van Erdigen, Y. M., van Hillegersberg, J., and Waarts, E.: ERP Adoption by European Midsize Companies. Communciations of the ACM, April 2000, Vol. 43, No. 4, pp. 27-31.

[21] Yang, M. and Sølvberg, A.: The new PPP: Its architecture and repository management. In Proceedings of the Fifth Workshop on The Next Generation of CASE Tools Utrecht, Holland, 1994.

[22] Zanchi, M., Su, X., and Gulla, J. A.: Modelling with APM in ERP Projects. Open Enterprise Solutions: Systems, Experiences, and Organizations Conference, Rome, Italy, 2001.

The Role of Business Models in Enterprise Modelling

Paul Johannesson

Stockholm University/Royal Institute of Technology, Kista, Sweden

Abstract. In order to cope with increasingly complex business and IT environments, organisations need effective instruments for managing their knowledge about these environments. Essential among these instruments are enterprise models that represent an organisation including its domain of work, processes, and context. Most enterprise models have focussed on information and process structures, but there has recently also been a growing interest in goal models, describing the intention of actors. We suggest that there is a need for an additional type of model, often called value model or business model, that focuses on the value created and interchanged between actors in a business environment. This kind of model provides a clear and declarative foundation for other kinds of enterprise models and they will become increasingly important in managing a complex environment characterised by collaboration, variety, and change.

1 The Roles of Modelling

Today's enterprises and IT systems are facing an increasingly complex environment characterised by collaboration, variety, and change. Enterprises are becoming more and more dependent on their business networks. In order to cope with tasks they cannot handle alone, enterprises need to collaborate with others in ever changing constellations. Organisations are experiencing ever more variety in their business, including products, customers, and enterprise infrastructure. Organisations have to manage an environment that is constantly changing and where lead times, product life cycles, and partner relationships are shortening. In order to cope with increasingly complex business and IT environments, organisations need effective instruments for managing their knowledge about these environments. Essential among these instruments are models, i.e. representations of aspects of an organisation including the domain of work, the processes, and the context. Models have been used for a long time in information systems design, and it is possible to identify three main ways of utilising models, [8]:

Models as sketches. Models are used as sketches to describe possible solutions to problems or to document existing solutions in order to facilitate communication among stakeholders. The idea is to use the models as informal support for explanation and communication.

Models as blueprints. Models are used as blueprints for implementing IT systems and services. The idea is that the models shall be sufficiently precise and formal for programmers, database designers and other IT experts to build a functioning system.

Executable models. Executable models take the idea of models as blueprints one step further. The models shall be formal enough to be automatically translatable into executable code. In this way, the coding step is eliminated, thereby reducing cost and risk for introducing errors.

The approach of executable models is not new but has been a vision for many years, [17]. Recently, it has got more momentum through OMG's launching of MDA, Model Driven Architecture, [14]. The purpose of MDA is to support model-driven engineering of software systems. System functionality is first to be defined in a platform-independent model (PIM), typically using UML as a modelling language. This PIM will then be transformed into a platform-specific model (PSM) adapted to a software environment like .Net or EJB.

Realizing the vision of MDA will require the solution of a number of difficult problems and issues including the modelling of dynamics, acceptance of standards by users and vendors, correct and reliable model transformation algorithms, and the spreading of expertise and skills in MDA. Another issue is the choice of model types to be used for PIMs in the context of information systems design. Most models for this purpose, also called enterprise models, have focussed on information and process structures. Recently, there has also been a growing interest in goal models, describing the intention of actors, [16]. In this Chapter, we suggest that there is a need for an additional type of model, often called value model or business model, that focuses on the value created and interchanged between actors in a business environment. We argue that this kind of model provides a clear and declarative foundation for other kinds of enterprise models and that they will become increasingly important in managing a complex environment characterised by collaboration, variety, and change. The Chapter is structured as follows. Section 2 gives a brief overview of enterprise models, in particular conceptual, process and goal models. Section 3 introduces business models, and Section 4 discusses how business models can be related to process and goal models. The final section concludes the paper and points out a number of research directions for business modelling.

2 Conceptual, Process and Goal Models

2.1 Conceptual Models

Describing a system by means of conceptual models means viewing the world as consisting of objects that belong to different classes, have distinct properties, and are related to each other in various ways. The objects are born, they are affected by events, they acquire and lose properties, they interact with other objects, and finally they die. This way of viewing a system provides a powerful representation and reasoning tool that has been put to use in many different contexts. It has been used for business engineering, requirements engineering, database design, information systems design, and many other applications. One of the first conceptual modelling languages was the ER approach, which was based on the notions of entities and relationships, [5]. Another influential language is NIAM and its successors, [11], that are based on a binary association approach and provides an expressive graphical notation for rule formulation. UML, which has its roots in software engineering, is today widely used also for conceptual modelling.

2.2 Process Models

Process models are used to represent the business processes of an organisation. A well-known definition of a business process is "a specific ordering of work activities across time and place, with a beginning, an end, and clearly-defined inputs and outputs; a structure for action", [6]. There are many other definitions, but in principle they all state that business processes are relationships between inputs and outputs, where the inputs are transformed into outputs using a series of work activities that add value to the inputs.

There exist a large number of languages and notations for process models, each focusing on different aspects of business processes. One kind of process model is the Data Flow Diagram, which shows the flow of data from one place to another. A Data Flow Diagram describes how data enters and leaves a process, the data produced and consumed by the activities of the process, the storage of the data within the process, and the organisational function responsible for the process. Another kind of process model is the Role Activity Diagram, which focuses on the roles responsible for different activities within a process and the interactions between theses roles. Still another kind of process model is IDEF0, which is a graphical notation for business processes showing their inputs, outputs, controls that govern the activities, and resources that are used to carry out the activities of the processes. There are also many other business process languages including EPC, BPMN and UML activity diagrams. Most of these languages are semi-formal and do not provide a precise semantics, but there have been attempts to formalise them using languages like Petri nets and pi-calculus. A formally defined and comprehensive process modeling language is YAWL, [25], which addresses control flow, data flow as well as resource aspects of business processes.

2.3 Goal models

Goal models have been used in requirements engineering to understand a problem domain and to map out the interests of different stakeholders. One of the most widely known languages for goal modelling is i*, [16], which provides constructs for modelling goals, tasks, resources, and dependencies between actors. While i* holds a strong position in the academic community, there are also goal modelling languages with a more practical orientation. One of these languages is the Business Motivation Model, BMM [4]. A basic notion in BMM is that of a goal, which expresses something a business seeks to accomplish, a desired future state of affairs or condition. Examples of goals are being the market leader in an industry or having a profit of more than 1 million euros. Goals can be decomposed, i.e. one goal can be a part of another goal.

Furthermore, BMM includes the notion of means, i.e. something that can be used to achieve a goal. Means can take different forms, as they can be instruments, devices, capabilities, techniques or methods. A means states what an organisation will do or use to achieve a goal, while a goal tells what the organisation views as desirable. There are two main kinds of means, course of action and directive such as business rules and policies. A course of action tells how an enterprise will behave to achieve a goal, while a directive governs or restrains the use of courses of actions. Another component of BMM is the influencer, i.e. something that can impact an enterprise in its employment of means or achievement of goals. An influencer expresses an objective state of affairs, while a goal is something that an organisation decides about – it wants to accomplish the goal. Similarly, a means is something that the organisation chooses itself – it decides to use a means in order to achieve a goal.

3 Business Models

A business model should help to answer a number of questions about a business idea and its realisation. The following are examples of such questions, formulated from one agent's perspective:

- Which is our value proposition?
- What do we offer to our customers?
- Why do the customers find this valuable?
- How do we go about to create this value and how do we market it?
- Can we deliver the value ourselves?
- Do we need to cooperate with other actors?
- Is our network of suppliers and partners sustainable?

These are some basic examples of questions that a business model should help to answer, and they illustrate that a business model is quite different from other types of models used in enterprise analysis and design. In particular, a business model is different from a process model. A business model gives a high level view of the activities taking place in and between organisations by identifying agents, resources and the exchange of resources between the agents. So, a business model focuses on the *what* in business. A process model, on the other hand, focuses on the *how*, as it deals with operational and procedural aspects of business communication, including control flow, data flow and message passing. In other words, a business model takes a declarative view, while a process model takes a procedural view.

There exist a number of languages for business models, where the three most comprehensive and well defined are REA, e^3value, and BMO. These three languages were originally developed for different and specific purposes, but there has also been recent work on expanding their applicability. REA was originally intended as a basis for accounting information systems [15] and focused on representing increases and decreases of value in an organisation. REA has subsequently been extended to form a foundation for enterprise information systems architectures, and it has also been applied to e-commerce frameworks [22]. e^3value focuses on modelling value networks of cooperating business partners and provides instruments for profitability analysis that help in determining whether a certain value network is sustainable [10]. Extensions of e^3value have been suggested that incorporate process related aspects as well as risk management [3] and [23] and strategic analysis, [24]. BMO differs from the two other approaches by being wider in scope, as it also addresses internal capabilities and resource planning. Furthermore, BMO incorporates marketing aspects describing value propositions as well as marketing channels [19].

3.1 The Resource-Event-Actor Framework

The Resource-Event-Actor (REA) framework was formulated originally in [15] and has been developed further, e.g. [9, 22]. Its conceptual origins can be traced back to business accounting where the needs are to manage and monitor businesses through a technique called double-entry bookkeeping. The core concepts in the REA ontology are Resource, Event, and Actor and the intuition behind them is that every business transaction can be described as two events where two actors exchange resources. To acquire a resource, an agent has to give up some other resource. For example, in a purchase the buyer has to give up money in order to receive some goods. There are two events taking place here from the buyer's perspective: one where the amount of money is decreased and another where the amount of goods is increased. A corresponding change of control of resources takes place at the seller's side, where the amount of money is increased while the amount of goods is decreased. Thus, an exchange occurs when an agent receives resources from another agent and gives resources back to that agent. REA does not model only exchanges but also conversions, which occur when an agent consumes resources in order to produce other resources.

3.2 The e^3value Ontology

The e^3value ontology, [10], aims at identifying exchanges of value objects, similar to the resources in REA, between the actors in a business case. It also supports profitability analysis of business cases. e^3value was designed to contain a minimal set of concepts and relations to make it easy to understand for business and domain experts. The basic concepts in e^3value are actors, value objects, value ports, value interfaces, value activities and value exchanges. An actor is an economically independent entity, typically a legal entity, such as an enterprise or a consumer. A market segment is a set of actors with similar preferences. A value object is something that is of economic value for at least one actor, e.g. cars, Internet access, and stream of music. A value port is used by an actor to provide or receive value objects to or from other actors. A value port has a direction, in or out indicating whether a value object flows into or out of the actor. A value interface consists of at least two in and out ports belonging to the same actor. Value interfaces are used to model reciprocity in business transactions. A value exchange is a pair of value ports of opposite directions belonging to different actors. It represents one or more potential trades of value objects between these value ports. A value activity, similar to conversions in REA, is an operation that can be carried out in an economically profitable way for at least one actor.

Fig. 1 gives an example of an e^3value model, which shows a business case for a Massively Multiplayer Online Game (MMOG). In this business model there are three principle actors involved - the game producer, the Internet Service Provider and the Customers. The game producer is responsible for producing the game content and selling and distributing its software on CD to the customers. In order to play the game, the customers need to have Internet access, which they get from the Internet Service Provider. They also need access to the game server, which is provided by the game producer. In the figure, actors are graphically shown by rectangles, value activities by rounded rectangles, value ports by triangles, value interfaces by oblong rectangles enclosing value ports, and value exchanges as lines between value ports with the names of value objects as labels.

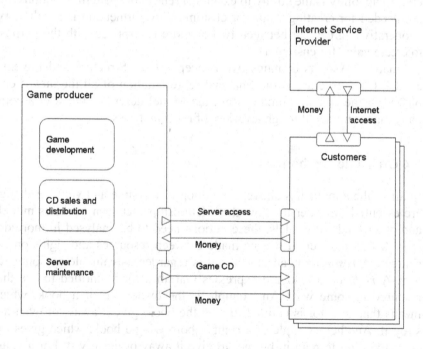

Fig. 1. An e^3value model for an MMOG case

3.3 The Business Model Ontology

The Business Model Ontology (BMO) as proposed in [18] provides an ontology that allows describing the business model of an enterprise precisely and in depth. BMO consists of nine core concepts in four categories. The categories are Product, Customer Interface, Infrastructure Management, and Financial Aspects. The single concept in Product is Value Proposition, which is an overall view of a company's bundle of products and services that are of value to a customer.

Customer Interface contains three concepts; Target Customer, Distribution Channel, and Relationship. A target customer is a segment of customers to which a company wants to offer value. A distribution channel is a means of getting in touch with the customers. A relationship is the kind of link a company establishes between itself and its customers.

Infrastructure Management contains three concepts; Value Configuration, Capability, and Partnership. A value configuration describes the constellation of activities and resources necessary to create value for customers. A capability is the ability to execute a repeatable pattern of actions that are needed for creating value for customers. A partnership is a voluntary, cooperative agreement between two or more enterprises with the purpose to create value for customers.

Financial Aspects contains two concepts; Cost Structure and Revenue Model. Cost structure is the financial representation of all the means employed in the business model. Revenue Model describes the way a company makes money through a variety of revenue flows.

3.4 On Value Exchanges

In all of the approaches above, the notion of resource and value exchange are essential. In order to show the relationships between business models and other kinds of models, these notions need to be analysed in more detail. A first distinction can be made between resources and rights on resources. A *resource* is an object that is regarded as valuable by some actors. A *right* on a resource expresses that an actor is entitled to use that resource in some way. An example is the ownership of a book, which means that an actor is entitled to read the book, give it away, or even destroy it. Another example of a right is borrowing a book, which gives the actor the right to read it, but not to give it away or destroy it. For a value exchange, both the resource being transferred and the right on the resource have to be specified. For example, the two value exchanges in which a car is sold and borrowed concern the same resource but differ in the rights being transferred.

Another component of a value exchange is the custody of the resource being exchanged from one actor to another. An actor has the *custody* of a resource if she has immediate charge and control of the resource, typically physical access to the resource. If an actor has the custody of a resource, this does not mean that she has any rights on the resource. For example, a distributor may have the custody of some goods, but he is not allowed to use the goods for any purpose. Providing custody of a resource is essential in a value exchange, as the buyer is typically unable to exercise the rights she gets unless she has custody of the resource.

A value exchange may also include the transfer of some evidence document that certifies that the buyer has certain rights on a resource. A typical example of an evidence document is a movie ticket that certifies that its owner has the right to watch a movie. Summarising, a value exchange can be seen as combining four components:

- The resource being exchanged from one actor to another, e.g., a book
- The right that the buyer obtains on the resource, e.g., the ownership of a book
- The custody of the resource, e.g., buyer's physical access to a book
- The evidence document, e.g., a ticket

4 Relating Business models to Other Kinds of Enterprise Models

In this section, we will discuss how business models relate to other kinds of enterprise models, in particular process models and goal models.

4.1 From Business Model to Process Model

A business model has a clearly declarative form and is expressed in terms that can be easily understood by business users. In contrast, a process model has a procedural form and is at least partially expressed in terms, like sequence flows and gateways, that are not immediately familiar to business users. Furthermore, it is often difficult to understand the reasons behind a certain process design and what consequences alternative designs would have. One way to address these problems is to base process modelling on a declarative foundation using business models. Such a foundation would provide justifications, expressible in business terms, for design decisions made in process modelling, thereby facilitating communication between systems designers and business experts. More concretely, a business model can be used as the starting point for designing a process model. However, this design cannot be automated as many different process models can realise the same business model, and additional knowledge about the intended process has to be introduced.

Designing a process model based on a business model can be viewed as a process consisting of three phases. First, the processes needed for realising the business model are identified, which results in a set of process names. Secondly, the internal structure of each process identified is designed according to a number of patterns. Finally, the designed processes are related to each other based on different kinds of dependencies. The following design process is based on and elaborates on the one proposed in [2], and it is assumed that the business model used as a starting point is in the form of an e^3value diagram.

Phase 1: Identifying processes

This phase consists of three steps, where the first two steps extend the business model and the third one identifies a set of processes based on the extended model.

Step 1: For each value exchange, determine whether the custody component of the value exchange exists and shall be modelled explicitly. If so, add one or more arrows to the model representing transfers of custody from one actor to another. This step can be viewed as "factoring out" the custody component of a value exchange and modelling it explicitly by additional flows in the model. It should be noted that several actors, and possibly also new actors, may be involved in transferring the custody from one actor to another.

Step 2: For each value exchange, determine whether the evidence document component of the value exchange exists and shall be modelled explicitly. If so, add one or more arrows to the model that represent transfers of evidence documents from one actor to another. Analogously to the step for custody, this step can be viewed as factoring out the evidence document component of a value exchange. Also in this case, several actors may be involved, e.g., when a ticket office supplies tickets on behalf of other service providers.

Step 3: Identify a set of processes based on the extended e^3value model from Step 2 and the Open-EDI transaction phases, [7].

- For each value transaction, one negotiation process is introduced
- For each arrow in the extended model, one actualization process is introduced
- For each arrow in the extended model, optionally one post-actualization process is introduced

Phase 2: Designing the internal structure of processes

The internal structure of each process identified in the previous phase needs to be designed, including control, data, and resource flows. This can be done from scratch but an attractive alternative is to base the design on a library of process patterns. As the number of patterns in such a library will be large, there is a need for structuring mechanisms that facilitate navigation and search. Two well-known structuring mechanisms are generalisation and specialisation, as employed in, for example, the MIT Process Handbook, [13]. Furthermore, the patterns need to be characterised so that a designer easily can choose between patterns for the same purpose. The list of possible characteristics is in principle open-ended, but for processes realising value exchanges, empirical research indicates that there are four main characteristics to be considered, [21]:

- risk - the risk one agent takes in an exchange, e.g. delivering a resource without getting paid
- type of resource - the type of resource being exchanged, e.g. goods, information or services
- time - the time needed for carrying out an exchange
- cost - the cost for carrying out an exchange, often called transaction cost

It is often necessary to make a trade-off between desirable characteristics of an exchange process. For example, the risk of an exchange may be reduced by introducing a letter of credit procedure, which on the other hand will increase costs and lead times. Furthermore, the needs and desires of different agents also have to be balanced, e.g. the risk for one agent may be reduced by requesting a down payment, but this will increase the risk for the other agent in the exchange.

Phase 3: Relating processes

In the two previous phases, a number of processes were introduced and designed. These processes may need to be related to each other, e.g. they may have to be put into sequence. One instrument for doing this is to use the notion of dependencies between activities as suggested in [1]. The two most relevant dependencies in this context are flow dependencies and trust dependencies. A flow dependency is a relationship between two activities, which expresses that the resources obtained by the first activity are required as input to the second activity. An example is a retailer who has to obtain a product from an importer before selling it to a customer. A trust dependency is a relationship between two activities, which expresses that the first activity has to be carried out before the other one as a consequence of low trust between the actors. Informally, a trust dependency states that one actor wants to see the other actor do her work before doing his own work. From these dependencies, relationships between the previously introduced processes can be added.

Basing process design on business models provides a number of advantages:

- Business Orientation. Instead of going directly into procedural details, a business model allows business experts to describe the underlying business reasons that govern the flow of processes. In particular, relations between activities can be specified in terms of notions like resource flow, trust, coordination, and reciprocity.
- Traceability. Components in a process model can be explained by and tracked back to business oriented notions and motivations expressed in a business model.
- Flexibility. The transformations from business model to process model give the main structure of a process model. However, the approach allows for flexibility by letting the internal structure of the processes be based on patterns. This means that the lower-level details of a process model can be tailored to the situation at hand by selecting appropriate patterns from a library.

4.2 Business Models and Goal Models

Goal models, similarly to business models, are typically used in the earliest phases of information systems design, where they help in clarifying interests, intentions, and strategies of different stakeholders. As suggested in [24], goal models often focus on the capabilities, customers, and competition of an enterprise. An enterprise formulates goals that it intends to obtain and uses its capabilities, i.e. internal resources, for this purpose. An important goal for any enterprise is to establish profitable relationships with its customers, which are actors or market segments that buy the products of the enterprise. An enterprise also has to closely watch the activities of its competition, i.e. other actors that address the same market segments. Thus, goal models are closely related to business models, as their subject matter naturally can be expressed in terms of the basic notions of business models. This relationship can be used for improving goal modelling as well as business modelling. For example, expressing goals, means and influencers in terms of agents, resources and economic events encourages precise and uniform formulations that make goal models more expressive and easier to understand. Another use is to design a to-be business model based on an as-is business model and a goal model expressing desired changes of a business. Thus, the goal model is used to suggest which actors, resources and exchanges that are needed to realise a business idea. The most important part of a goal model for this purpose are the means as they express how a business should be carried out and be changed in order to obtain certain goals. BMM makes a distinction between two kinds of means, courses of action and directives such as business rules and policies. A course of action tells how an enterprise will behave to achieve a goal, while a directive governs or restrains the use of courses of actions. After having surveyed a large number of goal models, we have found that almost all courses of actions concern the acquisition, production, maintenance, or provisioning of resources. In other words, means address the fundamental entities of business models - resources, events and agents. Thus, it becomes possible to formulate next to all means occurring in goal models according to a limited number of templates as given below ("resource" is here used as a synonym of "value object"):

1. offer <resource> to <actor | market segment>
2. stop offering <resource> to <actor | market segment>
3. procure <resource> from <actor | market segment>
4. stop procuring <resource> from <actor | market segment>
5. produce <resource> in <value activity>
6. stop producing <resource> in <value activity>
7. (increase | decrease) production of <resource> in <value activity>
8. outsource <value activity> to < actor | market segment>

An example of a goal model for the MMOG case, where the means have been formulated according to the templates above, is given in Fig. 2.

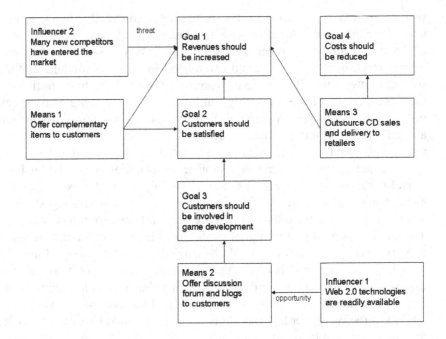

Fig. 2. A goal model for the MMOG case

Given an as-is business model and a goal model, containing a number of means formulated according to the templates above, it is straight-forward to construct a to-be business model that takes the means into account. The following rules can be applied for this purpose:

1. For a means of the form "offer <resource> to <actor | market segment>", add a value exchange for the resource in existing or new value interfaces
2. For a means of the form "stop offering <resource> to <actor | market segment>", remove a value exchange for the resource and possibly associated value interfaces
3. For a means of the form "procure <resource> from <actor | market segment>", add a value exchange for the resource and possibly associated value interfaces
4. For a means of the form "stop procuring <resource> from <actor | market segment>", remove a value exchange for the resource and possibly associated value interfaces
5. For a means of the form "(produce | create | launch | initiate | ...) <resource> in <value activity>", add a value activity producing the resource

6. For a means of the form "stop producing <resource> in <value activity>", remove the resource from the value activity and possibly also the value activity

7. For a means of the form "increase | decrease) production of <resource> in <value activity>", no changes are made to the business model

8. For a means of the form "outsource production of <resource> to <actor | market segment>", remove the resource from a value activity and possibly remove the value activity, add a new value exchange with associated value interfaces to a, possibly new, actor or market segment

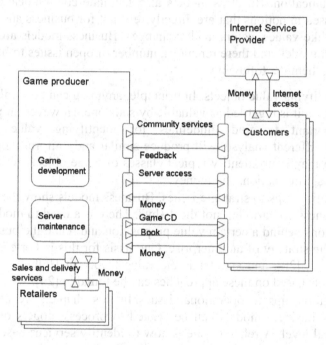

Fig. 3. A to-be e^3value model based on a goal model

Applying the means in the goal model of Fig. 2 to the as-is business model of Fig. 1 will result in the to-be business model of Fig. 3.

5 Concluding Remarks

In this chapter, we have discussed business models, their purpose and how they can be related to other kinds of enterprise models in business, requirements, and information systems engineering. It is envisaged that business models will play a major role in model driven architectures, as they possess important advantages compared to other types of models. In particular, they provide a compact view of a business scenario by focusing on its value aspects and disregarding procedural aspects. This means that business models can be quickly and easily comprehended also by business experts, and they thereby provide an adequate means for explanation and communication. Business models also facilitate communication by being expressed in notions that are directly relevant for business and domain experts, like values, actors, and exchanges. Business models are still a new kind of model, and there remains a number of open issues to be addressed, among them the following:

- Identifying value objects. In principle, anything can be a value object as long as it is regarded as valuable by someone. However, in practice it is important to find guidelines for identifying value objects so that different analysts will produce similar and uniform models. A first step may be to identify typical classes of value objects like goods, services, information, and money.
- Relationships to strategic issues. Business models show the "what" in a business scenario but not the "why". There is a need to model the motivations behind a certain value proposition and relate the business model to the strategy of an enterprise. One basis for this is Porter's five forces theory, [20], and another is the value theory of Holbrook, [12]. Initial results based on these approaches can be found in [24].
- Relationships to operational issues. In this chapter, we have outlined how business models can be related to process models on the operational level. A related issue is how to identify services based on a business model.

References

[1] Andersson, B., Bergholtz, M., Edirisuriya, A., Ilayperuma, T., Johannesson, P.: A Declarative Foundation of Process Models. In: *CAiSE05*, 18th International Conference on Advanced Information systems Engineering, Porto 2005 (Springer, Berlin Heidelberg New York 2005)

[2] Andersson, B., Bergholtz, M., Grégoire, B., Johannesson, P., Schmitt, M., Zdravkovic, J.; From Business to Process Models – a Chaining Methodology. In: *BUSITAL 2006*, A workshop on Business/IT Alignment and Interoperability, Luxembourg (2006)

[3] Bergholtz, M., Bertrand, G., Johannesson, P., Schmitt, M., Wohed, P. and Zdravkovic, J.: Integrated Methodology for linking business and process models with risk mitigation. In: *REBNITA05*, 1st International Workshop on Requirements Engineering for Business Need and IT Alignment, Paris, (2005)

[4] The Business Motivation Model, http://www.businessrulesgroup.org/bmm.shtml

[5] Chen, P.: The Entity-Relationship Model-Toward a Unified View of Data, ACM Transactions on Database Systems, (1976)

[6] T. Davenport: *Process Innovation: reengineering work through information technology*, Harvard Business School, (1992)

[7] Open-EDI phases with REA, UN-Centre for Trade Facilitation and Electronic Business, http://www.unece.org/cefact/docum/download/02bp_rea.doc

[8] Fowler, M.: *UML Distilled*, Addison Wesley, (2004)

[9] Geerts, G., McCarthy, W. E.: An Accounting Object Infrastructure For Knowledge-Based Enterprise Models. IEEE Intelligent Systems & Their Applications, pp. 89-94, (1999)

[10] Gordijn, J.: e-Business Model Ontologies. In: *e-Business Modelling Using the e3value Ontology*, Wendy Curry (ed.), pp. 98-128, Elsevier Butterworth-Heinemann, UK, (2004)

[11] Halpin, T.: *Conceptual schema and relational database design*, Prentice-Hall, Inc. Upper Saddle River, NJ, USA, (1996)

[12] Holbrook, M. B.: *Consumer Value – A Framework for Analysis and Research*, Routledge, New York, NY, (1999)

[13] Malone. T. et al.: *Towards a handbook of organizational processes*, MIT eBusiness Process Handbook, http://ccs.mit.edu/21c/mgtsci/index.htm

[14] OMG - Model Driven Architecture, http://www.omg.org/mda/

[15] McCarthy W. E.: The REA Accounting Model: A Generalized Framework for Accounting Systems in a Shared Data Environment. The Accounting Review, (1982)

[16] Mylopoulos, J., Chung, L., Yu, E.; From object-oriented to goal-oriented requirements analysis. Communications of the ACM, 42(1) (1999)

[17] Opdahl, A., Sølvberg, A.: Conceptual integration of information system and performance modelling. In: IFIP WG 8.1 Working Conference on Information System Concepts -- Improving The Understanding Alexandria, Egypt, April 13--15 (1992)

[18] Osterwalder, A.: *The Business Model Ontology. A Proposition in a Design Science Approach*. PhD-Thesis. University of Lausanne (2004)

[19] Osterwalder, A., Pigneur, Y., Tucci, C.: Clarifying Business Models: Origins, Present and Future of the Concept. Communications of the Association for Information Science (CAIS), Vol. 15, p. 751-775 (2005)

[20] Porter, M.: *Competitive Stategy*, New York, Free Press (1979)

[21] Schmitt M., Grégoire, B.: Risk Mitigation Instruments for Business Models and Process Models. In: *REBNITA05*, 1st International Workshop on Requirements Engineering for Business Need and IT Alignment (2005)

[22]   UN/CEFACT   Modeling   Methodology   (UMM)   User   Guide. http://www.unece.org/cefact/umm/.

[23] Weigand H., Johannesson P., Andersson B., Bergholtz M., Edirisuriya A., Ilayperuma T.: On the Notion of Value Object. In: *CAiSE06* 19th International Conference on Advanced Information systems Engineering, Luxembourg 2005 (Springer, Berlin Heidelberg New York 2005)

[24] Weigand H., Johannesson P., Andersson B., Bergholtz M., Edirisuriya A., Ilayperuma T., Strategic analysis using value modeling – the c3-value approach, In: Fourtieth Annual Hawaii International Conference on System Sciences (CD-ROM), January 7-10, 2007, Computer Society Press (2007)

[25] YAWL Foundation, http://www.yawlfoundation.org/

Capturing System Intentionality with Maps

Colette Rolland

Université Paris1 Panthéon Sorbonne

Abstract. Conceptual modelling has emerged as a means to capture the relevant aspects of the world on which it is necessary to provide information. Whereas conceptual models succeeded in telling us how to represent some excerpt of the world in informational terms, they failed to guide system analysts in conceptualising purposeful systems, i.e. systems that meet the expectations of their users. This chapter aims to investigate this issue of conceptualising purposeful systems and to discuss the role that goal driven approaches can play to resolve it. It considers the challenge of new systems having a multifaceted purpose and shows how intention/strategy maps help facing this challenge.

1 Introduction

Traditionally Information System (IS) engineering has made the assumption that an information system captures some excerpt of world history and hence has concentrated on modelling information about the Universe of Discourse [43]. This is done through conceptual modelling that aims at abstracting the specification of the required information system i.e. the conceptual schema, from an analysis of the relevant aspects of the Universe of Discourse about which the users' community needs information [9]. This specification concentrates on what the system should do, that is, on its functionality. Such a specification acts as a prescription for system construction. Whereas conceptual modelling allowed our community to understand the semantics of information and led to a large number of semantically powerful conceptual models [23] and associated tools [20], experience demonstrates that it failed in supporting the delivery of systems that were accepted by the community of their users. Indeed, a number of studies show [11, 24, 41] that systems fail due to an inadequate or insufficient understanding of the requirements they seek to address. Further, the amount of effort needed to fix these systems has been found to be very high [17]. To correct this situation, it is necessary to address the issue of building *purposeful systems*, i.e. information systems that are seen as fulfilling a certain purpose in an organisation. Understanding this purpose is a necessary condition for the conceptualisation of these purposeful systems. The foregoing suggests to go beyond the functionality based view of conceptual modelling and to extend the *'what is done by the system'* approach with the *'why is the system like this'*. This *why* question is answered in terms of organisational objectives and their impact on information systems supporting the organisation. The expectation is that as a result of a refocus on the *why* question, more acceptable systems will be developed in the future.

The objective of this chapter is to deal with the above issue of conceptualising purposeful systems and to show how a representation system called *Map* can help to this end. Map is a goal-driven approach similar to those developed in requirements engineering [1, 5, 6, 21, 28, 32, 34] business process reengineering [2, 22, 27, 44] and enterprise/business modelling with a holistic viewpoint [26, 38]. In these approaches goal-modelling proved to be an efficient means to capturing the *'Whys'* and establishing a close relationship with the *'Whats'*. The *Map* representation system conforms to goal models in the fact that it recognizes the concept of a goal (intention) but departs from those by introducing the concept of *strategy* to attain a goal. This choice was motivated by:

a) the fundamental distinction between *what to achieve* (the goal) and the *manner to achieve* it (the strategy),
b) *practice*: managers and stakeholders do not naturally make this distinction
c) *pitfalls* generated by this confusion:
    i.   strategies are expressed as goals, then unnecessarily increasing the size of the goal model,
    ii. alternative ways to make the business are more difficult to discover whereas reasoning about alternative ways of achieving a goal is easier,
    iii. recognizing stable elements in a business (intentions) versus more versatile ones (strategies) is difficult.
d) the *need to introduce variability* in the new generation of information systems. Whereas earlier, a system met the purpose of a single organization and of a single set of customers, a system of today must be conceived in a larger perspective, to meet the purpose of several organizations and to be adaptable to different usage situations and customer sets. The former is typical of an ERP-like de-

velopment situation whereas the latter is the concern of product-line development [4, 42] and adaptable software. In the software community, this leads to the notion of software variability which is defined as the ability of a software system to be changed, customized or configured to a specific context [13]. Whereas the software community studies variability as a design problem and concentrates on implementation issues [3, 26, 42], we believe like [14] that capturing variability at the goal level is essential to meet the multi-purpose nature of new information systems.

e) *the essential role of strategies in capturing variability in goal models*: Whereas traditional goal modelling concentrates on goal discovery, variability extends it to consider the many different ways of goal achievement For example, for the goal *Purchase Material*, earlier it would be enough to know that an organization achieves this goal by forecasting material need. Thus, *Purchase Material* was mono-purpose: it had exactly one strategy for its achievement. However, in the new context, it is necessary to introduce other strategies as well, say the Reorder Point strategy for purchasing material. *Purchase Material* is multi-purpose: it has many strategies for goal achievement. Our position is that variability implies a move from systems with a *mono-facetted purpose* to those with a *multi-facetted purpose* and points to the need to balance *goal-orientation* with the introduction of *strategies for goal achievement*. This is the essence of *intention/strategy maps* which we present here.

An *intention/strategy map*, or *map* for short, is a graph, with nodes as *intentions* and *strategies* as edges. An edge entering a node identifies a strategy that can be used for achieving the intention of the node. The map therefore, shows which intentions can be achieved by which strategies once a preceding intention has been achieved. Evidently, the map is capable of expressing variability in goal achievement and therefore, can help modelling the multi-facetted purpose of a system.

The remainder of this paper is organized in two main sections. The next section presents the *Map* representation system. In section 3 we illustrate the key aspects of *Map* with an excerpt of a real project conducted at DIAC, the financial branch of the Renault motor which grants credit to Renault customers and sells other related financial services. The *Map* approach was used to handle the standardization of practices in the various DIAC subsidiaries located in different countries in the world. In section 4 we conclude by summing up the lessons learnt from using *Map* in different European projects.

2 The *Map* representation system

In this section we introduce the *key concepts* of a map and their relationships and brought out their relevance to capture multi-facetted purposes.

Map is a representation system that was originally developed to represent a process model expressed in intentional terms [35]. It provides a representation mechanism based on a non-deterministic ordering of *intentions* and *strategies* that allows us to modelling the multi-facetted purpose of a system To-Be. The key concepts of the map and their inter-relationships are shown in the map meta-model of Fig.1 which is drawn using standard UML notations.

- A *map* is composed of several sections. A section is an aggregation of two kinds of intentions, *source* and *target*, linked together with a *strategy*.
- An *intention* is a goal that can be achieved by the performance of a process. An intention is according to Jackson [16], 'an optative' statement, it expresses what is wanted, a state or a result that is expected to be reached or maintained in the future. For example, *Make Room Booking* is an intention to make a reservation for a room in a hotel. The achievement of this intention leaves the system in the state, *Booking made*. Each map has two special intentions, *Start* and *Stop*, associated with the initial and final states respectively. We use a linguistic approach to define a template for formulating an intention. Our linguistic approach is inspired by Fillmore's case grammar [12] and its extension by Dik [8]. It views an intention statement as composed of a *verb* and different *parameters* which play specific roles with respect to the verb. The structure of an intention is the following:

  Intention: Verb <Target> [<Parameter>]*

Table 1 summarizes these parameters. In addition to the linguistic template, [29] proposed a classification of verbs and defined for each class, a *verb frame* which indicates the mandatory and optional parameters. For instance, the frame of the verb remain is *remain [Qual,(Ref),(Loc),(Time)]*. This frame means that « remain » is always followed by a quality and optionally followed by a referent, a location and a time point.

- A *strategy* is an approach, a manner or a means to achieve an intention. Let us assume that bookings can be made *on the Internet*. This is a way of achieving the room booking intention, i.e. a strategy. *By visiting a travel agency* is another strategy to achieve the same intention. It shall be noticed that the linguistic template for intention wording includes the parameter *way* which specializes into *manner* and *means*. Strategies in the *Map representation system* provide the means to capture variability in intention achievement.

- A *section* is an aggregation of the source intention, the target intention, and a strategy. As shown in Fig. 1 it is a triplet $<I_{source}, I_{target}, S_{source-target}>$. A section expresses the strategy $S_{source-target}$ using which, starting from the source intention, I_{source}, the target intention, I_{target} can be achieved. . The triplet *<Start, Make Room Booking, on the Internet>* is a section; similarly *<Start, Make Room Booking, by visiting a travel agency>* constitutes another section.

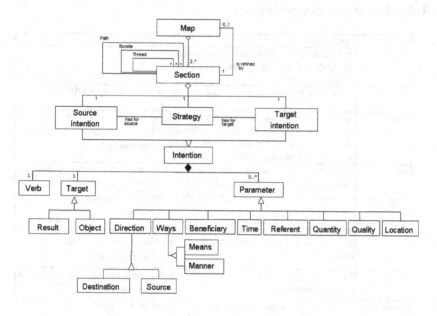

Fig. 1. The map meta-model

A section is the basic construct of a map which itself can be seen as an assembly of sections. When a map is used to model a multi-facetted purpose, each of its sections represents a facet. The set of sections model the purpose in its totality and we will see below that the relationships between sections and between a section and a map lead to the representation of the multi-facetted perspective.

A map section, a facet, highlights a consistent and cohesive characteristic of the system that stakeholders want to be implemented through some functionality. A facet in our terms is close to the notion of feature defined in FODA [19] as a "prominent or distinctive user-visible aspect, quality or characteristic of a system". However, our view of a facet emphasizes the intention that the underlying functionality allows to achieve. We believe that a facet is a useful abstraction to express variability in intentional terms.

A map is graphically represented as a directed graph from Start to Stop. Intentions are represented as nodes and strategies as edges between these. The graph is directed because the strategy shows the flow from the source to the target intention. The map of Fig. 2 contains six sections/facets MS0 to MS5.

Table 1. The intention parameters

Parameter	Description	Example
Target	The *Target* (Tar) designates an entity affected by the goal. We distinguish two types of target, object and result.	
Object	An *object* (Obj) exists before the goal is achieved.	'Check (room availability) $_{Obj}$ '
Result	*Result* (Res) can be of two kinds (a) entity which does not exist before the goal is achieved (b) abstract entity which exists but is made concrete as a result of goal achievement.	(a) 'Make (room booking) $_{Res}$ ' (b) 'Define (customer's request) $_{Res}$ '
Source	The two types of *direction* (Dir), namely *source* (So) and *destination* (Dest) identify respectively,	'Read (the validity date of card) $_{Obj}$ (in the card chip) $_{So}$ '
Destination	the initial and final location of objects to be communicated.	'Offer (booking facility) $_{Obj}$ (to the customer) $_{Dest}$ '
Means	*Means* (Mea) designates an entity which acts as an instrument using which a goal is to be performed.	Offer (booking facility) $_{Res}$ (to customers) $_{Dest}$ (with Internet booking system) $_{Mea}$
Manner	The *manner* (Man) defines the way in which the goal is achieved.	'Check (availability) $_{Obj}$ (in a real time process) $_{Man}$ '
Beneficiary	The *beneficiary* (Ben) is the person (or group of persons) in favour of whom the goal is achieved.	'Reduce (work load) $_{Obj}$ (for the hotel staff) $_{Ben}$ '
Referent	The *Referent* (Ref) is the entity with regard to which an action is performed, or a state is attained or maintained.	'Adjust(price) $_{Obj}$ (to inflation rate) $_{Ref}$ '
Quality	The *quality* (Qual) defines a property that has to be attained or preserved.	'Remain(more reliable) $_{Qual}$ (than our competitors) $_{Ref}$ '
Location	The *Location* (Loc) situates the goal in space. This case implies no movement, or movement within the same location.	'Make (room booking) $_{Res}$ (in a travel agency) $_{Loc}$ '
Time	The *Time* (Time) situates the goal in time.	'Remove (option booking) $_{Obj}$ (after 8 days) $_{Time}$ '
Quantity	*Quantity* (Quan) quantifies an evolution that should occur	'Reduce(price) $_{Obj}$ (by 3%) $_{Quan}$ '

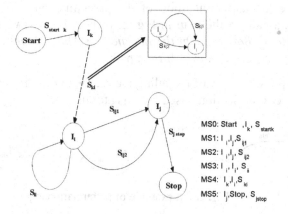

Fig. 2. The map as a graph

There are three relationships between sections (Fig. 4), namely *thread*, *path* and *bundle* which generate *multi-thread* and *multi-path* topologies in a map.

- *Thread relationship*: It is possible for a target intention to be achieved from a source intention in many different ways. Each of these ways is expressed as a section in the map. Such a map topology is called a *multi-thread* and the sections participating in the multi-thread are said to be in a *thread relationship* with one another. MS1 and MS2 are in a thread relationship in Fig. 2. Assume that *Accept Payment* is another intention in our example and that it can be achieved in two different ways, *By electronic transfer* or *By credit card*. This leads to a thread relationship between the two sections shown in Fig. 3.

It is clear that a thread relationship between two sections regarded as facets represents directly the variability associated to a multi-faceted purpose. Multi-faceting is captured in the different strategies to achieve the common target intention.

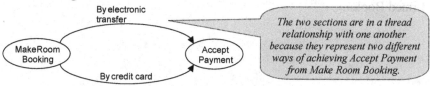

Fig. 3. An example of thread relationship

- *Path relationship*: This establishes a precedence/succession relationship between sections. For a section to succeed another, its source intention must be the target intention of the preceding one. MS0, MS1, MS4, MS5 is a path of the map in Fig. 2. In Fig. 4, the two sections <*Start, Make Room Booking, On the Internet*>, <*Make Room Booking, Accept Payment, By credit card*> form a path.

From the point of view of modeling facets, the path introduces a composite facet whereas the section based facet is atomic.

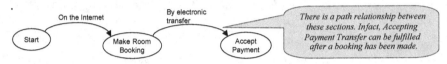

Fig. 4. An example of path relationship.

Given the thread and the path relationships, an intention can be achieved by several combinations of sections. Such a topology is called a *multi-path*. In general, a map from its *Start* to its *Stop* intentions is a multi-path and may contain multi-threads. Let us assume in our example that it is possible to *Stop* either because a customer retracts from making the booking (*By customer retraction*) or after payment (*Normally*). Fig. 5 shows the entire map with the purpose to *Make Confirmed Booking*. This map contains several paths from Start to Stop out of which two forming a multi-path are highlighted in Fig. 5.

Clearly, the multi-path topology is yet another way of representing the multi-facetted perspective. Multi-faceting in this case is obtained by combining various sections together to achieve a given intention of the map. Consider for instance the intention Accept payment in Fig. 5; there are four paths from Start to achieve it; each of them is a different way to get the intention achieved and in this sense, participates to the multi-faceting. Each path is a composite facet composed of two atomic facets. This can be extended to the full map which can be seen as composed of a number of paths from Start to Stop. This time these paths introduce multi-faceting but to achieve the intention of the map which in our example, is Make Confirmed Booking.

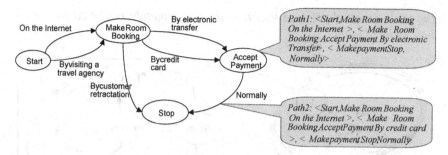

Fig. 5. The multi-path of the map Make Confirmed Booking

- *Bundle relationship*: A section that is a bundle of other sections expresses that only one of its sections can be used in realizing the target intention. Consider *Make Room Booking* and *Accept Payment* once again. Let it be that the hotel has entered into an agreement with an airline to provide rooms against miles earned by passengers. Accordingly, payment is accepted either normally or (exclusive) from the airlines miles. Notice that the difference between a thread and bundle relationship is the exclusive OR of sections in the latter versus an OR in the former.

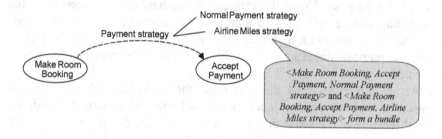

Fig. 6. The bundle relationship

- Fig. 4 also shows that a section of a map can be refined as another map through the *refinement relationship*. The entire refined map then represents the section as shown in Fig. 7. Refinement is an abstraction mechanism by which a complex assembly of sections at level $i+1$ is viewed as a unique section at level i. As a result of refinement, a section at level i is represented by multiple paths & multiple threads at level $i+1$.

From the point of view of multi-faceting, refinement allows to look to the multi-facetted nature of a facet. It introduces levels in the representation of the multi-facetted purpose which is thus, completely modelled through a hierarchy of maps.

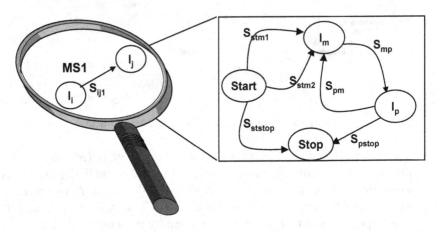

Fig. 7. The refinement relationship

*To sum up a)*The purpose of the artefact is captured in a *hierarchy of maps*. The intention associated to the root map is the high level statement about the purpose. Using the refinement mechanism each section of the root map can be refined as a map and the recursive application of this mechanism results in a map hierarchy. At successive levels of the hierarchy the purpose stated initially as the intention of the root map is further refined.

b)At any given level of the hierarchy, the multi-facetted dimension is based on *multi-thread* and *multi-path* topologies. Multi-thread introduces local faceting in the sense that it allows to represent the different ways for achieving an intention directly. Multi-path introduces global faceting by representing different combinations of intentions and strategies to achieve a given map intention. Any path from Start to Stop represents one way of achieving the map intention, therefore the purpose represented in this map.

Comparing Map with other goal modeling approaches

As process models, maps can be compared to the various types of process modelling languages and formalisms that have emerged supporting a variety of purposes. The existing formalisms can be roughly classified according to their orientation to activity-sequence oriented languages (e.g., UML Activity Diagram), agent-oriented languages (e.g., Role-Activity Diagram

[27]), state-based languages (e.g. UML state charts), intention-oriented languages (e.g. Maps).

The concept of goal is central in business process modelling and design. It is included in many definitions of business processes (e.g. "a business process is a set of partially ordered activities aimed at reaching a goal" [15]. However, most process modelling languages do not employ a goal construct as an integral part of the model. This is sometimes justified by viewing these models as an "internal" view of a process, focusing on *how* the process is performed and externalising *what* the process is intended to accomplish in the goal [7].

In contrast, intention-oriented process modelling focuses on what the process is intended to achieve, thus providing the rationale of the process, i.e. *why* the process is performed. Intention-oriented process modelling such as *Map*, follows the human intention of achieving a goal as a force which drives the process. As a consequence, goals to be accomplished are explicitly represented in the process model together with the alternative ways for achieving them, thus allowing variability in goal achievement to be modelled and facilitating the selection of the appropriate alternative for achieving the goal at enactment time.

3   Illustrating the use of *Map*

In this section we show the use of the *Map* representation system to capture the multi-facetted purpose of a system and take the financial information system of DIAC, the financial branch of Renault to illustrate this.

3.1 The DIAC Context

The DIAC company aims to sell products for financing the purchase of Renault vehicles. These are loans and leases. Business processes are organized into sales and post-sales administration. Sales processes include the definition of catalogues of products and contracting customers. Post-sales processes include treasury and information flow management. DIAC has a number of subsidiaries in different countries in Europe which have developed their own processes and their own information systems to support these activities.

The objective of the project was to standardize both the business processes and the supporting information systems across Europe. The DIAC headquarters in Paris were leading the project but the Spanish information system was selected as the basis for adaptation and further deployment in France, Spain, Portugal and Germany in a first stage. There were new business needs as well : (a) diversification of the sales channels to include for example, sales by the Internet in addition to regular vendors, (b) inclusion of additional financial services such as offering personal loans in addition to car loans, and (c) introducing a customer centric culture to replace the current contract centric one.

Our mission in the project was twofold (a) to help DIAC stakeholders capturing the intentionality behind the future DIAC business and supporting information system with maps and (b) to derive the information system specifications from these maps. In the following, we illustrate the use of *Map* as part of activity (a).

3.1.1 The Maps Construction Process

We were typically faced to a *system adaptation* problem bounded by the following constraints:

- No large scale deviations from the selected software system (the Spanish information system)
- Compliance with some of the functionality not found in the selected system but provided by others (the French system)
- Provision of functionality for handling the new business opportunities that were now recognized to be important.

From the foregoing it seemed to us that the adaptation process should be driven by *gaps* which identify what has to be changed/adapted to the new situation. In this change context, it is not so much the representation of the future situation that is important but the difference with the current situation. If gaps remain implicit, it is difficult to identify what has to be changed. Explicit gap representation seems to us, therefore, crucial to expressing change requirements. We developed a *gap typology* adapted to *maps* and organized the process for eliciting gaps between the As-Is situation and the To-Be situation as an iterative one as follows:

Repeat till all maps have been considered
1. Construct the *As-Is map* (if it does not exists yet)
2. Construct the To-Be by difference with the As-Is map taking into account the target selected system and the organization requirements for change. The *To-Be map* and the *Gaps* are modelled concurrently and then, documented,
3. Deliberate on each section of the To-Be map to decide if further refinement is required to identify more detailed gaps or not. Every section marked as '*to-be-refined*' will serve as starting point for a new

iteration of the elicitation process. Every section that does not require refinement gets the 'green' status.

The three steps were carried out in a *participative* manner. This allowed the consideration of different view points with the aim of reconciling them co-operatively, in the construction of the As-Is and To-Be maps as well as in the elicitation of gaps. Additionally, in step 3, the decision to refine elicited gaps at an iteration was also made co-operatively. As before, the refinements committed to in this step emerge as a consensus from among the different view points.

3.1.2 The Top Level Map

In its totality, the DIAC business and system can be seen to meet the purpose, *Satisfy Financial Needs of Renault Vehicle buyers Efficiently*. This is the intention of the root map shown in Fig. 8. The map shows that to meet this purpose three intentions have to be achieved, namely *Offer a product, Gain the customer,* and *Manage the customer relationship*. Evidently, there is an ordering between these intentions: the company cannot gain customers unless it offers products and it needs to maintain the customer relationships to be reimbursed of the customers' loans and pursue business with them.

The map of Fig. 8 shows a number of paths from *Start* to *Stop* that are constructed over 14 facets named C1 to C14 in the Figure. Thus, the map is able to present a global perspective of the diverse ways of achievement of the main purpose. When a more detailed view is needed, then it becomes necessary to focus more specifically on the multi-facetted nature of each intention found in the 'global' map. The detailed view of the intentions contained in Fig. 8 is brought out in turn below.

The multi-facetted nature of *Gain the customer* is shown in Fig. 8 by including three strategies for its achievement (a) *By prescribing* products it offers, (b) *By prospecting* new customers and (c). *By securing the customer loyalty*. The three facets are <*Offer a product,, Gain the customer, By prescribing*>, <*Offer a product,, Gain the customer, By prospecting*>, and <*Manage the customer relationship, Gain the customer, By securing the customer loyalty* >. Whereas the first of these three facets corresponds to a well established business strategy, the other two are novel. *By securing the customer loyalty* supports the company's essential requirement to keep customers as long as there is no need to *Stop* financing them *by exclusion*. It is completely innovating compared to the As-Is business model.

The intention of *Managing the customer relationship* is initiated *By demanding of the transfer* of the contracts signed with the pre-sales department to the post-sales administration. In DIAC's vision of the future way to hold the business, "customer relationship" means having business dealings with, and for customers. The intention name was thus introduced to emphasize a determining gap with the contract-wise management of customers currently prevailing in France and Spain. The customer relationship management requires, first of all, a unified handling of all contracts for a given customer. This corresponds to a change of culture for the company and an important change in the information system data structure and functionalities.

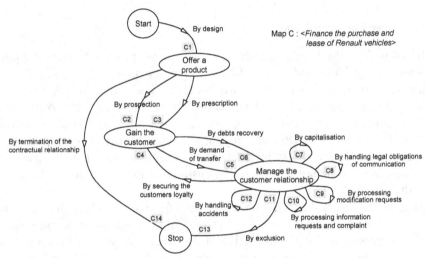

Fig. 8. Top level To-Be map of DIAC

As shown in Fig. 8, there are a number of different strategies to *Managing the customer relationship*. This multi-faceting highlights the new emphasis put by DIAC on the achievement of this intention in a set of diverse ways. Managing the relationship with customers should be done *By debts recovery* according to the contracts repayment schedules, and by managing multiple flows of customer-related information. This is shown in the map by the strategies: *By processing modification requests, By processing information and complaints requests*, and *By handling legal obligations of communication*. The latter strategy is imposed by the European and national laws on information privacy. Managing the customer relationship *By capitalization* of treasury, is an absolute requirement to ensure forthcoming financing. The strategy *By handling accidents* is important as well as, for some products, DIAC may propose to pay in the place of customers who have suffered damages that stop them to reimburse their debts.

4 Conclusion

The thrust of this chapter is to embedding systems in their larger usage context that is made possible by stepping back from merely anticipating the functionality that a system must provide (as done in conceptual modelling) to the determination of this functionality in a systematic manner. This is done by identifying the aims and objectives of different stakeholders and the activities they carry out to meet these objectives. The goal driven approaches that support this view lead to better understand the purpose behind the system To-Be and therefore, to more easily accepted systems in organizations.

The belief of the author is that goal-driven approaches are now facing the challenge of forthcoming multi-purpose systems, i.e. systems that incorporate variability in the functionality they provide and will be able to self adapt to the situation at hand. The goal/strategy maps have been introduced and discussed as an example of goal model that has been conceived to meet the aforementioned challenge.

A map expression provides a synthetic view of the variability of a system in a relatively easy to understand way. Variations are revealed in two ways, by the gradual movement down the different levels of a top map, and by the alternative strategies/paths available at a given map level. Variations express the multi purpose behind systems. Their expression relates more closely to the organizational stakeholders as different from system developers. Yet, this expression acts as a specification of what the new system should achieve.

Maps have been used in large scale industrial projects and in different areas such as business process modeling [25,33], change management [26, 37] , system evolution handling [36, 39], installation of ERP systems [30, 31, 45], process/system alignment [10, 40] and more recently in service definition and composition [18].

Finally, it is clear that the map needs to be supported by (a) a guidance mechanism that systematically helps the dynamic construction of maps, their verification and documentation and (b) an enactment mechanism that would present the different choices available for achieving an intention and aid in selecting one or more of these. These form the topic of current work.

References

[1] Antòn, A. I.(1996), *Goal based requirements analysis*. 2nd International Conference on Requirements Engineering ICRE'96, pp. 136-144.

[2] Antón, A. I., McCracken, W. M. and Potts, C.: Goal Decomposition and Scenario Analysis in Business Process Reengineering, Advanced Information Systems Engineering, 6th International Conference Proceedings (CAiSE '94), Utrecht, The Netherlands, (1994) 94-104.

[3] Bachmann Managing variability in software architecture. ACM Press, NY, USA. (2001)

[4] Bosch, *Variability issues in Software Product Lines*. 4th International Workshop on Product Family Engineering (PEE-4), Bilbao, Spain (2001)

[5] Bubenko, J., Rolland, C., Loucopoulos, P., de Antòn ellis V.(1994), *Facilitating 'fuzzy to formal' requirements modelling*. IEEE 1st Conference on Requirements Enginering, ICRE'94 pp. 154-158.

[6] Dardenne, A., Lamsweerde, A. v., and Fickas, S., (1993), *Goal-directed Requirements Acquisition*, Science of Computer Programming, 20, Elsevier, pp.3-50.

[7] Dietz J.L.G., "Basic Notions Regarding Business Processes and Supporting Information Systems", Proceedings of BPMDS'04, CAISE'04 Workshops Proceedings, Latvia, Riga, (2004).160-168,

[8] Dik, S.C. The theory of functional grammar, Foris Publications, Dodrecht, The Netherlands, (1989)

[9] Dubois E., Hagelstein J., Rifaut A., *Formal Requirements Engineering with ERAE*, Philips Journal of Research, Vol. 43, No 4. (1989)

[10] Etien, A., and Rolland, C.: Measuring the fitness relationship, *Requirements Engineering Journal (REJ)*, Springer, 10:3, pp. 184 - 197, (2005)

[11] European Software Institute, *European User Survey Analysis*, Report USV_EUR 2.1, ESPITI Project. (1996)

[12] Fillmore C. J., The case for case, in Universals in linguistic theory, Holt, Rinehart and Winston, Inc, E.Bach/R.T.Harms (eds) (1968)

[13] Van Gurp J., *Variability in Software Systems, the key to Software Reuse*. Licentiate Thesis, University of Groningen, Sweden (2000)

[14] Halmans J., *Communicating the variability of a software product family to customers. Software and System Modeling*, Springer-Verlag. (2003)

[15] Hammer M., and Champy J., Re-engineering the Corporation: A Manifesto for Business Revolution, Harper Collins Publishers, New York. (1993)

[16] Jackson M., *Software Requirements & Specifications – a Lexicon of Practice, Principles and Prejudices*. ACM Press. Addison-Wesley. (1995)

[17] Johnson J., *Chaos : the Dollar Drain of IT project Failures*. Application Development Trends, (1995) 41-47

[18] Kaabi, R.S, Souveyet, C., *Capturing intentional services with process business maps*, IEEE international Conference on RCIS (Research Challenges in Information Science), Ouarzazate, Maroc. (2007)

[19] Kang, K., Cohen, S., Hess, J., Novak, W., & Peterson, A.. *Feature-Oriented Domain analysis (FODA) Feasibility Study (Tech. Rep. CMU/SEI-90-TR-21),* Pittsburgh, PA, Software Engineering Institute, Carnegie Mellon University (1990)

[20] Krogstie J., Sølvberg A.: A classification of methodological frameworks for computerised information systems support in organisations, in Proc. IFIP 8.1/8.2 Conf. Method Engineering: Principles of Method Construction and Tool Support,August 1996, Atlanta, USA, Chapman&Hall, (1996)

[21] Lamsweerde, A.v.(2001), *Goal-oriented requirements engineering: a guided tour.* RE'01 International Joint Conference on Requirements Engineering, Toronto, IEEE,, pp.249-263

[22] Lee, J., "Extending the Potts and Bruns Model for Recording Design Rationale", Proceedings of the IEEE 13th International Conference on Software Engineering, Austin, Texas. (1991)

[23] Lindland O.I., Sindre G., and Sølvberg A.: Understanding quality in conceptual modelling', IEEE Software, March 1994 (1994) 42--49

[24] META Group *Research on Requirements Realization and Relevance,* report (2003)

[25] Nurcan, S., Rolland, C.: Meta-modelling for cooperative processes, The 7th European-Japanese Conference on Information Modelling and Knowledge Bases, Toulouse, (1997) 361-377.

[26] Nurcan, S., Rolland, C., A multi-method for defining the organisational change", Journal of Information and Software Technology, Elsevier. Vol. 45 N°2, (2003) 61-82

[27] Ould, M., Business Processes: Modelling and Analysis for Re-engineering and Improvement John Wiley & Sons. (1995)

[28] Potts, C., Takahashi, K., and Antòn , A. I. (1994), *Inquiry-based requirements analysis.* IEEE Software 11(2), pp. 21-32.

[29] Prat, N., *Goal formalisation and classification for requirements engineering.* 3rd International Workshop on Requirements Engineering: Foundations of Software Quality REFSQ'97, Barcelona, Spain, (1997) 145-156.

[30] Rolland C., Prakash N., *Bridging the gap between Organizational needs and ERP functionality.* Requirements Engineering journal 5 (2000).

[31] Rolland, C., Prakash, N., "Matching ERP System Functionality to Customer Requirements", Proceedings of the 5th IEEE International Symposium on Requirements Engineering, Toronto, Canada. (2001)

[32] Rolland C., Salinesi C.: *Modeling goals and reasoning with them,* Chap9 of the book Engineering and Managing Requirements , A. Aurum and C. Wohlin (eds), (Springer Verlag Pub, TBP 2005)

[33] Rolland, C., Nurcan, S., Grosz G.:A unified framework for modelling co-operative design processes and co-operative business processes, Proceedings of the 31st Annual International Conference on System Sciences, Big Island, Hawaii, USA. (1998)

[34] Rolland, C., Souveyet, C., and Ben Achour, C. (1998), *Guiding goal modelling using scenarios.* IEEE Transactions on Software Engineering, Special Issue on Scenario Management, 24(12)

[35] Rolland, C., Prakash, n., & Benjamen, A.. A Multi-Model View of Process Modelling. *Requirements Engineering Journal (REJ)*, (1999) 169-187
[36] Rolland, C., Salinesi, C., Etien, A.:Eliciting Gaps in Requirements Change, Requirements Engineering Journal (REJ), 9:1, pp. 1 - 15, 2004. (2003)
[37] Rolland, C., Loucopoulos, P., Kavakli, V., Nurcan, S.: Intention based modelling of organisational change: an experience report, Proceedings of the Fourth CAISE/IFIP 8.1 International Workshop on Evaluation of Modeling Methods in Systems Analysis and Design (EMMSAD'99), Heidelberg, Germany. (1999)
[38] Rummler, G.A., Brache, A. P., Improving Performance, Jossey-Bass Publishers (1995)
[39] Salinesi, C., Presso, M. J.: A Method to Analyse Changes in the Realisation of Business Intentions and Strategies for Information System Adaptation, Proceedings of the 6th IEEE International Enterprise Distributed Object Computing Conference (EDOC'02), Lausanne, Switzerland. (2002)
[40] Salinesi, C., Rolland, C.: Fitting Business Models to Systems Functionality Exploring the Fitness Relationship, Proceedings of the 15th Conference on Advanced Information Systems Engineering (CAiSE'03), Klagenfurt/Velden, Austria, (2003)
[41] Standish Group, *Chaos*. Standish Group Internal Report (1995)
[42] Svahnberg *On the notion of variability in Software Product Lines*. Working IEEE/IFIP Conference on Software architecture. (2001)
[43] Sølvberg, A.: Data and what they refer to, in P.P.Chen et al.(eds.): Conceptual Modeling, pp.211-226, Lecture Notes in Computer Science, Springer Verlag, (1999)
[44] Yu, E.S.K., Mylopoulos, J. :From E-R to 'A-R' - Modelling Strategic Actor Relationships for Business Process Reengineering, Proceedings of the 13th International Conference on the Entity-Relationship Approach, Manchester. (1994)
[45] Zoukar, I., and Salinesi, C.: Matching ERP Functionalities with the Logistic Requirements of French railways - A Similarity Approach, International Conference on Enterprise Information Systems (ICEIS), Porto, Portugal, 2004.

Conceptual Modeling and Software Design of Multi-agent Systems

David Kung[1] , Krishna Kavi[2]

[1]Univ. of Texas at Arlington, USA
[2]Univ. of North Texas, USA

Abstract. We present a framework for conceptual modeling, requirements analysis and design of agent-based systems. The framework is rooted in the Belief Desire Intention (BDI) formalism and extends the Unified Modeling Language (UML) to model multi-agent systems. We introduce several modeling constructs including Agent, Belief, Goal, Plan, FIPA Performative, KQML-Performative, and Blackboard. In addition, we introduce Agent Goal Diagram to model the relationships between the goals and the environment of an agent; Use Case Goal Diagram to model the relationships between use cases and goals; Agent Domain Model to facilitate understanding of domain knowledge of an agent; Agent Sequence Diagram to model interactions within an agent. Similarly, Agent Activity Diagram and Agent Statechart Diagram are introduced. We illustrate the framework through an agent-based intelligent elevator system.

1 Introduction

Over the last decade the popularity of agent-based systems have increased rapidly because agents bring intelligence, reasoning and autonomy to software systems. Agents are being used in an increasingly wide variety of applications from simple e-mail filter programs, such as MAXIS [21], to complex mission control and safety critical systems including air traffic control, such as OASIS [20]. Until recently few proposals for Agent Oriented Software Engineering and extensions to UML have been reported [7, 35, 29]. This should be contrasted with the object-oriented (OO) paradigm that is supported by modeling languages such as UML and a variety of CASE tools that aid during the analysis, design, implementation and validation phases of OO software systems: all of which contributed to the universal acceptance of the OO paradigm. In this paper, we propose a framework for conceptual modeling [31, 32, 33], requirements analysis, and design of multi-agent systems. It is an extension of the UML to support multi-agent systems (MAS) development. Our approach is rooted in the BDI formalism [28], but stresses the importance of conceptual modeling and practical software design methods instead of reasoning theories. In particular, we propose to extend UML [4] with conceptual modeling constructs called *Agent, Belief, Goal, Plan, FIPA Performative, KQML Performative,* and *Blackboard. Agent* is the super-type for all agent types. Belief, Goal and Plan model the reactive and proactive behaviours of agents. An agent has, among other data types, a collection of beliefs, goals and plans. *Beliefs* are the agent's observations and/or sensing of the environment and are updated by sensors or other agents. Changes in an agent's beliefs trigger the re-evaluation of the utility values of goals of the agent. Changes to goals' utility values result in pre-empting some plans and initiating new plans. Execution of plans affects the environment which in turn changes the beliefs, and so on. Agent communicates with each other through agent communication performatives such as FIPA [6] or KQML [9], or shared blackboards as in Linda or its extensions [22]. We introduce Agent Goal Diagram (AGD) to model the relationships between the goals and the environment, the Use Case Goal Diagram (UCGD) to relate use cases and goals, Agent Domain Model (ADM) to facilitate understanding of domain knowledge of an agent, Agent Sequence Diagram (ASD) to model interactions within an agent. Similarly, Agent Activity Diagram and Agent Statechart Diagram are introduced.

2 Extending UML

The framework is aimed to provide a modeling language to help application engineers to focus their effort on agent-oriented modeling. *Agent, Belief, Goal* and *Plan* are implemented as abstract classes in the proposed framework. Application specific BDI agent (resp. belief, goal, plan) types are implicitly defined as subclasses of *Agent* (resp. *Belief, Goal, Plan*); and hence, they inherit the model-defined structural and behavioural features and relationships. As in OO, concrete, application specific types must implement the inherited abstract features. In this way, the framework enforces the BDI model but also provides the flexibility for implementing application specific behaviour, including re-using an existing design or implementation.

In general, beliefs may be shared and modified by other agents. This can be achieved either by direct communication using KQML [9] or FIPA-ACL [6] messages, shared knowledge-bases or blackboards (e.g., Linda or its extensions such as LIME [22]). Goals can be proactive or reactive – proactive goals reflect the desires of an agent. These goals may impact how an agent reacts to external events (including the possibility of ignoring external stimuli — accomplished by ignoring/giving up goals with lower utility values). Reactive goals reflect how an agent can be situated in an environment.

2.1 New Modeling Constructs

The following provides (albeit an incomplete) list of new modeling constructs for MAS. An agent specification language (ASL) in BNF is given in [15].

Belief: *Belief* has a name for identifying *Belief* instances, a set of user-defined, application dependent annotations, and a list of goals that may be affected by changes to the belief. Examples of application dependent annotations are sampling frequency and probability of change of sensed values. *Belief* has methods for querying and updating a belief and relating goals with a belief. When a *Belief* instance is change, the affected Goal instances are informed, see below.

Goal: *Goal* has a name, a utility value, set and get functions, and a plan to accomplish the goal. The utility value of a goal indicates how valuable the goal is to the overall goal of the system. In addition, *Goal* has two abstract functions: *beliefChanged(b: Belief)* and *eval():real*. The former is automatically invoked by a changed belief that affects the goal. It allows the goal to respond to belief changes. The utility values are real values between 0 and 1 with 0 representing unreachable goals. The implementation of *eval()* is application dependent and can be a conventional decision tree, Computational Tree Logic (CTL) derivations as described in [27], or any other evaluation mechanism appropriate for the type of agent.

Plan: *Plan* has an identifying name and an abstract *execute()* method which can be invoked by a *Goal* object to start a plan. A subclass of *Plan* must implement the execute() method according to the concrete plan. The implementation may invoke KQML/FIPA performatives to communicate with other agents as well as perform conventional and knowledge based computations. In general, plans can be implemented by the command pattern [10]. The generic command class may implement Thread and the command subclasses each implement an action of the agent. A plan can be defined as a sequence of command objects and dynamically generated according to the reasoning steps. *Plan* also has a stop() method which can be invoked to terminate the plan.

Beliefs, Goals and *Plans*: These are collections of *Belief, Goal* and *Plan* objects and provide standard operations for querying, inserting, updating and deleting an element. These collections also have operations of their respective component types and delegate the call to each of the component type instances.

FIPA, and KQML Performatives: There are two Command Patterns [10] introduced to accommodate all the FIPA and KQML speech act performatives, respectively. Their subclasses are named after the performatives, each subclass implements the functionality of one performative. New speech act performatives can be supported by introducing additional command patterns.

FIPA, and KQML Interfaces: These interfaces define method signatures that correspond to FIPA and KQML performatives, respectively. Again, new speech act performatives can be supported by introducing additional interfaces.

Agent: *Agent* is the superclass for all agent types. It has *Beliefs, Goals, Plans* and methods to select the optimal goal. It has an abstract *goalValueChanged (g: Goal)* method, which is automatically invoked when a goal instance is changed. *Agent* implements *both FIPA and KQML Interfaces* and delegates the implementation of the performatives to the appropriate FIPA or KQML Performative subclasses. This way our framework accommodates both FIPA and KQML performatives and their extensions.

Blackboard: This is a concrete class, supported by the Singleton Pattern and Flyweight Pattern [10], to permit the use of shared blackboards. *Agent* can define polymorphic methods for reading, removing, writing, and appending to the blackboard (similar to Linda or LIME [22]).

Figure 1 shows the nations for above modeling constructs.

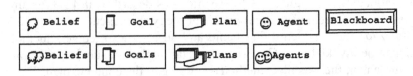

Fig. 1. Graphical notations

2.2 New Diagrams

In this section, we describe a number of new diagrams. Their use is illustrated in section 3:

Agent Goal Diagram (AGD): An AGD depicts the goals of an agent and their relationships to the environment. In addition, an AGD depicts relationships among the goals like goal-subgoal relationship. An AGD can also illustrate roles of an agent. For example, a goal of an auction agent playing the role of a buyer could be "minimize cost". The same agent when playing the role of a seller could have a goal to "maximize profit". Thus, the AGD for Auction-Agent/Buyer would contain "Minimize Cost" as a goal while the AGD for Auction-Agent/Seller would contain the goal "Maximize Profit".

Use Case Goal Diagram (UCGD): A UCGD combines the existing Use Case Diagram (UCD) and the AGD and shows the relationships between use cases and goals. That is, which use cases would affect which goal and vice versa. This information provides a high level guidance to Agent Sequence Diagram (ASD) construction. It can also be used to check the consistency between UCGD and ASD.

Agent Domain Model (ADM): In OO development, a System Domain Model (SDM) documents domain object classes and their attributes and relationships. The existing SDM is extended to include agents as domain concepts. Conceptual Modeling and Software Design of Multi-Agent Systems 5
Unlike an SDM, an ADM represents the domain knowledge that is internal to an agent, including the definitions of the agent's Beliefs, Goals and Plans and their intrinsic relationships.

Agent Sequence Diagram (ASD): An ASD depicts interactions among the beliefs, goals, plans and other objects of an agent to collectively carry out a task. It is a refinement of an agent.

Agent Design Diagram (ADD): ADD is introduced to document the design of an agent, derived from the corresponding ADM and ASD and implemented as a package in Java or a module in C++. This facilitates the re-use of an agent's design and/or implementation because an application can simply import a package or a module.

Agent Activity Diagram (AAD) and Agent Statechart Diagram (ASCD): These diagrams are introduced to model the internal activity and information flows and the internal state behaviours of agents.

2.3 Discussion

In our framework, flexible relationships as well as interactions among the agents are accomplished through FIPA performatives, KQML performatives, or Blackboard. The speech act performatives allow an agent to communicate with another agent of her choice. In particular, to query the capabilities of other agents and then request services. Agents can create and/or subscribe to a common blackboard to form a group. It is also possible to define group hierarchies through the use of blackboard messages. Role dependent beliefs, goals and plans of an agent can be accomplished by generalization/specialization or inheritance. That is, treating roles as derived agent types of a more general agent type. Instances of the derived types can be used to represent different roles of the agent (which is an instance of the more general agent type).

3 The Intelligent Elevator Case Study

The multi-agent intelligent elevator system (IES) consists of ordinary elevator hardware, an agent for each elevator car and a blackboard serving as a shared memory between the agents. The car agents communicate through the blackboard as well as directly with one another using an agent communication language. During the normal hours operation of the IES, a request by a passenger is posted with the Blackboard. Car agents can retrieve and update these requests asynchronously. The agent(s) decide how to satisfy the requests. Once inside the elevator car, passengers can enter a destination request. All the destination requests are maintained by the car agent and used to instruct the elevator to stop when the floor is reached. When an elevator reaches its final destination and there are no pending requests from the final destination floor, the car agent checks if it is during the rush hour. If so, the agent consults the blackboard and travels to a destination floor as appropriate; otherwise, the agent reads the blackboard for pending requests and consults the other elevator car agents to determine its next destination. The agent will go to serve a floor if and only if the following conditions hold:

- There is a pending request from the floor.
- It is the agent that can serve the request sooner than other agents.

If no floor needs to be served, the elevator enters the stand-by state and sleeps for a couple of seconds. When it wakes up, it repeats above process and goes to sleep again if no request needs to be served. During rush hours the demand for service is high and is usually in early morning, late afternoon and lunch time hours. The rush hour schedule is stored with the blackboard and periodically updated by an intelligent service log (ISL). The ISL uses data mining techniques to discover new demand patterns from its service log and computes the up-to-date rush hour schedule. The ISL does this once a while. The frequency is adaptive and adjusts to one that will provide the most suitable rush hour schedule. During a rush hour, the car agents direct their respective elevators to rush to floors whose demands have not been completely satisfied. The car agents use the anticipated rush hour demand and the demand that has been served to approximately determine how much demand remains to be served.

Applying the methodology described in the last section, we have the following (we have omitted steps 1-3) because these are the same as conventional software development):

Step 4.1. Identify use cases and goals from requirements.

A use case defines an application process to accomplish a task through interactions between an actor and the system under consideration. An actor may be a class of users, roles played by users, or other systems. A use case is initiated by a user with a particular goal in mind, and completes successfully when that goal is satisfied. A complete set of use cases specifies all the different ways to use the system, and therefore defines all required system behaviours.

The IES has the following use cases:

- Request Elevator: The passenger from outside of the elevator initiates this use case when the passenger wants to go to a particular floor. The agent can also initiate this use case during rush hour.
- Service Request in standby: This use case is initiated when the elevator car is idle.
- Service Request in motion: This use case is initiated when the elevator car is in transition and a new request comes in.
- Request Floor: This use case is initiated by the passenger inside the elevator car to go to the destination floor.
- Open Door: This use case is initiated by the Passenger or Timer.
- Close Door: This use case in initiated by the passenger or Timer, and the weight sensor.

Step 4.2. Refine use case diagrams and goal diagrams.

In this step, new use cases and goals are added and existing ones are revised. The use cases and goals are shown in use case diagrams and goals diagrams (see Figure 2), respectively. In particular, the figure shows a use case diagram on the left and a goal diagram on the right. The elevator subsystem box on the left shows the use cases and the actor (the passengers of the elevator). The diagram also contains a box on the right representing the Elevator Car Agent. Recall that the notation for an agent is the smiley face icon. The goals of the agent are shown as ovals with a curly paper icon. An association is drawn between the use case "Service Request in Standby" and the "Meet Required Response Time" goal signifying that when a passenger requests an elevator in standby the "Meet Required Response Time" goal will be affected. The agent's goals are sometimes conflicting wherein the agent takes a decision on which goal to pursue.

In addition to the goals, a goal diagram may also specify relationships among the goals using UML modeling constructs like inheritance, aggregation and association:

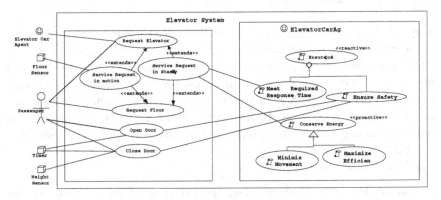

Fig. 2. Use Case Goal Diagram for the IES I

- Ensure QoS: This is a reactive Goal, which is responsible for ensuring the Quality of Service to the users. In order to accomplish this goal, both its subgoals, namely, "Ensure Safety" and "Meet Required Response Time" have to be achieved:
  - Ensure safety Goal: This Goal ensures safety of the Elevator system. This comes into picture during the Open Door and Close Door use cases. It considers following factors:
    - o   1. Motor Status whether it is ON or OFF.
    - o   2. Weight of the Elevator
    - o   3. Floor Sensor whether Elevator car is in a floor or in transition.
  - Meet Required Response Time: This goal is responsible for ensuring the required response time must be met.
- Conserve Energy: This proactive goal is responsible in conserving the energy of the elevators cars by either Minimize Movement goal or Maximize Efficiency goal:
  - Minimize Movement: This goal is responsible for minimizing the movement of the elevator Car. The utility value is evaluated based on the distance, since the Elevator car needs to travel to service a passenger from the elevator car's current position.

- Maximize Efficiency: This goal maximizes efficiency by serving the passengers in nearby floors that want to travel in the same direction as the current elevator direction.

Step 4.3. Refine system domain model and agent domain models.
In this step the system domain model — an ontological or conceptual model [2, 18, 31] for the application domain objects, their attributes and relationships—is constructed or refined for the current increment. The system domain model for the elevator example consists of objects representing various parts of an elevator. Since the domain model has been addressed elsewhere, we will not repeat here. We introduce the Agent Domain Model (ADM) to capture the application dependent beliefs, goals and plans of an agent and their properties and relationships. In our approach, an ADM is constructed for each type of application specific agent.

The agent domain model, shown in Figure 3, consists of a collection of timer, requests, weight, door status, last destination and motor status beliefs. Our application consists of Minimize Movement, Meet Required Response Time and Ensure Safety goals. The Elevator CarAgent has an ECAMaster-Plan. The change in the Requests belief notifies Minimize Movement and Meet Required Response Time goals. The change in beliefs related to state of elevator car notified the Ensure Safety goal.

The diagram indicates that the Elevator Car Agent has two beliefs: Elev-CarState and Requests. These beliefs are implicitly defined as subclasses of *Belief* indicated by the cloud icon. Changes to the Requests belief will affect the two goals as shown in the diagram. Similarly, the two goals are subclasses of *Goal* and hence must implement the *beliefChanged (b: Belief)* method. The diagram also indicates that the goals have plans and each plan delegates its task to a command object [10] that implements a thread.

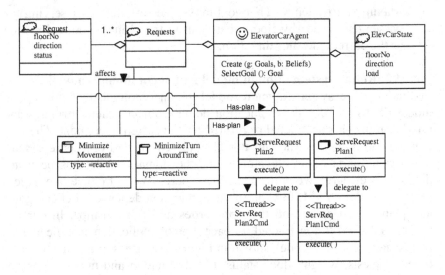

Fig. 3. Agent domain model

Step 4.4. Specify system and agent sequence diagrams

For each use case, at least one system level sequence diagram is constructed to document how the agents and other objects work together to accomplish the business process underlying the use case. This is the same as in OO modeling [19, 4] except that agents may communicate with other agents and interact with objects (e.g., opens/closes an elevator door). Similarly, Agent Sequence Diagrams are constructed to show the intrinsic interactions within an agent, as illustrated in Figure 4.

The Open Door Agent Sequence Diagram (Figure 4) begins with a state change in the motor. The Motor keeps updating its own status with the agent. The update of the motor status changes the motor belief, which in turn notifies the Ensure Safety goal subscribed to the motor belief. The Ensure Safety goal then evaluates a utility value (which in this case is 1 or 0) based on following parameters:

- The motor state being ON or OFF.
- The elevator is on a floor or is in transition.
- The total weight of the elevator should be less then a threshold.

The evaluated utility value is sent to the Elevator Car Agent. The agent then can either ask the goal to pursue or to abandon. If the agent decides to pursue, then the goal creates a plan for execution. The plan in turn opens the door of the elevator.

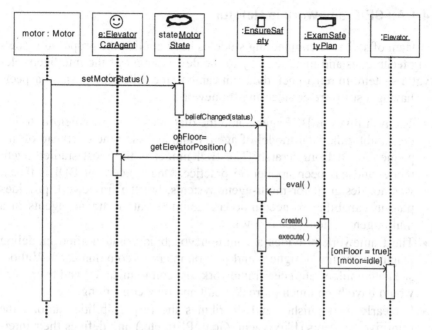

Fig. 4. Agent Sequence diagram for Open Door

Steps 4.5. Refine Design Class Diagrams and
Steps 4.6. Refine State and Activity Diagrams

In step 5, we derive the design class diagram from the system domain model and sequence diagrams and the Agent Design Diagrams from the Agent Domain Models and Agent Sequence Diagrams. In particular, the domain model provide information to define the structural aspect while the sequence diagrams provide information for the behavioural aspect. For agents, beliefs, goals and plans that have non-trivial activity and/or behaviour, the corresponding Agent Activity Diagrams and Agent Statechart Diagrams are also defined.

4 Lessons Learned

During the course of this project, several valuable lessons have been learned and will be presented in the following subsections. We believe that the lessons could benefit other research efforts on providing a software engineering framework for multi-agent systems because the most of the lessons are generic.

4.1 An SE Framework is Helpful

A team of software engineering students have applied the proposed modeling techniques and methodology to the development of the intelligent elevator system. In retrospect, the team came to the following positive aspects of having a software engineering framework:

- The primitives of BDI agents and the diagrams were very helpful to understanding the BDI model of agency and avoiding the overhead of implementing it from scratch. The BDI model is the most studied agent model and has been applied in practice. One concern of BDI is that it was not designed for multi-agent systems, but the framework provides plug-in capability to accommodate communication among agents in a multi-agent system (see below).
- The framework provides a common vocabulary and unified modeling language for the designers and programmers to communicate. Without such a common reference framework, the communication and teamwork would have been much more difficult and time consuming.
- It clearly distinguishes and distributes the responsibilities among the primitive concepts (like Agent, Goal, Plan, etc.) and defines their interactions/interfaces. This feature helped achieve separation of concerns and facilitated understanding on how the components work together. However, the current framework had not implemented the model-defined interactions among the beliefs, goals and plans of an agent. Therefore, the individual team members had to implement the interactions. It is hoped that such support would be in a future version of the framework.
- The framework provides a predefined, abstract multi-agent systems architecture for designing application specific agents while allowing application specific implementation.
- The framework allows use of any agent communication language and the ability to plug-in any implementation of the communication mechanism. The team was able to use JATLite's implementation of KQML communication for its elevator agents [14].
- The blackboard mechanism is a useful way of sharing information among agents. In regards to the elevator project, all outside elevator requests and the rush hour schedule were posted on the blackboard for the agents to learn from.

4.2 Using Design Patterns

Software design patterns [10] have roots in architectural patterns. According to Alexander, patterns repeat themselves, since they are effective solutions to specific problems [1]. The purpose of design patterns is to capture software design know-how and make it reusable. Design patterns can improve the structure of software, facilitate maintenance, and help avoid architectural drift. Design patterns also improve communication among software developers and empower less experienced personnel to produce high-quality designs. Successful reuse of well-designed and well-tested software components improves software quality and reliability. In this project, we have used and benefited from several design patterns. This experience could suggest the incorporation of these patterns into the software engineering framework.

4.3 Some Research Issues

In the multi-agent elevator system, utility values based on the current state of the environment were used to select a goal to pursue. The framework leaves the computation of the utility value entirely to the application developer. On the one hand, this flexibility is desirable because different applications have different ways to assess the utility of a goal. On the other hand, this shifts the burden to application developers. In our case, the utility values were calculated using ad-hoc algorithms invented by the team. It would be very helpful if the software engineering framework could provide default algorithms and their implementation for re-use.

A serious problem in the elevator system was concurrency. An agent's environment is constantly changing, thereby triggering several goals. The question now is what goal should be pursued? If the utility values of several goals triggered are the same, which one should be pursued next? If several goals are pursued and hence several plans are simultaneously executed, the system could quickly run out of resources and crash. This could be a topic of research in software engineering for multi-agent systems, especially for large multi-agent systems.

The framework provides flexibility for the multi-agent systems developers to plug-in any AI learning algorithm implementation. But the framework does not provide any APIs that implement any such algorithms. Therefore, the team members had to spend considerable time analyzing and implementing a learning capability. It would be very helpful if a software engineering framework for multi-agent systems can provide APIs that implement some of the existing AI learning algorithms so that the developer can easily re-use any of them.

Agent decision-making process was very crucial in the project. It brought up the issue of collaboration. Could agents come to a final agreement on an issue? Could one agent make decisions for other agents without violating the autonomy property? Or yet, should another agent be created to make final decisions for the agents themselves? As above, a software engineering framework could prefabricate agent decision making as well as agent coordination algorithms as APIs to facilitate the design and implementation processes.

5 Related Work

In this section we will limit our review of research projects in the area of agent oriented methodologies that are based on UML and/or BDI like agents. For more details on other methodologies we refer the reader to surveys in [34] and [12].

Rumbaugh et al's Object Modeling Technique (OMT) was adapted by Kinny et al [17] to translate the Belief, Goal, Plan and Agent Models to formal models like BDI, our approach provides modeling and implementation with the advantage of using application specific design and implementation alternatives. This is achieved by the use of abstract classes (Agent, Goal, Belief and Plan) and design patterns as the underlying implementation model to provide the power and flexibility to support all possible needs.

UML based modeling approaches have taken the front stage at International Workshops on Agent-Oriented Software Engineering (AOSE) [7] [35], The agent UML (AUML) approach proposed by Odell et al [24] introduces the Agent Interaction Protocol (AIP) for agent communication and constraints on messages. Yim et al. [36] proposed an architecture-centric design method based on OO design methods, design patterns and software architecture. They denote agent, agent messages, and other concepts using UML stereotypes. Bergenti and Poogi [3] treat agents as communicating entities. Similar to Yim et al, this approach uses UML to model MAS and requires no extension to UML. In addition, a Belief Model, a Goal Model and a Plan Model were proposed to specify the beliefs, goals and plans for agents. In contrast, we propose to extend UML from ground-up by introducing the concept of an Agent.

Methodology for Engineering Systems of Software Agents (MESSAGE/UML) proposed by Caire et al [5] describes an analysis process that consists of various levels with more detail added to the views at each level. The analysis model consists of different "views": 1) Organization view, consisting of entities in the system like agents, organizations, roles and relationships between them. 2) Goal/Task view, showing goals, tasks, situations and dependencies amongst them (this is similar to our Agent Domain Model). 3) Agent/Role view, describing agents and their roles. 4) Interaction view, describing the interactions amongst the agents/roles, the initiator of the interaction, the events that trigger the interaction. 5) Domain view, which is the same as a (System) Domain Model in our framework. Our modeling approach is use case centric and derives heavily from the Unified Process [19].

The Tropos methodology [11] covers a wide range of software development phases and emphasizes on requirements analysis. The methodology has a modeling language, which is not based on UML. It consists of the following phases: 1) the early requirements phase to identify goals, 2) the late requirements phase to identify the requirements for the actors, 3) the architectural design phase to assign goals and tasks to actors, 4) the detailed design phase to produce the details of actors and their communication and coordination protocols, and 5) the implementation phase. It is based on BDI concepts and framework and suggests that developers choose a framework for implementation.

6 Conclusions and Future Work

We have described a framework and the necessary extensions to UML to address the modeling and design of MAS including modeling constructs like Agent, Belief, Goal, Plan, FIPA Performative, KQML Performative, and Blackboard. Our approach draws from the BDI formalism. Agents are peers in the decision making process. The communication between agents is demonstrated by using a black board mechanism. Our approach allows the flexibility of using FIPA, KQML or any other agent communication languages. Various diagrams are introduced, based on UML notations. The modeling process uses Agent Goal Diagram to relate an agent's goals with its environment, Use Case Goals Diagram (UCGD) to associate use cases with goals, Agent Domain Model to describe application specific beliefs, goals, plans and their relationships. Our framework utilizes interfaces and abstract classes to provide flexibility in implementing application specific intelligent behaviours. The sequence diagrams from UML are used to portray interactions among agents. To model the decision making process and interactions within a agent, we proposed Agent Sequence Diagrams.

We are in the process to complete the implementation of the IES using the methodology discussed in this paper. We plan to apply the framework to modeling and design of intelligent agents for MavHome smart home project[8]. The MavHome consists of a hierarchy of intelligent agents that perceive the environment through sensors and act upon the environment to maximize the comfort of its inhabitants and minimize home maintenance costs. As future work, we will design and implement a Computer Aided Software Engineering (CASE) environment to provide modeling, design and analysis support to large-scale multi-agent systems development.

References

[1] Alexander C., Ishikawa S., Silverstein M., Jacobson M., Fiksdahl-King I. and Angel S., A Pattern Language, Oxford University Press, New York, 1977.

[2] Bubenko jr,, J.A.: Information modeling in the context of system development, Invited paper to IFIP Congress, pp. 395 - 411, 1980.

[3] Bergenti, F., Poggi, A.:Exploiting UML in the design of Multi-Agent systems, Proceeding of the ECOOP Workshop on Engineering Societies in the Agents World 2000 (ESAW 00), pp 96-103,2000.

[4] Booch, G., Rumbaugh, J., Jacobson, I.: The Unified Modeling Language User Guide, Addison Wesley, 1998.

[5] Caire, G., Leal, F., Chainho, P., Evans, R., Garijo, F., Gomez, J., Pavon, J., Kearney, P., Stark, J., Massonet, P.: Agent oriented analysis using MESSAGE/UML, Proc. of 2nd International Workshop on Agent Oriented Software Engineering, pp. 101-108, Montreal Canada, August 2001.

[6] Chiariglione, L.: FIPA 97 Specification, http:// leonardo.telecomitalialab.com/ fipa/ spec/ fipa97/ fipa97.htm.

[7] Ciancarini, P., Wooldridge, M. (eds.): Agent Oriented Software Engineering, Proc. First International Conference on Agent Oriented Software Engineering, Springer, 2000.

[8] Cook, D.: http://ranger.uta.edu/smarthome/links.html.

[9] Finn, T., Labrou, Y., Mayfield, J.: KQML as an agent communication language, in Software Agents, edited by J.Bradshaw, MIT Press, Cambridge, 1977.

[10] Gamma, E. et al.: Design Patterns: Elements of Reusable Object-Oriented Software, Addison-Wesley, 1995.

[11] Giunchiglia, F., Mylopoulos, J., Perini, A.: The Tropos software development methodology: process, models and diagrams, Proc. of International Conf. on Autonomous Agents and Multiagent Systems: Part 1, 2002, Bologna, Italy, 2002.

[12] Iglesias, C., Garijo, M., Gonzales, J.C.: A survey of agent-oriented methodologies. In Intelligent Agents V: Proceedings of the ATAL'98, volume 1555 of LNAI. Springer, 1999.

[13] Jennings, N.R., Sycara, K., Wooldridge, M.: A roadmap of agent research and development, in Autonomous Agents and Multi-Agent Systems, Kluwer Academic Publishers.

[14] Jeon, H., Petrie, C., Cutkosky, M.R.: JATLite: A java agent infrastructure with message routing, IEEE Internet Computing, Mar/Apr 2000.

[15] Kavi, K., Aborizka, M., Kung, D.: A framework for designing, modeling and analyzing agent based software systems, in Proc. of 5th International Conference on Algorithms & Architectures for Parallel Processing, October 23-25, 2002, Beijing, China.

[16] Kavi, K., Kung, D., Bhambhani, H., Pancholi, G., Kanikarla, M., Shah, R.: Extending UML to Modeling and Design of Multi-Agent Systems, Proc. of ICSE 2003 Workshop on Software Engineering for Large Multi-Agent Systems (SELMAS), Portland, Oregon, May 3–4, 2003.

[17] Kinny, D., Georgeff, M.: Modeling and Design of Multi-Agent Systems, In Proc. of the 3rd Int. Workshop on Intelligent Agents: Agent Theories, Architectures, and Languages, ATAL'96, pages 1–20, Budapest, Hungary, Aug. 1997.

[18] Kung, D.: Conceptual modeling in the context of software development," IEEE Trans. on Software Eng. Vol. 15, No. 10, pp. 1176 - 1187, (Oct. 1989).

[19] Larman, C.: Applying UML and Patterns, Prentice Hall, 2001.

[20] Ljunberg, M., Jucas, A.: The OASIS air traffic management system, Proc. of the 2nd Pacific Rim International Conference on AI, Seoul, Korea, 1992.

[21] Maes, P.: Agents that reduce work and information overload, Communications of the ACM, 37(7), pp 31-40.

[22] Murphy, A., Picco, G., Roman, G.C.: LIME: A middleware for physical and logical mobility, Proceeding of the 21 st International Conference on Distributed Computing Systems (ICDCS),April,2001,pp 524-533.

[23] Optimal Aircraft Sequencing using Intelligent Scheduling, http:/ /www.gsia.cmu.edu/andrew/course/45/865/2000/oasis.html.

[24] Odell, J., Van Dyke Parunak, H., Bauer, B.: Extending UML for Agents, AOIS Workshop at AAAI 2000.

[25] Odell, J.J., Van Dyke Parunak, H., Bauer, B.: Representing Agent Interaction Protocols in UML, in Proc. of First International Conference on Agent- Oriented Software Engineering, Paolo Ciancarini and Michael Wooldridge eds., Springer, Berlin, pp. 121-140, 2001.

[26] Van Dyke Parunak, H., Bauer, B.: Representing social structures in UML, Proc. of Autonomous Agents '01, Montreal Canada, May 28-June 1, 2001.

[27] Rao, A., Georgeff, M.: Modeling rational agents within a BDI architecture, Proceedings of the Second International Conference on Principles of Knowledge Representation and Reasoning, Cambridge, MA, 1991, pp. 473-484.

[28] Rao, A., Georgeff, M.: BDI agents: From theory to practice, Proceedings of the First International Conference on Multi-Agent Systems (ICMAS-95), San Francisco, pp. 312-319.

[29] 1st International Workshop on Software Engineering for Large-Scale Multi-Agent Systems, Orlando, Florida, USA, in conjunction with ICSE 2002, May 19, 2002,

[30] Garcia, A.F. (ed.): Software Engineering for Large Multiagent Systems, ICSE Workshop Proceedings, Portland, Oregon, May 2-3, 2003.

[31] Sølvberg A.: A Model for Specification of Phenomena, Properties, and Information Structures, IBM Research Lab. San Jose, Calif. 95193, RJ2027(28348)7/18/77

[32] Sølvberg A.: On the Specification of Scenarios in Information System Design, IBM Research Lab. San Jose, Calif. 95193, RJ2065 (28689) 8/15/77, 1977.

[33] Sølvberg, A.: A contribution to the definition of concepts for expressing user's information systems requirements, in Entity-Relationship Approach to System analyses and Design, P.P. Chen (ed.), Elsevier Science Publishing Comp., pp. 359 - 380, 1980.

[34] Tveit, A.: A Survey of Agent-Oriented Software Engineering. NTNU Computer Science Graduate Student Conference, Norwegian University of Science and technology, 2001.

[35] Wooldridge, M., Weib, G., Ciancarini, P. (eds.): Agent Oriented Software Engineering II, Proc. Second International Workshop, Montreal, Canada, May 29, 2001, Springer 2001.

[36] Yim, H., Cho, K., Jongwoo, K., Park, S. Architecture-Centric Object-Oriented Design Method for Multi-Agent Systems, in Proc. of the Fourth International Conference on Multi-Agent Systems (ICMAS-2000), 2000.

Agent Approach to Online Legal Trade

Antje Dietrich, Peter C. Lockemann, Oliver Raabe

Fakultät für Informatik, Universität Karlsruhe, Germany

Abstract. Large open electronic markets rely on some sort of self-organization, primarily those of a market economy. To function properly and continuously there must be an element of trust among the participants. Trust is achieved by imposing a legal framework within which all business is conducted. This paper examines how well the agent concept can, both as a design method and a software technology, support market participants in concluding legal contracts.

1 Introduction

Electronic markets are – aside from eventual physical transport of traded goods – large, distributed and often ubiquitous information systems. Consequently, the development of electronic markets should follow the rules of good information systems engineering. In a nutshell, information systems engineering insists that one acquires a sound and formal understanding of the application before building the supporting technical system, and that the steps from the conceptual design to the technical solution proceed along a solid methodology.

Many electronic markets are open: their participants may come and go. Large open systems cannot be governed by a cumbersome central authority if they are to function effectively and efficiently. Rather they have to rely on some sort of self-organization where the participants act autonomously but observe implicit or explicit rules that strike a balance between individual interests and the common good. For open electronic markets the rules are those of a market economy: The markets are controlled by supply and demand, driven by prices, and forced into efficiencies by competition. However, to function properly and continuously there must also be an element of trust among the participants. Society in general, and organizations in particular, achieve trust by imposing a legal framework within which all business is conducted, and enforcing sanctions if trust is broken. Participants in a business transaction can protect themselves if they enter into a legally effective contract.

Negotiations and legal advice have a strong flavour of non-determinism and could prove fairly resistant to a methodical, let alone formal engineering approach. We argue in this paper that software agents are well suited as a conceptual framework for the automated support of self-organizing markets. We proceed with the argument as follows. Section 2 introduces the market scenario underlying our work, and Section 3 software agents as the conceptual framework. Section 4 structures spontaneous negotiations in terms of this framework, and Section 5 does the same for legal advice. Section 6 briefly explores the technical challenges for a software agent solution. Section 7 concludes the paper.

2 A Scenario

2.1 Local Energy Markets

To trust the market participants one must first of all trust the legal system itself. Given today's state of the art chances are best if one confines business to a local market. The scenario underlying our work is a local grid of providers and consumers of electrical energy. Such markets are evolving because of the growing number of decentralized power generators such as combined heat and power plants (CHP) with electricity as a by-product, fuel cells, solar panels, wind power, or biomass plants.

By setting the right market mechanisms all parties involved should draw benefits. Suppose in our scenario a community of households or small enterprises that act on a market alternately as suppliers when they produce electricity beyond their current needs or as consumers when they operate under peak demand. Add a large electricity provider that guarantees a base supply and maintains the grid for power transmission. Now, if a participant wishes to offset some of its cost it will have to deliver electricity to the grid during peak loads when it can fetch an attractive price, and schedule its own appliances during times of low load with – hopefully – lower rates. As a supplier the participant may get some automated support by accessing an optimizer that computes a price it can fetch for its own energy, based on own profile, rates offered by competitors and load characteristics of the electrical grid. As a consumer the participant may employ another optimizer that schedules the appliances or one that selects the offer best suited to its needs if a good number of offers exist. Alternatively, a consumer may specify a rate structure it is willing to accept, and then invite bids from the various providers. Ultimately, the supplier will have found a consumer willing to take delivery, and both will have come to an agreement on the conditions of the energy transfer. From this point on the supplier may feed the excess energy into the grid provided it has negotiated a contract with of one of the large power suppliers for the power transmission.

The overall benefit of such a market is reduced need for non-reproducible resources like gas or coal. In other words, we claim that electronic markets provide mechanisms that are well suited to the conservation of natural resources by making more efficient and economical use of them.

2.2 Contractual Framework

The scenario offers ample opportunities for negotiations with legal consequences. Take the enterprise or household as a supplier. For one it will have to enter into a – presumably long-term – contract with a large provider to cover the transmission of its electric energy. And after it found a willing consumer it will have to negotiate a contract with it. Likewise, as a consumer it must conclude a contract with a supplier, and in case of group rebates also one covering the entire group.

The scenario is representative of what one could term a market of short-lived (or perishable) goods, i.e., goods that can not be stored or at best for a very short period, and that must find their consumers fairly quickly. Hence there is hardly time for obtaining professional legal advice. Also, the parties involved rarely have much of a legal background, i.e., as law laypersons have difficulties in judging the legal ramifications of a contract. Consequently, the scenario is typical for a situation where automated legal advice seems necessary.

3 Software Agents

3.1 Agent Characteristics

Open electronic markets fall into the class of loosely coupled distributed information systems. Agents are a useful design principle to describe the components in such a system if the emphasis is on the services that the components provide. Agents may describe both the real world where the physical participant is called the *principal* and the technical world with *software agents*. The two are related: The principal keeps major responsibilities but delegates others to particular software agents.

The usefulness of the agent approach derives from their property of autonomy: There is little or no central control in loosely coupled systems, instead each component must be capable of controlling its own progress. The autonomy is not unrestrained [22]. An agent provides a specified service. To render the service the agent must be capable of perceiving its environment (including other agents), and of responding somehow to the changes that occur (called reactive behaviour). Since the environment progresses somewhat unpredictably, the agent must be guided by goals given on its way, with goal deliberation and means-end assessment as parts of the overall decision process of practical reasoning. An agent may also have to be proactive, that is, to take the initiative in pursuance of its goals.

3.2 Multiagent Systems

A (distributed) system of software agents is called a multiagent system if the individual agent can attain its goals only with the help of others. Mutual support is contingent on existence of a shared (high-level) purpose, or goal. For example, in our scenario the individual goal of an agent is to obtain the best possible deal as a supplier or consumer, whereas the overall goal is to ensure that the decentralized energy market functions efficiently and conforms to legal norms.

To pursue the shared goal or procure help, a software agent must be capable of interacting with other agents. Due to the autonomy of the components, all communication between agents can only be asynchronous and, hence, message exchange is the primary means for the agents to cooperatively pursue the high-level goals. The agents must agree among themselves what the rules of engagement are. These rules define their *interaction protocol*. A well-known standard is the contract net protocol [22].

3.3 Agent Types

The notion of agent is too generic to be of immediate value to the conceptual design of loosely coupled information systems. Not all of the characteristics mentioned before may be needed, at least not to the same degree. Therefore, the literature differentiates among three types of agents [21].

The *reactive agent* emphasizes reactivity over proactivity and goal-directedness. Basically it works from rules "situation → action" that specify for each possible sensory input which action the agent should (immediately) perform upon this input. During execution, the agent takes its sensory input and matches it against the conditions for each action, taking (by inhibition) conflicts into account, that arise if more than one rule applies.

If the emphasis is on proactivity and goal-directedness while reactivity is of little importance, the solution is a *deliberative agent*. These agents store and maintain a model of their environment, and new sensory input is placed in the model as a perception. At some point in time the agent consciously starts a logical reasoning process. The best known among this agent type is the *belief-desire-intention (BDI) agent*. The agent takes its beliefs, i.e., the sensory input accumulated over time, and its desires, i.e., its goals, and forms intentions about what it is going to do in the future. Intentions are courses of action to which an agent commits itself.

A BDI agent shows poor reactivity because the reasoning process applied to a sensory input is so slow that the action may no longer be appropriate by the time it has been derived. Therefore, in order to combine both reactive and deliberative mechanisms a special *hybrid agent* makes more sense. A well-known example is the InteRRaP architecture that consists of three layers, each equipped with a database: A behavioural layer for reactive situation-action rules, a plan layer for goal-directed proactive planning, and a co-operation layer for modelling and handling interaction with other agents [13]. If an input cannot be handled on a layer, the situation is escalated to the next higher layer.

4 Negotiation

4.1 Basic Workflow

Contracts are a matter of bilateral or multilateral negotiation and agreement. Jennings et al. argue in a survey paper that negotiation is the most fundamental mechanism for managing inter-agent dependencies such that a group of agents comes to a mutually acceptable agreement on some matter [8]. Ludwig et al. distinguish between *negotiation protocol* and *negotiation strategy*, where the former determines the rules by which the parties must abide and thus the flow of messages between the parties, and the latter the way in which a given party acts within the rules to secure the best private outcome [14]. Our scenario differs from all these studies in that it embeds the negotiation proper into a legal framework: Laws ensure that contracts – however arrived at – meet certain societal norms. Consequently, two interleaving but distinctive tasks must be solved: Negotiating a contract and checking it for legal compliance. Following the proven software principle of separation of concerns we delegate each task to a separate agent – both with the same principal –, a contract negotiator and a legal advisor.

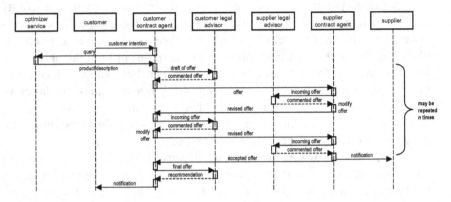

Fig.1. Workflow for contract negotiation

Figure 1 shows the negotiation process in the form of a basic workflow. Assumptions underlying the workflow are that suppliers publish standard contracts in the form of tariffs – perhaps for different classes of users and varying over days and hours within a day – and general terms and conditions (GTC), but that they allow to a certain degree to negotiate from them. Further, the legal basis is assumed to be Section 150 (2) BGB (the German civil code) where acceptance of an offer conditioned on further revision is considered a new offer. We note that, therefore, it is the consumer who starts with the first offer, and the supplier who closes with the final offer.

Figure 1 also indicates that the consumer – or more precisely, the consumer contract agent – may first engage an optimizer service. Provided the customer's load profile is known the optimizer ranks in monetary terms the suppliers on the basis of their published rates. This allows the consumer agent to select a specific supplier. The agent then starts with its offer by including further factors with no direct monetary valuation. The supplier contract agent may accept it, or it may return a counteroffer, which the consumer agent may now accept or counter with a new offer. Ultimately the two agents either may come to an agreement, or one may break off the process. Figure 1 also indicates that each agent may consult with its legal advisor agent when a new offer arrives (shown in the figure) or after it modified the incoming offer.

In general the workflow will be more complicated. For example, the consumer agent may return to the ranked list and select the next supplier if it is not satisfied with the negotiation. Usually the provider of the electric grid for transporting the energy must be included as a third party. Also, on a more technical level we would have to include a service for enforcing security during establishing the connection and the message exchange, and an archiving service for tracking and reconstructing the negotiation process.

4.2 Contract Agent

4.2.1 Agent Type

All participants have considerable leeway within which to act. As a result, the fellow negotiators' behaviour appears fairly unpredictable – non-deterministic – to each negotiator so that a heavy dose of goal-directedness and logical reasoning, and even some proactivity is needed. On the other hand, the workflow shows little in terms of reactivity. This suggests the BDI type as the best solution for the contract agent.

4.2.2 Beliefs

Beliefs represent the organized input accumulated over time. To function properly, the contract agent's beliefs must hold a *user model*, i.e., a model of its principal whose interests it has to pursue, and a *history* of the current negotiation as it evolves between the agent and the other party.

In our scenario the contract agent starts the negotiation with the optimizer input as the basis. Consequently, the negotiation concerns non-monetary factors only. Typically, many are of a business nature with legal ramifications. Take agreements on form, applicable law, jurisdiction, liability provisions, warranty terms, contract duration, or terms of notice. Others may have a social touch such as the percentage of energy from renewable sources. The user model assigns valuations to these factors. Therefore we refer to the user model as the user's *preferences*. Currently we allow six preferences. These are listed in Table 1.

Owing to the layperson nature of many principals the options for the preferences are given in linguistic terms. The standard approach to the interpretation of such terms is fuzzy sets [9,33]. To give very simple examples of rectangular membership functions, contract durations short, medium and long could be 8 months or less, 9 to 16 months, and 17 months or more, respectively.

Table 1. Preferences in the energy scenario

preference	options	comment
legal form	weak, advanced, qualified	proven strength of digital signature
applicable legal system	D, CH, AT	options for cross-border trade
successful outcome	important, unimportant	priority for closing the contract
contract duration	short, medium, long	
period of notice	short, medium, long	acceptable week range
consideration of renewable sources	high, low	

The same agent may sometimes act as a supplier and at some other time as a consumer. In this case we have to provide two sets of preferences.

We assume that the history does not extend beyond the current negotiation so that the agent does not show inexplicable behaviour due to earlier but uncontrolled learning. Given the user model, the history simply reflects the current valuations of the preferences, whether these are still subject to negotiation or have already been agreed upon by the two parties.

4.2.3 Desires

In the BDI concept desires play the roles of goals. The overall goal is straightforward: Given the optimal tariff, the two parties wish to maximize their own benefits in terms of the preferences. In all likelihood they will have to enter into some compromises. Therefore, it makes sense to compute the benefit from the preferences in terms of a utility function. The individual goals are reflected by the relative weight associated with each preference, possibly by weight functions if interdependencies must observed among the preferences (for example, between contract duration and period of notice), and by the threshold for an acceptable benefit.

The desires may also include the agents' attitudes. An agent may proceed in a greedy or cooperative fashion depending on how much understanding it is willing to develop for the other party, and it may be patient or impatient depending what upper time limit it tolerates for the negotiation.

4.2.4 Intentions

The courses of action are best explained by the view of the negotiation that the contract agent carries with him (Figure 2). Parameters are the kind of proposals generated, the content of the alternatives, the number of iterations pursued, and the break-off decisions.

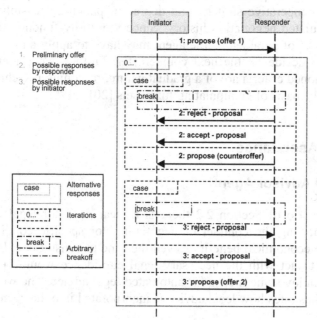

Fig. 2. Contract negotiation as intentions

4.3 Reasoning Process

The reasoning process implements the specific negotiation strategy of the agent and produces the actions. We assume that all strategies follow common ground rules:

- Each party (consumer and supplier) tries to negotiate a contract that maximizes its own utility.
- Neither party knows the current strategy (including the preferences) of the other party.
- Either party may break off the negotiation with acceptance or rejection.

The negotiation strategy can be seen as a decision-making model of the single agent while it is contemplating the next step. It follows from the assumptions that decisions must entirely be based on criteria owned by the agent itself. This is the main justification for the heavy reliance on preferences. Given one's own valuation of a preference, and a value or an interval as a counteroffer for the preference, the agent can compute a utility of this preference and the total utility over all preferences. Given this utility, the agent continues with the negotiation protocol on the basis of utility threshold, order of preferences if the preferences are mutually independent, greedy or cooperative strategy and degree of patience, possibly utilizing the accumulated negotiation history. Since the utility function contains a large number of parameters, the agent may have to apply an optimization function to decide on the next counteroffer. Further, since many of the aforementioned criteria are of a gradual nature, reasoning is technically realized on the basis of manipulating fuzzy sets [20].

5 Legal Assistance

5.1 Legal Advisor Agent

In the scenario of Section 2.2 there is a clear need for legal assistance while inspecting the contract or negotiating for specific conditions, but there is no economical benefit or even the time to consult one. Hence, the only way to act with the necessary legal confidence would be for both sides to employ some means for automated legal advice. The workflow of Figure 1 illustrates how legal advice is incorporated into the agent negotiations.

As Figure 1 shows the legal advisor agent is contacted by its own contract agent several times and for two or three distinctive purposes. Suppose the consumer, after having consulted the optimizer, initiates the negotiation with a non-binding offer. Before the consumer agent approaches the identified supplier it consults with its legal advisor to check the offer (initial check). After the consumer contract agent received a – possibly modified – offer from the supplier agent it again consults with its legal advisor who may suggest additional modifications and thus may cause a – now binding – offer to be returned to the supplier agent. This may continue several times until the consumer agent feels its preferences have been met, and the legal advisor in a final check recommends acceptance on legal grounds (the check may include further legal domains such as consumer protection law), or the negotiation has come to a dead end.

Likewise, the supplier contract agent will involve its own legal advisor agent. Whenever it receives a new offer from the consumer agent it will consult with its advisor and perhaps receive suggestions on how to modify the offer from a legal standpoint.

Clearly then, the legal advisor agent assumes a much more passive role than the contract agent. Whereas the contract agents are the ones driving the entire negotiation process, a legal advisor agent becomes active only upon explicit request by the contract agents. It is the typical reactive agent.

5.2 A Bird's Eye View of Legal Reasoning

5.2.1 Legal Norms

Legal reasoning is a highly complex intellectual process that is influenced by numerous factors such as the legal framework within which one operates (take the Continental European norm-based system of positive law and the Anglo-American case-law), cultural tradition, an attorney's specialization, a judge's experience and philosophical outlook, or the specificity or vagueness of a norm). Consequently, we have to begin by deciding on the framework – it is norm-based –, on the specificity of the norms – by relying on GTCs we will be able to avoid much vagueness – and also on the narrowness of the domain – we restrict ourselves to electronic energy trade and data protection.

To integrate legal reasoning into an agent we need an abstract model of the legal norms. Decisions are taken on the basis of primary norms. These norms determine a *legal consequence* (LC), given one or more *states of facts* (SF). Take as an example from the German Federal Data Protection Act (FDPA, in German: BDSG)[1]

[**Section 4a FDPA** Consent shall be effective (LC) when based on the data subject's free decision (SF1). [...] Consent shall be given in writing (SF2)[...].][2]

Not all norms fit this pattern. Rather some norms have a supporting function in that they explicate the meaning of a state of facts in some other norm (statutory definitions). Take

[**Section 4 FDPA** The collection, processing and utilization of person-related data shall be admissible only if permitted or prescribed by this Act [...] or if the data subject has consented.]

where a prior paragraph explicates

[**Section 3 FDPA** *"Person-related data"* means any information [SF1] concerning the personal [SF2] or material [SF3] circumstances of an identified [SF4] or identifiable [SF5] individual [...].]

---

[1] We take FDPA as an example because it is an excellent example for a modern law that supports automatic inferences. Further, its importance in our scenario derives from the fact that while parties to a contract may have to make personal data available, these must only be processed if a legitimate interest exists.

[2] Translated from the German original.

The example Sec. 4 FDPA includes another function: The second part is of a character akin to flow control in that it determines whether the norm applies at all, and if it does, it offers alternative routes of argument. Other norms have the purpose of determining exceptional situations where some other norm can be applied or should be excluded, or that impose further obligations on the parties involved.

5.2.2 Legal Reasoning

Legal reasoning is an intellectual affair, but fortunately there are a number of legal philosophies that try to explicate this process (for the German legal system see, e.g., [18]). We base our approach on the work by Larenz [10]). Somewhat simplified, the jurist – most likely by experience – has some idea of the legal consequence he or she wishes to attain. This in turn determines a limited set of primary norms from which to start. Each of these norms must now be inspected in order to determine whether the given situation matches the state of facts demanded by the norm. This may in turn require the jurist to look for statutory definitions. Other norms may refer the jurist to related norms that may him or her implore to pursue alternative routes or exceptions. Technically speaking, what the jurist eventually constructs is a (hopefully acyclic) graph of norms that ultimately allows a decision of whether the originally intended legal consequence can be reached.

If this sounds familiar to Artificial Intelligence researchers, there is indeed a strong similarity to theorem proving. Clearly the human mind will not be able to handle a comparable complexity, so jurists economize by learning how to prune the graph early enough, and to dynamically build up frequently occurring norm graphs during their daily practice.

5.2.3 Subsumption

According to Larenz, the norms in the positive law do not address singular cases but rather cover general classes of real-world situations. On the other hand, the jurist faces a specific real-world situation. Hence, before s/he even begins with legal reasoning s/he must try to find the norms whose general domain covers the situation (subsumes the situation). The jurist applies an intellectual process referred to as *subsumption*.

Subsumption is an interpretative process. Consequently, to mechanize subsumption the semantics must be considered, and these should go beyond thesauri. Ontologies hold particular promise because they reflect semantic relationships between terms, and these relationships can particularly be defined such that they directly support the subsumption process.

Lately, by providing a sound formal underpinning on the basis of description logic powerful inference mechanisms have become possible for ontologies.

5.2.4 Ontologies

Ontologies are tedious to build. Consequently there should be more and smaller ones. For example, for subsumption purposes we may have one for the legal domain and another for the application domain – in our case energy generation, consumption and trading. Take Figure 3. The legal ontology shown reflects the statutory definition Sec. 3 FDPA – except, though, for the legal terms "identifiable" and "identified". On the bottom is a small excerpt of the domain ontology. Provided we already know that someone is an individual) we should match, by subsumption, name and email address (that are shown to be personal information) to person-related data in the sense of the legal ontology.

Our most important contribution is to explicate the reasoning behind the match in a third ontology which incorporates judicial metaknowledge, i.e., operational knowledge guiding the subsumption process. Metaknowledge summarizes how a certain community of jurists arrives in several steps, by textual, historical, systematic and teleological interpretation, at associating concrete facts with a legal term that has no direct counterpart in the domain ontology and may thus be subject to judicial opinion. Take again Figure 3. The rule on top reflects the primary norm Sec. 4 FDPA and contributes to norm graph building. The rule relies on the statutory definition Sec. 3 FDPA. As indicated above, the legally appropriate interpretation of the terms "identifiable" and "identified" may be a matter of judicial opinion. The meta-knowledge in Figure 3 provides the necessary guidance together with the associated rule shown in the Figure. In essence, to be identifiable the information must objectively be knowable, and it must be made known with subjectively limited effort.

Ontologies are even more versatile. For example, one could translate some of the statutory definitions into the ontology and thus prune the norm graphs even further. Jurists may include in the ontology their own legal definitions of legal terms left consciously or unconsciously vague by lawmakers. Ontologies may even render help if the jurist must resort to conclusion by analogy because a given situation seems not covered by law. Ontologies may thus become powerful though not unlimited tools for automated legal advice, a promise that still has to be explored and understood at length. Some related work can be found in [5,19].

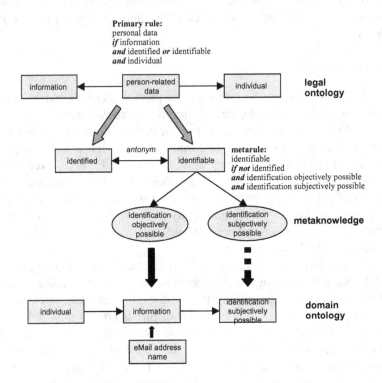

Fig. 3. Linked ontologies (explanation in the text)

5.2.5 Example

Suppose A stores B's name and email address. B has consented that A may pass on these data. A plans to give the data to C. C is a company affiliate of A. Case: May A pass on the email address?

Step 1: Determine the relevant primary norm. Sec. 4 FDPA is found.

Step 2: Preliminary check: Is the norm applicable? According to Sec. 4 FDPA, the legal consequence of permission to pass is given if passage of the email address is either collection, processing or utilization of person-related data. The statutory definition of person-related data is found in Sec. 3 FDPA. Subsumption via domain ontology: B is natural person, name and email address are distinctive information. Subsumption via legal ontology: Is person identifiable, i.e., can email address be associated with a specific person? Answer can be found via the metaknowledge in Figure 4. More specifically, can one tell purely from the address format whether it is legitimate? Does one happen to know or can one find out with modest effort whether it refers to a specific person (subjective identification)? This should be possible under the circumstances A is in. Hence, name and email address are person-related data. By further statutory definition, processing is storing, modification, deletion, or transmission. Next definitions: Transmission is information of a third party. Third party is any party outside the responsible party. Responsible party is the one that processes the data for its own purposes. Conclusion: Company affiliate is third party. Consequence: Sec. 4 FDPA is applicable.

Step 3: Application of the norm. Is the intended utilization permitted? According to Sec. 4 FDPA, A needs legal permission or the affected person's consent. Priority is on the latter. Sec. 4a FDPA explicates the formal conditions of consent. Subsumption: B's agreement meets the condition. Conclusion: A may give the data to C.

6 Implementation

It is often argued that the sole purpose of agent technology is for the conceptual design of loosely coupled distributed information systems. Indeed, it does not follow from such a design that the software implementation must necessarily follow the agent principle. There are some advantages if it does, though. In particular, it may be easier to verify that the implementation satisfies the design.

To gain first experiences we developed a quick prototype using the FIPA compliant agent platform JADE [1]. While JADE does not directly support BDI agents it allowed us to experiment with the organization of the contract agent. We used the methods of "Prometheus" [17] for specifying, designing and implementing the contract agent. Despite the relatively simple conceptual structure of the contract agent the implementation consists of close to 50 Java classes.

The legal advisor is much more demanding. We restricted ourselves to standard business transactions, i.e., those that follow specified standard contracts. For these chances are reasonable that the semantics can largely be formalized via an ontology, and norm graphs can evolve fairly quickly This is a conclusion that is borne out by earlier attempts to automate special sections of the law [2,6].

Figure 4 shows the basic architecture. It follows the reference architecture based on the layering pattern as proposed by Lockemann and Nimis [12,13]. Major layers are the ontology layer to support the subsumption process, and a behavioural layer for classical logical rule processing to model legal reasoning. Both layers include components for the domain and legal experts to build the ontology and the rule base.

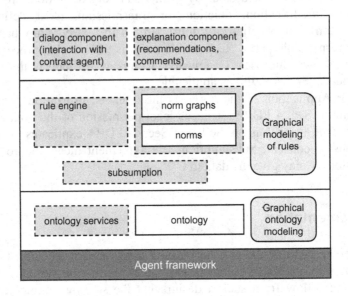

Fig. 4. Legal advisor agent architecture

The behavioural layer includes a rule engine, and the legal norms and summarized norm graphs are expressed as logical rules in the format required by the rule engine. In our first experiments the rules are translated into Java code, and rule processing is by means of the rule engine JESS. As noted in Sec. 5.2.2, legal reasoning starts from some legal consequence the jurist wishes to attain, and a primary norm that may support the consequence, and then works its way backwards to construct a norm graph. Consequently, inference by rule processing should primarily employ backward chaining (sometimes legal obligations must be derived by forward chaining). As a further complication, the order in which rules are applied, i.e., are arranged in the graph, is significant.

For managing ontologies we used the framework KAON [15]. Unfortunately, KAON only offers navigational means such as path expressions to exploit the semantic network. This is a far cry from any inference on the basis of description logic as suggested in Sec. 5.2.3. A successor to KAON, KAON 2 includes a description logic reasoner [7], although it imposes a number of restrictions on the logic to make reasoning decidable and tractable. Ontology reasoning seems important because rule processing and ontology processing should take place in an interleaved fashion.

7 Conclusions

The work reported in this paper is part of the SESAM project [4] which in turn is one of seven projects in the nationwide German initiative on an "internet economy". The scenario of Section 2 underlies the SESAM project. While it may sound futuristic we have the support of one of the large German energy providers who plans first experiments to test the prerequisite technical mechanisms and their acceptance.

For the proof of concept a demonstrator has been developed. The demonstrator includes technical guarantees that the processes in an open electronic market follow legal guidelines of trust and confidentiality [3].

Our foremost challenge is to carry our ontology approach to subsumption to much more depth. This requires a much more detailed study of linking ontologies. We hope to profit from recent studies by Lin, Sølvberg et al. [11].

One may ask oneself whether contracts negotiated by software agents have any legal standing at all, i.e., whether software agents can conclude legally valid contracts. Nitschke argues in [16] that even though the agent generates the contractual declaration, the declaration is generally based on the principal's will. For this reason and because a principal needs to willingly activate and instruct his agent in order to make it conclude contracts on his behalf, the agent's declarations can be ascribed to the principal and can therefore be regarded as declarations issued by the principal.

References

[1] Bellifemine, F.; Bergenti, F.; Caire, G.; Poggi, A.: JADE – a Java agent development framework. In Multi-Agent Programming ed by Bordini, R.; Dastani, M.; Dix, J.; El Fallah-Seghrouchni, A. (Springer, New York 2005) 125-147

[2] Bohrer, A.: Entwicklung eines internetgestützten Expertensystems zur Prüfung des Anwendungsbereiches urheberrechtlicher Abkommen, 2003

[3] Conrad, M.: Non-repudiation mechanism for peer-to-peer networks. Proc. 2nd Conf. On Future Networking Technologies (CoNEXT) 2006, 249-250

[4] Franke, M., Rolli, D., Kamper, A., Dietrich, A., Geyer-Schulz, A.Lockemann, P., Schmeck, H., Weinhardt, C.: impacts of distributed generation from virtual power plants. Proc. 11th Annual Internatl. Sustainable Development Research Conf., 2005, 1-12

[5] Gangemi, A., Sagri, M.-T., Tiscornia, D.: Metadata for content description in legal information. Proc. 5th Int. Conf. on Databases and Expert Systems 2003

[6] Haft, F., Lehmann, H.: Das LEX-Projekt: Entwicklung eines Expertensystems. Attempto 1991

[7] Hustadt,U., Motik,B., Sattler,U.: Reducing SHIQ description logic to disjunc-
     tive Datalog programs. Proc. 9th Int Conf. on Knowledge Representation and
     Reasoning. AAAI 2004, 152-162

[8] Jennings, N.R., Faratin, P., Lomuscio, A.R., Parsons, S., Sierra, C.,
     Wooldridge, M.: Automated negotiations: prospects, methods and challenges.
     J. of Group Decision and Negotiation 10(2), 199-215 (2001)

[9] Klir, G.J., Folger, T.A.: Fuzzy Sets, Uncertainty and Information (Prentice-
     Hall, Englewood Cliffs 1988)

[10] Larenz, K. Methodenlehre der Rechtswissenschaft (Springer, Berlin Heidel-
     berg New York 1991)

[11] Lin, Y., Strasunskas, D., Hakkarainen, S., Krogstie, J., Sølvberg, A.: Seman-
     tic annotation framework to manage semantic heterogeneity of process mod-
     els. Proc. 18th Conf. on Advanced Information Systems Engineering. Lecture
     Notes in Computer Science vol 4001 (Springer, Berlin Heidelberg New York
     2006) 433-446

[12] Lockemann, P.C.; Nimis, J.: Dependable multi-agent systems: layered refer-
     ence architecture and representative mechanisms. To appear in Lecture Notes
     in Artificial Intelligence (Springer, Berlin Heidelberg New York 2007)

[13] Lockemann, P.C., Nimis, J., Braubach, L., Pokahr, A. Lamersdorf, W.: Ar-
     chitectural design. In Multiagent Engineering ed by Kirn, S., Herzog, O.,
     Lockemann, P., Spaniol, O. (Springer, Berlin Heidelberg New York 2006)
     405-429

[14] Ludwig, S.A., Kersten, G.E., Huang, X.: Towards a behavioural agent-based
     assistant for e-negotiations. Proc. Montreal Conf. on E-Technologies
     (MCETECH), 2006

[15] Maedche, A., Motik, B., Stojanovic, L.: Managing multiple and distributed
     ontologies in the Semantic Web. The VLDB Journal 12(4), 286-302 (2003)

[16] Nitschke, T.: Legal consequences of agent deployment. In Multiagent Engi-
     neering ed by Kirn, S., Herzog, O., Lockemann, P., Spaniol, O. (Springer,
     Berlin Heidelberg New York 2006) 597-618

[17] Padgham, L., Winikoff, M.: Developing Intelligent Agent Systems – A Prac-
     tical Guide (Wiley, Chichester 2004)

[18] Ring, S. Computergestützte Rechtsfindungssysteme, Voraussetzungen, Gren-
     zen und Perspektiven, München 1994

[19] Senn, A., Schweighofer, E., Liebwald, D., Geist, A., Drachsler, M.: LOIS:
     Erfahrungen und Herausforderungen bei der Weiterentwicklung multilin-
     gualer Rechtsontologien. In e-Staat und e-Wirtschaft aus rechtlicher Sicht ed
     by Schweighofer et al. (Boorberg 2006) 290-295

[20] Weisbrod, J.: A new approach to fuzzy reasoning. Soft Computing 2, June
     1998

[21] Weiss, G. (ed.): Multiagent Systems, A Modern Approach to Distributed Ar-
     tificial Intelligence (MIT Press, Cambridge 1999)

[22] Wooldridge, M.: An Introduction to Multiagent Systems (Wiley, Chichester
     2002)

[23] Zadeh, L.A.: PRUF – a meaning representation language for natural lan-
     guages. Int. J. for Man-Machine Studies 10, 395-460 (1978)

Methods and Tools for Developing Interactive Information Systems

Anthony I. Wasserman

Carnegie Mellon West, USA

Abstract. This paper describes the evolution of hardware and software technology over the past three decades, focusing on approaches for building interactive information systems and web applications. Successive generations of technology have used advances in hardware and software technology, along with increasingly sophisticated development methods and tools, to reduce development times and to produce a better user experience. After describing the key technology characteristics of each generation, this paper also describes the evolution of a specific methodology, User Software Engineering, from its origins in the 1970's to its applicability to the development of modern Web applications.

1 Introduction

The processes and tools for developing interactive information systems (IIS) have changed drastically over the past three decades. Users of these systems have moved from slow, text-based systems in the 1970's to today's high-speed Web-based applications. Methods for developing these systems have evolved from the phased waterfall approach of the 1970's to more agile approaches commonly followed today. Similarly, the tools for creating these systems have evolved rapidly, reflecting changes in hardware technology, user interfaces, development notations and languages and mechanisms for collaboration among members of a team.

Looking back over the history of hardware and software technology, it is helpful to identify different generations of this technology that had a major impact on the processes used for building an IIS and the nature of the resulting system.

2 First Generation: Mainframes, Batch and Files

In the 1960's, most computing was batch-oriented, with few interactive systems. Graphical displays were available for some highly-specialized applications, such as radar tracking. Early database management systems used a hierarchical or network oriented view of data and were deployed on large mainframe systems. Terminal devices were slow (300 baud) and resembled teletypes, displaying text only in uppercase and printing on rolls of paper. The slow speed severely limited the amount of interaction. Among the first interactive applications were airline reservation systems, financial applications and military applications, such as radar tracking. These systems, in general, used file systems rather than a DBMS to store information, reflecting the need to obtain the best possible performance from the limited capabilities of the hardware. The first interactive programming environments, such as BASIC, also were developed at that time, making use of the early time-shared operating systems.

Development techniques for interactive systems were in their infancy, since there was almost no experience in building them. There were no analysis and design methods, no database modelling methods, or any of the other techniques that are now common. Modelling was at the procedural level, e.g., flowcharts, and at the logical level for files and data. In summary, the various hardware and software pieces for building an IIS weren't yet in place. For software professionals about to retire, the first generation reflects the situation at the beginning of their careers.

3 Second Generation: Time-Sharing, Terminals and Early DBMSs

The widespread presence of time-shared operating systems and alphanumeric video terminals transformed computing in the 1970's. Furthermore, this technology was available on minicomputers, such as those made by Digital Equipment Corporation, making it practical for almost every organization to obtain one. Primitive networks were in place to provide remote access to computing, including low-speed dialup.

The user interfaces were still text-based, but gradually moved from being line-oriented (glass teletype) to screen-oriented. While the first windowing systems were being developed in research settings, they were not generally available. Database systems had matured, but they remained very expensive. The first relational database management systems and the SQL query language were also introduced as research projects in the 1970's.

The first analysis and design methods also emerged in the 1970's, including Parnas' principles of modularity [10], Structured Design [15], Structured Analysis [4] and many more. Data modelling methods also appeared, including Chen's Entity-Relationship Modelling [3] and Bubenko's Inferential Abstract Modelling [2], though these were still primarily of interest to the research community and not to the average IIS developer. Sølvberg proposed techniques for integrating some of these models [16].

Nonetheless, all of the pieces were in place for the earliest interactive information systems. Bank tellers used terminals to process user transactions. Travel agents installed terminals for an airline reservation system and learned the arcane text commands for checking schedules and booking reservations. Similarly, companies began using interactive systems for managing their business, including accounting and order processing. While many of these systems were very primitive by today's standards, they were the vanguard of the transition to interactive computing.

4 The Origins of User Software Engineering

The User Software Engineering (USE) methodology was conceived during this period (1975-1980) [19]. USE added the user perspective to function and data design for overall system design. At that time, systems were frequently imposed on users, and users rarely participated in definition and design of a system. Systems were architected top-down or bottom-up.

However, users have little interest in the structure of the system; their only concern is whether the system makes it easier for them to get their job done. What was needed for an IIS was not top-down design, but rather outside-in design, where "outside" represents the user's perception of the system. *Outside-in modelling* is one of the most important concepts of the USE methodology. By emphasizing the external view of a system, it became much easier to communicate with users.

Each user interaction with the system was viewed as an event that could trigger an activity and/or a response. For example, the system could display a menu of choices to the user, with the user's input determining the program action, eventually leading to either program termination or another request for user input.

The user interaction and the system behaviour were modelled as a hierarchical set of transition diagrams. This approach had two major benefits. First, even on paper, it was possible to walk through a dialogue with a potential user of a system, validating the overall scenario. Second, and more significant, transition diagrams are a formal, executable model, making it possible to build an executable version of the emerging system.

The executable nature of transition diagrams led to the most important innovation of the USE methodology: *rapid prototyping of user interfaces*. The state transition diagrams, including specification of the user inputs and system outputs, were encoded in a transition diagram language TDL. This language also included the ability to specify executable program units. A tool, RAPID/USE, was built to interpret the TDL and execute the associated program units. In this way, RAPID/USE could be used both for prototyping the user interface and for running a complete program.

In this way, users could begin to work with the emerging system at a very early stage of development, to the extent that they could actively contribute to the definition of the system and the style of the user interface. This notion of *user involvement in the software development process* is, in many respects, the central idea of the USE methodology. The RAPID/USE system also gathered metrics on user behaviour, making it possible to track error conditions, task completion times and other measures of usability.

In general, developers would start by designing part of the user interface, implementing it and adding functions or pseudo-functions as place holders, as well as beginning design of the relational database model. This *incremental approach to application development* was a sharp contrast to the waterfall approach in widespread use at the time. This approach is very much in line with today's agile methodologies [7].

The ability to separate the user interface component from the program operations led to another significant concept of the USE methodology: *a three-tier architecture*. This notion was very similar to the Model-View-Controller (MVC) approach first presented by Reenskaug [11].

Fig. 1. The three-tier architecture of the USE methodology (from [24])

This architecture shows the separation between the various components of the information system, anticipating client-server systems of the early 1990's and modern n-tier architectures. In addition, it shows the possibility of associating multiple user interfaces with a set of system operations. Such an approach permitted separate interface designs for novice and expert users, as well as an application programming interface that could be used to drive test cases or to integrate the system with another system.

5 Third Generation: Personal Computers and WIMP

The third generation focused on three dramatic changes in computing systems: graphical user interfaces (GUIs), powerful personal computers and computer networking. Rudimentary GUIs were built for Pong, PacMan, Spacewar and other arcade games, but GUIs were not generally available for general purpose systems until the release of the Apollo and Sun workstations in 1982 and the Apple Macintosh™, with its integrated windowing system, in 1984. With the Macintosh, the user interface shifted from the alphanumeric screen of video terminals to a bitmapped display using an interface style known as WIMP (windows, icons, menus and pointer). The GEM GUI provided a similar interface for PC DOS about a year later and supported colour as well. Microsoft Windows was announced about the same time, but it was not until Windows 3.1 was released in 1992 that PC users had a widely used GUI.

The growth of personal desktop computing created a revolutionary change in applications. Previously, users had worked with "dumb" terminals, with all of the computing being done on a remote machine. Suddenly, the personal computer could run applications locally or emulate a terminal running a remote program. From a software perspective, the WIMP approach came with a set of libraries, application programming interfaces (APIs) and user interface guidelines for building applications using each windowing system, with the result that there was a great deal of commonality among GUIs on a particular computing platform. Many platform vendors offered incentives to software vendors to comply with the GUI guidelines, and users came to expect applications to comply with platform standards. By the early 1990's, new applications were being built with GUI interfaces, though many older enterprise applications still used alphanumeric interfaces.

In the same period, DBMSs became widely available. With the widespread adoption of Unix, C became an important programming language for IIS applications, with C-based APIs for the windowing systems and the DBMSs.

These advances led to significant changes in methods and tools for IIS development. Instead of a text-based interaction with a file system, developers now wrote C code to build GUI interfaces on personal computers and to connect their application to local and remote RDBMSs. The MVC architecture and the WIMP interface were well-suited to an object-oriented programming paradigm, for which the C++ language was widely adopted.

With these technology advances, the USE tools were no longer appropriate for prototyping of user interfaces. The WIMP interface could not be easily modelled with the hierarchy of state transition diagrams that worked for text-based systems, since there would be far too many states and transitions.

However, the *process* advocated in the USE methodology remained valid: use a succession of prototypes of the user interface to elicit user requirements and to implement increasing functionality of the IIS. From there, various user inputs could be associated with program actions that included the database operations for the various IIS functions. The emergence of standard mechanisms for database access and for GUI management led to common architectures for IIS development, making the development process more efficient and the resulting system more robust.

The USE methodology could be used with advanced 4GL systems, such as PowerBuilder (now owned by Sybase), a rapid application development system including screen design and database access mechanisms. Power-Builder, as with many other 4GL systems, was designed to be used in a client-server environment, providing the GUI interface on the user's local machine and network connectivity to a remote RDBMS.

In the area of software methods, structured approaches were being supplanted by object-oriented approaches, using hybrid notations such as OMT [12] and OOSD [23], pure OO notations such as Booch's clouds [1] and the use case approach of Jacobson [5]. The OO approach and the use case notation worked well for the design of an IIS, since there is a mapping between these logical concepts and the implementation.

Another key development of this generation was the growth of open source software, paralleling the development of the commercial software industry. Among the software packages released in source format were Berkeley Unix, the Ingres RDBMS, the USE rapid prototyping tools and the GNU software (Emacs, GCC etc.). Many of these free and open source components were suitable for inclusion in other packages, thereby reducing the time and effort needed to build new applications.

6 Fourth Generation: The World Wide Web and Multi-tier Systems

The next major advance in technology for IIS was driven by the invention of the World Wide Web (including the HTTP protocol, the HTML language and URLs) by Tim Berners-Lee and his colleagues at CERN in 1989, followed by the development and release of the Mosaic graphical Web browser, developed by Marc Andreesen and Eric Bina at the US National Center for Supercomputing Applications (NCSA) and released in late 1993. Andreesen and Bina commercialized their work at Netscape Communications, releasing the Netscape Navigator browser in 1994, a key milestone in the evolution of the Internet from a research tool to a ubiquitous resource for networked communications and services.

The Web brought forth a new generation of user interfaces and a new way of thinking about applications and their development. There was a vast investment in new Web-based businesses, virtually all of which had the characteristics of an IIS, using a Web browser as the "local" front end connected to a remote server that implemented program behaviour and accessed one or more databases and other remote services. The mediation between the web browser and the server-side application code was the Common Gateway Interface (CGI), a standard way for an HTTP server to pass a user request to an application program and to receive data back to forward to the user.

For existing client-server systems, the advent of the Web provided an opportunity to replace a platform-specific GUI with a browser-based GUI as a way to modernize their systems, keeping much of the server-side infrastructure in place. However, the vast majority of Web applications were written from scratch and therefore had no need to accommodate older technologies. What was most important for many of the new start-up businesses was to get their website up and running as quickly as possible, as a way to gain a competitive advantage on potential competitors and to generate revenue for their business. In an earlier paper [21], we showed how our original implementation to the CRIS Conference Management System example [20] could be modified to present a Web interface.

Interactive web systems could be divided into those that needed support for a large number of concurrent interactions and those that didn't. For the latter category, new scripting languages, including Perl, Python and PHP, emerged. Clicking on an image map or on a web form "Submit" button could be associated with a server-side action implemented in one of these (or other) languages. These actions often included access to remote files and databases, with retrieved data formatted into HTML and passed through the CGI for display in the user's browser.

High volume and critical systems, such as those for e-commerce, travel and financial applications, needed a more robust and secure infrastructure, including server-side load balancing, firewalls, routers and support for transactions. While these systems were logically three-tier systems, they were, in practice, N-tier systems, replicating the web servers and application servers, as well as adding clustered databases, content delivery systems, media streaming servers and/or online payment gateways. Many of these applications were built using what is now called Java Platform, Enterprise Edition (Java EE, formerly J2EE), which provides built-in support for access to shared resources and many other features needed for creating these sophisticated web applications.

Over time, standard approaches for building such systems have emerged. For example, Sun Microsystems, which has controlled the Java standard until recently, has led the creation of a set of development guidelines, patterns and blueprints for building Java EE applications [8].

As Web applications have grown to predominate older client-server applications, the term "Web application" has effectively supplanted the term "interactive information system", even though it is slightly narrower in some respects.

Design and development of Web applications presents some new technical challenges, which have been addressed by a broad variety of new tools. As with older applications, the skills needed for design of the GUI are quite different from those needed to implement the functionality of the system. Over the past decade, tools for design of the Web interface have evolved from text-based HTML editors to WYSIWYG design tools (e.g., NVU and FrontPage) to web site design tools capable of applying a template, cascading style sheets and links to CGI actions (e.g., Dreamweaver). Developers without graphical design experience can select from a vast number of pre-built site templates, making it quite straightforward to create a prototype of the user interface and to test it with several different web browsers on popular platforms (Windows, MacOS, Linux).

The design process for the conceptual data model, now often called "information architecture", has remained relatively unchanged over the years. The ideas pioneered by Chen, Bubenko and others not only remain in widespread use, but have also been incorporated into numerous other modelling notations, such as the Unified Modelling Language (UML) [13].

The widespread use of scripting languages for Web applications is very helpful for rapid prototyping and for the application of agile methodologies. One can iteratively define the database schema, adding new tables and columns to the schema as needed and writing the scripts to connect the actions specified in the HTML code to the appropriate computational and database modification actions.

7 Fifth Generation: Richer User Interface, Application Generation Tools and Open Source

Among the primary difficulties in building Web applications are building usable Web user interfaces and making the application robust, scalable and secure. Web application performance is critical to the success of a site, since users quickly grow impatient with slow response times. Poor performance may be caused by any or all of the following:

- large images or streaming media transferred to the user's browser;
- the nature of the HTTP protocol, which requires a separate call to the server for each item to be displayed in the browser
- inefficient database design or coding
- high traffic volume for the web site or a service used by the application, as well as high overall Internet traffic

While this list is not complete, it serves to illustrate the complexity of building Web applications and the importance of the user interface design. Over the past few years, there has been a great deal of effort expended on overcoming these problem areas. We discuss three of these efforts:

7.1 AJAX (Asynchronous JavaScript and XML)

The technologies comprising AJAX are intended to reduce the amount of data traffic between the server and the browser by avoiding the need to reload an entire web page each time the user requests a change, with the result being a richer user experience. Many "Web 2.0" websites, such as Gmail, Basecamp and Flickr, use this approach, which also facilitates the development and use of Web applications offered as a service, such as the Zoho Office Suite and productivity tools. There are more than 100 toolkits to aid in the development of these interfaces, including toolkits developed by IBM (Dojo), Yahoo, Google and numerous start-ups.

Use of such a toolkit is certainly a requirement for rapid prototyping of user interfaces, since hand coding of the Ajax interface can be extremely time-consuming and error-prone. Since the primary goal of prototyping is to gain a better understanding of the user requirements, it is difficult to justify additional time and effort on GUI design at the earliest stages of a project, and it is often better to defer tuning the GUI until the use cases and functional requirements have been determined.

7.2 Application Generation Tools

Automatic generation of applications is a longstanding goal of the software development community and many development tools (e.g., Software through Pictures [22]) and 4GLs (e.g., PowerBuilder) have aimed to generate part of all of an application from high level or visual development tools. The Object Management Group has been the primary sponsor for the

Model Driven Architecture project, which allows specification of the high-level architecture of a system independent of its implementation technology. Many companies have built products intended to generate an architecture from such a specification [9].

Automatic generation of a Web application is not easy, as it requires generation of the user interface, the database schema and the application logic in a way that links the separate pieces to one another. However, a vast body of knowledge about construction of Web applications has emerged, and there are now a variety of approaches. For many common types of Web applications, there are now website builder tools (e.g., City-Max and Caspio Bridge) with which one can quickly create a customized site. Similarly, Wiki tools (e.g., MediaWiki) and content management systems (e.g., Drupal) can be used to rapidly build specialized applications. Zou and Zhang [25] have described a framework for automatic generation of e-commerce web applications.

The Rails framework [17], built for the Ruby language [18], follows a different approach. Its creators describe Rails as "a full-stack framework for developing database-backed web applications according to the Model-View-Control pattern." When you create a new application with Rails, it generates the application framework automatically, using a database schema that you provide. It generates Ruby code to produce a basic web-based interface. Powerful Web applications, such as the Basecamp collaborative project management tool (http://www.basecamphq.com), have been developed with Rails.

For the CRIS conference management application, one could start by defining the mailing list table as follows:

```
CREATE table mailing_list
(name varchar (30) not null primary key,
affiliation varchar (63),
detail_address varchar (255),
postcode varchar (15),
city varchar (30),
country varchar (30));
```

The generation process creates a web-based form with the fields linked to the columns of the table, with the needed HTML code being generated by the Rails framework. Showing the use of Rails for the entire conference management system is beyond the scope of this paper; a significant amount of hand coding in Ruby is needed above and beyond the parts that can be generated automatically. Nonetheless, Ruby on Rails goes a long way toward automated generation of a Web application.

7.3 Open Source Software

Free, libre and open source software (FLOSS) products have been widely used for many years. Among the most prominent of these open source products are the GNU Emacs text editor, the GNU Compiler Collection, Berkeley Unix, the Apache web server, the Eclipse development framework, the MySQL and PostgreSQL DBMSs, the JBoss Java EE application server, various distributions of Linux and scripting languages, including Perl, Python, PHP and Ruby. Today, there are hundreds of widely used open source products and thousands of open source projects.

FLOSS products, both commercial and non-commercial, have made significant inroads into companies to support their software infrastructure. The Apache HTTP server, for example, is used for more than 60% of all websites. Beyond that, many FLOSS components have been integrated into leading software products. For example, SugarCRM is used with the Apache HTTP server, MySQL or PostgreSQL and PHP. In addition, many of the most heavily used websites, including Google and Yahoo, are built on FLOSS technologies, and the Windows operating system includes licensed open source components.

More than 60% of Java developers now use the Eclipse development environment, causing vendors of traditional closed source environments, such as BEA and Borland, to link their development tools to Eclipse. As FLOSS products have grown in use, they have found their way into virtually every organization, either intentionally or accidentally.

Early FLOSS projects were focused on development tools, small components and middleware. In many cases, the project would create a FLOSS replacement for a piece of commercial software, matching the external specifications so that the open version could serve as a replacement for the closed one. More recently, there has been a growth in FLOSS applications, such as SugarCRM and OrangeHRM, that build upon an open source infrastructure.

Rather than designing and writing the CRIS conference management application from scratch, one now has the option of using an open source conference management system. The SourceForge repository (http://www.sf.net) contains more than 140,000 open source projects (of varying quality and maturity). Among them is the IAPR COMMENCE Conference and Meeting Management System [14]. COMMENCE uses an HTTP web server, along with MySQL and PHP. Since those components were already running on my server, it was possible to download COMMENCE, install it in the HTTP server directory, run the setup script to create the database and immediately use the application. All of the software was freely available and the COMMENCE system comes very close to meeting the original requirements for the CRIS system. A screen of the COMMENCE application is shown in Figure 2.

The availability of this existing and freely usable open source project completely transforms the application development process. This unchanged version of the COMMENCE application can serve as a working prototype for the desired application, and the source code can be modified to improve the user interface, as well as to address missing requirements and remove unwanted functionality from the original version. The total time required to find and install the application was less than an hour. Methodologies such as User Software Engineering and the Rational Unified Process [6] become essentially irrelevant in this setting.

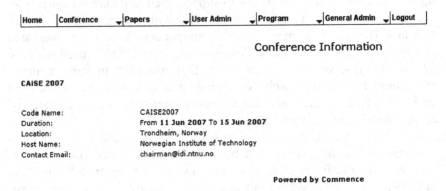

Fig. 2. Screen for COMMENCE Conference Management System

Open source software is transforming the software industry and shifting the traditional build vs. buy decision process. There are a growing number of open source alternatives to traditional closed source applications and tools. As their numbers grow, developers will increasingly look toward these open source packages as key components for systems that they are designing and developing. This growing inventory of high quality FLOSS components may have a bigger impact on Web application development than any other aspect.

8 Conclusion

The nature of interactive systems has changed drastically over the lifetime of today's computer science community. Severe limitations in storage capacity and processing speed are rarely an issue today. The nature of the user interface is much more intuitive, though also much more complex. The body of existing tools provides much more powerful application development capabilities than was previously. Furthermore, the presence of high quality existing applications and application frameworks means that fewer new applications need to be built from scratch, but rather by reusing and modifying existing software. Such an approach implies a revolutionary change in system development methodologies. For a method such as User Software Engineering, the key concepts remain valid, but may be less relevant as new development builds on existing code.

Future applications will certainly take advantage of new technologies in user interface development. Work is already well underway in developing web applications for mobile devices, addressing the challenge of providing a good user experience with the limited display area, restricted input mechanisms and relatively low bandwidth of current mobile devices. Among the approaches for overcoming these restrictions are voice-based applications, which remain quite limited in scope, but which could eventually overcome many of the current difficulties in using web applications.

Other advances are harder to predict, but continuing change is a certainty. It would have been nearly impossible to predict today's Web applications from the information systems of the 1960's described in Section 2. Forty years from now, future generations of information systems specialists will likely be using technologies that we cannot easily imagine.

References

[1] Booch, G. Object-Oriented Analysis and Design, 2nd ed. Reading, MA: Addison Wesley, 1993.
[2] Bubenko, JA, Jr. IAM: an Inferential Abstract Modelling Approach to Design of Conceptual Schema. ACM SIGMOD Toronto, Canada, 1977, 62-74.
[3] Chen, Peter P-S. The Entity-Relationship Model – Toward a Unified View of Data. ACM Transactions on Database Systems, 1976; 1: 9-36.
[4] DeMarco, T. Structured Analysis and System Specification. Prentice-Hall, Englewood Cliffs, NJ, 1979.
[5] Jacobson, I, Christerson, M, Jonsson, P, Overgaard, G. Object-Oriented Software Engineering-A Use Case Driven Approach. Addison-Wesley, Reading, MA, 1992.
[6] Kruchten, P. The Rational Unified Process: an Introduction. 3rd ed. Addison Wesley,Reading, MA, 2003
[7] Larman, C. Agile and Iterative Development: a Manager's Guide. Addison-Wesley, Reading, MA, 2003.
[8] http://java.sun.com/blueprints/enterprise/index.html
[9] http://www.omg.org/mda/committed-products.htm

[10] Parnas, DL. On the Criteria to be used in Decomposing Systems into Modules. Communications of the ACM, 1972; 15:1053-1058.

[11] Reenskaug, T. "Thing-Model-View Editor: an Example from a Planningsystem", Xerox PARC Technical Note, May, 1979 (available at http://heim.ifi.uio.no/~trygver/themes/mvc/mvc-index.html)

[12] Rumbaugh, J., et al. Object-Oriented Modelling and Design. Englewood Cliffs, NJ: Prentice-Hall, 1991.

[13] Rumbaugh, J, Jacobson, I, Booch, G. The Unified Modelling Language Reference Manual. Addison-Wesley, Reading, MA, 1999.

[14] http://sourceforge.net/projects/iaprcommence/

[15] Stevens, W, Myers, GJ, Constantine, LL. Structured Design. IBM Systems Journal, 1974; 13: 115-139

[16] Sølvberg, A. A Draft Proposal for Integrating System Specification Models. In: Olle, TW, Sol, HG, Verrijn-Stuart, AA (eds.) Information Systems Design Methodologies: a Comparative Review. North-Holland, Amsterdam, 1982.

[17] Thomas, D, Hansson, D, et al.. Agile Web Development with Rails. 2nd ed. Pragmatic Bookshelf, Raleigh, NC, 2006.

[18] Thomas, D, Fowler, C, Hunt, A. Programming Ruby, 2nd ed. Pragmatic Bookshelf, Raleigh, NC, 2005.

[19] Wasserman, A.I., "USE: a Methodology for the Design and Development of Interactive Information Systems," In: Formal Models and Practical Tools for Information Systems Design, ed. Schneider, H-J. North-Holland, Amsterdam, 1979, 31-50.

[20] Wasserman, AI, "The User Software Engineering Methodology: an Overview," In: Olle, TW, Sol, HG, Verrijn-Stuart, AA (eds.) Information Systems Design Methodologies: a Comparative Review. North-Holland, Amsterdam, 1982, 591-628.

[21] Wasserman, AI, "User Software Engineering: a Retrospective", In Brinkkemper, S, Lindencrona, E, and Sølvberg, A (eds.) Information Systems Engineering. Springer, Berlin, 2000, 149-158.

[22] Wasserman, AI, Pircher P, "A Graphical, Extensible Integrated Environment for Software Development," ACM SIGPLAN Notices, 22, 1 131-142. (Proc. ACM SIGSOFT/SIGPLAN Symposium on Practical Software Development Environments)

[23] Wasserman, AI, Muller, RJ, Pircher, P. "The Object-Oriented Structured Design Notation for Software Design Representation", IEEE Computer, 23(3)

[24] Wasserman, AI, Pircher, P, Shewmake, D, et al. Developing Interactive Information Systems with the User Software Engineering Methodology. IEEE Transactions on Software Engineering, 1986; 12: 326-345.

[25] Zou, Y, Zhang, Q, "A Framework for Automatic Generation of Evolvable E-Commerce Workplaces Using Business Processes", Proc. 2006 International Conference on Software Engineering, Shanghai, 2006, 799-802.

Conceptual Alignment of Software Production Methods

Óscar Pastor, Arturo González, Sergio España

Valencia University of Technology, Valencia, España

Abstract. From an Information Systems (IS) perspective, a myriad of specific approaches exist to deal with the different parts of a software production process. How to align them correctly taking a conceptual approach is still a very open problem. Instead of facing how to incrementally improve pre-existing methods, more and more proposals that are based on different paradigms or combine current IS concepts in some apparently innovative way are introduced. The conclusion of all of this is that, more than ever, we should concentrate on the essentials of IS modelling. A set of precise concepts is essential to be able to understand what each technique offers. A conceptual reference framework is needed to appropriately align the different proposals. This work presents a conceptual framework to be used for the conceptual alignment of software production methods. As a practical application, it is applied to the OO-Method, which is a conceptual model-based software production method, in order to show how the different pieces of the method fit the proposed framework conceptually.

1 Introduction

What is a software production process? It should be easy to answer such an apparently simple question. But if we ask this (apparently) simple question to either an academic or an industrial audience, there will probably be as many different answers as people. Again, if we add some simple adjectives, such as correct, or complete, or efficient (in relation to the software production process they describe), things will get even worse. The fact is that, after several decades of intensive theoretical and practical work, properly characterizing a specific software production process is still a very difficult task. Why is it so complicated?

Even though we obtained a huge number of different answers, we could conclude that there is some basic agreement on the fundamentals. No matter how a software production is defined, there is a set of phases that include a higher-level phase that deals with Requirements Modelling, a subsequent phase that deals with Conceptual Modelling, and a lower-abstraction level phase that is oriented to Design and Implementation.

However, even if this generic structure is accepted, things remain complicated. If we refer to Requirements Modelling, there is some confusion when Requirements Modelling is related to Business Modelling, or Business Process Modelling, or even Organizational Modelling. There are early and late requirements, different concepts and notations for business process modelling, goal-oriented techniques (KAOS, i*), scenario-oriented approaches (most of which are use case-based); the list could go on.

When an attempt is made to obtain a conceptual schema from any of these higher-level models, too many questions arise: how can a conceptual schema be derived from a requirements model? What if the process is started from a goal-oriented model? Is a functional, use case-based model ever useful in accomplishing this model transformation? How can non-functional requirements be properly represented? Can a goal model be directly transformed into a conceptual schema? Should this conceptual schema be object-oriented for the sake of understandability? Does it make sense to use aspect-oriented technology? If so, at what level? (Since the use of early aspects to deal with requirements generates aspect-oriented conceptual models.) Is object-oriented more convenient than aspect-oriented or vice versa? Or should both of them be ignored?

There are specific software production processes that are designed to provide an operational answer to the need for an appropriate solution. Normally, they come under the label of methods, and are based on a chosen paradigm. Examples of these are the OO-Method [18] for an object-oriented method; Tropos [3] for an agent-oriented method; Early Aspects [1,11] for an aspects-based proposal; and some generic proposals (normally based on UML [14]) which include the RUP [7] and Wisdom [13].

Finally, there are a myriad of specific techniques to deal with different parts of the process. However, there is still no proposal that deals successfully with the problem of correctly aligning these techniques. More than ever, it is necessary to concentrate on the essentials of Information Systems (IS) modelling. A set of precise concepts is essential to be able to understand what each technique offers. A conceptual reference framework that is based on a set of relevant and significant concepts is needed to confront this *methodological Tower of Babel*.

The use of basic frameworks of reference is a well-known, successful strategy, that is widely used in sound IS research. For instance, a basic framework for performance engineering during IS development is proposed in [15]. The strategy of IS modelling presented in [16] has been properly adapted to the context and objectives our work. Since the inherent complexity of IS is in the origin of the definition of diverse software development processes, and since different methods view the IS design and implementation from different perspectives, our goal is to identify a basic set of concepts of reference. Our final objective is to use this framework to characterize the different perspectives, strategies, and views of a given method. This characterization is called a conceptual alignment of a method with respect to the proposed framework, which shows how a given proposal relates to the basic concepts of our framework. This framework is used to classify any software production method from a unified conceptual base. It also will help us to understand the current situation of Software Engineering and to propose future lines of research from a very precise and well-analyzed context.

The conclusions obtained from the use of this framework are relevant because it highlights the various limitations of current software development methods. It also helps to clarify frequent misunderstandings that can be found in the literature, and it identifies deficiencies in the underlying criteria. For example, most methods offer poor communicational analysis of the IS. Communication is not always properly considered. Managing communication properly in IS development is fundamental, especially in the current socio-economic context where IS are more and more complex and need to be properly integrated and aligned with organizational needs. To fulfill our objectives, the main IS concepts are presented in Sect. 2, taking the FRISCO proposal [5] as a starting point. Sect. 3 presents an extension that properly incorporates the communicational perspective, which makes up a conceptual reference framework. Sect. 4 describes the application of this framework using the OO-Method, as an example. Finally, Sect. 5 presents further issues related to the application of the framework as well as some conclusions.

2 Core Elements Borrowed from FRISCO

As stated by Mylopoulos in [12], the use of conceptual models for Information Systems (IS) engineering was launched by Sølvberg in [20] and comprehensively represented in Bubenko's Conceptual Information Model [4]. A reasonable degree of maturity of the use of these models was attained during the 80's. The FRISCO reports are a good reflection of this. If a framework for IS is required, the FRISCO proposal is, in our opinion, a very appropriate starting point. Before introducing our proposal we present some basic definitions that were used as a source.

As their own name states, IS are systems. Therefore, they are better understood from a systemic perspective. The raison d'être of an IS is to support the mission of a particular organization. This Organizational System (OS) is interested in monitoring a certain Subject System (see Fig. 1). However, the imbrications between these systems can be quite varied, depending on the degree of overlapping. Also note that we do not make a distinction here between IS and Computerized Information (Sub-)Systems.

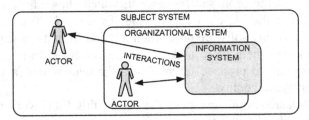

Fig. 1. The context of organizational management Information Systems

Organizations are often very complex systems. They are characterized by the existence of actors who require the adequate knowledge and resources to carry out their tasks. When something of interest happens in the environment of the organization, this event is reported to the IS by interacting with it. In order to reason unambiguously about IS, a framework of well-defined and related concepts is desirable. The following framework is based on the IFIP WG 8.1 Task Group results [5]. Several concepts are borrowed from the FRISCO conceptual framework, some of which are later extended to meet our needs.

According to FRISCO[1], A **transition** *is a special binary relationship between a pre-state and a post-state.*

A **transition occurrence** *is a specific occurrence of a transition. A set of transition occurrences is subject to strict partial ordering.*

An **action** *is a transition involving a non-empty set of actors in its pre-state, and, if not "destroyed" or "consumed" by the action, in its post-state as well, and involving a nonempty or empty set of other things (actands) as part of its pre-state, and having a nonempty or empty set of other things (actands) in its post-state.*

An **actor** *is a special thing conceived as being "responsible" or "responsive" and as being able to "cause" transitions.*

Let **actorOf** *be a function determining the actors performing an action.*

A **human actor** *is a responsible actor with the capabilities and liabilities of a normal human being, in particular capable of performing perceiv-*

---

[1] Definitions literally taken from the FRISCO proposal are shown in cursive.

ing actions, conceiving actions and representing actions. Then, let a non-human actor be any actor which is not human (e.g. sensors and other Computerized Information System components like a central processing unit).

An **actand** *is a thing involved in the pre-state or post-state of an action, not considered as an actor for that action.* An **input actand** (respectively **output actand**) *is a part of the pre-state (post-state) of an action, excluding the actors. The pre-state of an action is called its* **resources**.

Let **inputOf** *be a function determining the input actands of an action.*

Let **outputOf** *be a function determining the output actands of an action.*

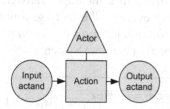

Notation
Triangles: Actors
Rectangles: Actions
Ovals: Actands
Lines: Actors perform actions
Arrows: Actands are input or output of actions

Fig. 2. FRISCO notation for the main elements and their relationships

The FRISCO notation for the main types of elements and their relationships (see Fig. 2) will be extensively used throughout the chapter.

The **goal** *of an action is a special input actand of that action, pursued by the actors of that action and stating the desired output state intentionally.*

Last, but not least, a **message** *is an actand composed of data, transmitted by one actor (the sender) via a channel (a medium), and intended for a non-empty set of other actors (the receivers).* Although a message transfer is a complex sequence of actions, we sometimes abstract some of its steps.

3 Towards a Precise Communicational View of IS

Some specializations of the concepts present in FRISCO help to achieve a better understanding of the complexity of Information Systems (IS).

We distinguish between external and internal actions. External actions are those which occur outside the boundaries of the IS. The changes that some external actions induce in the state of the Subject System are of great interest to the Organizational System. We refer to these external action occurrences as **events**. Since this word has been overloaded with different meanings, depending on the author, further explanation is necessary.

In the literature on real-time, embedded and control systems, the concept of event is often used in a broad sense: both external and internal transition occurrences are considered events. In programming environments, the term event designates any stimulus that interrupts a system component activity. In object-oriented techniques, events are also used in a generic fashion. An individual stimulus from one object to another is an event for Rumbaugh et al. [19]. According to Booch et al. [2], "in the context of state machine, an event is an occurrence of a stimulus that can trigger a state transition".

In contrast, we use the term event in a way similar to [6]. An event is a stimulus that occurs in the outside world to which the Organizational System must respond [21].

An **external message** is a message involved in a message transfer in which either the sender is communicating an event to the IS (e.g. a hotel clerk checking out a customer) or the IS is communicating facts upon petition of an actor belonging to the Organizational or Subject Systems.

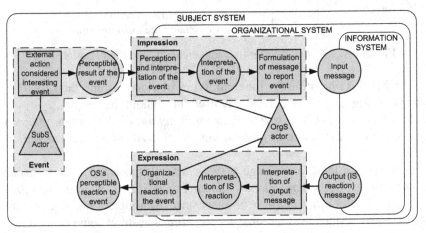

Fig. 3. Subject domain events trigger organizational responses

Fig. 3 shows an event occurring in the domain of the Subject System. An actor of the OS perceives this occurrence and reports it to the IS. The reaction of the OS to the event may have connative influence on the Subject System, but we preferred not to close the loop.

This figure makes use of FRISCO notation (see Fig. 1)[2]. Note that since the event is a transition occurrence, has no symbol assigned to it. It is, therefore, represented as an action that is performed by an actor of the subject domain, which is perceived as being of interest to the organization. FRISCO [5] defines the following OS external functions: **impression** is

---

[2] We extend the FRISCO notation with the use of rounded rectangles to denote the boundaries of the different systems involved. Also, in this particular diagram, dashed-lined geometrical shapes are used to denote a clustering of concepts.

the "conception of changes in the system domain as caused by the environment", and **expression** is the "conception of changes in the domain of the environment as caused by the system". These are related to the organizational actor's behaviour towards the event. For reasons of brevity, in some diagrams we do not include the sequence of actions that the event involves; that is, those elements outside the OS. Similarly, we will implicitly cluster the impression and expression actions in some of the subsequent diagrams. The focus will be placed on the interaction between organizational actors and the IS (which is not represented in Fig. 3).

3.1 From ISO82 to FRISCO98: It is all about Communication

Early in the 80's, an ISO report [6] presented a conceptual framework for IS, defining the basic interaction architecture shown in Fig. 4. According to this report, every IS reacts to messages with depending on different objectives. The objective of the IS is to memorize reported facts. The principle objective of the OS is to react to events.

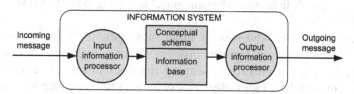

Fig. 4. Information System model according to ISO [6][3]

When it comes to comparing ISO and FRISCO[4] IS models, two issues should be addressed with respect to the ISO diagram (Fig. 4).

- **Intention**. ISO distinguishes between ingoing messages, which are intended to enter new information that the IS was not aware of, and outgoing messages, which are intended to recover information from the IS memory.
- **Communication**. Although bi-directionality is not explicitly drawn, ingoing and outgoing messages are, in actual fact, input and output dialogs, respectively. However, these dialogs are asymmetric. This is quite clear in the case of output dialogs: the objective of a listing is to retrieve facts from the system's memory, but some information input may be needed (e.g. report parameters like selection criteria). In general, this in-

---

[3] In Fig. 4, the diagram is not expressed in terms of the FRISCO notation, but according to the ISO report.

[4] In this chapter, when we refer to ISO, we mean [3]; by FRISCO, we mean [2]

put information is only used to generate the output, so it is not expected to be stored persistently.

FRISCO does not maintain this vision; their report presents a slightly different diagrammatic view of the IS, by focusing on the dialogical communication between the IS and its users. The input and output dialogs of ISO are generalized. Fig. 5 shows the FRISCO conception of the IS as a "channel for the message transfers between the various users" who want to "communicate about one and the same domain".

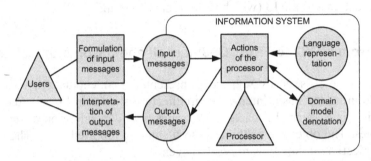

Fig. 5. Information System model according to FRISCO [5]

Users are actors who specify input messages to the processor and receive output messages from it. Processors are actors that are responsible for checking input messages, keeping the domain model denotation (i.e. the information base) logically consistent with the language representation (i.e. the conceptual model), and retrieving information to produce output messages; in short, a processor is responsible for the IS reaction to external stimuli. Both users and processors can be human or non-human.

FRISCO's description of the interaction between the users and the IS is a refinement of each of two dialogs defined by ISO. There is an implicit asynchrony between the ISO input and output dialogs, while in the FRISCO diagram, the interaction loop occurs synchronously. In summary, the diagrammatic view of an IS in ISO (Fig. 4) is projected in a forked fashion onto the FRISCO diagram (Fig. 5).

3.2 Further Refinement of the IS Model

Before refining the FRISCO IS model, we present an abstraction mechanism that is not addressed by FRISCO notation, but that will be used in subsequent diagrams. Some IS elements are generalized by placing them inside rectangles; these rectangles are marked by an icon that denotes the kind of elements they generalize (see Fig. 6.a). This syntactical resource is used for the sake of *diagrammatic economy*.

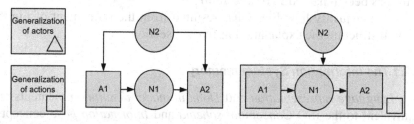

a) Generalizations   b) Diagram piece, no generalization   c) This one generalizes actions

Fig. 6. Generalization of Information System elements

Note that the pieces of diagram shown in Fig. 6 indicate two actions (A1 and A2) and two actands (N1 and N2). In Fig. 6.b, N2 is an input of both actions. In Fig. 6.c, the actions A1 and A2 have been generalized and the inputOf relationship between N2 and the generalization keeps the same semantics as in the former diagram: N2 is still an input for both actions.

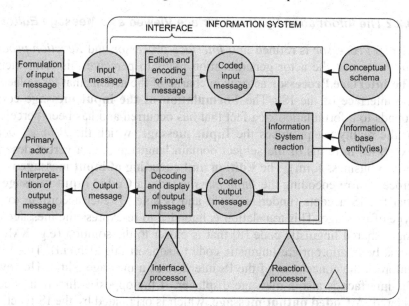

Fig. 7. Refined Information System model

Since our intention is to design a rich and expressive IS model, Fig. 5 is further decomposed by refining the IS processor and its actions. The following variations have been made to achieve Fig. 6. The interactive loop has been individualized to fit a single Subject System event reaction. Therefore, many elements are now named in singular terms; i.e. the *Users* actor has been renamed **Primary actor**.

To better justify how Fig. 7 has resulted from the refinement of Fig. 5, we will structure the explanation in five subsections.

3.2.1 The Information System memory

The *Language representation* and *Domain model denotation* elements are equivalent to the ISO *Conceptual schema* and *Information base* concepts, respectively. The **Conceptual schema** gathers the abstract knowledge of the OS; that is, the model of the IS memory, the types of facts the IS can register, and many rules about its behaviour. We highlight the fact that the information base is mainly composed of **Information base entities**; in the end, entities and their relationships are the IS memory imprints about Subject System facts. Due to the use that we make of the topological refinement, the *Conceptual schema* and the *Information base entities* are input for all the actions generalized inside the box.

3.2.2 The Information System Interface Viewed as a Message Editor

The IS *Processor* is refined into *Interface processor* and *Reaction processor* (note that the actor generalization helps to perceive this refinement). The **Interface Processor** actor is in charge of the actions that take place in the interface of the IS[5]. The **Formulation of the input message** corresponds to a formulation of a fact that has occurred and has been perceived in the reality[6]; it produces the **Input message**, which the *Primary actor* expresses in terms of the subject domain language (e.g. a verbal description, a business form). The **Edition and encoding of input message** is the process of re-encoding the *Input message* into a **Coded input message** so that the IS accepts (understands) it and is able to react according to the type of message. This translation is intended to re-express the message using a shared linguistic code [8] that is closer to the solution (e.g. XML is actually an appropriate linguistic code to support this element). This view enforces the conception of the IS interface as a message editor. However, the interface is also a message displayer, if the opposite direction is considered. A **Coded output message**, which is originated by the IS reaction, needs to be translated again to an external actor-intelligible **Output mes-**

---

[5] Note that one of the actorOf relationships crosses an action, for the sake of a nicer layout.

[6] The term reality should be taken from a Constructivist philosophical position.

sage and issued to the actor by means of a **Decoding and display of output messages** action. Note that both actions of the interface can make use of the information base (e.g., to help the user pick a business object without having to know its internal identifier).

3.2.3 The Information System Reaction

The *Actions of the processor* element in Fig. 5 has been decomposed into two interface actions (described above) and an *Information System reaction*. The **Reaction processor** performs the following steps of the **Information System reaction**: (1) it takes the *Coded input message* and checks if it corresponds to one of the expected types of messages (this knowledge is contained in the *Conceptual schema*); (2) then, it takes the needed facts from the information base; (3) it processes all this information according to a certain recipe of rules (i.e. an algorithm); (4) it updates the information base; (5) it produces the *Coded output message*. Obviously, the *Information System reaction* could be further refined to explicitly denote all these steps, but we chose to keep the diagrams simple.

3.2.4 The Organizational System Reaction

The OS reacts to Subject System events according to certain **Organizational Goals**, which are usually stated by organizational actors at the strategic level. Goals affect actions and can, therefore, be considered as input actands for any action being performed inside the boundaries of the OS. Fig. 8 shows a broad generalization of the organizational actions that are affected by *Organizational Goals*. Goals could be considered as the conceptual schema of an organization. A particular subset of these goals is the **Information System Goals**, which affects the IS actions.

Whenever one undertakes the modelling of any aspect of an IS, granularity emerges as an unavoidable issue to be tackled. Actions in general and organizational reactions in particular are susceptible to being treated at various granularity levels. The models presented in Fig. 7 and 8 are focused on interactions between an actor and the IS at the refinement level (granularity) of Subject System events. A so-called business activity could comprise several of these interactions, or even be decomposed into much lower granularity interactions. We will tiptoe round this thorny issue in this chapter, since it deserves to be tackled with great care and detail.

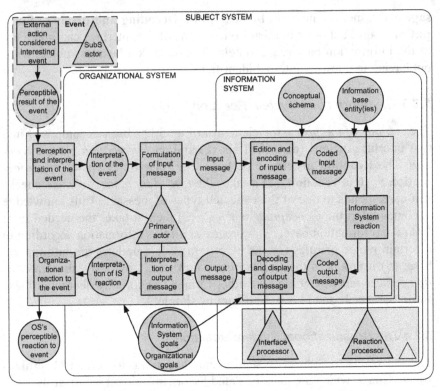

Fig. 8. Further refined Information System model

4 A Practical Application of the Conceptual Framework

The conceptual framework in Sect. 3 can be used to show the reasoning principles that are behind any specific software production method, independently of its core paradigm or its associated software process. As a practical example, we are going to apply the concepts to explain the OO-Method [18], which is a Conceptual Schema-Centric Software Development Method, that was developed at the Valencia University of Technology and that has been implemented commercially[7].

---

[7] OlivaNova model compiler by CARE Technologies http://www.care-t.com - Last visit: Jan-2007.

4.1 How IS Elements are Observed and Described

A software development method uses abstraction to reduce the complexity of the treated systems. Taking the system as a whole, the method defines a way to decompose it into smaller parts and proposes languages to describe these parts.

Each description of the IS in terms of modelling primitives is called a **perspective**. The primitives offered by the modelling language can be mapped to an upper-level conceptual framework like the one defined in Sect. 3. We call this mapping a **conceptual alignment**.

The model for an IS that we have presented constitutes an appropriate framework for dealing with IS components and their relationships. We considered two different strategies to represent it: a FRISCO-compliant (based on the concepts representation in Fig. 2 and on the abstraction mechanisms introduced at the beginning of Sect. 3.2), and a UML-like Class Diagram. We chose the FRISCO-based representation to define the conceptual alignment, because it is visually more intuitive for our purpose. We could also accomplish OCL-based navigations on the Class Diagram, but we believe the first option to be more understandable and practical from the conceptual point of view. In consequence, the conceptual alignment for a given method is represented as a view of the IS model (Fig. 8), where the IS elements are conveniently located, and are traversed (navigated) according to the techniques provided and applied by the method

When a given technique of a given method is analyzed, the navigation that corresponds to its conceptual alignment may not be complete. Many times, some elements are used and others are not. We refer to this as ellipsis. The **ellipsis** is the omission of certain type of IS elements in the description of an IS. This is an important issue because it allows us to better understand the particular characteristics of a method from the IS specification perspective. This ellipsis can be temporal or total. It is temporal when we do not consider a given element at a given instant in order to focus on other elements that associated with it, using the transitivity property. The ellipsis is total when the given method does not consider a particular IS element at all. In this case, there is a potential topic for discussion.

Before illustrating these issues using the OO-Method, is necessary to introduce the main characteristics of the method.

4.2 The OO-Method at a Glance

As briefly mentioned above, OO-Method is a software development method based on a clear separation between the Problem Space (**what** we want to build) and the Solution Space (**how** we are going to build it). The definition of a problem (the abstract description of an IS, represented in the corresponding Conceptual Schema) can be enacted regardless of any particular reification (concrete implementation of a software solution). This positions OO-Method as a sound methodological foundation on which to build tools that embrace the MDA directive of separating the logic of software systems from their (multiple) possible implementations.

The formalism underlying OO-Method is OASIS, a formal and object-oriented specification language for the specification of IS [17]. This formal framework provides a characterization of the conceptual elements needed to accurately specify an IS. It encompasses two main components: the Conceptual Model and the Execution Model. Since the Execution Model is the characterization of how a model is implemented in a target technology (e.g. Java, .NET), we will focus on the OO-Method Conceptual Model. The objective is to see how the method sets and provides the basic building units required to build a Conceptual Model for practical use.

The Conceptual Model comprises four complementary views: the Domain Model (or Object Model), the Dynamic Model, the Functional Model and the Presentation Model. All of them together constitute the whole Conceptual Model specification. These four views allow the definition of all structural and functional aspects of a system in an abstract (implementation-independent) yet accurate fashion by means of a set of modelling constructs. These conceptual primitives (or conceptual patterns) are conferred a precise semantics. Any of these conceptual patterns has a UML-based graphical notation, which hides the complexity of the underlying OASIS formal specification from the modeller. More details can be found in [18] and [10].

4.3 Conceptual Alignment of the OO-Method Conceptual-Modelling Phase

The following sequence of diagrams describes the OO-Method Conceptual Modelling phase in terms of its corresponding conceptual alignment. At each step, the same strategy is followed: we repeat the conceptual alignment graph of elements, and we "colour" its elements depending on the specification technique that is being considered. The notation contains:

- Elements that are being considered in the specification: a thick line with a grey background. This represents a basic element that is being described at that very step.
- Elements that are not considered in a given context: soft grey line and font. If these elements appear elements that are being specified, it is a

case of ellipsis. This case appears in the OO-Method between the elements *Interface processor* and *Information System reaction* when agents are assigned to class operations in Fig. 10.

- Elements already specified: they are represented as a normal dark line, with a grey background. It means that this element has been previously specified, and it is not relevant in the current specification step.

In accordance with this notation, we develop the following conceptual alignment of the OO-Method with respect to the reference framework.

4.3.1. Specification of the Information System Memory

We start by identifying the IS memory components. The specification of the static part of the OO-Method Domain Model is the natural starting point for the OO-Method proposal.

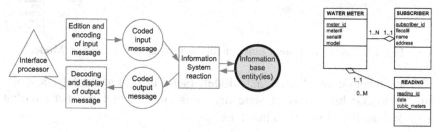

Fig. 9. Identifying the entities of the Domain Model

Fig. 9 shows how the specification of class attributes and class relationships constitutes the identification of the relevant entities of the Domain Model. It corresponds to the *Information Base Entities* in the conceptual framework. This is why this actand is represented with a thick line and grey background.

4.3.2 Specification of the Information System Reaction

Once the IS memory has been considered, it is time to assign system functionality to the entities of the Domain Model. We specify this under the umbrella of *Information System reaction*. This is covered in the OO-Method by determining class operations in the objectual Domain Model (see Fig. 10, right), by the state diagram that constitutes the OO-Method Dynamic Model (see Fig. 11, top right), and by the Functional Model, where the effect of every class operation on the object state is declaratively specified (see Fig. 11, bottom right).

In Fig. 10 we can see how the *Information System reaction* represents the action that directly interacts with the *Information base entities*, and how the *Interface processor* actor is responsible for specifying the operation that will be sent to the *Information System reaction* box. A clear example of ellipsis appears in the diagram. In this case the ellipsis was consciously introduced by the method, since the way the input message is edited and encoded is not the focus of these modelling components. As explained in Sect. 4.3.3, this is accomplished by a fourth OO-Method conceptual-modelling view named the Presentation Model.

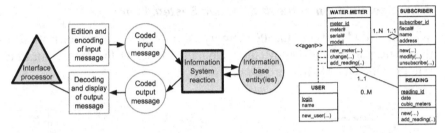

Fig. 10. Assigning system functionality to entities of the Domain Model

The Dynamic and Functional Models (see Fig. 11) accurately describe the behaviour by means of state diagrams and abstract instructions that specify how the IS reacts to input messages.

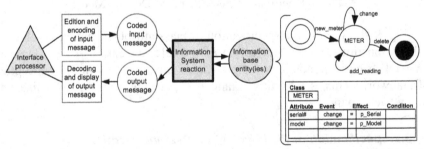

Fig. 11. Specifying behaviour and reaction in the Dynamic and Functional Models

4.3.3 Specification of the Information System Interface

Once static class architecture and system functionality (in the way of IS reaction) has been specified, the last step is the specification of the user interaction. In the OO-Method proposal, this is accomplished by creating the Presentation Model.

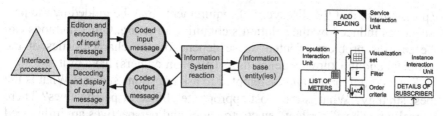

Fig. 12. Specifying edition and display of messages in the Presentation Model

Fig. 12 illustrates the corresponding conceptual alignment. In this case, the OO-Method Presentation Model (Fig. 12, right) is conceptually aligned with the actions of *Edition and encoding of input (output) messages*, which generates the *Coded input (output) message* actand. These messages are assumed to be properly processed by the IS, as specified in the models related to IS reaction (Sect. 4.3.2).

4.3.4 Specification of the Organizational System Reaction

It should be noted that the OS reaction, which is an element of the full conceptual framework, is not covered by the OO-Method Conceptual Modelling. This occurs because the requirements modelling phase is not subsumed by the conceptual modelling strategy provided by OO-Method. This can also be seen as an indication that the performed conceptual alignment could go beyond one specific phase (Conceptual Modelling) to cover other phases of a full software process associated to a given method. This inter-phase conceptual alignment can make the proposal even more powerful when applied to compare different methods.

This case study provides some interesting lessons that are discussed in the next section.

5 Concluding Remarks

The only way to properly confront the problem of understanding the essentials of any given software development method is to have a precise characterization of this set of concepts. The objective of this work is to establish this set of concepts.

Software production methods tend to suffer from a certain degree of rigidity with respect to their strategies. Some of them tend to be more method-centred; these are based on a sequential strategy of perspectives arranged by well-defined procedures. Others are more solution-centred; these emerge as a reaction to the dullness of method-centred attitudes and (pre)suppose that the discovery of requirements may be guided by the perspectives induced by the solution's cognitive structure. Other methods can be seen as problem-oriented; these depend on the characteristics of the problem and the knowledge the users (problem owners) have of it.

Even though one might be tempted to ask questions such as: What is the best strategy? What is the most appropriate choice of perspectives? There is really no "best" strategy, since strategies and perspectives are influenced by the problem to be solved. Having a common conceptual framework and performing the conceptual alignment of a method with respect to this common conceptual framework will enable us to understand the strategies and principles of any method.

The conceptual framework presented here follows the FRISCO tradition, and we have applied it to a specific software production method (the OO-Method). This framework can be applied to any other method. In future work, we are going to perform the same exercise with other well-known proposals based on different paradigms such as Wisdom [13] (UML, user-centred), Tropos [3] (agent-oriented), Early Aspects-based approaches [1,11], etc. This will open the door to further studies that deal with in-depth method understanding and comparison, which will help to identify weak points. In the case of OO-Method, we have detected the total ellipsis of the (external) communicational elements of the IS. This also appears to be common to other methods that we have begun to analyze, so we plan to give descriptive support to the usage of communicational-oriented perspectives, based on *Input* and *Output messages*. Since many definitions describe Information Systems as a tool for communication we believe it to be a promising line of research.

A comparison among various methods will also help to better understand the concept of quality in conceptual modelling, following the tradition of well-known previous works such as [9]. This comparison will enable an enhancement of the criteria underlying well-established methods. We hope that a better integration among the various strategies will provide a holistic integration which will benefit the current state of Software Engineering.

References

[1] Baniassad, E., Clements, P., Araújo, J., Moreira, A., Rashid, A., Tekinerdogan, B.: Discovering early aspects. IEEE Softw. **23**(1): 61-71 (2006)
[2] Booch, G., Rumbaugh, J., Jacobson, I.: *The Unified Modelling Language reference manual* (Addison-Wesley 1999)

[3] Bresciani, P., Perini, A., Giorgini, P., Giunchiglia, F., Mylopoulos, J.: TROPOS: an agent-oriented software development methodology. Autonomous Agents and Multi-Agent Systems 8(3): 203-236 (2004)

[4] Bubenko, J.: Information modelling in the context of system development. In: Proceedings IFIP Congress 1980, pp 395-411

[5] Falkenberg, E., Hesse, W., Lindgreeen, P., Nilsson, B., Oei, J., Rolland, C.;Stamper, R., Van Assche, F., Verrijn-Stuart, A., Voss, K.: FRISCO. A Framework of Information Systems Concepts. (IFIP WG 8.1 Task Grup Report 1998)

[6] Griethuysen, J.J.v. (ed): Information processing systems - Concepts and terminology for the conceptual schema and the information base. ISO TC97/SC5/WG3, publication ISO/TR 9007:1987 (1982)

[7] Jacobson, I., Booch, G., Rumbaugh, J.: *The Unified Software Development* (Addison-Wesley 1999)

[8] Jakobson, R.: The Speech Event and the Functions of Language. In: *On language*, ed by Monville-Burston, M., Waugh, L. R. (Harvard University Press 1990) pp 69-79

[9] Lindland, O.I., Sindre, G., Sølvberg, A.: Understanding quality in conceptual modelling. IEEE Softw. 11(2): 42-49 (1994)

[10] Molina, P.J., Meliá, J., Pastor, O.: JUST-UI: A user interface specification model. In: *Computer-Aided Design of User Interfaces III*, ed by Kolski, Ch., Vanderdonckt, J., 4th International Conference on Computer-Aided Design of User Interfaces CADUI'2002 (Kluwer 2002) pp 63-74

[11] Moreira, A., Rashid, A., Araújo, J.: Multi-dimensional separation of concerns in requirements engineering. In *Proceedings of RE 2005*, 13th IEEE International Conference on Requirements Engineering, Paris, France, August-September 2005 (IEEE Computer Society Washington DC 2005) pp. 285- 296

[12] Mylopoulos, J.: Information modelling in the time of the revolution. Inf. Syst. 23(3-4): 127-156 (1998)

[13] Nunes, N.J., Cunha, J.F.e.: Wisdom: a software engineering method for small software development companies. IEEE Softw. 17(5): 113-119 (2000)

[14] Object Management Group: Unified Modelling Language: Superstructure v. 2.0. http://www.omg.org/docs/formal/05-07-04.pdf (2005) Cited Jan 2007

[15] Opdahl, A.L., Sølvberg, A.: A framework for performance engineering during information system development. In *Proceedings of CAiSE 1992*, ed by Loucopoulos, P., 4th Conference on Advanced information Systems Engineering, Manchester, England, May 1992. Lecture Notes in Computer Science, vol 593. (Springer Berlin Heidelberg New York 1992) pp 65-87

[16] Opdahl, A.L., Sølvberg, A.: Conceptual integration of information system and performance modelling. In *Proceedings of IFIP WG 8.1 Working Conference on Information Systems Concepts: Improving the Understanding*, ed by Falklenberg, E.D, Rolland, C., Nasr-El-Dein El-Sayed, E.S., Alexandria, Egypt, April 1992. (North-Holland 1992) pp 273-294

[17] Pastor, O., Hayes, F., Bear, S. (1992) OASIS: An object-oriented specification language. In *Proceedings of CAiSE 1992*, ed by Loucopoulos, P., 4th Conference on Advanced information Systems Engineering, Manchester, Eng-

land, May 1992. Lecture Notes in Computer Science, vol 593. (Springer Berlin Heidelberg New York 1992) pp 348-363

[18] Pastor, Ó., Gómez, J., Insfrán, E., Pelechano, V.: The OO-method approach for information systems modelling: from object-oriented conceptual modelling to automated programming. Inf. Syst. **26**(7): 507-534 (2001)

[19] Rumbaugh, J., Blaha, M., Premerlani, W., Eddy, F., Lorensen, W.: *Object-oriented modelling and design.* (Prentice-Hall 1991)

[20] Sølvberg, A.: A contribution to the definition of concepts for expressing users' information systems requirements. In *Entity-Relationship Approach to Systems Analysis and Design*, ed by Chen, P., 1st International Conference on the Entity-Relationship Approach, Los Angeles, USA, (North-Holland 1980) pp 381-402

[21] Yourdon, E., *Modern structured analysis.* Yourdon Press Computing Series (Prentice-Hall 1989)

The Co-Development of System Requirements and Functional Architecture

Klaus Pohl[1,2], Ernst Sikora[1]

[1]Software Systems Engineering, University of Duisburg-Essen, Germany

[2]Lero - The Irish Software Engineering Research Centre

Abstract. It is widely recognized that in system development, innovative requirements and innovative architectural solutions need to be co-developed. Yet, no comprehensive method exists to support the co-development of requirements and architecture. This chapter describes the COSMOD-RE method for supporting the co-development of requirements and architectural artefacts at four distinct levels of abstraction. An overview on the method is provided, and the activities for supporting the development of system requirements and the functional system architecture are described.

1 Introduction

The evolution of information systems from centralized architectures into distributed architectures has already been observed, for instance, in [18]. Since then, information systems have evolved further. Today, innovative software-intensive systems have to incorporate both, information system and embedded system components in order to provide the required functionality. A recent example is the radio frequency identification (RFID) technology which integrates information systems (e.g. inventory systems) with a network of software-intensive embedded systems (smart tag readers). Furthermore, systems that were traditionally designed purely as (real-time) embedded systems have to incorporate information systems technology in order to realize innovative functionality. For example, the increased amount of data that needs be processed in a modern vehicle has raised the need for persistent data storage and reliable data retrieval capabilities (see e.g. [19]). Similar examples can be found in various other domains such as telecommunications or building automation. In short, a convergence of information systems and embedded systems can be observed in innovative systems development. The convergence facilitates new system functionality but also increases the complexity of the resulting systems and therefore imposes a new challenge for the developers.

When the development of an innovative software-intensive system is initiated, typically not much more is known about the planned system than a vision of the changes (or enhancements) that the system should bring about in its application domain (cf. [9]). An example of a vision is: "Develop a driver assistance system that maintains a safe following distance on motor-ways".[1] The stakeholders (customers, users, requirements engineers, managers, architects, etc.) have different needs and wishes concerning, e.g., the system usage, the technology that the system will be based on, or the development process. In order to facilitate the implementation of the system, the stakeholders must achieve a consolidated view of the system including the specification of the system's functionality, behaviour, and technical structure(s). Traditionally, two kinds of processes are performed to support the specification task:

- *The requirements engineering process*: This process is predominantly concerned with the problem space. In this process, the stakeholders develop the requirements for the new system by collaboratively performing elicitation, negotiation, documentation, and validation activities.
- *The architectural design process*: This process is predominantly concerned with the solution space. In this process, the stakeholders develop a (core) technical solution for the planned system including, for instance, the technical system structure which defines the configuration of interacting embedded system and information system components.

The development of a new system can be regarded as a learning process, in which the stakeholders explore the problem, define requirements for the planned system, and incrementally build a solution structure. The emerging solution points to areas of the problem space that require a more in-depth exploration. The new insights gained typically entail further iterations of exploring the problem space, defining requirements and elaborating on the solution. In this spirit, Nuseibeh [13] has proposed twin-peaks, a simple spiral model for the co-development of requirements and design. According to the twin peaks model, the development proceeds in a spiral from coarse-grained to detailed requirements and architectural definitions.

However, presently, no method exists to support the co-development of requirements and architectural artefacts. The twin-peaks model itself does

---

[1] The "adaptive cruise control" system (ACC) is used as an example throughout this chapter. For details about the ACC system, see [3].

not provide methodical guidance. For instance, it does not define what coarse or detailed means with respect to requirements and design artefacts and activities. It does not indicate how the gap between coarse and detailed artefacts can be bridged and what relations exist between requirements and architecture. Other approaches that are applied to support the transition from requirements to architecture such as architecture description languages, goal-based approaches, and problem frames have been analyzed by Galster et al. with the result that none of the approaches closes the gap between requirements and architecture (for details, see [5]).

The remainder of this contribution is structured as follows. Section 2 presents the key principles of our method COSMOD-RE (sCenario and gOal based SysteM develOpment methoD) for supporting the co-development of requirements and architectural artefacts for software-intensive systems. Section 3 defines the activities for part of our method. Section 4 summarizes this contribution.

2 Overview of the COSMOD-RE Method

The main goal of the COSMOD-RE method is to support the refinement of an overall system vision into a coherent set of requirements and architectural artefacts. In order to manage high system complexity, the COSMOD-RE method structures the development artefacts and activities by means of a hierarchy of abstraction layers. The development artefacts at the different abstraction layers are produced by three distinct co-design processes. Each co-design process includes the co-development of two viewpoints, the requirements viewpoint and the architecture viewpoint.

In the following, we briefly characterize the abstraction layers and the two viewpoints (Section 0), define key requirements and architectural artefacts at two layers (Section 0), and structure the development process in three co-design processes and five sub-processes (Section 0).

2.1 Abstraction Layers for Requirements and Architecture

The use of layers (constituting different levels of abstraction) is an established concept to manage a high system complexity. By considering the planned system at a high level of abstraction, a comprehensive view of the system and its benefits for the users can be conveyed to all stakeholders. At lower layers, details are specified that are required by engineers and software developers to construct the system. The layers defined in the COSMOD-RE method are shown in Fig. 1.

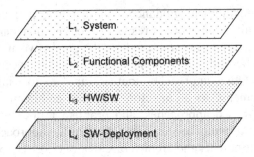

Fig. 1. The four abstraction layers defined in the COSMOD-RE method

The hierarchy depicted in Fig.1 is a means-ends hierarchy, i.e. a hierarchy in which layer L_{i+1} provides the means to achieve the ends (solve the problem) imposed by the artefacts at layer L_i. The four abstraction layers can be characterized as follows:

- L_1: At the system layer, the relationships between the system and its environment are considered. The system itself is regarded as a black box that interacts with external actors through a set of well-defined interfaces. The system level emphasizes the usage of the system.
- L_2: The functional components layer includes the functional decomposition of the system, i.e., a decomposition into units of coherent functionality. These units, or functional components, have well-defined interfaces which are used to connect the components to each other.
- L_3: At the HW/SW (hardware/software) components layer, the decomposition of the system into HW and SW components is defined. System functions defined at L_2 are assigned either to hardware or to software.
- L_4: The SW-deployment layer assigns SW components to programmable HW components.

As depicted in Fig. 2, each COSMOD-RE abstraction layer consists of a requirements viewpoint and an architecture viewpoint. To each viewpoint, distinct development artefacts are assigned. For instance, the requirements viewpoint at the system layer includes requirements artefacts pertaining to the entire system such as models describing the externally visible system behaviour. At the functional components layer, the requirements viewpoint includes requirements artefacts pertaining to individual functional components.

Some definitions such as the identifiers of the functional components are shared between the requirements viewpoint and the architecture viewpoint. This fact is indicated in Fig. 2 by the overlap between the two viewpoints.

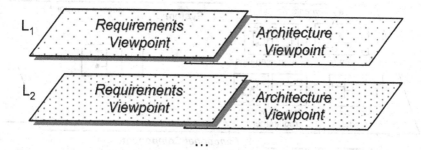

Fig. 2. Requirements viewpoint and architecture viewpoint

A characterization of the requirements viewpoint and the architecture viewpoint is provided in Table 1. Section 0 describes key requirements and architectural artefacts at two abstraction layers.

Table 1. Characterization of the requirements viewpoint and the architecture viewpoint at each abstraction layer

Layer	Requirements	Architecture
L_1 - system	- Interactions between system and external actors - Functional and quality requirements pertaining to the entire system	- Design specifications of external system interfaces
L_2 – functional components	- System-internal interactions - Functional and quality requirements for each functional component	- Design specifications of functional component interfaces - Configuration of the functional components
L_3 – HW/SW	- Interactions of HW and SW components - Functional and quality requirements for each HW and SW component	- Design specifications of HW/SW component interfaces - Configuration of the HW/SW components
L_4 – SW-deployment	- Requirements pertaining to the deployment of individual SW components	- Specification of the SW-deployment

2.2 COSMOD-RE Artefacts

An overview of the key requirements and architectural artefacts at the system layer and the functional components layer is shown in Fig. 3. The role of the artefacts shown in Fig. 3 is described in Section 0, and the activities that produce, consume, and modify the artefacts are presented in Section 0.

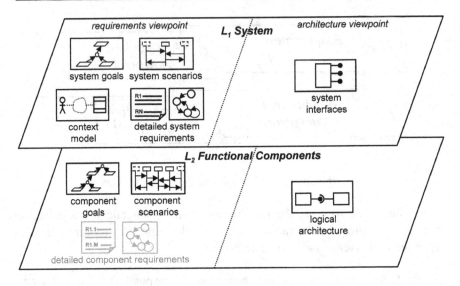

Fig. 3. COSMOD-RE artefacts at the system and functional components layers

2.2.1 Requirements Artefacts at the System Layer

The requirements viewpoint at the system level represents mainly the concerns of the users or customers of the planned system. It encompasses the following types of artefacts:

- *Context model*: The context model documents the embedding of the envisioned system into its environment. The context model defines the external actors (entities in the system environment) that interact with the system. An actor represents a human user or a system. In addition, the context model denotes the principle nature of the interactions between the system and the external actors.
- *System goals*: System goals refine the overall system vision. A system goal documents an intended high-level property of the system, for instance, concerning its usage by external actors. Goals are typically hierarchically structured. Sub goals are related to super goals by means of AND/OR refinement relationships (see e.g. [10]). An example of a system goal is: "The system shall inform the driver about important events." Each system goal is associated to at least one system scenario which concretizes the system goal (cf. e.g. [6]). Typically, several (detailed) requirements can be derived from a system goal.

- *System scenarios*: System scenarios define interactions between external actors and the system (cf. "type B" and "type C" scenarios in [14]). The documentation of system scenarios is based on use case templates (cf. e.g. [7]) or a model-based technique (cf. e.g. [8]). The use of goals and scenarios in COSMOD-RE is motivated by their successful application in innovative development (see e.g. [2], [11], [15], [17]).
- *Detailed system requirements*: The detailed system requirements subsume functional requirements (function, structure, and behaviour) and quality requirements such as performance, safety, or security requirements. System requirements are documented using a natural language and/or requirements modeling languages (cf. [4] for examples).

2.2.2 Requirements Artefacts at the Functional Components Layer

The requirements at the functional components level refine the system-level requirements into requirements for individual functional components:

- *Component goals*: Component goals define required properties of individual functional components. Like system goals, component goals are hierarchically structured. In addition, the component goals refine the goals defined at the system layer. Component goals are associated with component scenarios which concretize the goals.
- *Component scenarios (system-internal scenarios)*: Component scenarios or system-internal scenarios (see "type A" scenarios in [14]) refine the system scenarios. A component scenario defines the interactions between the functional components that are required to realize the external interactions of the system (i.e. the interactions with external actors).
- *Detailed component requirements*: The detailed component requirements include functional requirements and quality requirements for the individual components. The development of detailed component requirements is not in the scope of this chapter.

2.2.3 Architectural Artefacts

The architecture viewpoint represents mainly the concerns of engineers, system architects, and other technical stakeholders. The architectural artefacts considered in COSMOD-RE (at the system layer and the functional components layer) can be characterized as follows:

- *System interfaces*: System interfaces are the locations where interactions between the system and its environment, i.e. the exchange of information, energy, or material, take place. The interface definitions describe the functions or services that the system provides to its users and to external systems. A complex software-intensive system typically has several different types of interfaces such as human-machine interfaces and network interfaces.

- *Logical architecture*: The logical system architecture defines a decomposition of the overall system into a set of functional components. Each component has well-defined interfaces through which it can interact with other functional components or external actors (humans and systems). The logical architecture abstracts from certain aspects such as the partitioning of the system into software and hardware.

2.3 COSMOD-RE Process Structure

The COSMOD-RE process structure includes three co-design processes (Section 0). Each co-design process is subdivided into five sub-processes (Section 0). In addition, COSMOD-RE defines a set of activities that are performed within the five sub-processes. The activities are presented in Section 0.

2.3.1 Three Co-Design Processes

Based on the hierarchy of abstraction layers, COSMOD-RE defines three co-design processes with the following responsibilities (see Fig. 4):

- *System-level co-design*: The objective of this process is to develop the system requirements (L_1) and the logical system architecture (L_2).
- *Function-level co-design*: This process produces the functional-component requirements (L_2) and the HW/SW architecture (L_3).
- *HW/SW-level co-design*: The objective of this co-design process is to develop the HW/SW requirements (L_3) and the SW-deployment (L_4).

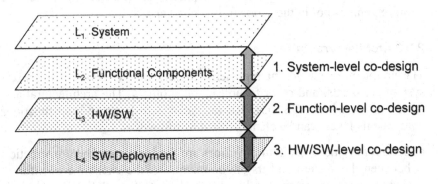

Fig. 4. Assignment of the co-design processes to the four abstraction layers

2.3.2 Five Sub-Processes

Each co-design process includes five sub-processes which support the co-development of innovative requirements and an innovative architectural solution. In the following, we briefly characterize the five sub-processes. The description of the five sub-processes is based on the system-level co-design process:

- SP_1: *Development of the requirements viewpoint at the system layer:* The goal of this sub-process is to develop innovative actor-system interactions and to define these interactions in terms of overall system goals and system scenarios.
- SP_2: *Development of the architecture viewpoint at the functional components layer.* The goal of this sub-process is to develop an innovative functional architecture for the intended system which, e.g., embeds new technologies and thus can provide innovative functionality or quality.
- SP_3: *Comparison of the requirements and the architecture viewpoints.* The main goals of this sub-process are (1) to check if the architecture supports the identified requirements, and (2) to identify new requirements based on the proposed architecture by comparing the results of the sub-processes SP_1 and SP_2. The comparison of the two viewpoints is driven by the refinement of system scenarios into component scenarios and the refinement of the associated goals.
- SP_4: *Consolidation of the requirements and the architecture viewpoints.* The main goal of this sub-process is to consolidate the requirements viewpoint and the architecture viewpoint based on the inconsistencies detected and the ideas developed in the sub-process SP_3.
- SP_5: *Definition of detailed requirements.* The goal of this sub-process is to produce textual requirements as well as models of function, data/structure, and behaviour that can be integrated into (one or multiple) requirements documents. The requirements are developed based on the consolidated set of goals, scenarios, and architectural artefacts.

The sub-process SP_5 accounts for the fact that detailed requirements cannot be defined at the desired level of detail without making explicit or implicit assumptions about the intended solution. When the system requirements are defined, the system goals, system scenarios, and the logical system architecture have already been established and consolidated in an iterative process. A (partial) system architecture can thus be used as an input for the definition of the system requirements in the system-level co-design process. Furthermore, the definition of detailed requirements can initiate further iterations of the other sub-processes, e.g. if missing or incomplete goals and scenarios are detected.

3 Activities in the System-Level Co-Design Process

This section describes the key activities of the system-level co-design process. The primary goal of the system-level co-design process is to specify the system from a usage perspective and to establish a (partial) coarse-grained solution. The system-level co-design process includes the activities shown on the left of Fig. 5. In addition, Fig. 5 shows the assignment of the eight activities to the five sub-processes defined in Section 0. The content of each cell indicates the relevance of the activity in the respective row for the sub-process in the respective column. The symbol "$\oplus\oplus$" means the activity is highly relevant for the sub-process. The symbol "$\oplus$" means the activity is somewhat relevant. "$\varnothing$" indicates that the activity is of little or no relevance for the sub-process. In the following, we describe each activity.

3.1 Context Elicitation

The goal of this activity is to identify context entities and to determine the relevance of each context aspect for the planned system. The procedure of identifying context aspects can be described as follows:

1. Identify relevant requirements sources such as stakeholders, documents, and existing systems.
2. Use the requirements sources to identify relevant context entities.
3. Iterate the above steps until a sufficiently detailed model of the system context has been established.

The following structuring of the context into four context facets can be used to support the identification of context entities:

- *Usage facet*: The usage facet contains all context objects and aspects that are related to the usage of the system by humans and other systems. The context analysis activity should identify, for instance, the business processes that must be supported by the planned system and determine the external actors (people and systems) that use the planned system.
- *Subject facet*: The subject facet comprises the "real-world" entities that must be represented in the planned system and acquired, stored, and processed by the system. Based on the analysis of the subject facet, a data model of the system can be developed.

	SP1 Development of the requirements viewpoint	SP2 Development of the architecture viewpoint	SP3 Comparison of the requirements and the architecture viewpoints	SP4 Consolidation of the requirements and the architecture viewpoints	SP5 Definition of detailed requirements
context elicitation	⊕⊕	⊕	∅	⊕	⊕
scenario elicitation	⊕⊕	∅	⊕	⊕	∅
scenario refinement	∅	∅	⊕⊕	⊕	∅
goal elicitation	⊕⊕	∅	⊕	⊕	∅
goal refinement	∅	∅	⊕⊕	⊕	∅
specification of detailed requirements	∅	∅	∅	∅	⊕⊕
architectural design	∅	⊕⊕	∅	⊕	∅
requirements and design evaluation	∅	∅	⊕⊕	∅	∅

Fig. 5. Overview of the main development activities in the system-level co-design process including the assignment to the five sub-processes

- *IT-system facet*: The IT-system facet includes all objects and aspects pertaining to the technical infrastructure in which the planned system is embedded as well as the relevant strategies and policies related to the infrastructure. When analyzing this facet, the stakeholders should identify, for instance, innovative technologies and technological trends that might affect the planned system.
- *Development facet*: The development facet comprises regulations and standards concerning the development process. This facet affects, for example, the tools and techniques that the developers must use.

Any object or aspect that is identified by this procedure is assigned to one of the following two categories:

- The aspect/object is within the relevant system context since it uses the system or affects the system in some other way. An example is a source providing data to the planned system in a specific format or using a specific protocol which the system must adhere to.
- The aspect/object is not relevant for the planned system. In some cases, a negotiation process is required to determine whether an aspect/object is relevant for the planned system or not. The stakeholders should document the results of the negotiation to make them transparent for other development activities.

The context knowledge elicited and documented at the system layer is refined at the functional components layer. The refinement is performed to support goal refinement and scenario refinement (see Sections 0 and 0). For instance, an external system may be refined into its functional components in order to identify those functional components that interact with the planned system.

3.2 Goal Elicitation

The objective of this activity is to elicit system goals. Typically, different stakeholders have different goals for a system. Managers have business goals. Users have goals pertaining to system usage. Engineers have goals concerning the technical solution.

Goals are identified using requirements elicitation techniques such as interviews or group discussions. For innovative systems, the development of goals should be supported by creativity techniques such as brainstorming (cf. e.g. [12]). Typically, some of the identified goals conflict with each other. To support the identification of conflicts, goals should be structured into different categories. The four context facets (see Section 0) can be used as a rough classification scheme for goals. After performing the classification, conflicts can be identified, firstly, within each category. If a conflict is detected, negotiation activities are performed in order to resolve the conflict. After the conflicts within each category have been resolved, the stakeholders should check for conflicts among goals in different categories (which can be more subtle and therefore more difficult to detect).

In addition to positive goals the stakeholders should identify negative goals (anti goals). Negative goals are goals that the system must prevent from being satisfied. An example of a negative goal is "the system shall (not) cause an accident". By identifying scenarios that result in the satisfaction of negative goals and by conceiving means to prohibit such scenarios, the identification of safety and security requirements is supported.

3.3 Goal Refinement

The objective of this activity is to refine system goals that have been identified in the goal elicitation activity in order to (eventually) produce a set of component goals. The goal refinement activity produces sub goals that are related to the initial goals by AND/OR refinement relationships. In the case of AND refinement, all sub goals must be satisfied to satisfy the super goal. For instance, the goal "maintain safe distance" can be refined (AND refinement) into the two sub goals "measure distance" and "reduce speed". The OR refinement relationship indicates that satisfying one sub goal is sufficient to satisfy the super goal. The responsibility for satisfying a sub goal can be with the system or with a functional component:

- If the system has the responsibility for satisfying the sub goal, the sub goal is assigned to the system layer.
- If a single functional component is responsible for satisfying the sub goal, this sub goal is assigned to the functional components layer and related to the respective functional component.

Goal refinement can be used to support the design of functional components. For instance, if a functional component lacks the required interfaces or connections for satisfying a sub goal that is assigned to the component, a redesign of the component is needed. If the goal "reduce speed" is refined into two sub goals "actuate brakes" and "reduce engine torque", the stakeholders must check if the functional component that is responsible for reducing the speed is able to interact with the component that controls the engine torque, for example.

The goal refinement activity is closely related to the scenario refinement activity (see Section 0). If a system scenario is refined into a component scenario, the goals associated to the system scenario should also be refined. The resulting sub goals should be assigned to the component scenario.

3.4 Scenario Elicitation

The objective of this activity is to develop system scenarios, which are, in most cases, system usage scenarios. Each system (usage) goal that is elicited in the goal elicitation activity should be concretized by at least one system scenario. For instance, the stakeholders might concretize the goal "maintain save following distance" by the following scenario:

1. The driver activates the ACC (adaptive cruise control) system.
2. The ACC recognizes a relevant vehicle ahead.

3. The ACC signals the detection of the vehicle to the driver.

4. ACC reduces the speed in order to maintain a safe following distance.

Scenarios for innovative systems should be developed collaboratively by an interdisciplinary team (cf. e.g. [11]). Initially, the scenario development should focus on the main scenarios, i.e. the scenarios that are most likely to occur. Subsequently, the main scenarios should be analyzed in order to identify alternative and exceptional scenarios and thus to obtain a more complete set of scenarios. Alternative scenarios describe alternative ways of satisfying the goal of the main scenario. An alternative scenario for the ACC system might be, for example:

3. (...see main scenario...)

4a. The driver operates the brake pedal.

5a. The operation of the brake pedal deactivates the ACC.

Exceptional scenarios describe sequences of interactions that are performed when an error occurs (e.g. when a user enters incorrect data or a hardware component fails). An exceptional scenario terminates without satisfying the scenario goal.

In addition to the above-mentioned scenarios, the stakeholders should identify negative scenarios. Negative scenarios describe sequences of interactions which must be actively prevented by the system. Negative scenarios are, for example, scenarios, in which a user gains illegal access to privileged system functions, or scenarios, in which humans sustain damage due to system failure.

To provide more detailed guidance for the development of goals and scenarios, established goal- and scenario-based requirements engineering approaches can be applied (cf. e.g. [1], [6], [11], [16]).

3.5 Scenario Refinement

The objective of the scenario refinement activity is to refine system scenarios into component scenarios. The refinement of the system scenario presented in Section 0 is depicted in Fig. 6. In the component scenario, functional components and (system-internal) interactions between the components are shown.

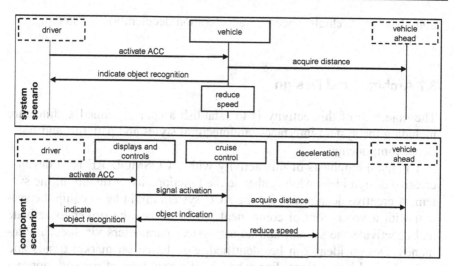

Fig. 6. Sample refinement of a system scenario into a component scenario

The scenario refinement supports the development and evaluation of the logical architecture. The possible results of the scenario refinement include the identification of additional functional components, the identification of additional component interactions as well as the identification of additional interactions with external actors. The consistency between the resulting component scenario and the original system scenario should be checked at the end of the refinement.

3.6 Specification of Detailed Requirements

The objective of this activity is to develop functional and quality requirements for the planned system. The inputs to this activity include goals, scenarios, and a (coarse-grained) logical architecture. Thereby, explicit architectural knowledge can be considered when defining the detailed system requirements.

The requirements artefacts produced by this activity are comprehensive specifications of the externally observable system behaviour, functionality, and structure/data. Concerning the system behaviour, major system states such as "inactive mode", "standby mode", "active mode", and "failure mode" are defined. Concerning the system functionality the major functions that are available at the system interfaces are described (e.g. "activate ACC", "adjust set speed", and "adjust set distance"). Concerning structure/data, major structural and data elements are described (e.g. the "motion data" – "vehicle speed", "acceleration/deceleration", "steering angle").

3.7 Architectural Design

The objective of this activity is to establish a coarse-grained architecture including the system interfaces, architectural styles and patterns, and functional components.

The main emphasis of this activity within COSMOD-RE is to develop creative design ideas which enhance the functionality or quality of the system. A creative design idea for the ACC system might be to equip the system with a voice control component which allows the driver to activate and deactivate the system and adjust system parameters via speech commands. Design ideas can be identified, e.g., based on market trends and technological innovations. For example, if a new type of network appears on the market, the system engineers might conceive ways of exploiting the new network technology for the planned system.

The design ideas developed in this activity are, initially, documented using simple architectural models such as boxes-and-lines models. Typically, an architectural model includes several design ideas that are integrated into an overall candidate architecture. The result of the architectural design activity is a (partial) logical architecture consisting of system interfaces, key functional components, and their interconnections.

3.8 Requirements and Design Evaluation

The objective of this activity is to identify inconsistencies between the system-level requirements artefacts and the logical architecture. The comparison of the system-level requirements artefacts with the logical architecture is facilitated by refining system goals into component goals and the refinement of system scenarios into component scenarios (see Sections 0 and 0). The following questions should be raised during the evaluation:

- Does the architecture satisfy the system goals and system scenarios?
- Does the proposed architecture offer potentials for innovative goals and scenarios that have not been conceived yet?
- Do the system goals and scenarios account for feature interactions and failure states that become evident through the analysis of the logical architecture?

By resolving the detected inconsistencies, the stakeholders improve the completeness of the specification and the consistency of requirements and architecture. In addition, answering the above questions may lead to creative ideas for enhancing the requirements and architectural definitions.

4 Summary

In this chapter, the key principles of the COSMOD-RE have been presented. COSMOD-RE supports the co-development of requirements and architectural artefacts for innovative software-intensive systems. The method defines four abstraction layers for requirements and architecture. The co-development of requirements and architectural artefacts is supported by means of five interrelated sub-processes which include the development of innovative goals and scenarios, the development of innovative design ideas, and the consolidation of requirements and design. The main emphasis of this chapter has been on the description of the activities for developing goals and scenarios at the system level, refining the goals and scenarios, designing a coarse-grained, logical system architecture, evaluating the architecture against the requirements artefacts, and developing detailed requirements based on consolidated goals, scenarios, and architectural artefacts. Overall, the COSMOD-RE process structure and the associated set of activities provide a systematic support for incorporating and exploiting architectural knowledge in the requirements engineering process and consolidating requirements and architectural definitions.

We are currently working on a formalization of our method as a basis for developing tools that support the COSMOD-RE activities and the management of the artefacts produced by the activities.

Acknowledgments. This research was partly founded by the BMBF project REMsES, grant no. 01 IS F06 D. The writing of this chapter was partly founded by SFI grant no. 03/CE2/I303_1.

References

[1] Antón, A.I., Dempster, J., Siege, D.: Deriving Goals from a Use Case Based Requirements Specification for an Electronic Commerce System. In: Proc. 6th Int. Workshop on Requirements Engineering: Foundation for Software Quality, REFSQ'00 (2000) pp 10-19

[2] Beyer, H., Holtzblatt, K.: *Contextual Design: Defining Customer-Centered Systems* (Morgan Kaufmann, San Francisco 1998)

[3] Robert Bosch GmbH: *ACC Adaptive Cruise Control* (The Bosch Yellow Jackets, Edition 2003) available via http://www.christiani-tvet.com

[4] Davis, A.M.: *Software Requirements: Objects, Functions, and States* (Prentice Hall, Englewood Cliffs 1993)

[5] Galster, M., Eberlein, A., Moussavi, M.: Transition from Requirements to Architecture: A Review and Future Perspective. In: Proc. 7th ACIS International Conf. on Software Engineering, Artificial Intelligence, Networking, and Parallel/Distributed Computing, SNPD'06 (2006) pp 9-16

[6] Haumer, P., Pohl, K., Weidenhaupt, K.: Requirements Elicitation and Validation with Real World Scenes. IEEE Trans. on Softw. Eng. **24**(12), 1036-1054 (1998)

[7] Halmans, G., Pohl, K.: Communicating the Variability of a Software Product Family to Customers. Software and Systems Modeling **2**(1), 15-36 (Springer, Berlin Heidelberg New York 2003)

[8] ITU-T Recommendation Z.120: Message Sequence Chart (MSC). International Telecommunication Union (2004)

[9] Jarke, M., Pohl, K.: Establishing Visions in Context: Towards a Model of Requirements Processes. In: Proc. 14th Int. Conf. on Inf. Systems, Orlando, Florida (1993) pp 23-34

[10] Van Lamsweerde, A.: Goal-Oriented Requirements Engineering: A Guided Tour. In: Proc. 5th IEEE Int. Symp. on Req. Eng., RE'01, Toronto, Canada (IEEE Computer Society Press 2001) pp 249-262

[11] Maiden, N.; Alexander, I. (eds.): *Scenarios, Stories, Use Cases: Through the Systems Development Life-Cycle* (Wiley, Chichester, West Sussex 2004)

[12] Maiden, N; Robertson, S.; Robertson, J.: Creative Requirements: Invention and Its Role in Requirements Engineering. In: Proc. 28th Int. Conf. Softw. Eng., ICSE'06, 20-28 May, Shanghai, China (ACM 2006) pp 1073-1074.

[13] Nuseibeh, B.: Weaving Together Requirements and Architectures. IEEE Computer **34**(3), IEEE Computer Society (2001) pp 115-117

[14] Pohl, K., Haumer, P.: Modelling Contextual Information about Scenarios. In: Proc. 3rd Int. Workshop on Requirements Engineering: Foundation for Software Quality, REFSQ'97, Barcelona (Presses Universitaires, Namur 1997)

[15] Puschnig, A.; Kolagari, R.T.: Requirements Engineering in the Development of Innovative Automotive Embedded Software Systems. In: Proc. 12th IEEE Int. Req. Eng. Conf., RE'04, Kyoto, Japan (IEEE Computer Society 2004)

[16] Rolland, C., Souveyet, C., Achour, C.B.: Guiding Goal Modeling Using Scenarios. IEEE Trans. on Softw. Eng. **24**(12), 1055-1071 (1998)

[17] Rolland, C., Grosz, G., Kla, R.: Experience with Goal-Scenario Coupling in Requirements Engineering. In: Proc. 4th IEEE Int. Symp. on Requirements Eng., RE'99, Limerick, Ireland (IEEE Computer Society 1999) pp 74-81

[18] Sølvberg, A.. Research Issues in Integrated Distributed Information Systems. Keynote Speech CAiSE'93 (1993)

[19] Zhu, Q., Medjahed, B.: Developing In-Vehicle Database Management Techniques for Efficient Vehicular Applications, Technology Day 2006, Henry W. Patton Center for Engineering Education and Practice, University of Michigan – Dearborn (2006)

Capturing Dependability Threats in Conceptual Modelling

Guttorm Sindre[1], Andreas L. Opdahl[2]

[1] NTNU, Trondheim, Norway
[2] University of Bergen, Bergen, Norway;

Abstract. To improve the focus on security and other dependability issues it might be useful to include such concerns into mainstream diagram notations used in information systems analysis. In particular, there have been proposals introducing inverted icons to depict functionality *not* wanted in the system (e.g., misuse cases) or actors with malicious intent (in i* diagrams), thus addressing security issues in such notations. But there are many other modelling notations also used in early systems development, and the focus on dependability could be strengthened if these provided similar means to incorporate dependability issues. This paper looks at the possibilities for addressing dependability in information models and workflow models. To maintain visual consistency with the abovementioned proposals, it is suggested to apply inverted icons also here. In information models this can be used to represent misinformation, and in workflow models malicious or fraudulent actions attacking the business process. In both cases, inversion of icons contributes to clearly distinguishing between what is wanted in the system and what must be avoided, thus enabling a visual representation of dependability concerns.

1 Introduction

Often, malicious attacks or accidents have disastrous effects in organizations because they happen in ways that were not imagined when automated information systems and manual routines were developed. For instance, some computer criminals can perform attacks with a persistence and ingenuity which is very hard to protect against [2, 16] – especially since the system must succeed every time, while the attacker needs to succeed only once. And even the most elaborate technological protection will be futile if the organization's employees are duped by social engineering attacks [17] to give away confidential information. Similarly, safety concerns may have been taken into account in the development of a system, but unforeseen combinations of external events, system faults, and human failure may sometimes lead to disastrous effects [13].

Hence, increased focus on supporting early discussions to identify possible threats to a system could be much needed[3, 8], but mainstream techniques for security analysis such as [7] tend to be formal and heavyweight, not easily including a broad range of stakeholders. To the extent that informal modelling techniques are used in systems analysis, these primarily deal with system functionality, while security is often delayed to later phases. This often leads to expensive rework or losses due to security breaches [12]. Therefore there is a need to integrate dependability concerns into mainstream early phase techniques for systems development.

There are two notable proposals that have both made use of inverted icons to capture attackers and security threats. Use case diagrams were extended with inverted actor and use case icons into misuse case diagrams[21], and i* diagrams were similarly extended with inverted actor icons to capture attackers and inverted goal icons for the malicious goals of these attackers [15].

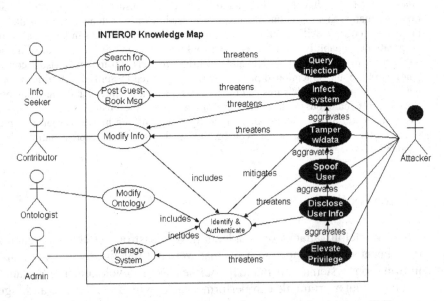

Fig. 1. Misuse case diagram with security threats, adapted from [19]

The diagram of Fig. 1 shows some normal use cases for a Knowledge Map application, as well as the Actors using this functionality. Additionally, there are misuse cases (inverted), as well as the actor for the misuse cases, in this case a generic "Attacker". Misuse cases can threaten normal use cases, and more use cases can then be introduced to mitigate the misuse cases. The misuse cases in this example are security-related, since they are initiated by a malicious attacker. But accidental mistakes by legitimate actors can be modelled in much the same way. As suggested by [1], misuse cases can also be applicable in cases of health and environmental safety, and non-human threats such as bad weather, floods, and fires can be anthropomorphized so that the same inverted actor symbols can still be used. The example of Fig. 2 shows a boiler system controlled by a computer and an operator. On the left are the normal, successful actions of these two actors. On the right, there are possible mistakes and failures that threaten the normal operation of the system.

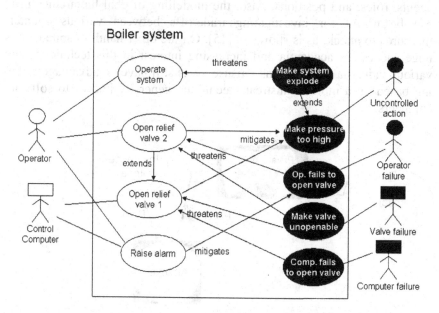

Fig. 2. Safety-oriented misuse case diagram.

The example of Fig. 2 is adapted from [13], but there it was modelled with a Cause-Consequence Diagram, which is a safety-specific technique not utilizing inverted icons. The point here is not that misuse cases is better than CCD's for capturing safety issues (it may easily be the other way around, since the latter technique was specifically designed with safety in mind), but misuse cases do have the advantage of being just a minor extension of a notation which is already known by many software developers, and which is used anyway in a huge number of projects. Thus the threshold for introducing safety concerns in a mainstream project would be smaller.

Another technique where the use of black icons have been suggested to deal with security issues is i* [15]. The example of Fig. 3 shows an excerpt from an i* diagram illustrating the basic extensions. Unlike misuse case diagrams, the symbols are not directly inverted but embedded in black rectangles, otherwise the idea is analogous: The Attacker has malicious intent, in this case trying to hurt the soft-goal of preserving the privacy of patient data. The diagram also shows that this attacker role may be played by an actor which is otherwise a legitimate actor in the system, namely an Insurance Company. Here, i* has an advantage over misuse cases in providing more powerful concepts for modelling the various relationships between agents, roles, and positions. Also, the modelling of goal hierarchies in i* can be useful for investigating trade-offs between various countermeasures to attack, as is shown in [15]. On the other hand, in spite of i*'s huge success in academia and increasing interest in this technique with various industrial applications, misuse cases still have an advantage in being based on a more mainstream technique generally known to software engineers.

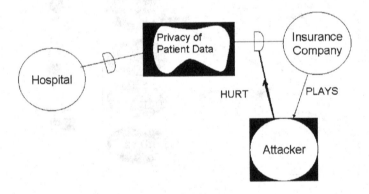

Fig. 3. Example of an i* diagram with an attacker, excerpt from [15]

Both misuse cases and the elaboration of security issues with i* (or the related Tropos, cf. [18]) have shown a lot of promise, and there is no reason to stop at this, as there are several other modelling paradigms where the inclusion of inverted icons could also be considered. In the rest of the paper we will look at various opportunities for this. Section 2 considers the usage of inverted icons in information models. Section 3 similarly looks at inverted icons in models for business processes or workflow. Finally, section 4 provides some discussion and conclusions to the paper.

2 Modelling Information and Misinformation

The WWW has made a wealth of information freely available for almost anyone. Often the problem is that a search returns too much information, and that some of the information is of poor quality. In some cases, such poor information quality is only a minor annoyance, but in other cases there may be serious safety issues involved when people take action based on misinformation. One notable example is web information containing medical advice, where misinformation [9] may cause people to hurt themselves or their children, or in the case discussed in [24]: their pets. As emphasized by [6] medical misinformation comes not only from unserious charlatans marketing bogus drugs or therapies, but even to some extent from medical journals, as one study is often contradicted by later ones[11].

While it is undoubtedly useful to model information (e.g., for the purpose of building a database or ontology), it could be questioned whether it is useful to model also misinformation (which would normally not be wanted in the database anyway). However, making a concept model that includes frequent types of misinformation may be a first step towards providing automatic support for detecting and systematizing web documents that contain misinformation, and investigate how misinformation spreads from one document to the next. It might also provide assistance for ranking online documents based on the ratio of information vs. misinformation. For instance in the domain of medical advice, the huge number of documents available on the web, with varying quality, suggests that a concept model supporting the identification of information as well as misinformation could be most helpful.

In other cases, where misinformation is used for fraud against business processes, such as embezzling funds through fake invoices, concept models including misinformation could be useful in discussing business process reengineering, audit procedures or security protection mechanisms to reduce the possibility for fraud.

In systems analysis information is often modelled with ER-diagrams or similar notations, such as UML class diagrams. For the purpose of this paper we will look at one particular notation for information modelling, namely Sølvberg's Referent Model [22], and extending this to represent misinformation. The motivation for choosing the Referent Model instead of ER or UML class diagrams is that it has been demonstrated to be well suited for modelling the contents of documents, cf. [4, 5], in particular semi-structured information on the web, such as medical information.

For simplicity the example of Fig. 4 displays only a smaller part of what a medical advice document on the internet might contain. The white Referent sets denote accepted phenomena (e.g., in accordance with best medical knowledge), whereas the black Referent sets denote misinformation. The white part of the diagram indicates that the universe of discourse concerns symptoms that have causes. Often, several symptoms occur together, hence a symptom collection is an aggregation of symptoms often co-occurring, and it is for such symptom collections (which may in some cases still consist of a single symptom) that diagnoses may be suggested. Notice that the referent set Diagnosis Options, which associates symptom collections with causes, does not contain instances of *the* diagnosis, as established for one specific patient by one specific doctor. Instead it contains sets of diagnoses, i.e., all the candidate diagnoses given a certain symptom collection. Finally, the diagnosed causes may be either diseases or normal states (e.g., having a headache after working all night with a conference paper or being slightly depressed when the paper is still rejected). This is of course a gross simplification as there are a number of health problems that are not diseases, e.g., injuries or back problems, but the diagram would be far too big if attempting a complete ontology of the domain. Finally, some action may be recommended for a suggested cause, such as immediately consulting your doctor or dentist, seeking some alternative treatment, buying some drug, performing some self-treatment, or (e.g., in the case of the work all night headache) just taking a rest, so a more complete model would also indicate various types of treatment, how these treatments could be obtained, their costs, side-effects etc.

The inverted part of the diagram concerns itself with some types of misinformation that may be present in this domain. First of all, there may be misinformation about symptoms. A document may contain discussion of bogus symptoms, i.e., something presented as a symptom without being medically recognized as such. This is shown by the fact that the example instance S2 which is a member of Bogus Symptom, is *not* a member of the Symptom referent set. On the other hand, an Inaccurate Symptom is a member of the Symptom set, thus representing a medically recognized symptom. The problem here is that the description of the symptom is imprecise, so that the reader of the document may easily misinterpret it, for instance failing to recognize the symptom even if having it, or on the other hand getting unsubstantiated fear of displaying the symptom when it is really not present. This lack of precision is indicated by the fact that the description value of the symptom instance S1 does not correspond to any description in the corresponding value set (rectangle with a triangle in the lower right corner).

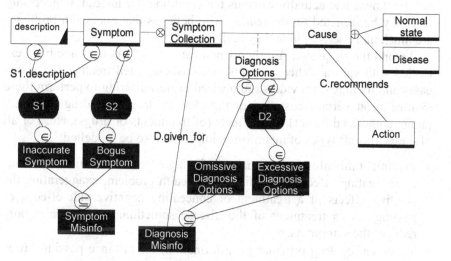

Fig. 4. Example of Referent Model including misinformation

Diagnosis Misinformation is probably an even more serious problem than Symptom Misinformation. One medical advice website would not be expected to offer diagnoses for all possible symptom collections, so it makes little sense to talk about misinformation for symptoms and causes that the document is not at all dealing with. However, *if* diagnoses are suggested for a certain symptom collection, then one can talk about two different kinds of misinformation:

- Omission: The document offers some candidate diagnoses, but not all the known candidate diagnoses for the symptom collection, i.e., some candidate diagnoses are ignored. Or alternatively, the document starts with the cause (e.g., discussing a certain disease), but does not provide all the possible symptom collections relevant for this disease.
- Excess: The document offers some diagnoses that are discredited / not accepted, i.e., bogus relationship instances between symptom collections and causes. One option here may be that both the symptom collection and cause are medically recognized, but that no relationship really exists between them. Another option would be the suggestion of a completely bogus cause (e.g., being the victim of a witch spell or under the influence of a demon inhabiting your computer keyboard).

If the reader performs some kind of self-diagnosis based on such misinformation, several problems may occur. For instance, a serious health problem may be mistaken for a less serious one, so that the patient fails to seek the needed medical assistance in time, or instead embarks on some self-treatment that actually worsens the condition. Or instead, unnecessary fear may be inflicted on the reader, who believes that his health problems are much more serious than they really are.

Beyond the suggested Action given a cause, Fig. 4 could have been extended with various other concepts, such as suggested treatments for diseases and treatment providers (authorized or not) offering to perform these treatments at certain cost and quality levels, drugs and drug providers (again authorized or not), side-effects (of treatments or drugs), etc. For all of these, various types of misinformation could also be modelled:

- Treatment misinformation, such as offering a treatment which really has no mitigating effect on the diagnosed health problem, exaggerating the positive effects of a treatment or concealing negative side-effects, or passing off as treatment of the disease something which really only reduces the symptoms.
- Treatment or drug provider misinformation, for instance passing off as authorized a provider or vendor who is not.
- Drug misinformation, such as inaccurate dosage information, concealment of side-effects, or trying to sell fake products.

Such misinformation could be modelled in a way similar to the example in Fig. 4. Another example of misinformation is given in Fig. 5, more directly linked to fraudulent behaviour against a particular business process. Assume that in University X it is common procedure for professors to pay for minor research expenses (e.g., books, equipment, conference trips) out of their own pocket and later get refunded, because this is administratively simpler than having to apply up front to have the university cover the expense immediately. The model shows that an expense is incurred by exactly one professor, whereas each professor may have had several expenses. Similarly, a claim is made by exactly one professor, who can make several claims. A claim may be related to one or more expenses, and at the bottom, claims are specialized according to the various stages they go through (un-submitted, submitted, checked, accepted or rejected, and if accepted then later reimbursed). Assuming that some professors might try to embezzle funds through this reimbursement process, some misinformation sets have been added to the model, most notably "Illegitimate Claim". As can be seen, there are several subtypes of illegitimate claims:

- Private claim c (def.): $c.made\_for(e) \wedge e \in PrivateExpense$
- Excessive claim c (def.): $c.made\_for(e) \wedge c.amount > e.amount$

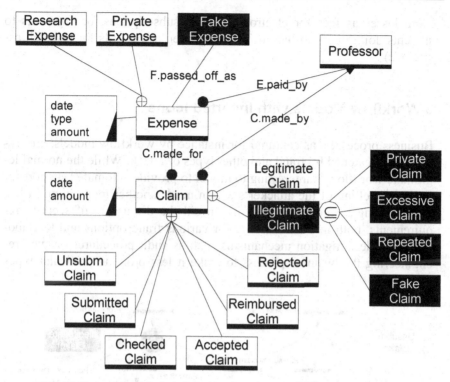

Fig. 5. Potential misinformation in an expense reimbursement process

- Repeated claim c (def.; some other claim which is already submitted has involved the same expense):

  $c.made\_for(e) \wedge$

  $((\exists c' \in Claim) : c' \neq c \wedge c'.made\_for(e) \wedge c' \notin UnsubmClaim)$

- Fake claim c (def.): $c.made\_for(e) \wedge e \in FakeExpense$

Some of these definitions might have been possible to illustrate diagrammatically, but the diagram would easily become clumsy if trying to do too much just with visual symbols. Notice that Fake Expense is not a subset of Expense, since a fake expense does not at all correspond to a real expense incurred by the professor (could for instance be "proven" by a receipt retrieved from the trash bin of the university bookshop, thus really being paid by another person) – this in contradiction to a private expense, which was paid for by the professor, but includes goods or services for private use rather than for research purposes. Notice that the Private Expense rectangle is not inverted. A private expense is not illegitimate as such, but becomes illegitimate only if a claim is made for it as a research expense (e.g., passing off a strip club bill as a seminar fee, internet gambling losses as fees for electronic journal subscriptions, or payments to students doing work in the professor's garden as rewards for research assistance)[1].

3 Workflow Models with Inverted Icons

Business processes, as captured for instance by workflow models, are frequently threatened by fraud and other types of attack. While the normal legitimate workflow is interesting to model to provide automated support for it, the modelling of the attacker's action needs another motivation. Still it is interesting to model because it can aid the discussion of security requirements, both in brainstorming for various fraud options and to elaborate possible mitigation mechanisms such as audit procedures or even reengineering the business process to make it less prone to particular types of attack.

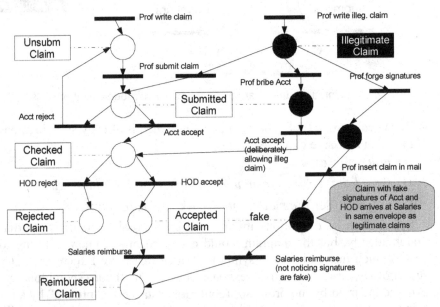

Fig. 6. Behaviour Network Model of the reimbursement process, including fraud

An early formalism for the modelling of system activity was that of Petri nets [20], which are still used for the modelling of workflows. There

---

[1] Note that all these examples are fictitious and not related to any real professor that we know of.

are many different dialects of Petri nets to choose from. For our particular purpose we select the Behaviour Network Model [14, 23], due to the fact that it is integrated with ER-style information modelling.

Fig. 6 shows a BNM diagram for the reimbursement process related to the Referent Model of Fig. 5. Apart from the normal ingredients of Petri nets (places and transitions) BNM provides the possibility to link places to entity classes, thus showing the type of tokens.

The diagram of Fig. 6 can be explained as follows: The normal process starts with the professor writing a claim, then submitting it. It is then checked by an accountant to see if all claimed expenses are validated (e.g., with receipts) and if the sums add up correctly. If there is some problem, the accountant returns the claim to the professor for corrections or requesting additional information. If OK, the accountant signs the claim as checked and forwards it to the Head of Department. The HOD does not make any detailed check of receipts (which was the accountant's responsibility) but rather considers if the expense is a research expense in accordance with department policy. If the expense is considered private, the HOD will reject it. Otherwise the HOD signs it as accepted and forwards it to Salaries for reimbursement.

As for the inverted part of the diagram, this initially shows the professor entering an illegitimate claim into the system. Then the diagram depicts three different ways that fraud can be attempted: (a) submit the illegitimate claim into the normal process using the transition "Prof submit", hoping that the control is sloppy enough or any fake receipts clever enough that the fraud will not be discovered, (b) collude with the accountant using the transition "Prof bribe Acct". Here, the accountant knowingly accepts an illegitimate claim, for instance under a deal of splitting the profits. Since the HOD's inspection of the claims is rather superficial, this may have good hope of succeeding. (c) try to bypass the department's internal control altogether, via the transition "Prof forge signatures". Here the professor does not submit his claim the normal way but instead himself signs for the accountant and HOD so that the claim appears to have passed acceptance. Then, it is simply slipped into the envelope that the department sends to Salaries every second week, containing claims for various professors in the department. This can fairly easily be achieved if the professor has a key to the mailroom and is familiar with the routines, thus knowing when this envelope is likely to be waiting to be picked up from the department outbox.

In BNM it would also be possible to make formal expressions for preconditions and post-conditions of the transitions, which might be particularly appropriate for security analysis, but this is beyond the scope of this paper. Even without including such formal conditions, the above diagram may support a discussion of possible ways to mitigate the fraud – for instance by annotating various options directly onto the diagram. For the simplest fraud (where the Prof submits an illegitimate claim in the normal way) the most obvious mitigation would be a more thorough control by the accountant or HOD. The collusion between professor and accountant could possibly be mitigated by process redesign, such as swapping claims between various accountants in a way not predictable to the professors in advance (i.e., not using the same accountant for claims from Prof X every time), or by sometimes double-checking claims by two accountants. The final fraud variation, where the professor forges the signature of the accountant and HOD could be mitigated in several ways: (1) by changing to electronic claim forms with digital signatures (the Prof would then need to obtain the HOD's password rather than simply forging a handwritten signature), (2) by sending the claims from the HOD to Salaries in another way (i.e., avoiding that the envelope waits in the Dept Outbox for some time), (3) having the Acct and HOD keep lists of the claims that have really been accepted, then comparing with a list from Salaries of which claims were actually reimbursed (will not prevent the fraud, but ensures that it is detected within a month). All the above-mentioned mitigation options could easily be positioned in the BNM diagram, which could thus be a useful basis for initial discussion of various possibilities. Then, the most promising possibilities could be taken further, comparing the cost of mitigations to the assumed cost of the fraud.

4 Discussion and Conclusions

The paper has looked at the expression of security threats and related issues of misinformation and fraud in conceptual models. Through some examples the paper has demonstrated that inverted icons are not only interesting with use case and i* diagrams, for which such proposals have been made some years ago, but also for quite different types of diagrams, such as information models and Petri nets. Of course, the same information models could have been made without the use of inversion, just relying on the node names to tell which parts of the diagram were about information, and which were about misinformation. However, it is our belief that the models become much clearer if the important distinction between information and misinformation is made explicit. The same applies to the Petri net, but again a model where the malicious actions were not visually distinguished from the legitimate actions would easily have become confusing for the stakeholders. Moreover, the presence of the inverted nodes strongly invites a focus on dependability aspects early on, calling such issues to the attention of those who discuss the diagrams.

A challenge to the proposed approach is that models quickly grow quite complex when both positive and negative elements are to be shown together, especially with Petri nets, for which this is often a problem even without the inclusion of malicious actions. This kind of modelling will therefore rely on diagramming tools with good support for filtering and decomposition. For the modelling of fraudulent business processes one could of course consider other modelling languages with more powerful abstraction mechanisms than Petri nets, for instance the Extended Enterprise Modelling Language (EEML), which gradually developed from work on the PPP modelling approach in Arne Sølvberg's research group in the late 80's [10]. This must potentially be investigated in future work.

Other topics for future work are a better evaluation of the proposed approaches in terms of industrial case studies or controlled experiments, as well as tool development to facilitate their potential industrial application. Additionally, it could be interesting to investigate how to integrate lightweight approaches based on inverted icons with more formal and heavyweight approaches to dependability requirements.

References

[1] Alexander, I., Misuse Cases: Use Cases with Hostile Intent. IEEE Software, 2003. 20(1): p. 58-66.
[2] Andrews, M. and J.A. Whittaker, How to Break Web Software. 2006, Upper Saddle River, NJ: Addison-Wesley.
[3] Bauer, M.D. Fear and loathing in information security. 2005 11 Feb [cited 2006 1 Oct]; Available from: http://www.oreillynet.com/pub/a/network/2005/02/11/mbauer_1.html
[4] Brasethvik, T. and J.A. Gulla. A Conceptual Modeling Approach to Semantic Document Retrieval. in 14th International Conference on Advanced Information Systems Engineering (CAiSE'02). 2002. Toronto: Springer Verlag.
[5] Brasethvik, T. and A. Sølvberg. A Referent Model of Documents. in 1th ERCIM Database Research Group Workshop on Metadata for Web Databases. 1998. Sankt Augustin, Germany: ERCIM.
[6] Burney, M. Don't Believe Everything You Read - Even in Medical Journals. HealthFactsAndFears.com   2005   [cited 2006 1.1.]; Available from: http://www.acsh.org/factsfears/newsID.591/news_detail.asp
[7] CCIMB, Common Criteria for Information Technology Security Evaluation. 1999, Common Criteria Implementation Board.

[8] CSC. How CSC's Bill Tafoya Applies Creative Thinking to IT Security. 2002 [cited 2006 1 Oct]; Available from: http://www.csc.com/features/2002/117. shtml

[9] Detwiler, S., Charlatans, Leeches, and Old Wives: Medical Misinformation. Searcher, 2001. 9(3).

[10] Gulla, J.A., O.I. Lindland, and G. Willumsen. PPP: A Integrated CASE Environment. in Advanced Information Systems Engineering, CAiSE'91. 1991. Trondheim, Norway: Springer (Lecture Notes in Computer Science 498).

[11] Ioannidis, J.P.A., Contradicted and initially stronger effects in highly cited clinical journals. Journal of the American Medical Association, 2005. 294: p. 218-228.

[12] Jürjens, J., Secure Systems Development with UML. 2004, Berlin: Springer.

[13] Leveson, N.G., Safeware: System Safety and Computers. 1995, Boston: Addison-Wesley.

[14] Kung, C.H, Sølvberg, A.: Activity Modeling and Behavior Modeling. in IFIP WG 8.1 Working Conference on Comparative Review of Information Systems Design Methodologies: Improving the Practice (CRIS '86). 1986. Noordwijkerhout, The Netherlands: North-Holland.

[15] Liu, L., E. Yu, and J. Mylopoulos. Security and Privacy Requirements Analysis within a Social Setting. in 11th International Requirements Engineering Conference (RE'03). 2003. Monterey Bay, CA: IEEE Press.

[16] Mitnick, K.D. and W.L. Simon, The Art of Intrusion. 2006, Indianapolis: Wiley.

[17] Mitnick, K.D. and W.L. Simon, The Art of Deception: Controlling the Human Element of Security. 2002, Indianapolis: Wiley Publishing, Inc.

[18] Mouratidis, H., P. Giorgini, and G. Manson. Integrating Security and Systems Engineering: Towards the Modelling of Secure Information Systems. in 15th Conference on Advanced Information Systems Engineering (CAiSE'03). 2003. Velden, Austria: Springer LNCS 2681.

[19] Petit, M., Knowledge map of research in interoperability in the INTEROP NoE. 2004, Univ. Namur, Belgium. p. 278.

[20] Petri, C.A., Kommunikation mit Automaten. 1962, University of Bonn.

[21] Sindre, G. and A.L. Opdahl. Eliciting Security Requirements by Misuse Cases. in 37th International Conference on Technology of Object-Oriented Languages and Systems (TOOLS-PACIFIC 2000). 2000: IEEE CS Press.

[22] Sølvberg, A., Data and what they refer to, in Conceptual Modeling, Current Issues and Future Directions (Selected Papers from the Symposium on Conceptual Modeling, Los Angeles, CA, held before ER'97). P.P. Chen, et al., Editors. 1999, Springer Verlag: Berlin. p. 211-226.

[23] Sølvberg, A. and D.C. Kung. On Structural and Behavioral Modeling of Reality. in IFIP WG 2.6 Working Conference on Data Semantics (DS-1). 1985. Hasselt, Belgium: North-Holland.

[24] Tabaka, C. Medical misinformation on the internet and how it can harm your tortoise.2003 [cited 2006 1.1.]; Available from: http://www.chelonia.org/articles/Medical_misinformation.htm

What Is Being Iterated?
Reflections on Iteration in Information System
Engineering Processes

Nicholas Berente, Kalle Lyytinen

Case Western Reserve University, Cleveland, U.S.A

Abstract. Iteration is a fundamental principle of information system engineering, yet the concept remains under-theorized in the literature. In this chapter we articulate a lens for studying iteration through four types of iterating artifacts: concepts, representations, instantiations, and methodologies, and we apply this lens to a variety of prescriptive approaches to system development. Our review of these approaches suggests that iteration across one artifact or set of artifacts may substitute for iterations across another. We conclude with a reflection on how it is not the presence of iteration that distinguishes between methodologies, as iteration can be assumed in all system development efforts. Rather, the *attitude toward iteration* that various methodologies imply, and the *audience of iterations* across specific artifacts that the various approaches prescribe do more to differentiate between methodologies.

1 Introduction

Although "iteration" is often stressed as a fundamental principle of modern software development practices [18], the concept of iteration is not new. Information system engineering has always been an iterative process: from the formulations of earliest methodologies, concepts relating to iteration have been inherent in the discussions among researchers [32]. Yet, surprisingly, researchers have not addressed the types of iterations that occur across the various methodologies in any depth or the reasons for iteration.

The term "iteration" is not always used to denote the same aspect of design. For example, iteration most commonly refers to the cyclical generation of functional software code and it's testing [5]. But iteration also connotes repetition of a phase of development due to rework [20], the progressive design of "perceivable" subsystem structures [32], or successive sub-phases within a main phase [29]. Less common applications of the word also abound. For example, Checkland and Scholes [16] indicate that the cyclical comparison of conceptual models to the real world forms an iteration. Iterative activities also often go by different names, such as "prototyping" to iteratively elicit user input [1], "rounds" of iterative design activities to reduce risk [9], or even a "dance" of human interactions toward increased mutual understanding [10].

The concept of iteration is fundamental to design activity and therefore inherent in each design methodology. However, it is rarely articulated carefully in information system development literature. We follow Dowson in viewing iteration as a "generic" term implying "change to previous decisions and actions, and to the objects that have resulted from these actions. It is important to note that the need for these changes does not arise solely (or even mainly) from previous mistakes and errors; it is an inevitable part of the refinement and evolution of a software system" [22: p.36].

This chapter explores the concept of iteration as it pertains to information systems engineering processes, and seeks to understand the types of iterations, that is, the "artifacts" that iterate, and the configurations in which iterations emerge. In order to do this, we will establish four broad categories of artifacts that undergo iteration during development processes, and then address prescriptive literature to understand how these artifacts are treated across a variety of approaches.

2 What is Being Iterated?

According to Simon [49], the fundamental activity in design processes involves iterative "generate-test" cycles which traverse cognitive and representational spaces during the design process. March and Smith [41] build upon Simon's ideas and enlist the "artifacts" associated with information system development as: constructs (concepts), models (representations), methods (processes), and instantiations (software code), which all can be mapped either to cognitive or representational spaces. Our conceptualization of these four artifacts can be summarized as follows:

- *Conceptual artifacts* are representations of constructs that support the design process; such as stages in the process, or representations of a methodology.
- *Representational artifacts* are representations of the system-in-development, or software code.
- *Instantiation artifacts* are manifestations of the code itself, and
- *Methodological artifacts* are conceptual artifacts relating specifically to the process from a meta level.

We will use this classification to analyze what is being iterated and make sense of alternative forms of iteration. We examine what happens when we are iterating through conceptual, representational, or methodological artifacts, or through instantiations of the system itself [41]. Finally, we examine the expected impact of prescriptive iterative practices for each type of iteration.

2.1 Concepts

The most common conceptual artifact present in the design is the step, stage, or phase of the design. Stages are iterated if they are repeated. Stages and phases of the process are constructs that are prescribed by a methodology, but are not directly related to the designs or code instantiations. Other terms for such repeating steps in the methodology are "rounds" [9] and "iterations" [5,31,34]. Iterations over stages have traditionally been considered an inevitable, necessary evil [20,48], but are now more commonly thought to enhance the system quality across multiple dimensions [3,5,7,14,18,23,30,35,44]. Such stages can be formal, such as the requirements determination phase, which results in "frozen" requirements [21], or they can be fairly indeterminate, such as "time-boxed" steps [2,6].

Beyond stages some researchers describe other forms of conceptual iterations. The perceptions of individual designers change throughout the design, at different levels of the design [32]. For example, systems design has been likened to a hermeneutic circle [11], where a designer iteratively compares an artifact to its context in order to understand its meaning. Checkland [15] recommends specific representations, such as rich pictures and holons, to guide a system developer in iterative cognitive cycles between the representations, personal mental models, and perceptions of reality that progressively refine his underlying concepts. As conceptual models of reality cannot have a direct, one-to-one mapping to the system, Sølvberg [50,52] suggests iterating across conceptual models while communicating and developing requirements, then translating these models into data models that represent the design model.

Researchers have also likened forms of system development to dialectic cycles [17]. Such cycles are evident in participatory approaches that encourage dialogs between system developers and the user community [24,45]. These dialogs result in a series of iterative agreements concerning system functionality, the anticipated environment, or appropriate methodologies [45]. They typically involve cycles of cooperation and conflict that are intended to improve user-related outcomes such as user satisfaction and system use.

2.2 Representations

System engineering processes are rife with representational artifacts that depict the information system or its environment. These representations are intended to describe aspects of the entire system, or portions of it. For example, requirements definitions, specifications, and data models depict slices of the system from a certain perspective and using a particular abstraction level. Other representations are intended to illustrate only aspects or parts of the system, for example, use cases, user-interface mock-ups, or user views. Throwaway prototypes [4], if actually thrown away, would be considered representational artifacts even though they are representations made up of software code.

Early representations in the design process need to accommodate the "fuzzy" cooperative thinking necessary while requirements and needs are being articulated, while later representations involve formal, detailed specifications that guide programming [53]. Over the course of design, representations change and evolve or translate into other representations, such as "as built" software documentation. Because of this need for downstream documentation, no software development methodology can overlook iteration across documents entirely, although some, such as XP [5], do look to remove documentation from the critical path of development.

Iteration across a representation can imply changes to that representation that refine or improve it, but can also indicate different alternatives of which only one will be incorporated in the final design [33,50]. The extant literature addresses various forms of iteration related to representations – some to a great degree, such as requirements determination [21] and related data models [50] in general, as well as the wide array of documentation within formal methodologies [7,9,20,28,31,45,51].

2.3 Instantiations

Software code evolves through multiple instantiations in some development approaches including versions of a completed system, or evolutionary prototypes. The common usage of "iterative development" refers to software development that proceeds through "self-contained mini-projects", where each produces partially completed software [34]. This has traditionally been referred to as evolutionary prototyping [1,6,23], or explorative programming [51]. Although iterative development has been associated with stepwise refinement of a blunt system [56], it is most often equated with evolutionary enhancement, where a subset of the final code is developed to evolve into the final system [3].

The justification for evolutionary prototyping centers on trial and error learning (i.e., learning by doing) about both the problem and solution. Users and developers do not know what they need until they see something useful. Generation of prototypes assists learning about the product and to communicate it in ways that is often superior to traditional documentation, thus supporting mutual learning [1,3,5,7,14,18,23,30,35,44].

Although evolutionary prototyping is the idea most often associated with iterative development, all application software iterates over the course of its life-cycle even if the methodology is not referred to as iterative. In this sense, each version of a software system can be considered an iteration. As bugs are fixed or enhancements added to code in a linear, even in a supposedly "non-iterative" evolutionary process, each new instantiation of code can be considered an iteration. An iteration of the software can also be tested. When all or some portion of the code is compiled, the result is an iteration of compiled code. Anytime a designer replaces or adds to any part of working code resulting in some form of instantiation, he has developed an iteration of that code.

2.4 Methodologies

System designers work within implicit or explicit normative frameworks that guide their work. The explicit representations of such frameworks are known as methodologies. Such frameworks offer stability and resist change: organizations are known to not change their methodologies even after numerous failures [39]. Since all methodologies have limitations [18], a conclusion that many have reached is that a contingency approach to selection of development methodologies is a necessity [18,19,21,26,42]. In this approach, selection of the appropriate methodology depends upon critical project variables such as the project's level of uncertainty [21], innovativeness, criticality, number of users [26], and risk [42], as well as the size of the development team [18], and organizational fit [19]. In an effort to find an appropriate methodology, if a team were to change its methodology between projects, it might implement entirely different methodologies, or perhaps merely implement a few practices from current vogue methodologies. As methodologies change between projects, one could say the methodologies and their representations iterate toward the goal of an ideal fit with the specific context.

An articulation of each variant of a methodology would be the iterating artefact. A better and more fine-grained example of methodological iteration is the idea presented in method engineering literature [12,47,54]. Because methodologies cannot specify all of the tasks to be done in a development project, and problems change during development, designers must reflect on their actions [15]. Through this reflection, designers will learn and continuously evolve their practices [47]. As practices evolve and designers learn, capturing that process knowledge and rationale for method-related decisions can reduce errors and facilitate proper evolution of development methods [47]. When developers articulate changes in their development processes, they are iterating their methodology.

Any change to the development methodology may or may not improve specific outcomes. In this sense, changes are essentially experiments associated with trial and error learning around a methodology and development process. A series of changes that take advantage of learning from iterations would conceivably lead to improvements. Incremental refinement of methodologies can lead to better outcomes than radical changes to methodology, because incremental refinements take process experience and continuous evolution into consideration.

3 Prescriptive Software Engineering Approaches

Five general approaches were identified as classes of information system engineering methodologies: traditional, evolutionary, hybrid, socio-technical, and sense-making. In the next section, these five approaches will be briefly addressed and their treatment of iteration for each class of methodologies will be explored.

3.1 Traditional Approaches: Waterfall and SDLC

There are numerous system development life-cycle methodologies (SDLC). The life-cycle approach is based on the assumption that all development should follow a series of stages that center on activities of definition, development and implementation, with varying sub-steps [20]. The life-cycle structure emphasizes the documents and approvals that must be completed during each step. Iterations typically follow review processes that connect steps and determine whether the project can go on to the next step, or whether a step must be performed again. Reasons for iteration during the formal review process of a life-cycle approach include technical uncertainty, quality concerns, and budget problems [51].

The Waterfall model is the most well known a life cycle methodology and is often characterized as top-down, unidirectional, and non-iterative [48]. Contrary to this popular claim, even in its earliest manifestation Royce suggested that unwanted changes and their resulting iterations are inevitable, and he recommended a number of practices to address such unanticipated problems, including piloting any sizable software project with a "preliminary program design" [48: p.331]. This concept was later popularized by Brooks when he stressed to "plan to throw one away; you will, anyhow" [14: p.116]. Royce also suggested iterative maintenance of design documentation. He understood that requirements change over time as the developer learns from the design, and therefore the requirements should evolve through a series of at least five documents to the final documentation of the design "as built." Updates to design documentation occur for two primary reasons: to guide or to track development.

3.2 Evolutionary/Agile Approaches

Iterative development practices emerged soon after Waterfall. The idea of "stepwise refinement" involved a blunt, top-down design of the main system, then a phased decomposition and modular improvement of the code – largely to increase system performance [57]. Stepwise refinement was criticized for requiring "the problem and solution to be well understood," and not taking into consideration that "design flaws often do not show up until the implementation is well underway so that correcting the problems can require major effort" [3: p.390]. To address these issues, Basili and Turner recommended an "iterative enhancement" method of software development. They suggested that designers start small and simple, by coding a "skeletal sub-problem of the project." The team should develop a "project control list" that details all of the expected tasks that the system is expected to achieve. Then developers incrementally add functionality by iteratively extending and modifying the code, using the control list as a guide, until all items on the list have been addressed. Each iteration involves design, implementation (coding & debugging), and analysis of the software. When analysis finds a given iteration to be acceptable, the control list is modified accordingly, and the developers are on to the next task on the list. This idea of iterative enhancement established the foundation for evolutionary prototyping and many modern agile development methods.

Modern manifestations of evolutionary development practices are labeled "agile," or lightweight methodologies [18]. Agile methodologies are based on the assumption that communication is necessarily imperfect [18], and that software development is a social activity among multiple developers and users of the system. According to proponents of agile methods, increased documentation is not necessarily the answer to the weaknesses of evolutionary development practices. Rather, certain complementary activities must be in place to augment evolutionary development and to increase the quality or scope of iterations, such as pair programming, time-boxing, test-first development, etc. [5].

Anticipated benefits of evolutionary development are many. By growing the design in this matter software can be developed more quickly [13]. Beyond speed, evolutionary development enables a "more realistic validation of user requirements," the surfacing of "second-order impacts," and increased the possibility of comparing several alternatives [7: p.656]. Prototyping can demonstrate technical feasibility, determine efficiency of part of the system, aid in design/specification communication, and organize implementation decisions [23]. Prototyping is thought to mitigate requirements uncertainty [21], aid in innovation and increase participation [26], reduce project risk [9,40,42], and lead to more successful outcomes [35]. Because developers generate code rather than plan and document, they are expected to be more productive [3,5,34]. Therefore projects using evolutionary prototyping can be expected to cost less [3,5,18,35].

One problem with strict evolutionary design, however, is the lack of "iterative" planning for each prototype. Starting with a poor initial prototype could turn users away; prototyping can contribute to a short-term, myopic focus for the project; and "developing a suboptimal system" could necessitate a great deal of rework in later phases [7]. Exhaustive design documentation will still be required even if prototyping is the primary process [28]. The output of evolutionary development often resembles unmanageable "spaghetti code" that is difficult to maintain and integrate, similar to the "code and fix" problems that Waterfall was originally intended to correct [9]. Also, by using the software code itself to guide discussions of requirements, conversations tend to focus mainly on detail, rather than business principles associated with the information system [51]. Many continuing problems associated with evolutionary development include "ad hoc requirements management; ambiguous and imprecise communication; brittle architectures; overwhelming complexity; undetected inconsistencies in requirements, designs, and implementation; insufficient testing; subjective assessment of project status; failure to attack risk; uncontrolled change propagation; insufficient automation" [31: ch.1].

Therefore, many caution that evolutionary development practices will not be suited to every situation as such approaches make often unrealistic assumptions. Evolutionary methods assume that projects can be structured according to short-term iterations, face-to-face interaction is tenable and superior to formal documentation, and the cost of change remains constant over the project [55]. Issues such as scaling, criticality, and developer talent often require hybrid methodologies – or some combination of evolutionary prototypes with more formal methods [18,36]. Also, evolutionary development requires complementary innovations to succeed [5,7].

3.3 Heavyweight/Hybrid Approaches

While the bulk of software engineering approaches recognize the power of prototyping, many do not believe strict evolutionary development to be a universal answer to all needs of development. Rather, they argue that formal planning, documentation, and discipline is the answer, and thus developed "heavyweight" methodologies.

Boehm [7] described his COCOMO process as the waterfall model using incremental development. Boehm's process involved three explicit "increments of functionality": the first of which provided "a basic capability to operate and gain experience with the model"; the second is intended to add "valuable capabilities"; and the third added "nice to have features" [7: p.42]. Within each increment, however, development was expected to proceed linearly with distinct start and endpoints. Boehm was detailed about the number of documents that were expected to be produced in each phase, and they were fixed after they were produced within incremental trajectories, but modified between increments. One recent example of the adapted Waterfall method is McConnell's "survival" process, which recommends essentially a repackaged Waterfall process with prototyping in the requirements definition phase, and staged delivery and testing in the implementation phase [43].

Boehm's spiral model [9] involves a great deal of planning and formal reviews, but it is based rounds of development and allows for a number of prototypes. Rather than three clear increments [7], the spiral model allows any number of increments, which are guided by a hierarchy of risks. Early in development, when user-interface risks are particularly salient, evolutionary rounds of prototyping may occur until these specific risks are reduced. Later rounds, when interface-control risks might dominate, the rounds might entail a series of mini-waterfall processes. A modern descendent of the spiral model is the rational unified process, or RUP [31].

A noteworthy software engineering practice that stresses high formality is the capability maturity model of software development, or CMM [28]. The fundamental premise of CMM is that only statistically measured processes can be improved to reach consistency with cost, performance, and schedule expectations. In order to accomplish accurate measurement that is essential for consistency, the process must be mature. Different development teams have different levels of maturity. The failure of immature teams (levels 1&2) are not typically because of technical failure, but rather the "confused and incoherent process" due to lack of consistent management is typically at fault [28: p.28]. More mature teams have orderly, measured processes, actively developed standards, advanced tools and languages, etc. CMM is a top-down philosophy that stresses continuous process improvement and repeatable processes within well defined phases. The process itself is incrementally (iteratively) improved through the five CMM levels, with well-defined assessment methods at each level.

A fundamental assumption of each formal methodology is that certain aspects of the development process can be frozen, documented (and therefore communicated) adequately, and built-on with subsequent phases. The spiral model's rounds build upon frozen previous rounds. Although Humphrey warns not to freeze requirements too soon, he indicates that requirements should in fact be frozen at an appropriate time.

3.4 Participatory & Socio-Technical Approaches

Many information development researchers are concerned with system design as a social process, which involves communication, participation, and power. The multidimensionality of information solutions needs to be addressed. Although they are certainly technical systems, information systems are "more primarily, organizational and social communication systems" [29]. A view of information systems as socio-technical systems, complete with a multiplicity of perspectives, and as potential vehicles for control or emancipation [27] is not addressed in much of the information system engineering literature.

A growing segment of the information system engineering research and practitioner community believe that "passive" user participation is not sufficient to gain an adequate fit between the business process and the IS. Therefore, user involvement in the development process and the resulting knowledge of the system leads to better information system design, and a more successful implementation [46]. The socio-technical approaches, also known as participatory design approaches, not only involve users, but give them control over the development process. System designers act more like consultants to users who develop systems. The presence of 'neutral' facilitators is also required to manage the diversity and inevitable conflict in participatory exercises. Socio-technical development approaches seek to balance social and technical aspects of the development system [27,45].

ETHICS is a popular socio-technical, participatory methodology which resembles the life-cycle approaches in that is primarily linear in its view of stages and it tries to have clear understandings of the problems, objectives, etc. before the start of the design [45]. However, within each stage, a great deal of organic, discussion-based interaction takes place to define the steps, multiple alternatives are encouraged, adding a level of iteration reminiscent of early evolutionary approaches [i.e.,30]. But it is not evolution of the design itself, rather, the evolution of interpersonal agreements about the design and the design process. Ideas of groups of people, discussion, diverse goals, and conflict add to illustrate the interpersonal tensions associated with design. If cooperation and conflict do not emerge early, the result can be a potentially ineffective solution – with less cooperation and more conflict after implementation, when it is more difficult to make changes. Agreements on the design and its process thus can change iteratively throughout the development process.

Based on ETHICS, as well as a number of other participatory methodologies from the Scandinavian school [24], STEPS was developed as a sort of culmination of participatory methods [24]. One important contribution of STEPS is formal documentation of expected work practices resulting from implementation of the system, and changes in planned work practices aligning with the evolution of the system [24,25]. Participatory methods often resemble the highly formalized hybrids of linear SDLC methodologies with prototyping principles. However, they can add unique theoretical twists to their prescriptive methodologies. For example, the PIOCO methodology [29] requires iterative problem solving within levels of abstraction. Rather than freezing portions of the design through predetermined linear phases, developers are allowed to engage in explicit non-linear iterative activity throughout the design, and then freeze the design at specific level of abstraction before tackling lower levels of abstraction.

3.5 Sense-Making Approaches

Sense-making approaches to information system design emerged around issues concerning problem formulation. Problems, or requirements, do not exist objectively on their own in the world. But rather they are thought to be "constructed between various stakeholders adhering to various perspectives" [27: p.37]. Such approaches criticize other methods for taking simplistic, unrealistic view of meaning attached to the system, and a mechanistic view of organizations [37]. The most well-known sense-making approach is the soft systems approach (SSA), developed by Peter Checkland [15].

SSA is concerned with influencing a problematic situation by focusing on the "planning process" involved around problem identification [16]. This process involves refinement of a designer's conceptual model of the problem through multiple cycles. The conceptual models are based on a designer's understanding of the salient relationships, perceptions of the problem, political dimensions, and social roles, norms and values. To document this understanding, Checkland recommends conceptual representations called "rich pictures," "holons" and "root definitions." The designer's conceptual models are linked together and extended to approach the problem formulation in an iterative fashion - between conceptual models and the real world. The analyst can cycle through all stages of SSA, among a few stages, or within any stage a number of times. To understand an ensuing process, the analyst iterates cognitively between perceptions of the social world external to him, his internal ideas, various representations, and the instantiations of the methodology [16].

Although this form of inquiry is likely to offer a richer view of the social and cognitive phenomena surrounding design, it is apparent that there is little focus on overall cost and rework associated with iterations beyond what can be articulated through the perceptions and interests of individuals. Also, due to the cyclical nature of the methodology, no formal "universal" steps are addressed to provide a sense of progress. Rather, the inquiry resembles evolutionary methods, where convergence is the goal rather than an attempt to fit the outcome into neatly planned steps.

4 Reflections: What is Being Iterated?

From the above analysis, it is apparent that different methodologies vary in the iterations they address, and the reasons for iteration. For example, to address changing user requirements, traditional approaches iterate representational artifacts such as documentation, whereas evolutionary approaches iterate the instantiation. Both methods iterate to capture requirements, but they do so using different artifacts.

The philosophy associated with the iteration is also distinct across approaches. For example, traditional, heavyweight, and participatory methods encourage "freezing" requirements, which is expected to put an end to the iteration of requirements. Evolutionary and sense-making approaches question whether such freezing can ever really occur. Table 1 summarizes the iterating artifacts that are addressed in the different approaches, and their expected impacts.

The information systems development process can be defined as a change process of an object system to achieve certain objectives [27]. In this sense, designers are addressing issues of the current system and identifying and mobilizing resources that will enable movement from the current socio-technical system to a new one of the future. Due to uncertainty and ambiguity this is by necessity iterative. Information systems are dynamic and always evolving, under revision, and behaving differently in unique contexts due to learning and idiosyncratic practices. We assert that there is no single entity that *is* the system in a given development process, rather we view the system to be an elusive idea that can only be approximated through representations [38]. Early in the design process, the information system may be little more than an idea generated by a handful of people whose only tangible artifact is a vague conceptual model of some sort [53]. Later in the process the information system may be represented by lines of incomplete code, dozens of use cases, system models, and a great number of varying expectations of the system's utility. Yet throughout the process, individuals can all discuss the information system as if it were a single, discrete entity, although all individuals only have a partial view [56].

Since all system development is iterative, one might question the actual difference between modern "iterative" development and traditional methodologies. The answer appears to be in the way that these methodologies view the idea of iteration, and their audience for a given iteration. The first distinc-

Table 1. Iterating Artifacts Across Information Systems Engineering Approaches.

App.	Iterating Artifact Type	Description	Expected Impacts
Tra-dition	Conceptual Stages - formal	Phases in linear process	Discourage costly & inevitable problem fixes
	Representational: Doc.	Capture solutions to problems	Track changes to code
	Representational: Process Track.	Capture progress of project	Monitor proj.through phases
	Instantiation: Software Code	Fix prob. according to phases	Fix problems
Evo-lution	Conceptual Stages - cycle	Scheduled and informal iterations	Enables enhancement of code
	Representational: Process Track.	Capture progress of project	Monitor project over time
	Instantiation: Software Code	Enhance code, fix problems	Better code, less cost, strong. user-related outcomes
	Method: Between projects	Change method	Contingency alignment; learning and experience
	Method: Within projects	Refine method	Refinement
Hy-brid	Conceptual Stages – formal	Phase within cycle is repeated	Enables disciplined enhancement/problem fixes
	Conceptual Stages – cycle	Scheduled repetition of entire cycle	Enables enhancement of code
	Representational: Requirements	Requirements can iterate before frozen	Guide specifications
	Representational: Specifications	Specifications can iterate before frozen	Guide development of code
	Representational: Doc.	Code documentation	Track development of code
	Representational: Process tracking	Formal process documentation	Monitor project through phases
	Instantiation: Software code	Enhance code, fix problems	Better code, stronger user-related outcomes
	Method: Within project	Adapt process within method	Better fit to support code development
Part.	Conceptual Stages – formal	Phases in linear process	Discourage costly and inevitable problem fixes
	Conceptual: Agreements	Document cooperation/conflict results	Accommodate multiple perspectives
	Representational: Doc.	Capture solutions to problems	Track changes to code
	Representational: Process tracking	Capture progress of project	Monitor project through phases
	Instantiation: Software code	Enhance code, fix problems	Better code, stronger user-related outcomes
	Instantiation: Object system	Address object system context	Accommodate multiple perspectives
	Method: Between projects	Improve method	Accommodate multiple perspectives
	Method: Within projects	Refine method	Accommodate multiple perspectives
Sense-Mak	Conceptual: Stages - cycle	Cycling between designer and context	Enables the progressive improvement of understanding
	Conceptual: Problem understanding	Iterations btwn representation and world	Refine understanding
	Representational: Requirements	Object system representations iterated	Tool for improvement of understanding
	Instantiation: Object system	Active explicit interaction with object system	Improve and refine understanding
	Method: Within project	Refine method based on understanding	Supports designer understanding

tion lies in the view, or *attitude toward iteration*. Traditional methodologies attempt to avoid or minimize iteration, viewing it as an inevitable evil that can only be managed through better proactive planning. Evolutionary, or iterative, development processes embrace iteration as the mechanism by which developers can reach better outcomes. Traditional methodologies have attempted to deal with iteration as a reaction to an error or problem, whereas modern methodologies proactively seek the value of planned iteration. The other difference between iterative and traditional development is the intended *audience for the iteration*. Iterative development creates iterations specifically for garnering feedback from some portions of the clientele, whereas traditional development keeps its iterations within the developer community until the review process is expected at the end of a given phase, or until a complete release is made.

The first distinction, the proactive view of iteration, is addressed by foundational researchers through notions such as iterative enhancement [3] and evolutionary prototyping [1,23], and has now been embraced by agile methodologies [5,16,34]. The second distinction, which is the visibility of iteration has not been addressed, and can only be understood through understanding the varied roles of the artifacts used in a design process. Obviously there are many artifacts and past research has not been very clear about their roles. In this paper we have attempted to tease out iterations associated with system development by identifying sets of artifacts that are described in the extant literature. This exercise is intended to guide researchers' thinking about iteration in the future. By establishing a more detailed understanding of the information that each artifact makes visible, the role of the various artefacts and the relationships between these artifacts, better methodologies can be designed.

The four artifacts we have identified are located at different levels of abstraction and they overlap. For example, a given methodology can be considered a function of cognitive understanding [12,18,47], and might therefore be considered a conceptual artifact which iterates. Likewise, all representational artifacts typically represent conceptual, or methodological facets, or instantiations of the system itself. Instantiations can be self-evident (evolutionary prototypes), or they can be characterized by representational artifacts (such as throw-away prototypes), or they can be mental constructs of the designers.

4 Conclusion

In this essay, we have identified several iterating artifacts that are present in information system engineering processes based on the type of artefact. Through this effort, we look to remind researchers and practitioners that iteration forms the first principle of *any* system development project, regardless of methodology. Simon [49] argues that design cannot exist without iteration, as an activity without iteration cannot rightly be called design. The only questions become then: What is iterated? Why is it iterated? How long is it allowed to iterate? For whom and by whom it is iterated? And, of course, what are the effects of this iteration?

Our primary contribution has been to lay foundations for establishing a more refined view of iteration by introducing the four types of iterating artifacts, and by illustrating their application across five broad classes of information systems engineering methodologies. The construct of an iterating artifact can be leveraged in the future to aid in the design of methodologies and the tools that support these methodologies. It can be also used as a construct in studying empirical system design processes and their outcomes. By distinguishing different forms of iterating artifacts we offer a conceptual baseline for future treatments of these artifacts across methodological approaches and empirical investigations.

References

[1] Alavi, M.: An assessment of the prototyping approach to information systems development, Communications of the ACM, 27(6): 556-563 (1984).

[2] Auer, K., Meade, E., and Reeves, G.: The rules of the game. In: Extreme Programming and Agile Methods, Lecture Notes in Computer Science, Vol. 2753, ed by Maurer, F., Wells, D. (Springer, Berlin Heidelberg New York 2003).

[3] Basili, Turner: Iterative enhancement: a practical technique for software development. IEEE Transactions on Software Engineering. 1(4): 390-396 (1975).

[4] Baskerville, R.L., Stage, J.:Controlling prototype development through risk analysis," MIS Quarterly 20(4): 481-504 (1996).

[5] Beck, K.: Extreme Programming Explained: Embrace Change. The Agile Software Development Series, (Addison-Wesley 2002).

[6] Beynon-Davies, P., Tudhope, D., Mackay, H.: Information systems prototyping in practice. Journal of Information Technology. 14(1): 107-120 (1999).

[7] Boehm, B.: Software Engineering Economics, (Prentice-Hall 1981).

[8] Boehm, B., Gray, T.E., Seewaldt, T.: Prototyping vs. specification: a multiproject experiment. IEEE Transactions on Software Engineering, 10(3): 290-302(1984).

[9] Boehm, B.: The spiral model of software development and enhancement. Computer, 21(5): 61-72 (1988).

[10] Boland, R.J.: The process and product of system design. Management Science, 24(9) 887-898 (1978).

[11] Boland, R.J., Day, W.F.: The experience of system design: a hermeneutic of organizational action. Scandinavian Journal of Management, 5(2): 87 (1989).

[12] Brinkkemper, S.: Method engineering: engineering of information systems development methods and tools. Information and Software Technology, 38(4): 275-280 (1996).

[13] Brooks, F.P.: No silver bullet: essence and accidents of software engineering. Computer, 20(4): 10-19 (1987).

[14] Brooks, F.P.: The Mythical Man Month: Essays on Software Engineering (Addison-Wesley 1995).
[15] Checkland, P.: Systems Thinking, Systems Practice (Wiley 1981).
[16] Checkland, P., Scholes, J.: Soft Systems Methodology in Action, (Wiley 1999).
[17] Churchman, C.W.: The Design of Inquiring Systems (Basic Books 1971).
[18] Cockburn, A.: Agile Software Development, The Agile Software Development (Addison-Wesley 2002).
[19] Cooperider, J.G., Henderson, J.C.: Technology-process fit: perspectives on achieving prototyping effectiveness. Journal of Management Information Systems, 7(3): 67-87 (1991).
[20] Davis, G.B.: Management Information Systems: Conceptual Foundations, Structure, and Development (McGraw Hill 1974).
[21] Davis, G.B.: Strategies for information requirements determination. IBM Systems Journal. 21(1): 4-30 (1982).
[22] Dowson, M.: Iteration in the software process; review of the 3rd International Software Process Workshop. In: ICSE 1987, Proceedings of the 9th international conference on software engineering, Monterey, California, 1986.
[23] Floyd, C.: A Systematic Look at Prototyping. In Approaches to Prototyping, ed by Budde et al (Springer, Berlin, Heidelberg, New York 1984).
[24] Floyd, C., Mel, W.M., Reisin, F.M., Schmidt, G., Wolf, G.: Out of scandinavia: alternative approaches to software design and system development. Human-Computer Interaction. 4(4): 253-350 (1989).
[25] Floyd, C.: STEPS - a methodical approach to PD. Communications of the ACM. 36(6): 83 (1993).
[26] Hardgrave, B., Wilson, R., Eastman, K.: Toward a contingency model for selecting an information system prototyping strategy. Journal of Management Information Systems. 16(2): 113-136 (1999).
[27] Hirschheim, R., Klein, H., Lyytinen, K.: Information Systems Development and Data Modeling: Conceptual and Philosophical Foundations (Cambridge University Press 1995).
[28] Humphrey, W.S.: Managing the Software Process (Addison-Wesley 1989).
[29] Iivari, J., Koskela, E.: The PIOCO model for information systems design. MIS Quarterly. 11(3): 401 (1987).
[30] Keen, P.G.W., Scott Morton, M.S.: Decision Support Systems: An Organizational Perspective (Addison-Wesley 1978).
[31] Kruchten, P.: The Rational Unified Process An Introduction, 2nd edn (Addison-Wesley 2000).
[32] Langefors, B.: Theoretical Analysis of Information Systems (Auerbach 1973).
[33] Langefors, B.: Information and Data in Systems (Mason/Charter 1976).
[34] Larman, C.: Agile and Iterative Development, A Manager's Guide (Pearson 2004).
[35] Larman, C., Basili, V.: Iterative and incremental development: a brief history," Computer. 36(6): 47-56 (2003).
[36] Lindvall, M., Basili, V., Boehm, B., et al: Empirical findings in agile methods. In: Extreme Programming and Agile Methods – XP/Agile Universe 2002, Lecture Notes in Computer Science 2753, ed by Maurer, F., Wells, D. (Springer, Berlin Heidelberg New York 2003).

[37] Lyytinen, K.: Information Systems Development as Social Action: Framework and Critical Implications. Dissertation (Jyvaskyla Studies in Computer Science, Economics and Statistics ISBN 0357-9921; 8, 1986).

[38] Lyytinen, K.: A taxonomic perspective of information systems development: theoretical constructs and recommendations. In: Critical Issues in Information Systems Research, ed by Boland, R.J., Hirschheim, R. (Wiley 1987).

[39] Lyytinen, K., Robey, D.: Learning failure in information systems development, Information Systems Journal. 9(2): 85 (1999).

[40] Lyytinen, K., Mathiassen, L., Ropponen, J.: Attention shaping and software risk - a categorical analysis of four classical risk management approaches, Information Systems Research. 9(3): 233-255 (1998).

[41] March, S., Smith, D.: Design and natural science research on information technology. Decision Support Systems. 15(4): 251-266 (1995).

[42] Matthiassen, L., Seewaldt, T., Stage, J.: Prototyping and specifying: principles and practices of a mixed approach. Scandinavian Journal of Information Systems. 7(1): 55-72 (1995).

[43] McConnell, S.: Software Project Survival Guide (Microsoft Press 1998).

[44] McCracken, D.D., Jackson, M.A.: A maverick approach to systems analysis and design. In: Systems Analysis and Design. A foundation for the 1980's, ed by Cotterman, W.W, et al (North-Holland 1981).

[45] Mumford, E.: Redesigning Human Systems (Idea Group 2003).

[46] Oppelland, H.J., Kolf, F.: Participative development of information systems: methodological aspects and empirical experience. In: The Information Systems Environment, ed by Lucas, H., et al [IFIP 1979] (North-Holland 1980).

[47] Rossi, M., Ramesh, B., Lyytinen, K., Tolvanen, J.P.: Managing evolutionary method engineering by method rationale. Journal for the Association of Information Systems. 5(9): 356-391 (2005).

[48] Royce, W.W.: Managing the development of large software systems. Proceedings of IEEE WESCON. (1970).

[49] Simon, H.: The Sciences of the Artificial, 3rd edn (MIT Press 1996).

[50] Sølvberg, A.: Software requirements definition and data models. Fifth International Conference on Very Large Databases (1979).

[51] Sølvberg, A., Kung, D.C.: Information Systems Engineering, an Introduction. (Springer, Berlin Heidelberg New York 1993).

[52] Sølvberg, A.: Data and what they refer to. In: Conceptual Modeling, Current Issues and Future Directions. Lecture Notes in Computer Science, Vol. 1565, ed by Chen, P.P., Akoka, J. (Springer, Berlin Heidelberg New York 1999).

[53] Sølvberg, A.: Co-operative concept modeling. In: Information Systems Engineering, State of the Art and Research Themes, ed by Brinkkemper, S., et al (Springer, Berlin Heidelberg New York 2000).

[54] Tolvanen, J.P., Lyytinen, K.: Flexible method adaptation in CASE. The Metamodeling Approach. Scandinavian Journal of Information Systems. 5(1): 551-578 (1993).

[55] Turk, D., France, R., Rumpe, B.: Assumptions underlying agile software development processes. Journal of Database Management. 16(4): 62 (2005).

[56] Turner, J.: Understanding the elements of system design. In: Critical Issues in Information Systems Research, ed by Boland, R.J., Hirschheim, R. (Wiley 1987).

[57] Wirth, N.: Program development by stepwise refinement. Communications of the ACM. 14(4): 221-227 (1971).

Systems Development in a GRIDs Environment

Keith G. Jeffery

CCLRC Rutherford Appleton Laboratory, UK

Abstract. Over the past 30 years or more information systems engineers have attempted to improve the cost effectiveness of systems development by improving requirements capture and analysis, by structured design, by utilising design languages that can be verified for consistency more or less formally and in some cases matched formally to requirements. While data design methods improved significantly with relational and extended relational paradigms, program design was not so successful. Jackson input-process-output and hierarchic design methods gave way to functional. Object-orientation soon came up against the inability of hierarchic/inheritance mechanisms to represent the real world requirements which has more complexity. Aspect-oriented programming was intended to resolve this problem but appears to have caused even more confusion. Meantime, a bringing together of functional and object-oriented process design as service-oriented architecture, together with relational data design principles, has given some hope for progress. Early system design achieved device independence of programs and then (with relational technology) true data independence. However, general virtualisation of computing, data storage and communications resources has hitherto not been possible. The GRIDs paradigm achieves this latest step forward. Starting with metacomputing (linked supercomputers) in the USA, the European vision of GRIDs is a general IT 'surface' with which the end-user interacts intelligently to determine her requirement and the system behind the surface offers a 'deal' to fulfil the request. Beneath the 'surface' various architectures have been attempted. The GLOBUS architecture provides computational scheduling, but does not virtualise generally computation, data or network resources. The bringing together of WS (web services) with the GRIDs environment led to OGSA (Open Grids Services Architecture). Work with OGSA has exposed two major problems: the operating system facilities provided today are inadequate in various areas including security and resilience and the multiple layers in the service-oriented architecture expose too much complexity. The latest thinking revolves around SOKU (Service Oriented Knowledge Utilities) which are composed of self-managing, self-assembling, self-organising and self-destroying processes with exposed parametric and data input/output interfaces as well as its service description including non-functional aspects. The key is metadata (describing the SOKU processes and the data resources) and its use.

1 A Short History of Computing: A Personal View

From the earliest stages of using computers there has been the concept (although not the name) of systems engineering. Even the earliest programmers planned out their program before coding it. The software systems development methods developed along two parallel lines: one emphasising efficiency of developer time and fidelity to informally-defined user requirements with associated techniques of prototyping and fourth generation languages; the other emphasising correctness of the program, formal verification and formally-defined specifications. The former led to the so-called design methodologies, the latter to formal methods in software engineering, proof systems and in particular their application in the safety-critical environment.

An alternative and complementary viewpoint emerged in the sixties where systems development concentrated on the data. This was no surprise since large corporations were using computers for business processing and required to represent their business world of interest.

The problems with these approaches used in the seventies and eighties are well-documented. Software development was slow and error-prone and the use of formal methods made it slower. Data-centric approaches failed to map correctly the objects and their relationships in the real world: well-known examples include early database systems which could only map hierarchies, not fully-connected graph structures.

With the relational theory of data, and attached concept of the relational algebra (and calculus) a new age dawned. By the late eighties the first kind of software engineering came together with data engineering providing unprecedented speeds of system development, conformance to informally-stated user requirements and ability to adapt. Security issues emerged and were solved and there were attempts at distribution and the provision of business continuity. Furthermore, entity-relationship modelling based on the relational approach provided a further level of abstraction and a communications environment between the designer/developer and the end-user. Earlier work on artificial intelligence became encapsulated as knowledge engineering and aided the modelling process by providing a formalism for expressing the semantics of the information and for specifying constraints. In this era Arne Sølvberg and his team produced excellent R&D results demonstrating formal systems engineering from requirements specification to running system.

However, early systems had problems with performance, and errors made in the data modelling led to many work-arounds and modifications to the associated software. The systems became expensive to maintain. Steps were taken to formalise requirements and to generate systems – both data structures and software – using predefined component software fragments. The concept now known as services emerged.

To overcome the data-process gap, object-orientation was introduced reaching acceptance in the late eighties. Based on much earlier software engineering principles (e.g., those of Simula in the sixties) object-orientation encapsulated the static data model aspects of the application with the dynamic process aspects. Information Systems developed using this paradigm proved to be lacking in performance and additionally there were problems in both data modelling (related to hierarchic restrictions on inheritance) and process-modelling (repetition of the same code for many objects). The latter was to some extent overcome by aspect-oriented pro-gramming at the end of the nineties but by then the world was returning (indeed, many had never left) to relational database technology (improved with some object-oriented aspects).

The emergence of the world-wide-web rekindled interest in old tech-nologies in information retrieval and hypermedia. Progressively the web systems developed and heightened the visibility of technologies such as mobile code, service-oriented architecture and hypermedia. The web of-fered new possibilities in user interface design and in thin clients. Linking with the emergence of wireless technology and widespread use of mobile phones it was a short step to the concept of ambient, pervasive computing. Tim Berners-Lee emphasised the importance of semantics and trust rekin-dling interest in knowledge engineering.

In the USA in the late nineties the need for massive computation power to simulate various physical phenomena (from nuclear explosions to cli-mate) led to the metacomputing (linked supercomputers) concept popular-ised as 'the GRID'. In Europe a wider concept emerged simultaneously – GRIDs. It is in this context that systems engineering – and specifically in-formation systems engineering – is now discussed.

2 Requirements Today and Tomorrow

2.1 User Perspective

Users demand systems that are easy to use. The end-user has a low atten-tion span and requires immediate satisfaction. The threshold barrier to achieve usage of the system must be very low, else impatience precludes usage. The system should be capable of handling heterogeneous character sets, languages (information syntax) and semantics (knowledge). The system must be easy to understand and intuitive in its operation. The system must be knowledge-assisted – providing contextual hints, help, explanation. It must also be knowledge-assisted to assist in reducing the effort of input and update and to ensure constraints are in place to assure data quality. The end-user must have choice in the end-user device used implying that the system must be device-independent, adaptive to changing user modes of interaction through various media and be adaptable for variously abled persons. Naturally the system must handle the problems of intermittent connection, synchronisation and data transfer optimisation required in a mobile, ambient, pervasive environment. This requires particular expertise in user interface design.

2.2 System Perspective

The system should provide adequate performance, achieved by (re-)scheduling, parallelism, and distribution with appropriate optimisations and reconfiguration. The system should provide appropriate security, trust, privacy. For security of future use, the system should provide appropriate curation, preservation, which may be linked with appropriate failover and business continuity facilities. All this implies that systems have to be 'self-*' or autonomic: self-managing, self-configuring, self-organising, self-tuning, self-scheduling, self-maintaining, self-adapting. With millions of nodes and massive processing requirements it will be simply uneconomic for persons to 'be in the loop' of systems management.

3 The GRIDs Paradigm

The concept of the GRID was initiated in the USA in the late 1990s. Its prime purpose was to couple supercomputers in order to provide greater computational power and to utilise otherwise wasted central processor cycles. Starting with computer-specialised closed systems that could not interoperate, the second generation consists essentially of middleware which schedules a computational task as batch jobs across multiple computers. However, the end-user interface is procedural rather than fully declarative and the aspects of resource discovery, data interfacing and process-process interconnection (as in workflow for a business process) are primitive compared with work on information systems engineering involving, for example, databases and web services.

Through GGF (Global GRID Forum, now OGF Open GRID Forum) a dialogue has evolved the original GRID architecture to include concepts from the web services environment. OGSA (Open Grid Services Architecture) with attendant interfaces (OGSI) is now accepted by the GRID community, and OGSA/DAI (Data Access interface) provides an interface to databases at rather low level.

In parallel with this metacomputing GRID development, an initiative started in UK has developed an architecture for GRIDs that combines metacomputing (i.e. computation) with information systems. It is based on the argument that database R&D (research and development) – or more generally ISE (Information Systems Engineering) R&D - has not kept pace with the user expectations raised by WWW. Tim Berners-Lee threw down the challenge of the semantic web and the web of trust [1]. The EC (European Commission) has argued for the information society, the knowledge society and the ERA (European Research Area) – all of which are dependent on database R&D in the ISE sense. This requires an open architecture embracing both computation and information handling, with integrated detection systems using instruments and with an advanced user interface providing 'martini' (anytime, anyhow, anywhere) access to the facilities. The GRIDs concept [6] addresses this challenge, and further elaboration by a team of experts has produced the EC-sponsored document 'Next Generation GRID' [3].

It is time for the database community (in the widest sense, i.e. the information systems engineering community) to take stock of the research challenges and plan a campaign to meet them with excellent solutions, not only academically or theoretically correct but also well-engineered for end-user acceptance and use.

3.1 The Idea

In 1998-1999 the UK Research Council community was proposing future programmes for R&D. The author was asked to propose an integrating IT architecture [6]. The proposal was based on concepts including distributed computing, metacomputing, metadata, agent- and broker-based middleware, client-server migrating to three-layer and then peer-to-peer architectures and integrated knowledge-based assists. The novelty lay in the integration of various techniques into one architectural framework.

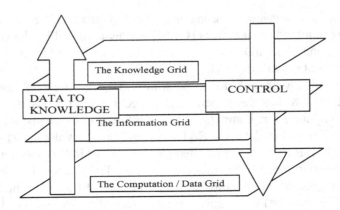

Fig. 1. Grids Architecture

3.2 The Requirement

The UK Research Council community of researchers was facing several IT-based problems. Their ambitions for scientific discovery included post-genomic discoveries, climate change understanding, oceanographic studies, environmental pollution monitoring and modelling, precise materials science, studies of combustion processes, advanced engineering, pharmaceutical design, and particle physics data handling and simulation. They needed more processor power, more data storage capacity, better analysis and visualisation – all supported by easy-to-use tools.

On the other hand, much of commercial IT (Information Technology) including process plant control, management information and decision support systems, IT-assisted business processes, entertainment and media systems and diagnosis support systems all require ever-increasing computational power and expedited information access, ideally through a uniform system providing a seamless information and computation landscape to the end-user. Thus there is a large potential market for GRIDs systems.

The original proposal based the academic development of the GRIDs architecture and facilities on scientific challenging applications, then involving IT companies as the middleware stabilised to produce products which in turn could be taken up by the commercial world. During 2000 the UK e-Science programme was elaborated with funding from 04 2001.

3.3 Architecture Overview

The architecture proposed consists of three layers (Fig.1). The computation/data grid has supercomputers, large servers, massive data storage facilities and specialised devices and facilities (e.g. for VR (Virtual Reality)) all linked by high-speed networking and forms the lowest layer. The main functions include compute load sharing/algorithm partitioning, resolution of data source addresses, security, replication and message rerouting. This layer also provides connectivity to detectors and instruments. The information grid is superimposed on the computation/data grid and resolves homogeneous access to heterogeneous information sources mainly through the use of metadata and middleware. Finally, the uppermost layer is the knowledge grid which utilises knowledge discovery in database technology to generate knowledge and also allows for representation of knowledge through scholarly works, peer-reviewed (publications) and grey literature, the latter especially hyperlinked to information and data to sustain the assertions in the knowledge.

The concept is based on the idea of a uniform landscape within the GRIDs domain, hiding complexity by easy-to-use interfaces.

3.4 The GRID

In 1998 – in parallel with the initial UK thinking on GRIDs – Foster and Kesselman published a book generally known as 'The GRID Bible' [4]. The essential idea is to connect together supercomputers to provide more power – the metacomputing technique. However, the major contribution lies in the systems and protocols for compute resource scheduling. Additionally, the designers of the GRID realised that these linked supercomputers would need fast data feeds so developed GRIDFTP. Finally, basic systems for authentication and authorisation are described. The GRID has encompassed the use of SRB (Storage Request Broker) from SDSC (San Diego Supercomputer Centre) for massive data handling. SRB has its proprietary metadata system to assist in locating relevant data resources. It also uses LDAP as its directory of resources. The GRID corresponds to the lowest grid layer (computation/data layer) of the GRIDs architecture.

4 The GRIDs Architecture

The idea behind GRIDs is to provide an IT environment that interacts with the user to determine the user requirement for service and then, having obtained the user's agreement to 'the deal' satisfies that requirement across a heterogeneous environment of data stores, processing power, special facilities for display and data collection systems (including triggered automatic detection instruments) thus making the IT environment appear homogeneous to the end-user.

Referring to Fig. 2, the major components external to the GRIDs environment are:

- users: each being a human or another system;
- sources: data, information or software
- resources: such as computers, sensors, detectors, visualisation or VR (virtual reality) facilities

Each of these three major components is represented continuously and actively within the GRIDs environment by:

1) metadata: which describes the external component and which is changed with changes in circumstances through events

2) an agent: which acts on behalf of the external resource representing it within the GRIDs environment.

As a simple example, the agent could be regarded as the answering service of a person's mobile phone and the metadata as the instructions given to the service such as 'divert to service when busy' and/or 'divert to service if unanswered'.

Finally there is a component which acts as a 'go between' between the agents. These are brokers which, as software components, act much in the same way as human brokers by arranging agreements and deals between agents, by acting themselves (or using other agents) to locate sources and resources, to manage data integration, to ensure authentication of external components and authorisation of rights to use by an authenticated component and to monitor the overall system.

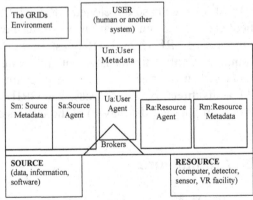

Fig. 2. The GRIDs Components

From this it is clear that they key components are the metadata, the agents and the brokers.

5 Systems Development in a GRIDs Environment

The architecture sketched above depicts the middleware necessary for applications to be constructed and executed. The EC NGG1 (Next Generation Grids Expert Group 1) confirmed this set of requirements and architecture characterised as 'the invisible GRID' i.e. hidden from the end-user but available and performing. However the requirements outlined earlier demand 'so-called non-functional' characteristics of the system which are not at this level but which concern the lower levels of the architecture – in particular the provision of performance and trust /security. This led the NGG2 expert group of the EC to an architecture for systems development with operating systems enhanced with foundationware to bring them up to the required interface standard including provision of trust and security, performance and self-* features. Above the foundationware is the service-oriented middleware providing the basic services required by end-user applications which themselves sit on top of the middleware layer and are developed essentially by composition of services including, where necessary because of unavailability, the provision of new services.

It was then realised by the NGG3 expert group of the EC that this layered architecture was too complex and that a simplification was possible. The foundationware and middleware layers could both be implemented as components providing services, and these components had to have certain characteristics. Essentially the components had to be active, that is they had to be themselves self-motivating such that they could compose themselves into applications based on requirements, and since they are self-managing they could reorganise (self-tune, self-schedule) with changing resource availability opportunities and changing user requirements. The SOKU (service-oriented knowledge utility) concept was defined.

5.1 SOKU

The concept of SOKU is based on a service. The service can be discovered, composed into larger-scale services, replicated for parallelism and distributed, modified by parametric input. In order for this to be achieved the service needs to be wrapped by rich metadata such that these actions can be automated and not require human intervention. The key question then is what metadata is required for these autonomic actions to be achievable at execute time and for systems development at system build time.

5.2 Environment

The problem is how to specify, design and construct such systems – or system components – based on SOKUs. Traditional system development technologies are only partly appropriate to this new environment. Instead of the traditional requirements specification, iterative development and delivery of an end-to-end system - which may or may not include preconstructed components – the emphasis is on the development of preconstructed components that can be automatically or semi-automatically composed at both system development time and at execute time. This requires a different kind of analysis of requirements utilising an approach that considers a much wider context than the system being specified in order to optimise the future utilisation of components being developed. In other words the requirement is for the development of generic components that meet the specification of the system currently being developed but also can be re-used in other systems. This approach has been discussed in the past – usually in an object oriented environment with the class concept – but has rarely if ever been achieved. The contention of this paper is that this is because the metadata associated with the components was inadequate for the re-use purpose.

6 Metadata is the Key Technology

Metadata is data about data [7]. An example might be a product tag attached to a product (e.g., a tag attached to a piece of clothing) that is available for sale. The metadata on the product tag tells the end-user (human considering purchasing the article of clothing) data about the article itself – such as the fibres from which it is made, the way it should be cleaned, its size (possibly in different classification schemes such as European, British, American) and maybe style, designer and other useful data. The metadata tag may be attached directly to the garment, or it may appear in a catalogue of clothing articles offered for sale (or, more usually, both). The metadata may be used to make a selection of potentially interesting articles of clothing before the actual articles are inspected, thus improving convenience. Today this concept is widely-used. Much e-commerce is based on B2C (Business to Customer) transactions based on an online catalogue (metadata) of goods offered. One well-known example is www.amazon.com.

B2B (Business to Business) is more complex, often involving negotiation to reconcile metadata differences in syntax and semantics including metadata associated with trust and security.

What is metadata to one application may be data to another. For example, an electronic library catalogue card is metadata to a person searching for a book on a particular topic, but data to the catalogue system of the library which will be grouping books in various ways: by author, classification code, shelf position, title – depending on the purpose required.

6.1 Current Availability and Usage

A database schema is a well-known example of metadata. However, it does little more than provide an interface to provide independence between software and data and a naming system for data objects to be used in software. Database schemas do provide information on syntax (structure) at both logical and physical levels but fail to address the semantic (meaning) level.

A URI provides metadata pointing to the actual object of interest. URIs can be rather complex, including not just an internet address but also parameters or even a query.

DC (Dublin Core) is a well-known metadata standard for describing objects, initially designed to describe web pages. It has a set of extensions (qualified DC) which makes interoperation difficult as different developers interpret differently the semantics (and in some cases the syntax) of DC.

There have been various attempts at trust negotiation and rights management/trading using metadata and standards for recording rights have been proposed. The management of rights associated with created works has been discussed extensively [8]. This extends to IPR (intellectual property rights) as understood in this environment. However, the management of rights in a B2B transaction (or a business relationship with multiple transactions e.g. within a supply chain) is more complex. Setting up the relationship involves trust negotiations which in turn require access to conditions of business, background information on the organisation and possibly references concerning the organisation. From this basis an appropriate trust/security policy can be put in place for transactions with the organisation concerned and encoded as metadata which wraps the transactional information in order to ensure the security systems in the organisation operate correctly. A basic trust model is presented in [9] while a more business-oriented approach is that of TrustCom project [10].

Dictionaries, thesauri, domain ontologies are all required for interpretation of semantics and are used in association with other metadata to support the IT processes, and their users, in understanding and interaction. They are also used for interoperation between heterogeneous systems.

Procedure calls and functional signatures provide some metadata information about the functional properties of a software component. However the information is usually very limited and commonly the information is only encoded as comments within the component. A further problem is that, in general, non-functional properties (such as performance, limitations of use, precision/accuracy etc) are not declared and documented.

O-O classes and KE frames provide metadata again concerning the properties of a software component or software/data component. Herein lies the problem, the confusion between software and data properties and how they should be described or exposed for utilisation by other systems. In general these technologies are being superseded by service-oriented components.

6.2 Kinds of Metadata

It is increasingly accepted that there are several kinds of metadata. The classification proposed (Fig. 3) is gaining wide acceptance and is detailed below.

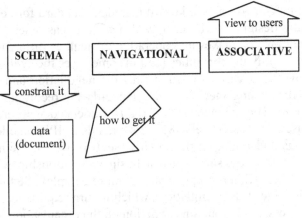

Fig. 3. Metadata Classification

Schema Metadata: Schema metadata constrains the associated data. It defines the intension whereas instances of data are the extension. From the intension a theoretical universal extension can be created, constrained only by the intension. Conversely, any observed instance should be a subset of the theoretical extension and should obey the constraints defined in the intension (schema). One problem with existing schema metadata (e.g. schemas for relational DBMS) is that they lack certain intensional information that is required [11]. Systems for information retrieval based on, e.g. the SGML (Standard Generalised Markup Language) DTD (Document Type Definition) experience similar problems.

It is noticeable that many ad hoc systems for data exchange between systems send with the data instances a schema that is richer than that in conventional DBMS – to assist the software (and people) handling the exchange to utilise the exchanged data to best advantage.

Navigational Metadata: Navigational metadata provides the pathway or routing to the data described by the schema metadata or associative metadata. In the RDF model it is a URL (universal resource locator), or more accurately, a URI (Universal Resource Identifier). With increasing use of databases to store resources, the most common navigational metadata now is a URL with associated query parameters embedded in the string to be used by CGI (Common Gateway Interface) software or proprietary software for a particular DBMS product or DBMS-Webserver pairing.

The navigational metadata describes only the physical access path. Naturally, associated with a particular URI are other properties such as:

- security and privacy ;
- access rights and charges
- constraints over traversing the hyperlink mapped by the URI;
- semantics describing the hyperlink such as 'the target resource describes the son of the person described in the origin resource'

However, these properties are best described by associative metadata which then allows more convenient co-processing in context of metadata describing both resources and hyperlinks between them and – if appropriate - events.

Associative Metadata: In the data and information domain associative metadata can describe:

- a set of data (e.g. a database, a relation (table) or a collection of documents or a retrieved subset). An example would be a description of a dataset collected as part of a scientific mission;
- an individual instance (record, tuple, document). An example would be a library catalogue record describing a book ;
- an attribute (column in a table, field in a set of records, named element in a set of documents). An example would be the accuracy/precision of instances of the attribute in a particular scientific experiment ;
- domain information (e.g. value range) of an attribute. An example would be the range of acceptable values in a numeric field such as the

capacity of a car engine or the list of valid values in an enumerated list such as the list of names of car manufacturers;

- a record/field intersection unique value (i.e. value of one attribute in one instance) This would be used to explain an apparently anomalous value.

In the relationship domain, associative metadata can describe relationships between sets of data e.g. hyperlinks. Associative metadata can – with more flexibility and expressivity than available in e.g. relational database technology or hypermedia document system technology – describe the semantics of a relationship, the constraints, the roles of the entities (objects) involved and additional constraints.

In the process domain, associative metadata can describe (among other things) the functionality of the process, its external interface characteristics, restrictions on utilisation of the process and its performance requirements/characteristics.

In the event domain, associative metadata can describe the event, the temporal constraints associated with it, the other constraints associated with it and actions arising from the event occurring.

Associative metadata can also be personalised: given clear relationships between them that can be resolved automatically and unambiguously, different metadata describing the same data may be used by different users.

Taking an orthogonal view over these different kinds of information objects to be described, associative metadata may be classified as follows:

- descriptive: provides additional information about the object to assist in understanding and using it;
- restrictive: provides additional information about the object to restrict access to authorised users and is related to security, privacy, access rights, copyright and IPR (Intellectual Property Rights);
- supportive: a separate and general information resource that can be cross-linked to an individual object to provide additional information e.g. translation to a different language, super- or sub-terms to improve a query – the kind of support provided by a thesaurus or domain ontology;

Most examples of metadata in use today include some components of most of these kinds, but neither structured formally nor specified formally so that the metadata tends to be of limited use for automated operations thus requiring additional human interpretation.

6.3 What is Needed Now

The roadmap for moving forward requires several components:

1. a generally agreed understanding of the purposes, uses and needs for metadata in a GRIDs/ambient environment
2. the definition of metadata that is machine understandable as well as machine readable
3. the definition of metadata for description, restriction, correctness, navigational access and system support
4. standardisation of (2) and (3) with widespread deployment and use
5. a process for updating (4)

Clearly (1), (2) and (3) will require more research and development including extensive testing for effectiveness before we can move to (4). I foresee this R&D effort lasting for some years, and keeping active researchers in the area very busy!

7 Conclusion

The GRIDs architecture will provide an IT infrastructure to revolutionise and expedite the way in which we do business and achieve leisure. The Ambient Computing environment will revolutionise the way in which the IT infrastructure intersects with our lives, both professional and social. The two architectures in combination will provide the springboard for the greatest advances yet in Information Technology. This can only be achieved by excellent R&D leading to commercial take-up and development of suitable products, to agreed standards, ideally within an environment such as W3C (the World Wide Web Consortium) and/or OGF (Open GRID Forum). The current efforts in GRID computing have moved some way away from metacomputing and towards the architecture described here with the adoption of OGSA (Open Grids Services Architecture). However, there is a general feeling that Next Generation GRID requires an architecture rather like that described here, as reported in the Report of the EC Expert Group on the subject [3]. To develop instances of this architecture will require advanced information systems engineering. The key is advanced, machine-understandable metadata to describe the architectural components.

Acknowledgements: Although the author remains responsible for the content, many of the ideas have come from fruitful discussions not only with the author's own team at CCLRC-RAL but also with many members of the

UK science community and the UK Computer Science/Information systems community. The author has also benefited greatly from discussions in the contexts of ERCIM (www.ercim.org), W3C (www.w3.org) and the EC NGG Expert Group.

There is one special acknowledgement. I was working on - or more accurately struggling with - how best to manage the systems development process for advanced information systems applications when I met Arne. We have been colleagues and -I am proud to say- friends for approximately 25 years. We have served together on boards and committees, most recently as president and vice-president of ERCIM. Arne has been mentor and guide, opponent and partner (in discussions and debate), supporter and critic. We have worked together on developing a strategy for IT in Europe (and wider) and we have worked together on projects. Whether in a professional context, or as host (and raconteur) Arne is always excellent company. He has surely been a major influence on my career.

References

[1] Berners-Lee,T.: 'Weaving the Web' 256 pp Harper, San Francisco 1999
[2] http://purl.oclc.org/2/
[3] www.cordis.lu/ist/grids/index.htm
[4] Foster, I., Kesselman, C. (Eds). The Grid: Blueprint for a New Computing Infrastructure. Morgan-Kauffman 1998
[5] Jeffery, K.G.: 'An Architecture for Grey Literature in a R&D Context' Proceedings GL'99 (Grey Literature) Conference Washington 2 October 1999
[6] Jeffery, K.G.: Original Paper available at http://www.cclrc.ac.uk/Publications/1433/KnowledgeInformationData20000124.htm
[7] Jeffery, K.G. 'Metadata': in Brinkkemper,J; Lindencrona,E; Sølvberg,A: 'Information Systems Engineering' Springer Verlag, London 2000.
[8] http://www.dlib.org/dlib/july98/rust/07rust.html
[9] http://jan.netcomp.monash.edu.au/publications/IC2002_69.pdf[10]
[10] http://www.eu-trustcom.com/
[11] Jeffery, K. G., Hutchinson, E. K., Kalmus, J. R., Wilson, M. D., Behrendt, W. , Macnee, C. A.: 'A Model for Heterogeneous Distributed Databases' Proceedings BNCOD12 July 1994; LNCS 826 pp 221-234 Springer-Verlag 1994

Adaptive Information Systems[1]

Barbara Pernici

Politecnico di Milano, Italy

Abstract. Adaptivity in information systems is proposed in the context of mobile and multichannel applications of information systems. Adaptivity may range from interaction functionality to variable ways of providing services according to a variable context of use. The paper will focus on adaptivity of process-based service provisioning, following a service oriented approach, to information system development, in which services are selected, deployed, and invoked in variable contexts. Support to self-healing features of service-based information systems will also be discussed.

1 Introduction

New technologies available for the development of information systems allow dynamically composing services to provide advanced personalized value added services and ubiquitous and mobile access from the users with a variety of access devices. To support the development of such information systems, a clear requirement emerges for flexibility and adaptability.

Flexibility for information systems processes has been studied in the context of workflow systems for building systems that are flexible regarding both business and corresponding IT infrastructure transformation [7].

To provide adaptability in information systems and in particular context-awareness, the Service Oriented Architecture (SOA) [1] provides a conceptual and technological infrastructure that facilitates the development of adaptive systems.

---

[1] Part of this work has been funded by the EU STREP-FET Project WS-Diamond and FIRB 2005 Tekne project.

In the MAIS (Multichannel Adaptive Information Systems) project [15], model-based development has been considered both to develop front-end and back-end services. The adaptation process operates at several levels: selecting the most appropriate contents (e.g., according to user interests), building an adequate layout for web pages according to layout capabilities of the client device, developing adaptive and flexible processes which select services based on the context of execution, both at the user side and the service side.

The quality of the design of the information system is particularly critical in adaptive and flexible systems. In fact, while high quality for conceptual modeling would require properties such as validity and completeness of the developed models, the trade off between desirable properties and cost impact becomes significant. In [13], the concept of feasibility is introduced and, in particular, feasible validity, feasible completeness, and feasible comprehensibility. On the other end, a feasible design requires mechanisms which allow adapting the system at run time to cope with situations which have not been completely considered at design time.

The goal of this paper is to discuss how process flexibility can be achieved, and to discuss it with respect to the relation between design time and run time aspects of the design of adaptive information systems. We focus in particular on process-related aspects, and on methods to achieve flexibility through dynamic service invocation, negotiation, and self-healing properties introduced in the information system.

The structure of the paper is as follows. In Section 2, we discuss flexible processes. In Section 3, we introduce negotiation and re-optimization as adaptivity mechanisms. In Section 4, we present the concept of self-healability of processes. Finally in Section 5 we discuss related work.

2 Flexible Processes

In the MAIS project, a major research question which has been addressed is the development of interactive information systems on a multi-channel platform [15]. In Fig. 1, we illustrate the context-aware process execution scenario considered in the MAIS project. A variable service execution context is assumed, including different user profiles, different and variable interaction devices and interaction contexts, variable service provisioning contexts, and variable and context-dependent network characteristics. Adaptivity can be provided at different levels: service provisioning, network, and front-end.

Process support technologies are a natural choice for enabling interaction machines. Such technologies are typically based of process models, which need to be flexible enough for people to adapt them to support their emerging goals. Service Oriented Architectures (SOA) favour the development of systems to support processes in a mobile environment, providing a general infrastructure to access services: a communication infrastructure to invoke services, based mainly on the SOAP protocol; the publication of services in a service registry (or broker) by the service providers; retrieval of services from the registry by user applications; a direct interaction between requestor and provider, without the intervention of the service broker.

MAIS Platform Scenario

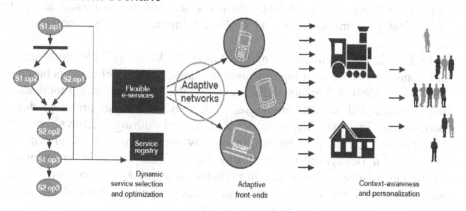

Fig. 1. MAIS context-aware processes

In MAIS, services can be composed to develop applications using workflow-like languages. In particular, processes are modelled and executed using an extension of the Business Process Execution Language (BPEL), which allows the definition of composed services as web services. BPEL provides the basic coordination constructs for process definition, such as sequence, iteration, and selection, allowing both synchronous and asynchronous interaction. Innovative solutions have been developed for service provisioning on multiple channels. The focus of the research is adaptivity to channel and context characteristics at the service level and an optimized selection of micro-services to dynamically create value-added flexible macro-services. The focus is mainly on web-services, i.e., e-services that are provided using a web infrastructure on an Internet connection provided on variable types of connection. An adaptive service execution has been studied, with the goal of providing flexible e-services and focusing on dynamic semantic-based selection and composition of services from an extended UDDI registry. This is achieved by taking into account functional and quality-of-service parameters, and dynamic service substitution and execution mechanisms [6].

A service is characterized both by functional aspects (i.e., the provided capabilities) and by non-functional aspects (i.e., quality-of-service levels), and the same service might be offered with a different quality of service.

Processes are realized by composing services offered by different providers. Specifically, a MAIS process describes the composition of different services to obtain a flexible e-service, where service selection, and in some cases dynamic composition, may be performed at run time, during process execution. The execution of a flexible service depends on the context of execution and the quality of service of the component services. The MAIS approach allows services to be dynamically selected or substituted, and to be dynamically composed in a high-performance process orchestration environment.

In Fig. 2, the architecture of the MAIS back-end flexible Web service environment is shown through its main modules. Service selection is based on the MAIS Service Registry, which extends the UDDI registry functionality with service and domain ontologies. The same ontologies are used during publication by the Semantic Publisher and during retrieval by the Matchmaker. Dynamic composition of new services is performed with the support of a Behavioral Compatibility Engine. The semantic and syntactic mediation of services is of key importance in dynamic composition. This is why the MAIS Service Registry also stores a Wrapper Repository, where semantic and syntactic wrappers are stored.

The flexible invocation and orchestration environment is illustrated in the upper part of the figure. MAIS flexible services are invoked by external end users and Web applications through a Platform Invoker module, which provides an interface to the MAIS back-end environment. Services are invoked by a Concrete Service Invoker, which provides the basic mechanisms for adaptivity: it retrieves from the MAIS Service Registry the services to be invoked, invoking them through wrappers, if needed; context information for context-aware service invocation is provided by support from the MAIS Reflective Architecture, a middleware component to exchange context information.

The process orchestration provided by the Process Orchestrator is based on an abstract description of the processes, and actual services are invoked through the Concrete Service Invoker. The Concretizator module performs selection of services for an abstract composed process orchestrated by the Process Orchestrator using optimization and negotiation techniques, and using recommendations for personalized service selection from the Recommendation Environment. A number of support tools have also been developed within the MAIS environment to support service design [15].

The MAIS Process Language allows the definition of flexible processes in terms of the following elements provided as annotations to an abstract BPEL process specification:

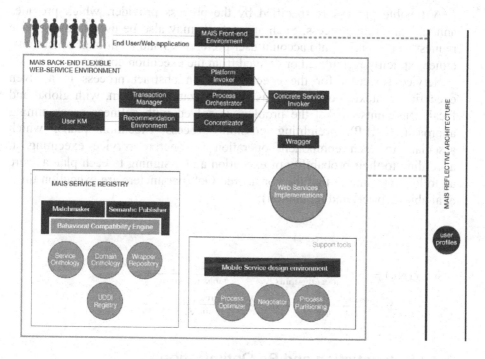

Fig. 2. MAIS back-end environment

- Component services: the requested abstract service operations of component services;
- Quality constraints: quality constraints may be specified on the process (global constraints) or on component services (local services).
- Selection constraints: preferred concrete services may be associated with the requested abstract services; selection constraints may also be used to specify that two operations in the process must be executed by the same service.
- Probability of executing a given execution path: for optimizing service selection, it is useful to take into consideration information about the probabilities of possible executions. This is particularly important when cycles and alternative execution paths are present. Probabilities of execution are associated with switches in the flow, and cycles are associated with the maximum number of expected iterations and, at times, with a probability of executing the ith iteration; such information may be derived from execution logs.
- Negotiation: negotiation preferences may be associated with each service invocation activity (e.g., the auction type, and negotiation attributes). Negotiation preferences are expressed using WS-Policy.

A flexible process is specified by the process provider, which provides annotations to the process. Such annotations may also be used in the service request phase, taking into account user preferences and additional constraints, either explicitly formulated or derived from the execution context.

Service selection for the execution of an abstract process in a given execution context is considered as an optimization problem, with global and local constraints. In [2] the problem is solved with a linear programming approach (MILP), weighting possible process execution plans, which associate to each component operation a concrete service executing it, according to their probability of execution and assigning to each plan a score as follows (assuming that the considered QoS parameters are execution time, availability, price, and reputation):

$$\max \sum_{l=1}^{L} freq_l score(ep_l)$$

$$score(ep_l) = w_1 \frac{\max Q_1^l - exeTime_l}{\max Q_1^l - \min Q_1^l} + w_2 \frac{avail_l - \min Q_2^l}{\max Q_2^l - \min Q_2^l}$$
$$+ w_3 \frac{\max Q_3^l - price_l}{\max Q_3^l - \min Q_3^l} + w_4 \frac{rep_l - \min Q_4^l}{\max Q_4^l - \min Q_4^l}$$

3. QoS Negotiation and Re-Optimization

3.1 QoS agreement

To achieve more flexibility and adaptivity, QoS negotiation can be adopted both during service selection and at run time.

For service selection performed with a QoS optimization approach mentioned above, QoS negotiation can be adopted to relax QoS constraints in case no feasible solution can be found by the optimization algorithm. The constraints which are the best candidates for negotiation can be identified, and bilateral negotiations with candidate service providers may help reaching a feasible solution. The flexibility of the process is thus obtained relaxing the original global constraints in a limited way and allocating a minimum number of additional resources to the process, according to the results of negotiation with candidate providers.

In addition negotiation can be used to agree the QoS level of the invoked services [10]. In fact, usually both service requestors and service providers specify ranges for QoS characteristics in service requests and service publication. After service selection for the process, a contract should be established among the parties which specifies which is expected the service QoS level. Such level can be used to monitor process performance and to perform adaptation operations at run time in case the parameters levels specified in the contract are not respected.

In [10], two approaches to automated contract negotiation of QoS and prices in service oriented architectures are proposed. In the first one, negotiation is automated only on the service provider side. The manual interaction of the service consumer is still required. In the second one, the negotiation is automated on both sides; the provider and the consumer delegate the execution of the negotiation to a negotiation broker. The Negotiation Broker performs the automated negotiation using the strategies specified by providers and consumers through policies.

The result of the negotiation process is a contract, which is formalized using WS-Agreement. The contract allows the architecture to monitor the service provisioning phase, enforcing penalties and recovery actions when the contract is not fulfilled by one or both parties.

3.2 Re-optimization

At run time, an adaptive mechanism consists in updating the global plan identified by initially solving the optimization problem in order to take into account the variability of Web services and of end users context. Re-optimization is performed periodically and is triggered in the following cases:

- The current value of the quality attributes of the composed service can be evaluated after the end of execution of every task. If the current QoS value differs more than a given threshold value from the corresponding prediction which can be evaluated from the global plan, then the re-optimization is performed.
- If a Web-service invocation fails, then re-optimization identifies a substitute service.
- Re-optimization is triggered by end user's context switch, since different channels can be associated with different constraints and set of weights.

Re-optimization requires some information on the current state of the composite service execution and starts revising the process instance specification.

4 Self-Healing Processes

While the flexible process execution environment developed in MAIS allows the development of information systems according to the feasible design principles, the resulting applications may incur in situations which are not anticipated in the developed models.

We distinguish here between expected exceptions, which are part of the models, and unexpected exceptions, which cannot be anticipated at run time or for which the additional cost for considering them at design time would not be justified.

The problem of exception modeling and handling has been studied extensively in the workflow literature and in particular in the WIDE project [8] the concept of exception pattern has been proposed to make exception design easier. In the WAMO system [12] a constructive approach to handle unanticipated exceptions at run time has been proposed, to define possible process repair plans according to predefined rules. In BPEL, several exception, event, and message handling mechanisms are proposed to support a sophisticated approach to considering exceptions in the design phase.

However, modeling of exception and repair rules might also become a design activity with costs which cannot be justified and with a severe impact on comprehensibility, violating the feasible comprehensibility requirement [13].

An innovative proposal to provide self-healing properties to service-based processes is being developed within the WS-Diamond[2] project. While the normal behaviour of the process and its expected exceptions are modelled, an environment to support unexpected exceptions is provided. The environment is based on two main components: a monitoring and diagnosis component, which analyze the process behaviour to identify failures and possible causes of errors [3], and a repair component, which supports repair actions (Fig. 3). Repair actions are performed on the processes underlying the services through a service management interface defined for the process.

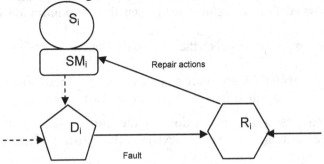

Fig. 3. Self-healing processes

A process is considered repaired when normal execution flow can be resumed. In the WS-Diamond project a set of repair actions on process instances has been defined [14]. They can be classified into actions which act

---

[2] Web-Service Diagnosis, Monitoring, and Diagnosability, EU FET-STREP Project, http://wsdiamond.di.unito.it/

of single services, such as retry an operation invocation, redo an operation with different parameters, or service substitution, and repair actions on the process flow or data, such as changes of variable values, changing the point of execution of the process (e.g., going back and forward in the process flow), selecting alternative execution paths. An extreme process repair action is the migration to a different process in case the process being executed cannot be repaired. In WS-Diamond, repair actions can be either manually invoked, or an execution plan could be automatically defined, along the lines proposed in [12] for workflow dynamic exception handling.

5 Related Work

Several methodological approaches and systems have been proposed to support process-based service composition, by extending traditional process management system technology to distributed, Internet-based scenarios.

In [9] dynamic and adaptive composition of e-services is proposed. In SELFSERV [5], services can be composed and executed in a decentralized way and a first approach to QoS based service selection has been proposed in [16]. The evaluation of quality of flexible process models in discussed in [7].

Flexible and context aware mechanisms are needed in future systems. In [11] a layered architecture for flexible e-service invocation is proposed based on substitution mechanism. Moreover, for the more general use of mobile applications, it is important to be able to adapt these systems to the user at hand, thus making a case for simple user models to guide the adaptation. Banavar and Bernstein [4] highlight the importance of semantic modeling in this respect.

6 Concluding Remarks

Flexibility and adaptation techniques for processes in adaptive information systems have been discussed in the paper. The trade-off between model completeness and flexibility and adaptivity at run time has been discussed, focusing on ways for enhancing the information system process specification with mechanisms to provide adaptivity at run time. In particular, in mobile information systems, the main requirement is for flexible and adaptive system behaviour in the execution of process, since the context of invocation may be very variable: a multitude of services are available across the network, providers and services may vary in time, and changes in the context are frequent. The traditional view of requirement engineering, where a requirement specification is developed early on in a project and then undergoes only minor changes during development and further system evolution, only partially applies. Rather, it is important to deal with ever evolving, unclear, and inconsistent user requirements that change and emerge through actual use.

References

[1] Alonso, G., Casati, F., Kuno, H., Machiraju, V.: *Web Services*. (Springer Verlag, Berlin Heidelberg New York 2004)

[2] Ardagna, D., Pernici, B.: Dynamic Web Service Composition with QoS Constraints, International Journal of Business Process Integration and Management (IJBPIM), accepted for publication

[3] Ardissono, L., Console, L., Goy, A., Petrone, G., Picardi, C., Segnan, M., Theseider Dupré, D.: Enhancing Web Services with Diagnostic Capabilities. In: *Proc. of ECOWS 2005 - 3rd IEEE European Conference on Web Services*, Vaxjo, Sweden, 2005, pp 182-191

[4] Banavar G., Bernstein, A.: Software infrastructure and design challenges for ubiquitous computing applications. Commun. ACM **45**(12):92-96 (2002)

[5] Benatallah, B., Sheng, Q.Z., Dumas, M.: The Self-Serv environment for web services composition. IEEE Internet Computing **7**(1):40-48 (2003)

[6] Bianchini, D., De Antonellis, V., Melchiori, M., Pernici, B., Plebani, P.: Ontology based methodology for e-service discovery. Information Systems **31**(4-5):361-380 (2006)

[7] Carlsen, S., Krogstie, J., Sølvberg, A., Lindland, O.I.: Evaluating Flexible Workflow Systems. In: *Hawaii International Conference on System Sciences (HICSS-30)*, Maui, Hawaii (1997)

[8] Casati, F., Castano, S., Fugini, M.G., Mirbel, I., Pernici, B.: Using Patterns to Design Rules in Workflows. Trans. on Software Engineering **26**(8):(2000)

[9] Casati, F., Shan, M.: Dynamic and adaptive composition of e-services. Information Systems **26**(3) (2001)

[10] Comuzzi, M., Pernici, B.: An Architecture for Flexible Web Service QoS Negotiation. In: *Proc. EDOC 2005*, Enschede, The Netherlands (2005), pp 70-82

[11] De Antonellis, V., Melchiori, M., De Santis, L., Mecella, M., Mussi, E., Pernici, B., Plebani, P.: A layered architecture for flexible e-service invocation", Software & Practice Experience. Software Practice & Experience **36**(2):191-223 (2006)

[12] Eder, J., Liebhart, W.: The Workflow Activity Model. In:*Proc. CoopIS 1995*

[13] Lindland, O.I, Sindre, G., Sølvberg, A.: Understanding Quality in Conceptual Modeling. IEEE Software, **11**(2):42-49 (1994)

[14] Modafferi, S., Mussi, E., Pernici, B.: SH-BPEL - A Self-Healing plug-in for Ws-BPEL engines. In: *MW4SOC: Workshop of the 7th International Middleware Conference 2006*, Melbourne, Australia (2006)

[15] Pernici, B. (ed.): *Mobile Information Systems – Infrastructure and design for adaptivity and flexibility*. (Springer, Berlin Heidelberg New York 2006)

[16] Zeng, L., Benatallah, B., Ngu, A.H.H., Dumas, M., Kalagnanam, J., Chang, H.: QoS-Aware Middleware for Web Services Composition. IEEE Trans. On Software Engineering **30**(5): 311-327 (2004).

Modelling of the People, by the People, for the People

John Krogstie

IDI, NTNU, Trondheim, Norway

Abstract. Modeling approaches as we know them today started to be used in a large scale around 30 years ago, using DFDs and ER-diagrams. Still the main focus is for intermediaries to document the knowledge as held by different stakeholders for further use, rather than for people themselves to use these means for knowledge representation for their own needs. Although useful e.g. in systems development, for modeling to have a larger effect, we propose a move the field to enable all knowledge workers to be active modelers. This chapter provides an overview of interactive models as an approach to support this vision, and gives an overview of the necessary future development to make this a reality on a large scale.

1 Introduction

It can be argued that the main reason that humans have excelled, is their ability of representing and transferring knowledge across time and space, inventing new knowledge on the way. Whereas in most areas of human conduct, one-dimensional (textual) languages being either informal (natural language) or formal (as in mathematics) have traditionally been used for this purpose, we see the use of two and many-dimensional representational forms to be on the rise. One such technique is traditionally termed *modelling*, although this term is used in different senses in different areas. Our background is primarily the use of modelling in the development of enterprises and enterprise information systems in particular.

Although useful e.g. in systems development, for modelling to have a larger effect, we propose a move of the technologies and approaches for this to enable also 'normal' knowledge workers (i.e. not only system developers) to be active modelers, both in restricted situations, and also towards the adaptations of the applications they are using to support their work task. One approach towards this is the application of what we term *interactive models* (also termed Active Knowledge Models [13]). Although interactive models can be used across a large range of knowledge creation and knowledge representation tasks, our focus in this chapter is the use of these techniques relative to provide IT-support in an enterprise.

The use of interactive models is about discovering, externalizing, capturing, expressing, representing, sharing and managing enterprise knowledge. A model is *active* if it directly influences the reality it reflects, i.e. changes to the model also change the way some actors perceive reality. Actors in this context include users as well as software components. [6] argue that active models can enable IS to meet many business needs that current technologies fail to support.

Model activation is the process by which a model affects reality. Model activation involves actors interpreting the model and to some extent adjusting their behaviour accordingly. This process can be

- *Automated*, where a software component interprets the model,
- *Manual*, where the model guides the actions of human actors, or
- *Interactive*, where prescribed aspects of the model are automatically interpreted and ambiguous parts are left to the users to resolve (through modeling in an guided environment).

Fully automated activation implies that the model must be formal and complete, while manual and interactive activation also can handle incomplete and partly informal models. Completing this terminology, we define a model to be *interactive* if it is interactively activated. That a model is interactive entails a co-evolution of the model and its domain. A model that does not change will not be able to reflect aspects of reality that changes, nor can it reflect evolution of a human actor's understanding. Consequently, an interactive model that does not evolve will deteriorate. It contributes to change, but does not reflect this change. The process of updating an interactive model is called *articulation*. The interplay of articulation and activation reflects the mutual constitution of interactive models and the social reality they reflect. The software components that support intertwined articulation and activation are termed *model activators*.

The most comprehensive theoretical approach to this field is Peter Wegner's interaction framework [23, 24]. Its development was triggered by the realisation that machines involving users in their problem solving, could solve a larger class of problems than algorithmic systems computing in isolation [23]. The primary characteristic of an *interaction machine* is that it can pose questions to users during its computation. The process can be a multi-step conversation between the user and the machine, each being able to take the initiative. The notion of an interaction machine is further extended to that of *multi-stream distributed interaction machines*, enabling multiple users and external systems to interact simultaneously, e.g. in groupware systems. DEUDU (Design of End-user Design in Use) [3] is a similar concept for system adaptability by user intervention – as a contributing designer – at use time.

Interactive models allows us to capture and benefit from situated, work-generative knowledge that otherwise will only be captured as tacit knowledge in the minds of those involved if at all. Active and situated knowledge has some very important intrinsic properties, and the only way we can benefit from these properties is by supporting users interactive modelling using the technology to model and execute models.

The industrial community has not been offered much new in terms of IT approaches and solutions over the last fifteen years. The few exceptions that spring to mind are enterprise modelling (EM), industrial portals and more recently web services and Service Oriented Architecture. This has left industry with a long list of unsolved problems. The situation has been described in the IDEAS project [8]:

- Aligning business, ICT and knowledge management (KM),
- Reducing expenses for application portfolio management and applications integration,
- Achieving cheaper and faster solutions development, delivery, deployment and integration,
- Achieving predictability, accountability, adaptability and trust in networked organizations,
- Achieving ease of re-engineering, reuse and management of solutions,
- Supporting concurrency, context-sensitivity and multiple simultaneous life-cycles of products and processes,
- Providing self-organizing, self-managing and re-generating solutions,
- Automating or semi-automating information and knowledge management,
- Supporting learning-by-doing
- Achieving independence of system experts,
- Harmonizing user environments and designing personalized workplaces

Continuous, on-demand industrial computing solutions are urgently needed in order to meet the business demands and opportunities of the new global economy. These solutions must offer qualities, capabilities and services that dramatically reduce the costs of developing, deploying, operating and managing customer solutions.

One approach to interactive models is termed Active Knowledge Modelling (AKM) technology [5, 7, 12, 19]. AKM is offering new roles for Enterprise Modelling to address the above issues: developing visual scenes for pro-action learning, modelling actions to capture context, creating contextual descriptions of work, and supporting knowledge evolution.

Recent platform developments [1] will support integrated modelling and execution platforms as one common platform, thereby enabling what in cognitive psychology is denoted as "closing the learning cycle". We will return to this approach after describing briefly the history and state of the art in the field of IS and enterprise modelling. We will then conclude looking at some of the potential pitfalls and problems of this approach.

2 State of the Art and State of Practice Within IS and Enterprise Modelling

Modelling approaches as we know them today within the information system field started to be used in large scale around 30 years ago, with developments such as DFDs and ER-diagrams, including e.g. the Phenomena model [17]. From the start a focus was to develop conceptual modeling languages that would focus on the important concepts of the world, typically containing a few, general concepts, depicted with simple and abstract visual icons. The languages were to be used to develop models by experts, although being meant to be used as a communication-artefact with different types of 'domain experts'. In the eighties, there were a large number of proposals for THE right modelling notation. In IFIP WG8.1 there was a number of conferences (the so-called CRIS–conferences – Comparative Research on Information Systems, e.g. [15]) starting out a long tradition in this, being followed up in the EMMSAD workshop series related to the CAiSE-conference since 1996. Understanding that language appropriateness was to a large extent based on the situation and goals of modelling, meta-modelling approaches started to appear around 1990 with tools such as RAMATIC making it possible for projects and organizations to extend existing notations, or in fact creating whole new notations from scratch. Successful approaches of metamodeling are e.g. MetaEdit [10]. Also Microsoft is currently pursuing this approach with the focus on DSL – Domain Specific Languages. The development of UML profiles can be looked upon as a variant of this. Still the main focus in the application of these techniques is for intermediaries (e.g. analysts, designers) to document the knowledge as held by different stakeholders for further use, rather than for people themselves to use these powerful means for knowledge representation and creation for their own needs.

Whereas the first modelling approaches where focused on software development, the area of *enterprise modelling (EM)* provided in the eighties the use of similar techniques to a somewhat broader scope. Five main categories for enterprise (process) modeling inspired by [4, 18, 21] is:

1. Human-sense making and communication to make sense of aspects of an enterprise and to communicate with other people
2. Computer-assisted analysis to gain knowledge about the enterprise through simulation or deduction.
3. Business Process Management.
4. Model deployment and activation to integrate the model in an information system.
5. Using the model as a context for a system development project, without being directly implemented (as it is in category 4).

State-of-practice in EM has progressed furthest in certain manufacturing industries, and in particular with respect to these three areas:

- Enterprise Architecture is currently the most vivid and fastest growing market particularly in the US.
- Business Process Modelling looked like a fast growing market already around 1998, but new requirements for web-service security have slowed it down. As for BPM (Business Process Management), the area appears to be on the rise once again.
- Enterprise Performance Analyses is another market that has as yet to really take off.

We believe that the major reasons for this slow acceptance and modest market penetration are mainly to be found in the fact that also EM is still a tool-based effort for experts, lacking scientifically based methodologies and respective visual languages.

The characteristics of the EM models, approaches and usage of models by industry are:

- The enterprise knowledge that can be represented is predetermined by vendor proprietary languages,
- The modelling approach, roles of modellers, and views to create are also predetermined,
- Modelling is not an integral part of engineering or product development, but performed in isolation by specialists,
- The user interface is systems engineer oriented, and supports just one style of modelling,

- There is limited support for knowledge externalization, sharing, and management,
- Most models are collections of diagrams and functional views and give no support for adaptation and extension of meta-models,
- Models and modelling environments are detached from solution execution platforms.

In short it is fair to say that so far EM is just another technology island in the non-interoperable industrial tools and systems landscape. Current standardization activities have little effect on industry. Although many such activities are going on, present standards (e.g. ENV 12204 or DIS 19439) are rarely used within industry. With respect to other, de-facto standards (e.g. BPMN from BPMI.org and OMG), industry does not perceive a clear distinction between conceptual and execution-oriented standards.

Now this situation is about to change. The goal is to make explicit knowledge that add value to the enterprise and can be shared by business applications and users for improving the agility and performance of the enterprise. Here we propose that this is best achieved in what we define as Enterprise Visual Scenes (EVS) as will be described in the next section.

3 Towards Enterprise Visual Scenes

EM can contribute to solve interoperability difficulties by increasing the shared understanding of the enterprise structures, rules and behaviour. EM provides methodologies for the identification of connected roles, objects and processes between enterprises from different perspectives. Sets of software applications used in the enterprises and their relationships can be identified with EM, and their degree of interoperability can be analyzed. Many languages and tools exists that support some form of EM with partially overlapping approaches. Today, several attempts to combine languages are known. For example, the Unified Enterprise Modeling Language project [20] has prototyped an integrated approach for exchange of enterprise models among EM tools, work that has been continued within the EU NoE INTEROP [16] and ATHENA [2].

As indicated above, enterprise modelling shows various inadequacies in a number of areas. The solution to these fallacies is to develop and share core languages, services, modelling constructs, models and meta-model structures by use of a comprehensive modelling infrastructure. An example of a comprehensive modelling infrastructure is given in Figure 1, depicting the solution platform as a platform providing services to help one or more networking companies perform practical work and achieve business goals. The core of the AKM is its approach, its CPPD (Collaborative Product and Process Design) methodologies – POPS innovative knowledge space, EKA structures, collaboration spaces, and its MUPS (model-configured and user-composable services) and industrial solution platforms. We will return to all of these areas below. The layers of platforms and services are illustrated in Figure 1, where the two lowest layers are identical with the products developed and delivered by Troux Technologies or other vendors, and the layers above are enabled by task, view, role and collaboration space management added by AKModelling.

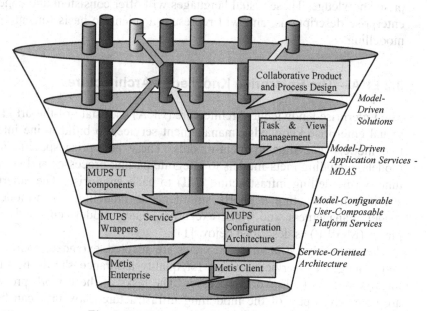

Fig. 1. Integrated modeling infrastructure

3.1 POPS as Core Modelling Languages

It can be argued that the core knowledge of any enterprise is the four inseparable dimensions of product, organization, process and system (POPS). Reflective views, recursive work processes, repetitive tasks and solutions, and replicable meta-models and templates are intrinsic properties of these dimensions. Business and other aspects and views are derived from these core enterprise knowledge dimensions. This core knowledge integrates and provides the qualities that future solutions depend on.

This core description is required in order to define, calculate and manage parameters and balance attributes and value sets across disciplines. Any EM language must be a derivation from this core. Otherwise it will not produce quality, manageable models and solutions. The partial, complementary languages can be used separately, and there is no demand to use more than one language from any of the four dimensions.

In the ATHENA project we have developed a first version of such a unified enterprise modelling language to enable the exchange of enterprise models independent of tools [26]. The partners have provided new solutions for open, tool-independent visual languages to model the core enterprise knowledge. These visual languages will offer consistent and coherent enterprise descriptions, and will represent a scientific basis for enterprise modelling.

3.2 EKA – The Enterprise Knowledge Architecture

The Enterprise Knowledge Architecture (EKA) uses state-of-the-art IT and visual enterprise knowledge management services to build inline interactive models and situated meta-models. These enterprise specific meta-models, including meta-models to integrate partner processes and systems, tune the modelling infrastructure (MI) to each enterprise. The enterprise specific infrastructure supports simultaneous modeling, meta-modeling, model management and work execution, using model-generated workplaces (MGWP) as described below [11].

The knowledge structures and views are adapted, extended, coordinated and managed by services, which for quality assurance should be implemented as repeatable work processes. The tasks of these work processes are themselves part of the modelling infrastructure. Any task can be invoked and executed as need arises, supporting unpredictable situations. Execution of these tasks may vary between automatic and highly interactive depending on the context. This means that self-adaptive, self-organizing solutions are possible, since situated knowledge can be modelled and activated.

3.2.1 Model-Generated Workplaces (MGWP) and Model-Configured and User-Composable Services (MUPS)

A model-generated workplace (MGWP) is a working environment for the business users involved in running the business operations of the enterprise. It is a user platform that provides the graphical front-end for human users to interact with software services supporting their day-to-day business activities.

The workplace can be tailored to meet the specific requirements of different roles or persons within an enterprise, providing customized presentation and operation views. This is achieved through model-configured and user-composable services (MUPS). These services make use of models to generate business-oriented and context-aware graphical user interfaces.

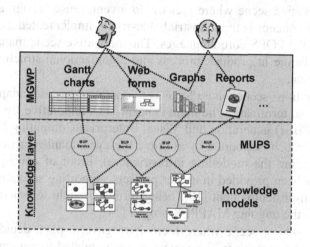

Fig. 2. Operational view of a model-generated workplace

Fig. 2 depicts an operational view of a model-generated workplace, exemplified with two different persons accessing ICT services and knowledge assets using different model-generated views, e.g. Gantt charts for project monitoring, web forms for activity reporting, bar graphs visualizing budget spending, and Web documents reporting on activities. The different views may reflect the same knowledge asset in a different form or manner that best suit the role or person using that asset in a given business context. Information represented in the different views is based on the same models ensuring information consistency. The models of the MGWPs are themselves knowledge models. MGWPs will typically be implemented as Web portals and MUPSs specify Web elements that can be generated in such portals.

3.2.2 EVS - Enterprise Visual Scenes

An enterprise has many knowledge spaces. These spaces can be implemented as Enterprise Visual Scenes (EVS). Enterprise visual scenes are ensembles of views to interrelated interactive models supporting arche-typical work in an organization.

We see four major enterprise visual scenes required to continuously in-novate, operate, evolve and transform, and govern and manage future en-terprises. In addition there will be a multitude of smaller, more project and task specific scenes to support situated project work. The four Visual scenes for future enterprising are briefly defined as:

- The Innovative scene where focus is to invent, reuse, design and learn. The main concept is the industrial War-room, implemented as an appli-cation of the POPS core languages. The innovative scene manages con-tinuous change in product, process and organizational structures of the organization.
- The Operations scene where focus is to operate, generate, adapt, extend, manage and terminate; The main concept is Collaborative Business So-lutions (CBSs) generation and Visual Enterprise Computing (VEC) de-livery approach, supported by multiple life-cycle management (adapting and extending the modelling infrastructure). Proof of concept for this scene has been provided in earlier projects supporting solutions genera-tion and user deployment [19], being further brought to practical appli-cations in the ongoing MAPPER project [14].
- The Governance scene where focus is to govern, plan, decide, assign, measure and strategize; The main concept is related to aggregation and propagation of parameters, attributes and values, achieving the "real-time enterprise".
- The Evolutions scene where the focus is to analyze, configure, change, transform, align, and manifest; The main concept is continuous collabo-rative business management (CBM).

3.2.3 The Power of Visual Scenes

There is a need to enhance the way people think about computing, and there is a need to extend information systems and enterprise modeling from being a tool-based exercise for experts, isolated from operational business solutions, to become visual environments for a new style of com-puting supported by an integrated modelling infrastructure. Visual pat-terns, scenes and languages, have at least six properties that natural lan-guage and current software methods will never acquire. We believe these properties are fundamental in driving a new approach to systems engineer-ing, and for solving the challenges facing industry and IT providers:

1. Being able to collapse life-cycle stow-piping, i.e. play with abstractions of the time-dimension, removing the phases of material and information flows,
2. Providing methods for concurrently evolving concepts, content, context and actions,
3. Correlation of conceptual views (meta-views), several content and functional views, and finally contextual views, and their dependencies,
4. Defining and applying business and working services and rules that are valid in given contexts,
5. Performing innovative works, and being able to create meta-models by executing tasks,
6. Supporting pro-action learning in visual scenes for role-playing and dry-runs.

When we can support these properties then maybe we can truly support design, problem-solving and organizational team learning with the use of computers.

3.2.4 How to Represent – Building the EKA

The EKA (Enterprise Knowledge Architecture) is a set of inter-dependent knowledge representations, that allow us to separately define, de-couple and manage enterprise knowledge structures and constructs. It provides adaptable visual languages, and supports interoperable solutions. The six major enterprise knowledge representation aspects (UEMLST) are composed of:

- *U*ser enterprise views,
- *E*nterprise models and sub-models, and structures of integrated solution models,
- *M*eta-model definitions of various types of models,
- *L*anguage; core visual constructs as basis for modeling languages,
- *S*tructures of meta-model objects and constructs, and finally
- *T*ype-hierarchies representing standardized industrial knowledge.

These enterprise knowledge model representations are vital for the formation, integration and operation of intelligent enterprises and smart organizations, and must be visually editable and manageable in a portal environment in order to harvest the full benefits of visual scenes.

The portal acts as an integrator and as an environment to plug in and perform applications and services over the device of choice. Application services are work processes, single or cascaded tasks, stored in the repository for re-activation and repetitive execution. The services provided in the portal, supported by the modelling infrastructure, are services to build knowledge models, to cooperate and collaborate, to perform work and project simulation, services to do work management, and finally services to do work execution.

Most existing enterprise modeling frameworks like Zachman [25], CIMOSA [22], and GERAM [9] represent useful methodology views, but all of them are lacking meta-views, support for appropriate meta-modeling languages and meta-model design and management structures. These are crucial knowledge constructs and structures for enterprise integration, and for linking to execution engines. None of them are aware of the key capabilities and services provided by a comprehensive modelling infrastructure, and of the integrating properties of a logically consistent, coherent and complete EKA layer. This layer must be designed for each enterprise, but the design is based of extensive reuse of constructs and structures and re-activation of tasks as design services.

4 Concluding Remarks

The importance of interactive models will slowly be appreciated, as the change from legacy systems and solutions delivery will demand full integration of these.

Most projects do modelling by using professional model builders and consultants, whereas engineering and industrial users are rarely involved. This is partly due to the user interfaces of the EM tools, but also relates to the value contributed by the modelling process. If EM is externalizing and sharing knowledge, then it should be the knowledge of the people possessing the core enterprise knowledge.

Involvement of stakeholders in sharing knowledge and data is a key issue. Think of inter-relating all stakeholder perspectives and life-cycles views from requirements, expectations and constraints on design to maintenance and decommissioning or re-engineering. Being able to interrelate and analyze, build this "big picture" and make it active or drive execution depends mainly on two conditions:

1. The real designers and engineers must work with real customer product deliveries, and
2. The product and process are designed/modelled and worked out (executing tasks) in concert by the real users.

This implies closing the gap between modeling and execution. Many might argue that modeling is inherently difficult, and thus can not be expected to be done by traditional knowledge workers. We agree that modeling on the *type* level, where you try to perceive a large number of cases in the future, is difficult. Modeling in the interactive modeling approach is mainly on the *instance* level, which should be manageable by most knowledge workers, given that they have an appropriate working environment (read MGWP). There are still large challenges for such an approach, especially on the interoperability of modeling infrastructures that need to be tackled.

References

[1] AKModelling http://www.akmodeling.com/ . Cited 1 Mar 2007
[2] ATHENA Integrated Project, IST –2002- 50678, project A1, see www.athena-ip.org. Cited 1 Mar 2007
[3] Bøving, K.B. and Petersen, L.H. (2002) Design for Dummies: Understanding Design Work in Virtual Workspaces. In *Proceedings of PDC2002*, Malmö, Sweden, 23-25 June.
[4] Curtis, B., Kellner, M., Over, J.: Process Modelling, Communication of the ACM, **35**(9), 75-90 (1992).
[5] Elvekrok, D.R. et al, Active Knowledge Models of Extended Enterprises. In *Proceedings of CE 2003*, Madeira, July 2003
[6] Greenwood, R.M., Robertson, I, Snowdon, R.A. and Warboys, B.C. (1995) Active Models in Business, *5th Conference on Business Information Technology, CBIT '95* .
[7] Haake, J. and Lillehagen F., Supporting evolving Project-based Networked Organizations. In *Proceedings of CE 2003*, Madeira, July 2003.
[8] IDEAS, IST-2001-37863, Deliverable D2.3 Goals and Challenges for the 21st Century. http://www.ideas-roadmap.net. Cited 1 Mar 2007
[9] IFIP-IFAC Task Force on Architectures for Enterprise Integration. GERAM: Generalised enterprise reference architecture and methodology. Technical Report Version 1.6.3, March 1999. Available at http://www.cit.gu.edu.au/~bernus/taskforce/geram/versions/. Cited 1 Mar 2007.
[10] Kelly, S., Lyytinen, K., and Rossi, M. MetaEdit+: a fully configurable Multi-User and Multitool CASE and CAME environment. In *Proceedings CAiSE 1997*. Barcelona, Spain, June 1997.
[11] Krogstie, J. and Jørgensen, H. D. Interactive Models for Supporting Networked Organisations. In *16th Conference on advanced Information Systems Engineering*. 2004. Riga, Latvia: Springer Verlag.
[12] Lillehagen F. The foundation of the AKM Technology. In *Proceedings of CE 2003*, Madeira, July 2004
[13] Lillehagen, F., J. Krogstie, and Solheim, H. G. From Enterprise Modelling to Enterprise Visual Scenes. International Journal of Internet and Enterprise Management, 2005.

[14] MAPPER 6FP project, Model-based Adaptive Product and Process Engineering, http://193.71.42.92/websolution/UI/Troux/07/Default.asp?WebID=260&PageID=1 . Cited 1 Mar 2007.

[15] Olle, B., Sol, H., and Verrijn-Stuart, A. editors, *Information System Design Methodologies: A Comparative Review*. North-Holland, 1982.

[16] Opdahl, A and Berio, G. A Roadmap for UEML. In *Proceedings of I-ESA'06*, Bordeaux,France, March 2006.

[17] Sølvberg, A. A contribution to the definition of concepts for expressing users' information systems requirements. In *Entity-Relationship Approach to Systems Analysis and Design*. North-Holland, 1980.

[18] Totland, T. (1997). Enterprise Modelling as a means to support human sense-making and communication in organizations. IDI. Trondheim, NTNU.

[19] Tinella S. et al Model Driven Operational Solution: The User Environment Portal Server. In *Proceedings of CE 2003*, Madeira, July 2003.

[20] UEML thematic network IST–2001–34229, WP1 State-of-the-art, see www.ueml.org. Cited 1 Mar 2007.

[21] Vernadat, F. B. *Enterprise Modelling and Integration: Principles and Applications,* (Chapman & Hall, 1996)

[22] Vernadat, F. B. The CIMOSA languages. In: *Handbook of Architectures of Information Systems*. Ed P. Bernus, K. Mertins, and G. Schmidt, editors, (Springer Berlin, Heidelberg, New York, 1998).

[23] Wegner, P. Why interaction is more powerful than algorithms, Communications of the ACM, **40**(5), 80-91 (1997).

[24] Wegner, P. and Goldin, D. Interaction as a Framework for Modeling. In: *Conceptual Modeling. Current Issues and Future Directions*, ed by Chen P. P., Akoka J., Kangassalo H, and Thalheim B. Lecture Notes in Computer Science 1565 (Springer Berlin, Heidelberg, New York, 1999)

[25] Zachman framework website. http://www.zifa.com. Cited 1 Mar 2007.

[26] Ziemann, J., Ohren, O., Jaekel.F-W., Kahl, T. and Knothe, T. Achieving Enterprise Model Interoperability Applying a Common Enterprise Metamodel. In *Proceedings of I-ESA 2006* - March 2006

A Research Agenda for Conceptual Schema-Centric Development

Antoni Olivé[1], Jordi Cabot[2]

[1]Universitat Politècnica de Catalunya, Spain
[2]Universitat Oberta de Catalunya, Spain

Abstract. Conceptual schema-centric development (CSCD) is a research goal that reformulates the historical aim of automating information systems development. In CSCD, conceptual schemas would be explicit, executable in the production environment and the basis for the system's evolution. To achieve the CSCD goal, several research problems must be solved. In this paper we identify and comment on sixteen problems that should be included in a research agenda for CSCD.

1 Introduction

The goal of automating information systems (ISs) building was established in the 1960s [51]. Since then, the goal has been reformulated many times, but the essential idea has remained the same: to automatically execute the specification of an information system in its production environment.

Forty years later, it is clear that this goal has not been achieved to a satisfactory degree. The main reason is that a number of major problems remain to be solved [41]. Most of these problems are technical, but others are related to the lack of maturity in the information systems field, such as the lack of standards. The insufficient standardization of languages and platforms has hampered advances in the automation of systems building. Fortunately, however, the last decade has seen the emergence of new standards related to information systems development. The progress made in standardization provides an opportunity to revive the goal of automation [50].

In [37] we proposed to call the goal "conceptual schema-centric development" (CSCD) in order to emphasize that the conceptual schema should be the focus of information systems development.

To achieve the CSCD goal, numerous research problems must be solved. In this paper we propose a research agenda with sixteen main research problems that we believe it is necessary to solve in order to achieve that goal. This agenda extends, refines and updates the one proposed in [37].

The paper is organized as follows. In the next section we briefly review the role and contents of conceptual schemas. In Section 3 we characterize the CSCD goal. We then present the proposed research agenda in Section 4. Finally, in Section 5 we summarize the conclusions of this paper.

2 Conceptual Schemas

In this section, we first review the main functions of ISs and then analyze the knowledge required by a particular IS to perform these functions. Through this analysis we will be able to define and establish the role of conceptual schemas.

2.1 Functions of an Information System

Information systems can be defined from several perspectives. For the purposes of conceptual modeling, the most useful is that of the functions they perform. According to this perspective, an IS has three main functions [3, p.74]:

- *Memory*: To maintain a consistent representation of the state of a domain.
- *Informative*: To provide information about the state of a domain.
- *Active*: To perform actions that change the state of a domain.

The memory function is passive, in the sense that it does not perform actions that directly affect users or the domain, but it is required by the other functions and it constrains what these functions can perform.

In the informative function, the system communicates some information or commands to one or more actors. Such communication may be explicitly requested or implicitly generated when a given generating condition is satisfied.

With the active function, the system performs actions that change the state of the domain. Such actions may be explicitly requested or implicitly generated when a given generating condition is satisfied.

2.2 Knowledge Required by an Information System

In order to perform the above functions, an IS requires general knowledge about its domain and knowledge about the functions it must perform. In the following sections, we summarize the main pieces of knowledge required by each function.

If the memory function of an IS has to maintain a representation of the state of the domain, the IS must know the entity and relationship types to be represented and their current population. The entity and relationship types that are of interest are general knowledge about the domain, while their (time-varying) population is particular knowledge.

In conceptual modeling, an Information Base (IB) is the representation of the state of the domain in the IS. The representation of the state in the IB must be consistent. This is achieved by defining a set of conditions (called integrity constraints) that the IS is required to satisfy at any time. Such integrity constraints are general knowledge about the domain.

The domain state is not static. Most domains change over time, so their state must also change. When the state of a domain changes, the IB must change accordingly. There are several kinds of state changes. If they are caused by actions performed in the domain, they are called external domain events. If they are caused by actions performed by the IS itself, they are called generated domain events. The IS must know the types of possible domain event and the effect of each event instance on the IB. This is also general knowledge about the domain.

If the informative function has to provide information or commands on request, the IS must know the possible request types and the output it must communicate. On the other hand, if there are generated communications then the IS must know the generating condition and the output it has to return when the condition is satisfied.

In general, in order to perform the informative function, the IS needs an inference capability that allows it to infer new knowledge. The inference capability requires two main elements: derivation rules and an inference mechanism. A derivation rule is general knowledge about a domain that defines a derived entity or relationship type in terms of others. The inference mechanism uses derivation rules to infer new information.

If, in the active function, the IS has to perform a certain action on request, then the IS must know the possible request types and the action it has to perform in each case. On the other hand, if a certain action must be performed when a generating condition is satisfied, the IS must know this condition and the action it has to perform.

2.3 Conceptual Schemas

The first conclusion from the above analysis is that in order to perform its required functions, an IS must have general knowledge about its domain and about the functions it has to perform. In the field of information systems, such knowledge is referred to as the Conceptual Schema (CS).

Every IS embodies a CS [29, 34, 48, p.417+]. Without a CS, an IS could not perform any useful functions. Therefore, developers need to know the CS in order to develop an IS.

The main purpose of conceptual modeling is to elicit the CS of the corresponding IS. As we have seen, given that all useful ISs need a CS, we can easily reach the conclusion that conceptual modeling is an essential activity in information systems development.

3 Conceptual Schema-Centric Development

In this section we reformulate the vision of the conceptual schema-centric development (CSCD) of information systems. To achieve this vision, we must be able to specify the initial conceptual schema, to execute it in the production environment and to evolve it in order to support the new functions of the IS. We call these three main distinguishing characteristics *explicit, executable* and *evolving schema*.

Explicit schema. Once the functions of the IS have been determined, there must be an explicit, complete, correct and permanently up-to-date conceptual schema written in a formal language. We need a development environment with tools that facilitate the validation, testing, reuse and management of (potentially large) schemas.

Executable schema. The schema is executable in the production environment. This can be achieved by the automatic transformation of the conceptual schema into software components (including the database schema) written in the languages required by the production environment, or by the use of a virtual machine that runs over this environment. In either case, the conceptual schema is the only description that needs to be defined. All the others are internal to the system and need not be externally visible.

According to the conceptualization principle [27], conceptual schemas exclude all aspects related to information presentation. Therefore, the software responsible for handling user interactions (the presentation layer) is outside the scope of CSCD.

Evolving schema. Changes to the functions of the IS require only the manual change of its conceptual schema. The changes to this schema are automatically propagated to all system components (including the database schema and data) if needed.

4 Towards a Research Agenda for CSCD

CSCD is still an open research goal. There are many research problems that must be solved before CSCD can become a widely used approach in the development of industrial information systems. In this section, we identify some of the research problems found related to the three CSCD features presented above. Our starting point is the agenda presented in [37], which we extend, refine and update here. We highlight the problems related to CSCD; see [9, 14, 55] for other relevant research agendas in conceptual modeling.

4.1 Explicit Schemas

Very large conceptual schemas. The conceptual schema of a large organization may contain thousands of entity types, relationship types, constraints, and so on. The development and management of (very) large conceptual schemas poses specific problems that are not encountered when dealing with small conceptual schemas. Conceptual modeling in the large is not the same as conceptual modeling in the small. The differences are similar to those observed between programming in the large and programming in the small [16]. We need methods, techniques and tools to support conceptual modellers and users in the development, reuse, evolution and understanding of large schemas.

So far, work on this topic has focused mainly on conceptual schemas for databases [1, 11, 46]. In CSCD we have to deal with ISs and take into account both the structural (including constraints and derivation rules) and behavioral schemas.

Business rules integration. A business rule is a statement that defines or constrains certain aspects of a business. From the information systems perspective, business rules are elementary pieces of knowledge that define or constrain the contents of and the changes to the information base. Business rules are the main focus of a community that advocates a development approach in which the rules are explicitly defined, directly executed (for example in a rules engine) and managed [8, 42]. Given that business rules are part of conceptual schemas, we can state that the community already follows the CSCD approach as far business rules are concerned.

It is both useful and necessary to integrate the business rules and CSCD approaches. It should be possible to extract the rules embedded in a schema and to present them to users and conceptual modellers in a variety of ways and languages, including natural language. Automated support for this extraction and presentation is necessary. It should also be easy to pick up on a particular rule and to integrate it into the schema. Automated support for this integration is desirable.

Similarly, the workflow community fosters the use of workflow specifications as the primary artefact in the software development process. Workflow specifications define a set of activity ordering rules that control the workflow execution. These rules are usually executed and managed with the help of dedicated workflow management systems. Workflow specifications should be also integrated with the CSCD approach.

Schema integration. A conceptual schema is very rarely developed by a single conceptual modeller [47]. Instead, several sub-schemas are (separately) developed by different modellers, each of whom addresses a specific part of the IS. To apply the CSCD approach, these sub-schemas must subsequently be integrated in a single schema that represents the overall view of the IS.

A first step in integrating the schemas is to identify and characterize the relationships between the different sub-schemas (schema matching [40]). Once these have been identified, matching elements can be linked in a coherent schema (schema merge [39]).

Previous research on this topic focuses on the integration of database schemas [6, 38]. More recently, the problem has been studied at a more abstract level (for example, [4] presents general operators for model matching and merging). Nevertheless, much work remains to be done on schema integration in the presence of general integrity constraints and derived elements. Moreover, research on the integration of behavioural schemas is still in a preliminary stage [49].

Complete and correct conceptual schemas. Several factors affect the quality of a conceptual schema, as stated in the framework presented in the seminal paper [28] and validated in [32, 33]. Completeness and correctness are two of the quality factors of conceptual schemas. A complete conceptual schema includes all knowledge relevant to the IS. A correct conceptual schema contains only correct and relevant knowledge. Correctness is also referred to as validity. Consistency is subsumed by validity and completeness. In CSCD, completeness and correctness are the principal quality factors. They can be achieved by using a very broad spectrum of approaches, including testing and verification. It should be possible to test and verify conceptual schemas to at least the same degree that has been achieved with software.

Several studies have focused on testing conceptual schemas [25, 30, 20, 57]. There are automatic procedures for the verification of some properties of conceptual schemas in description logics [10]. Model checking is being explored as an alternative verification technique [18]. Nevertheless, in all these topics, a lot of work remains to be done [35].

Refactoring of conceptual schemas. In general, several complete and correct conceptual schemas may exist for the same IS. However, some are better than others in terms of quality. Therefore, in some cases an initial conceptual schema may be improved if it is first transformed into a better (semantically-equivalent) alternative schema.

For this purpose, the application of refactorings at the model level has been proposed. Refactoring was initially proposed at the code level [19] as a disciplined technique for improving the structure of existing code (using simple transformations) without changing the external observable behaviour. More recently, work has been done to apply this technique to design models instead of to the source code [31]. In CSCD, we need specific refactoring operations that take into account all the components in a conceptual schema. General guidelines have not yet been developed to determine *when* and *where* to apply refactorings in order to improve the quality of the conceptual schema.

Reverse engineering. Most legacy applications do not have an explicit conceptual schema. To benefit from the CSCD approach, we must elicit the explicit conceptual schema from the internal schema embodied in the software components that form the legacy application. This process is known as reverse engineering.

Reverse engineering applied to entity and relationship types and to the taxonomies of conceptual schemas has been extensively studied for relational databases [15] and object-oriented languages [53]. However, much work remains to be done regarding the reverse engineering of general integrity constraints and derived elements of schemas. Moreover, a complete understanding of the application code in order to elicit the behavioural part of the schema is also needed. Ideally, the interactions between the application's various software components should also be considered during the reverse engineering process.

4.2 Executable Schemas

Materialization of derived types. In general, conceptual schemas contain many derived entity and relationship types, with their corresponding derivation rules [36]. For reasons of efficiency, some of these types must be materialized. The process to determine the derived types that need to be materialized should be as automatic as possible. Moreover, changes in the population of base types may require changes in that of one or more materialized types. The propagation of these changes should be completely automatic.

The work done on the selection of database views that need to be materialized in data warehouses [23] is highly relevant to the determination of the derived types to materialize in ISs. Similarly, the large body of work on the incremental maintenance of materialized database views [22] is highly relevant to the more general problem of change propagation in ISs.

Enforcement of integrity constraints. Most conceptual schemas contain a large number of integrity constraints. The IS must enforce these constraints efficiently. This can be achieved in several ways [52]. The main approaches are integrity checking, maintenance and enforcement. In integrity checking and maintenance, each constraint is analyzed in order to (1) determine which changes to the IB may violate the constraint; (2) generate a simplified form of the constraint, to be checked when a particular change occurs; and, (3) (in maintenance) generate a repair action. In integrity enforcement, each event (transaction) is analyzed in order to (1) determine which constraints could be violated by the effect of the event; and, (2) generate a new version of the event effect that ensures that none of the constraints will be violated.

In CSCD, the analysis—regardless of the approach taken—should be fully automatic and able to deal with any kind of constraint. A general method for this analysis does not yet exist. However, a great deal of research and development work has been carried out on the enforcement of constraints in the database field for relational, deductive and object-oriented databases [12, 44]. The general method is likely to be an extension of this work. A recent step in this direction (for the integrity checking strategy) is [13].

From declarative to imperative behaviour specifications. There are two different approaches for specifying the effect of the domain events of an IS: the *imperative* and the *declarative* approaches [56]. In an imperative specification, the conceptual modeller explicitly defines the set of changes (insertions of entities and relationships, updates of attribute values, etc.) to be applied over the IB. In a declarative specification, a contract for each domain event must be provided. The contract consists of a set of pre and postconditions. A precondition defines a set of conditions on the event input and the IB that must hold when the domain event is issued, while postconditions state the set of conditions that must be satisfied by the IB at the end of the domain event.

In conceptual modeling, the declarative approach is preferable since it allows a more abstract and concise definition of the event effect and conceals all implementation issues [56]. Nevertheless, in order to execute the conceptual schema, these declarative specifications must be automatically transformed into their equivalent imperative specifications. The main problem of declarative specifications is that they may be non-deterministic, i.e. there may be several possible states of the IB that verify the postcondition of a contract. This implies that a declarative specification may have several equivalent imperative versions, which hampers the transformation process.

Up to know, there is no general method that automatically provides this translation. Current solutions are mainly limited to deal with the *frame problem* [7], which discusses the possible IB states for types that are not referred to in the event contract. The automatic transformation for types that do appear in the contract needs further investigation.

Reusability. The possibility of reusing previously developed software pieces in the implementation of a new IS is one of the long-standing goals in the software community. In CSCD, reusability could help to reduce the effort required to transform the conceptual schema into an appropriate set of software components by means of studying the commonalities between the schema and a given set of existing software elements [2].

The main obstacle to a broader adoption of the reusability goal is the problem of selecting the right software component/s to reuse. Currently, the selection process is not completely automatic and requires a formal definition of the software components and a semantic comparison between the components and the conceptual schema [43]. This kind of analysis is still under development, particularly for two specific types of software components: commercial-off-the-shelf (COTS) components and web services. Ideally, the selection process should also consider possible non-functional requirements of the IS and the cost of integrating the selected component into the rest of the system.

4.3 Evolving Schemas

Concept evolution. The most fundamental changes to a conceptual schema are the addition or removal of concepts (entity, relationship or event types or states in state machines) and the addition or removal of edges in the concept generalization hierarchy. In CSCD, evolution must be automatically propagated to the logical level [26]. Therefore, these changes must be propagated to the logical schema(s) of the database(s) (and/or to other software components generated for the execution of the CS) and to its (their) instances. Changes to the generalization hierarchy may induce a change (increase or decrease) in the population of some concepts such that certain integrity constraints are violated. The IS should (efficiently) detect these violations and produce an appropriate response. Further work on these topics must take into account the considerable amount of existing work on database schema evolution, which focuses mainly on concept evolution [5].

Furthermore, concept evolution may also affect other elements in the conceptual schema. For instance, changes to a generalization hierarchy may affect the general integrity constraints defined in the schema (some constraints may become unnecessary while others may now be required). Additionally, the formal definition of constraints, derivation rules and domain events may need to be adjusted after a concept evolution since they may refer to elements that no longer exist in the schema or whose specification (cardinality, data type, changeability, etc.) has been changed during the evolution process.

Constraints evolution. Adding a constraint may turn the IB inconsistent. Changing a constraint may be considered as a removal (which cannot lead to any inconsistencies) plus an addition. When a constraint is added, the IS has to check whether or not the current IB satisfies it. For very large IBs, the checking procedure may need to be efficient. If one or more fragments of the IB violate the constraint, the IS has to produce a response (to reject the constraint, to ignore the inconsistency, to repair the fragment or to handle the fragment as an exception).

In the database field, the problem of adding constraints has been studied for particular constraints and database models [54]. In CSCD, we need to be able to deal with particular constraints (like cardinalities) but also with general constraints expressed in a conceptual modeling language, including base and/or derived types.

Derivability evolution. The derivability of entity and relationship types may change. A base type may become a derived type or vice versa. Furthermore, a derivation rule may also change. Changing the derivability of a type may produce a change in its population and, indirectly, in that of other types. If the change affects a materialized type it must be recomputed. For large IBs, recomputation may need to be efficient. Changing the population of a type may also induce the violation of certain integrity constraints. The IS should (efficiently) detect these violations and produce an appropriate response.

Some work has been carried out on this topic [21], but much more needs to be done. A partially similar problem in the database field is that of "view adaptation" after view redefinition [24].

Completeness and correctness of the evolved schema. After evolving the CS, it is necessary to check that the conceptual schema is still complete and correct. This verification should be done efficiently. In particular, it is only necessary to consider the evolved subset of the schema (together with other schema elements that may have been affected by the evolution-induced effects).

Approaches for the efficient verification of evolved schemas focus on the detection of *consistency* (see, for example, [17]). These approaches state that a conceptual schema is consistent if it satisfies a set of integrity constraints (usually referred to as well-formedness rules) predefined by the conceptual modeling language used in the specification of the schema. These constraints restrict the possible structure of schemas defined with that modeling language. Efficiency is achieved by checking the relevant constraints on the evolved part of the schema. A constraint is relevant to an evolved schema if changes in the schema could induce a violation of this constraint.

Much work is required to efficiently verify other quality factors of the evolved schema.

4.4 Other Research Problems

Benchmarks for CSCD. In most areas of computer science (databases, computer architectures, programming and so on), an extensive set of benchmarks have been developed to test the performance (or the covering or any other property) of a method that addresses a research goal in that area. Benchmarks are also useful for comparing different proposals tackling the same goal.

In CSCD, benchmarks could help to measure the progress of the community regarding the different research goals presented in this study. Additionally, conceptual modellers could benefit from benchmarks when selecting a tool to specify the conceptual schemas. Several benchmarks are needed, depending on the research goal concerned.

Education for CSCD. When the conceptual schema is placed at the centre of the development process, the focus of software engineering education needs to be shifted from code-centric to model-centric. As expressed in [45], each role in the software development process requires appropriate education. In CSCD, the main role is that of the conceptual modeller. Therefore, we must develop appropriate teaching/learning techniques to leverage the modeling abilities of software engineering students and practitioners. This is a critical factor in the success of the CSCD approach.

We are currently witnessing an increase in the number of available modeling courses (both virtual and traditional face-to-face courses), particularly for the popular Unified Modeling Language. However, most of these courses focus on the notational aspects of modeling languages. Instead, in CSCD education, we must concentrate on clearly explaining the semantics of the different modeling constructs and how they can be combined to construct complete and correct conceptual schemas. A body of examples of "good" and "bad" schemas for well-known domains would therefore be very useful.

5 Conclusions

Conceptual schema-centric development (CSCD) is a reformulation of the goal of automating information systems building that highlights the central role of conceptual schemas in the automatic development of information systems. In CSCD, conceptual schemas would be explicit, executable in the production environment and the basis for the system evolution.

To achieve the CSCD goal, numerous research problems must be solved. The main purpose of this paper was to identify and comment on a list of sixteen open problems that should be included in a research agenda for CSCD.

We believe that this research agenda must be carried out before the CSCD approach can become widely used in practice.

Acknowledgements

We wish to thank the GMC group (Jordi Conesa, Dolors Costal, Cristina Gómez, Enric Mayol, Joan Antoni Pastor, Anna Queralt, Maria-Ribera

Sancho, Ruth Raventós and Ernest Teniente) for many useful comments on previous drafts of this paper. This work was partially supported by the Ministerio de Ciencia y Tecnologia and FEDER under project TIN2005-06053.

References

[1] Akoka, J., Comyn-Wattiau, I.: Entity-relationship and object-oriented model automatic clustering. Data & Knowledge Engineering, 20, 1996, pp. 87-117

[2] Basili, V., Briand, L.C., Melo, W.: How reuse influences productivity in object-oriented systems. Communications of the ACM 39 (10), 1996, pp. 104-116

[3] Boman, M., Bubenko, J.A. jr., Johannesson, P., Wangler, B.: Conceptual Modelling. Prentice Hall, 1997, p. 269

[4] Bernstein, P.A.: Applying Model Management to Classical Meta Data Problems. In Proc. CIDR 2003, pp. 209-220

[5] Banerjee, J., Kim, W., Kim, H-J., Korth, H.F.: Semantics and Implementation of Schema Evolution in Object-Oriented Databases. In Proc. ACM SIGMOD 1987, pp. 311-322

[6] Batini, C., Lenzerini, M., Navathe S.B.: A Comparative Analysis of Methodologies for Database Schema Integration. ACM Comput. Surv. 18 (4), 1986, pp. 323-364

[7] Borgida, A., Mylopoulos, J., Reiter, R.: On the frame problem in procedure specifications. IEEE Transactions on Software Engineering 21, 1995, pp. 785-798

[8] BRCommunity.com (Eds.): A Brief History of the Business Rule Approach. Business Rules Journal, 6 (1), January 2005

[9] Brinkkemper, S., Lindencrona, E., Sølvberg, A. (Eds.): Information Systems Engineering. State of the Art and Research Themes, Springer, 2000

[10] Calvanese, D., Lenzerini, M., Nardi, D.: Description Logics for Conceptual Data Modeling. In Chomicki, J., Saake, G. (Eds.): Logics for Databases and Information Systems. Kluwer, 1998, pp. 229-263

[11] Castano, S., de Antonellis, V., Fugini, M.G., Pernici, B.: Conceptual Schema Analysis: Techniques and Applications. ACM TODS, 23 (3), 1998, pp. 286-333

[12] Ceri, S.; Fraternalli, P.; Paraboschi, S.; Tanca, L. "Automatic Generation of Production Rules for Integrity Maintenance". ACM TODS, 19 (3), 1994, pp. 367-422

[13] Cabot, J., Teniente, E.: Incremental Evaluation of OCL Constraints. In Proc. CAiSE 2006, LNCS 4001, pp. 81-95

[14] Chen, P., Thalheim, B., Wong, L.Y.: Future Directions of Conceptual Modeling. In Proc. ER 1997, LNCS 1565, pp. 287-301

[15] Davis, K.H., Aiken, P.H.: Data Reverse Engineering: A Historical Survey. In Proc. Working Conference on Reverse Engineering, 2000, pp. 70-78

[16] DeRemer, F., Kron, H.: Programming-in-the-Large Versus Programming-in-the-Small. IEEE Trans. Software Eng. 2 (2), 1976, pp. 80-86

[17] Egyed, A. Instant consistency checking for the UML. In Proc. ICSE 2006, pp. 381-390

[18] Eshuis, R., Jansen, D.N., Wieringa, R.: Requirements-Level Semantics and Model Checking of Object-Oriented Statecharts. Requirements Engineering 7 (4), 2002, pp. 243-263

[19] Fowler, M.: Refactoring: Improving the design of existing code. Addison-Wesley, 1998, p. 464

[20] Gogolla, M., Bohling, J., Richters, M.: Validation of UML and OCL Models by Automatic Snapshot Generation. In Proc. UML 2003, LNCS 2863, pp. 265-279

[21] Gómez, C., Olivé, A.: Evolving Derived Entity Types in Conceptual Schemas in the UML. In Proc. OOIS 2003, LNCS 2817, pp. 33-45

[22] Gupta, A., Mumick, I. S.: Materialized Views. Techniques, Implementations and Applications. The MIT Press, 1999

[23] Gupta, H., Mumick, I.S.: Selection of Views to Materialize in a Data Warehouse. IEEE Trans on Knowledge and data engineering, 17 (1), 2005, pp. 24-43

[24] Gupta, A., Mumick, I.S., Ross, K.A.: Adapting Materialized Views after Redefinitions. In Proc. ACM SIGMOD 1995, pp. 211-222

[25] Harel, D.: Biting the Silver Bullet. Toward a Brighter Future for System Development. Computer, January 1992, pp. 8-20

[26] Hick, J-M., Hainaut, J-L.: Strategy for Database Application Evolution: The DB-MAIN Approach. In Proc. ER 2003, LNCS 2813, pp. 291-306

[27] ISO/TC97/SC5/WG3: Concepts and Terminology for the Conceptual Schema and the Information Base, J.J. Van Griethuysen (Ed.), March 1982

[28] Lindland, O.I., Sindre, G., Sølvberg, A.: Understanding Quality in Conceptual Modeling. IEEE Software, March 1994, pp. 42-49

[29] Mays, R.G. "Forging a silver bullet from the essence of software". IBM Systems Journal, 33 (1), 1994, pp. 20-45

[30] Mellor, S.J., Balcer, M.J.: Executable UML. A Foundation for Model-Driven Architecture. Addison-Wesley, 2002, p. 368

[31] Mens, T., Tourwé, T.: A Survey of Software Refactoring. IEEE Trans. Software Eng. 30 (2), 2004, pp. 126-139

[32] Moody, D.L., Sindre, G., Brasethvik, T., Sølvberg, A.: Evaluating the Quality of Process Models: Empirical Testing of a Quality Framework. In Proc. ER 2002, LNCS 2503, pp. 214-231

[33] Moody, D.L., Sindre, G., Brasethvik, T., Sølvberg, A.: Evaluating the quality of information models: empirical testing of a conceptual model quality framework. In Proc. ICSE 2003, pp. 295-307

[34] Mylopoulos, J.: The Role of Knowledge Representation in the Development of Specifications. In Proc IFIP 1986, pp. 317-319

[35] Mylopoulos, J.: Information Modeling in the Time of the Revolution. Information Systems 23(3/4), 1998, pp. 127-155

[36] Olivé, A.: Derivation Rules in Object-Oriented Conceptual Modeling Languages. In Proc. CAiSE 2003, LNCS 2681, pp. 404-420
[37] Olivé, A.: Conceptual Schema-Centric Development: A Grand Challenge for Information Systems Research. In Proc. CAiSE 2005. LNCS 3520, pp. 1-15
[38] Parent, C., Spaccapietra, S.: Issues and approaches of database integration. Communications of the ACM 41 (5), 1998, pp. 166-178
[39] Pottinger, R., Bernstein, P.A.: Merging Models Based on Given Correspondences. In Proc VLDB 2003, pp. 826-873
[40] Rahm, E., Bernstein P.A.: A survey of approaches to automatic schema matching. VLDB Journal 10 (4), 2001, pp. 334-350
[41] Rich, C., Waters, R.C.: Automatic Programming: Myths and Prospects. Computer, August 1988, pp. 40-51
[42] Ross, R.G. (Ed.): The Business Rules Manifesto. Business Rules Group. Version 2.0, November 2003
[43] Schumann, J. M.: Automated Theorem Proving in Software Engineering, Springer, 2001, p. 228
[44] Schewe, K-D., Thalheim, B.: Towards a theory of consistency enforcement. Acta Informática 36, 1999, pp. 97-141
[45] Shaw, M.: Software Engineering Education: A Roadmap. In Future of Software Engineering, Proc ICSE 2000, pp. 371-380
[46] Shoval, P., Danoch, R., Balabam, M.: Hierarchical entity-relationship diagrams: the model, method of creation and experimental evaluation. Requirements Eng., 2004, 9, pp. 217-228
[47] Sølvberg, A.: Co-operative Concept Modeling. In [9], pp. 305-326
[48] Sowa, J.F.: Knowledge Representation. Logical, Philosophical and Computational Foundations. Brooks/Cole, 2000, p. 594
[49] Stumptner, M., Schrefl, M., Grossmann, G.: On the road to behavior-based integration. In Proc. APCCM 2004, pp. 15-22
[50] Steimann, F., Kühne, T.: Coding for the Code. ACM Queue, 3 (10), 2006, pp. 45-51
[51] Teichroew, D., Sayani, H.: Automation of System Building. Datamation, 17 (16), 1971, pp. 25-30
[52] Teniente, E., Urpí, T.: On the abductive or deductive nature of database schema validation and update processing problems. Theory and Practice of Logic Programming 3 (3), 2003, pp. 287-327
[53] Tonella, P., Potrich, A.: Reverse Engineering of Object Oriented Code. Springer, 2005, p. 210
[54] Türker, C., Gertz, M.: Semantic integrity support in SQL: 1999 and commercial (object-)relational database management systems. VLDB Journal, 10, 2001, pp. 241-269
[55] Wand, Y., Weber, R.: Research Commentary: Information Systems and Conceptual Modeling – A Research Agenda. Information Systems Research, 13 (4), 2002, pp. 363-376
[56] Wieringa, R.: A survey of structured and object-oriented software specification methods and techniques. ACM Computing Surveys 30, 1998, pp. 459-527

[57] Zhang, Y.: Test-Driven Modeling for Model-Driven Development. IEEE Software, September/October 2004, pp. 80-86

Bibliography

[1] Andersen, R., Bubenko jr. J.A., Sølvberg, A. editors: *Proceedings of the Third International Conference on Advanced Information Systems Engineering (CAiSE'91)* number 498 in Lecture Notes in Computer Science, Trondheim, Norway, May 1991. Springer-Verlag.

[2] Andersen, R., Conradi, R., Krogstie, J., Sindre, G., Sølvberg, A.: Project courses at the NTH : 20 years of experience. In J.L. Diaz-Herrera, editor, *7 th Conference on Software Engineering Education (CSEE'7)* pages 177–188. Springer Verlag (LNCS 750), 1994.

[3] Andersen, R., Sølvberg, A.: Software configuration management an its database implications. In *Proceedings of DAISEE '87 - Datastøttet Systemutvikling* Oslo, Norway, November 12-13 1987.

[4] Andersen, R., Sølvberg. A.: Support for development teams in information systems engineering. In *Proceedings of the 3rd European Workshop on the Next Generation CASE Tools* Manchester, England, 1992.

[5] Andersen, R, Sølvberg, A.: Conflict management in systems development groups. In N.Prakash, C.Rolland, and B.Pernici, editors, *Information Systems Development Process (IFIP 8.1)* pages 207–227, Como, Italy, 1993. North Holland.

[6] Bergheim, G., Sandersen, E., Sølvberg, A.: A taxonomy of concepts for the science of information systems. In Falkenberg and Lindgren, editors, *Information Systems Concepts: An In-Depth Analysis* San Diego, USA, 1989.

[7] Brasethvik T., Sølvberg A.: A Referent Model of Documents ERCIM Workshop on Web-bases & Meta-data, St. Augustin, Bonn, May 1998

[8] Brataas, G., Hughes, P., Sølvberg, A:. Integrating management of human and computer resources in task processing organizations: A conceptual view. pages 703–712, Volume 4, Maui, Hawaii, January 4–7 1994. IEEE.

[9] Brataas, G., Hughes, P., Sølvberg, A.: Performance Engineering of Workflow Systems With an Integrated View of Human and Computerised Work Processes. Proc. CAiSE'97

[10] Brinkkemper S., Lindencrona E., Sølvberg A.(eds.): Information Systems Engineering: State of the art and Research Themes, Springer, June 2000

[11] Bubenko, J., Impagliazzo, J., and Sølvberg, A.: History of Nordic Computing: Springer-Verlag 2005. ISBN 0-387-24167-1. 488 p

[12] Carlsen, S., Jørgensen, H.D., Krogstie, J., Sølvberg, A.: Flexible Support of Work Processes - Balancing the Support of Organisations and Workers. In Proceedings of EURAM - 2nd Annual Conference on Innovative Research in Management, Stockholm, Sweden, 2002

[13] Carlsen, S., Krogstie, J., Sølvberg, A. and Lindland, O. I.: Evaluating Flexible Workflow Systems, Hawaii International Conference on System Sciences (HICSS-30), Maui, Hawaii, 1997.

[14] Farshchian B. A., Krogstie J., Sølvberg A.: Integration of User Interface and Conceptual Modeling, in Stephanidis, C. (ed.) Proceedings of the Workshop on User Interfaces for All, European Research Consortium for Informatics and Mathematics, ICSFORTH, Heraklion, Greece, 1995

[15] Krogstie, J., Sølvberg, A.: Software maintenance in Norway: A survey investigation. Best paper at ICSM'94, September 1994.

[16] Krogstie J., Sølvberg A.: A classification of methodological frameworks for computerised information systems support in organisations, in Proc. IFIP 8.1/8.2 Conf. Method Engineering: Principles of Method Construction and Tool Support, August 1996, Atlanta, USA, Chapman&Hall, 1996

[17] Lin, Y., Strasunskas, D., Hakkarainen, S., Krogstie, J., Sølvberg, A.: Semantic Annotation Framework to Manage Semantic Heterogeneity of Process Models. Proceedings of the 18th Conference on Advanced Information Systems Engineering(CAiSE*06), Luxemburg,2006, Springer-Verlag, LNCS.

[18] Lindland, O.I., Willumsen, G., Gulla, J.A. Sølvberg, A.: Prototyping in transformation-based case environments. In *Proceedings of the 5th International Conference on Software Engineering and Knowledge Engineering (SEKE'93)* pages 696--603, Hotel Sofitel, San Francisco Bay, USA, 1993. Knowledge Systems Institute.

[19] Lindland, O.I., Sindre, G., Sølvberg, A.: Understanding Quality in Conceptual Modeling, IEEE Software, 11(2):42–49, March 1994.

[20] Lunde, Ø., Brasethvik, T., Sølvberg, A.: A model-based approach to data-warehousing. NOKOBIT-97 (Norsk konferanse om organisasjoners bruk av IT), Bodø, Norway, 1997

[21] Moody, D.L.; Sindre, G., Brasethvik, T., Sølvberg, A.: Evaluating the Quality of Process Models: Empirical Testing of a Quality Framework. In S. Spaccapietra, S.T. March, and Y. Kambayashi (Eds.): ER 2002, LNCS 2503, pp. 214–231, 2002.

[22] Moody, D.L.; Sindre, G., Brasethvik, T., Sølvberg, A.: Evaluating the quality of information models: empirical testing of a conceptual model quality framework. In Proc. 25th International Conference in Software Engineering (ICSE'03), Portland, OR, USA, 3-10 May 2003.

[23] Moody, D.L.; Sindre, G., Brasethvik, T., Sølvberg, A.: An instrument for empirical testing of conceptual model quality frameworks. In Proceedings of EMMSAD'02, Toronto, Canada, May 2002.

[24] Opdahl, A.L., Sølvberg, A.: Conceptual integration of information system and performance modelling. In *Proceedings of IFIP WG 8.1 Working Conference on Information System Concepts – Improving The Understanding* Alexandria, Egypt, April 13--15 1992.

[25] Opdahl, A.L., Sølvberg, A.: A framework for performance engineering during information system development. In *Proceedings CAiSE'92: The Fourth Conference on Advanced information Systems Engineering* Manchester, England, 1992. Springer Verlag.

[26] Opdahl, A.L., Vetland, V., Brataas, G., Sølvberg, A.: CASE tool support for efficient utilisation of computing resources. In *Proceedings of the 3rd European Workshop on the Next Generation CASE Tools Workshop* Manchester, England, May 1992.

[27] Opdahl, A.L., Vetland, V., Sølvberg, A.: An integrated environment for performance evaluation and possible information systems engineering applications. In *Proceedings of Norsk Informatikk Konferanse (NIK '89)* November 14–15 1989.

[28] Sindre, G., Moody, D.L., Brasethvik, T., Sølvberg, A.: Introducing Peer Review in an IS Analysis Course. Journal of Information Systems Education, 14(1):101–119, 2003.

[29] Sindre, G., Moody, D.L., Brasethvik, T., Sølvberg, A.: Students' Peer Review in Modelling Exercises. In Proc. Informing Science + Information Technology Education Joint Conference (InSITE 2003), Pori, Finland, 24–27 Jun 2003.

[30] Sølvberg A.: On the Specification of Scenarios in Information System Design, IBM Research Lab. San Jose, Calif. 95193, RJ2065 (28689) 8/15/77

[31] Sølvberg A.: A Model for Specification of Phenomena, Properties, and Information Structures, IBM Research Lab. San Jose, Calif. 95193, RJ2027(28348)7/18/77

[32] Sølvberg, A.: A contribution to the definition of concepts for expressing users' information systems requirements. In P.P. Chen, editor, *Entity-Relationship Approach to Systems Analysis and Design*. North-Holland, 1980.

[33] Sølvberg, A.: A draft proposal for integrating system specification models. In Olle, Sol, and Verrijn-Stuart, editors, *Information System Design Methodologies: A Comparative Review*. North-Holland, 1982.

[34] Sølvberg. A.: A framework for data base design. In *Proceedings of the Second Scandinavian Research Seminar on Information Modelling and Database Management* Tampere, Finland, 1983.

[35] Sølvberg. A.: Behaviour-specification in an information systems analysis cntext. In E.A. Oxborrow, editor, *Proceedings of the Fifth British National Conference on Databases (BNCOD5)* pages 71–85. Cambridge University Press, 1986.

[36] Sølvberg. A.: Guidelines for data administration. In *Proceeding of IFIP 10th World Congress* pages 23--26. North-Holland, 1986.

[37] Sølvberg. A.: Integrated modelling and support environments for information systems. In B.Randell, editor, *23rd Newcastle-upon-Tyne International Seminar on the Teaching of Computer Science at University Level* Newcastle-upon-Tyne, England, 1990.

[38] Sølvberg. A.: Research issues in integrated distributed information systems. Keynote Speech CAiSE`93, June 1993.

[39] Sølvberg. A. et al.: Research and curricula development at Norwegian universities. I: History of Nordic Computing. USA: Springer Publishing Company 2005. ISBN 0-387-24167-1. pages 137–154

[40] Sølvberg, A.: Co-operative Concept Modeling, in Brinkkemper S., Lindencrona E., Sølvberg A.(eds.): Information Systems Engineering: State of the art
and Research Themes, Springer, June 2000

[41] Sølvberg A.: Conceptual Modeling in a World of Models in R.Haschek (ed.):
Entwicklungsmethoden fuer Informationssysteme und deren Anwendung,
pp.63-77, B.G.Teubner, 1999

[42] Sølvberg A.: Data and what they refer to, in P.P.Chen et al.(eds.): Conceptual
Modeling, pp.211–226, Lecture Notes in Computer Science, Springer Verlag,
1999

[43] Sølvberg, A., Krogstie, J., Seltveit, A.H.(eds:): Proceedings of the IFIP8.1
WC on Information Systems Development for Decentralized Organizations
(ISDO'95), Trondheim, Norway, 21-23 August 1995. Chapman & Hall.

[44] Sølvberg, A., Kung. C.H.: An exercise of integrating data base design tools.
In *Proceedings of the Third Scandinavian Research Seminar on Information
Modelling and Database Management* Tampere, Finland, 1984.

[45] Sølvberg, A., Kung. C.H.: Activity modelling and behaviour modelling. In
Olle, Sol, and Verrijn-Stuart, editors, *Information Systems Design Methodologies: Improving the Practice.* North-Holland, 1986.

[46] Sølvberg, A., Kung. C.H.: On structural and behaviour modelling of reality.
In Steele and Meersman, editors, *Database Semantics.* North-Holland, 1986.

[47] Sølvberg, A., Kung. C.H.: *Information Systems Engineering.* Springer-
Verlag, 1993.

[48] Steinholtz, B., Sølvberg, A., Bergman, L. editors: *Proceedings of the Second
Nordic Conference on Advanced Information Systems Engineering
(CAiSE'90)* number 436 in Lecture Notes in Computer Science, Stockholm,
Sweden, May 1990. Springer-Verlag.

[49] Vestli, M., Nordbø, I., Sølvberg, A.: Developing well-structured knowledge-
based systems. In *Proceedings of the Sixth International Conference on Software Engineering and Knowledge Engineering* pages 366–373, Jurmala, Latvia, June 21-23 1994.

[50] Vestli, M., Nordbø, I., Sølvberg, A.: Modeling control in rule-based systems.
IEEE Software pages 77–81, March 1994.

[51] Vetland, V., Hughes, P., Sølvberg, A.: A composite modelling approach to
software performance measurement. In *Proceedings of SIGMETRICS '93*
pages 275--276, Santa Clara, California, May 10–14 1993. Extended Abstract.

[52] Vetland, V., Hughes, P., Sølvberg, A.: Improved parameter capture for simulation based on composite work models of software. In *Proceedings of the
1993 Summer Computer Simulation Conference* Boston, USA, July 19–21
1993.

[53] Yang, J., Sølvberg, A.: Intelligent ODA/ODIF documents: Perspectives for
the petroleum industry. In *Proceedings of Offshore Information Conference*
pages 161–188, Glasgow, Scotland, September 26–28 1990.

[54] Yang, M., Sølvberg, A.: The new PPP: Its architecture and repository management. In *Proceedings of the Fifth Workshop on The Next Generation of
CASE Tools* Utrecht, Holland, 1994.

Index

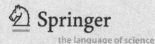
Oscar Pastor • Juan Carlos Molina

Model-Driven Architecture in Practice

XII, 292 p. Hardcover
ISBN 978-3-540-71867-3

Formal specification languages, object-oriented methods, CASE tools, component-based software production, agent-oriented, aspect-oriented ... During the last two decades many techniques have been proposed from both research and industry in order to generate a correct software product from a higher-level system specification. Nevertheless, the many failures in achieving this goal have resulted in scepticism when facing any new proposal that offers a "press the button, get all the code" strategy. And now the hype around OMG's MDA has given a new push to these strategies.

Oscar Pastor and Juan Carlos Molina combine a sound theoretical approach based on more than 10 years' research with industrial strength and practical software development experience. They present a software process based on model transformation technology, thus making the statement "the model is the code" – instead of the common "the code is the model" – finally come true. They clearly explain which conceptual primitives should be present in a system specification, how to use UML to properly represent this subset of basic conceptual constructs, how to identify just those diagrams and modeling constructs that are actually required to create a meaningful conceptual schema, and, finally, how to accomplish the transformation process between the problem space and the solution space.

Their approach is fully supported by commercially available tools, and the subsequent software production process is dramatically more efficient than today's conventional software development processes, saving many man-days of work. For software developers and architects, project managers, and people responsible for quality assurance, this book introduces all the relevant information required to understand and put MDA into industrial practice.

Contents: The OO-Method and Software Production from Models.- Conceptual Modeling: About the Problem Space.- Conceptual Model Compilation: From the Problem Space to the Solution Space.- Conclusions, References.

Klaus Pohl • Günter Böckle
Frank J. van der Linden

Software Product Line Engineering

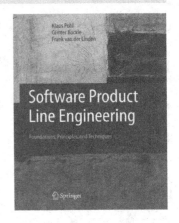

XIX, 467 p. Hardcover
ISBN 978-3-540-24372-4

This textbook addresses students, professionals, lecturers and researchers interested in software product line engineering. With more than 100 examples and about 150 illustrations, the authors describe in detail the essential foundations, principles and techniques of software product line engineering. The authors are professionals and researchers who significantly influenced the software product line engineering paradigm and successfully applied software product line engineering principles in industry. They have structured this textbook around a comprehensive product line framework.

Software product line engineering has proven to be the paradigm for developing a diversity of software products and software-intensive systems in shorter time, at lower cost, and with higher quality. It facilitates platform-based development and mass customisation. The authors elaborate on the two key principles behind software product line engineering: (1) the separation of software development in two distinct processes, domain and application engineering; (2) the explicit definition and management of the variability of the product line across all development artefacts.

As a student, you will find a detailed description of the key processes, their activities and underlying techniques for defining and managing software product line artefacts. As a researcher or lecturer, you will find a comprehensive discussion of the state of the art organised around the comprehensive framework. As a professional, you will find guidelines for introducing this paradigm in your company and an overview of industrial experiences with software product line engineering.

Contents: Part I Introduction. Introduction to Software Product Line Engineering. A Framework for Software Product Line Engineering. Overview on the Example Domain: Home Automation.- Part II Variability. Principles of Variability. Documenting Variability in Requirements. Documenting Variability in Design. Documenting Variability in Realisation.- Part III Domain Engineering. Product Management. Domain Requirements Engineering. Domain Design. Domain Realisation. Domain Testing. Using COTS Components as Domain Artefacts.- Part IV Application Engineering. Application Requirements Engineering. Application Design. Application Realisation. Application Testing.- Part V Organisation Aspects. Organisation. Transition Process.- Part VI Experiences. Experiences with Software Product Lines.- Appendix.

Barbara Pernici

Mobile Information Systems

XVI, 354 p. Hardcover
ISBN 978-3-540-31006-8

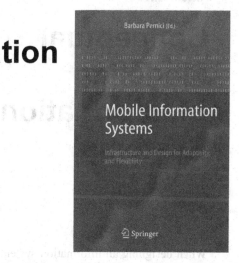

Mobile devices allow users to access information resources and services over many different distribution channels – anywhere, anytime, anyhow. Technical and usage characteristics of mobile systems are highly variable with respect to user capabilities and context characteristics, therefore an immense level of flexibility is required.

Barbara Pernici – with contributions by the research groups involved in the project – presents here a framework for mobile information systems, focussing on quality of service and adaptability at all architectural levels, ranging from adaptive applications to e-services, middleware, and infrastructural elements, as it was developed in the "Multi-channel Adaptive Information Systems (MAIS)" project. The design models, methods, and tools developed in the project allow the realization of adaptive mobile information systems in a variety of different architectures.

The book is divided into three parts: core technologies for mobile information systems (e.g., adaptive middleware and flexible e-services), enabling technologies (like data management on small devices or adaptive low-power hardware architectures or wireless networks), and methodological aspects of mobile information systems design (such as service profiling or user interface and e-service design for context-aware applications). It provides researchers in academia and industry with a comprehensive vision on innovative aspects which can be used as a basis for the development of new frameworks and applications.

Contents: Part I: Core Technologies for Mobile Information Systems.- Basic Concepts.- Reference Architecture and Framework.- E-Services.- Middleware and Architectural Reflection. Part II: Enabling Technologies.- Adaptive Networks.- Data Management on Micro Devices.- Low Power Architectures for Mobile Systems. Part III: Mobile Information Systems Design.- Methods and Tools for the Development of Adaptive Applications.- Development of Services for Mobile Information Systems.- Knowledge-Based Tools for E-Service Profiling and Mining.- Applications.

Antoni Olivé

Conceptual Modeling of Information Systems

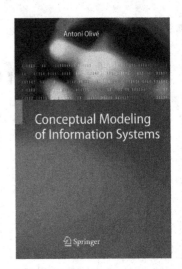

Approx. 450 p. Hardcover
ISBN 978-3-540-39389-4

When designing an information system, conceptual modeling is the activity that elicits and describes the general knowledge the system needs to know. This description, called the conceptual schema, is necessary in order to develop an information system. Recently, many researchers and professionals share a vision in which the conceptual schema becomes the only important description to be created, as the system implementation will be automatically constructed from its schema – this is e.g. the basic idea behind OMG's Model Driven Architecture.

Olivé's textbook explains in detail the principles of conceptual modeling independently from particular methods and languages and shows how to apply them in real-world projects. He covers all aspects of the engineering process from structural modeling over behavioral modeling to meta-modeling, and completes the presentation with an extensive case study based on the osCommerce system, an online store-management software program freely available under the GNU General Public License. His presentation is based on well-known industry standards like UML and OCL as a particular conceptual modeling language, yet also delivers the basics of the formal logical language background.

Written for computer science students in classes on information systems modeling as well as for professionals feeling the need to formalize their experiences or to update their knowledge, Olivé delivers here a comprehensive treatment of all aspects of the modeling process. His book is complemented by lots of exercises and additional online teaching material.

Contents: 1. Introduction to Conceptual Modeling of Information Systems.- Part I: Structural Modeling.- 2. Entity Types - 3. Relationship Types - 4. Cardinality constraints - 5. Particular Kinds of Relationship Types - 6. Reification - 7. Generic Relationship Types - 8. Derived Types - 9. Integrity Constraints - 10. Taxonomies.- Part II Behavioral Modeling.- 11. Domain Events - 12. Action Request Events - 13. State Transition Diagrams - 14. Statecharts - 15. Use Cases.- Part III: Building Conceptual Schemas.- 16. A Case Study.- Part IV: Metamodeling.- 17. Metamodeling - 18. MOF and XMI.